Lord of a Visible World

LORD
of a
VISIBLE
WORLD

An Autobiography in Letters

H. P. Lovecraft

Edited by S. T. Joshi and David E. Schultz

OHIO UNIVERSITY PRESS

Athens

CPL

Ohio University Press, Athens, Ohio 45701
© 2000 by Ohio University Press
Printed in the United States of America
All rights reserved

Ohio University Press books are printed on acid-free paper ∞ ™

09 08 07 06 05 04 03 02 01 00   5 4 3 2

Permission to quote portions of letters and other documents by H.P. Lovecraft has been
granted by Robert C. Harrall, Administrator of the Estate of H. P. Lovecraft.

The photograph of H.P. Lovecraft, used on the jacket and frontispiece, appears courtesy
of Brown University Library.

Library of Congress Cataloging-in-Publication Data
Lovecraft, H. P. (Howard Phillips), 1890–1937.
    [Correspondence. Selections.]
    Lord of a visible world: an autobiography in letters / H. P. Lovecraft; edited by
    S.T. Joshi and David E. Schultz.
        p. cm.
    Includes bibliographical references and index.
    ISBN 0-8214-1332-5 (alk. paper) — ISBN 0-8214-1333-3 (pbk.: alk. papeer)
    1. Lovecraft, H.P. (Howard Phillips), 1890–1937. 2. Lovecraft, H.P. (Howard
Phillips), 1890–1937—Correspondence. 3. Authors, American—20th century—
Biography. 4. Authors, American—20th century—Correspondence. 5. Horror tales—
Authorship. I. Schultz, David E., 1952– II. Joshi, S.T., 1958– III. Title.

PS3523.O833 Z48 2000
813'.52—dc21
    [B]   00-0125961

Contents

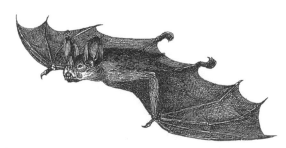

Introduction

As early as 1937, a few months after H. P. Lovecraft's death, his old friend
Maurice W. Moe, recipient of nearly twenty-five years' worth of correspondence, wrote: "if there is ever a survey to determine the greatest letter-
writer in history, the claims of Lovecraft deserve close investigation."[1] In
context, Moe's use of the word "greatest" does not refer to number —
although, certainly, Lovecraft wrote a great many letters — but to quality.
Is it so preposterous to claim that Howard Phillips Lovecraft — who, at the
time of his death, was a nearly forgotten "pulp writer" who had had only
one pitifully misprinted book of a single story published by an impecu-
nious small press — ranks with Cicero, Horace Walpole, Voltaire, H. L.
Mencken, and other canonical writers as a master in the art of letter writing? Perhaps this volume will offer readers a chance to make their own
judgment.

The actual number of Lovecraft's letters has probably been somewhat
exaggerated, and the figure of a hundred thousand casually bandied about
since the 1970s is probably much too high. But even if that figure is lowered to a more realistic seventy-five thousand — including thousands of
postcards, many of which contain more text than an average person's letter — it still gives Lovecraft a high rank in sheer quantity. And when we
take into consideration that on a number of occasions his letters ran to
thirty, forty, or even fifty closely written pages, the figure bulks still larger.
Of course, only a tiny percentage of his total correspondence survives; but
the editors have amassed nearly three thousand letters, totaling roughly
four million words — an amount that in sheer wordage dwarfs his collected
fiction, poetry, and essays combined.

But what makes Lovecraft among the most exhaustively self-docu-
mented individuals in human history is the remarkable content of his

letters. Lovecraft might be said to be one of the most *revealing* letter writers in history. With the exception of a very few subjects of extreme sensitivity, he has no compunction in chronicling the most minute particulars of his life, in recalling memories of all phases and periods of his existence, and in outlining at great length and detail his views on philosophy, aesthetics, science, history, politics, economics, and the myriad other subjects that engaged his attention. And then there are the delightfully piquant asides triggered by some chance mention by his correspondent: learned disquisitions on different types of doughnuts or baked beans or cheese; paeans to the many cats he has known throughout his life; the almost manic detail in which he chronicles the purchase of a suit from a discount clothing store; and on and on and on. It is these qualities in his far-flung correspondence that have made the compilation of this book possible.

While it is true that many of Lovecraft's colleagues, early and late, have left accounts of their memories and impressions of him and that diligent researchers and biographers have unearthed many important documents pertaining to his life, it remains a fact that for many particulars of Lovecraft's life we are reliant upon his own testimony. Every responsible scholar must of course regard this testimony with a certain skepticism; but if Lovecraft's words seem generally to harmonize with the external evidence and to match our overall impression of Lovecraft from other sources, then there is no reason not to accept them. We are particularly at Lovecraft's mercy in his accounts of his childhood, recounted in many letters over the course of his life; and yet, the picture they paint is in accord with the available evidence, and they merely add a wealth of fascinating detail to the basic outline.

Born in Providence, Rhode Island, on August 20, 1890, to a family that was both well-to-do financially and a part of the informal social aristocracy of the city, Lovecraft spent what is by all accounts an idyllic childhood, even if a somewhat lonely one. The succession of intellectual and aesthetic interests that came to him from earliest infancy—a natural sense of meter at the age of two; reading at the age of four; enthusiasm for the *Arabian Nights* at five, for classical myth at six, for music at seven, for chemistry at eight, and for astronomy at eleven—testifies to an innately curious and adventuresome mind, while his delightful stories of play (the building of toy landscapes on tabletops; the construction of elaborately designed playgrounds in the vacant lot next to his birthplace) bespeak more than simply a wholesomely "normal" childhood and point to a creative instinct that led him to write his first stories at the age of six. Because of highly strung nerves and other ailments, Lovecraft did not attend grammar school until he was eight; and the two years that he did attend the Slater Avenue School (1898–99 and 1902–3) were widely spaced, the intervening period occupied with private tutors.

Even as a boy Lovecraft was aware of the family's dwindling finances; and in early 1904 the calamity struck. His grandfather, the successful industrialist Whipple Van Buren Phillips, died, and the subsequent mismanagement of his estate forced the family to move out of its large quarters at 454 Angell Street into a smaller house at 598 Angell Street. The effect of the move on Lovecraft was twofold: firstly, the chief adult male presence in his life was removed (his father, stricken with a form of syphilis in 1893, spent the rest of his life in a sanitarium and died in 1898); secondly, the loss of his birthplace was cataclysmic to one who had already developed a keen sense of place. If we are to believe Lovecraft, he seriously contemplated suicide at this time. What prevented him was not so much the creative instinct (even though he was writing voluminously, both stories and scientific work) as intellectual curiosity. Too many things about the world remained unknown; so how could a young gentleman remove himself without knowing a bit more? Perhaps a year or two of high school could be endured before making an exit.

Although his term at Hope Street High School (1904–8) was interrupted by health problems, Lovecraft found the experience far pleasanter than he had expected. He was given the freedom to pursue a wide range of studies, and he formed lasting friendships with other boys in the school. It was at this time that he broke into print with astronomy columns for several local papers.

Exactly what caused Lovecraft's withdrawal from high school after the completion of only his third year (he had been absent for nearly the whole of the 1905–6 term) remains unclear: the succeeding "blank" period (1908–13) is one of the topics about which Lovecraft refused to speak in correspondence. Clearly he was ashamed at his failure to matriculate at Brown University, as his family expected. At a time when his peers were going to college or establishing themselves in remunerative positions in society, Lovecraft was vegetating—no doubt reading voluminously, taking a few correspondence classes that led nowhere, writing occasionally and largely for himself, but otherwise remaining shut up in an increasingly stifling environment with a mother who was herself slowly losing her grasp of reality and breaking down under the strain of her husband's death and her son's manifest inability to support himself. It is for this period—and this period alone—that Lovecraft truly earned the designation of "eccentric recluse" that careless biographers have applied to the whole of his life.

Lovecraft emerged from this hermitry in a peculiar way. For years he had been leavening his reading of the standard classics with an equally enthusiastic thirst for cheap popular magazines, especially several in Frank A. Munsey's extensive chain—predecessors to the pulp magazines of the succeeding decade. The prolific romance writer Fred Jackson was much beloved by readers of these magazines, and they took umbrage when, in 1913, Lovecraft attacked Jackson's sentimentality in a long and archaically worded letter to the editor. Shortly thereafter the controversy took an odd direction, and several writers including Lovecraft began to write salvos in verse. Lovecraft, ever the Anglophile and literary archaicist, resurrected the verse satire of Dryden and Pope in a series of stinging squibs with the general title *Ad Criticos*. The controversy lasted more than a year, and in the course of it Lovecraft was contacted by Edward F. Daas, a recruiter for the United Amateur Press Association (UAPA), and invited to join the association.

The world of amateur journalism—into which Lovecraft poured most of his energies for the period 1914–22—is so little understood today that many readers have difficulty appreciating his involvement in and his devotion to it. The UAPA and its older rival, the National Amateur Press Association (NAPA), were nationwide organizations of budding writers who either published their own papers—sometimes at great expense—or contributed to papers published by others. In both literary quality and physical appearance they rank somewhere between the "little magazines" and the "fan magazines" of a later generation. The word "amateur" ideally referred merely to the fact that the writers were not interested in remuneration. While it may be true that the great majority of amateurs were in fact tyros, and while Lovecraft is the only amateur to have truly emerged as a figure in general literature, several other amateur writers—including Lovecraft's colleagues Edith Miniter, Samuel Loveman, and Edward H. Cole—can bear comparison with the established writers of their time. Some of these writers published work professionally at the same time that they continued writing for the amateur papers.

What did Lovecraft mean when he wrote in a 1921 essay that amateur journalism had given him "life itself"? Clearly he was referring to its aid in his emergence from the torpidity of his post–high school years. Also, the realm of amateur journalism was small enough (neither the UAPA nor the NAPA ever had more than 250 members at any given time) that Lovecraft, still highly diffident about his own work, would not feel intimidated. Moreover, amateurdom's noncommercial stance harmonized with Love-craft's own aesthetic, with its emphasis on "self-expression" and its scorn for writing for pay. The hierarchical nature of amateurdom—with annual elections for such offices as president, vice-president, official editor, and the like—allowed Lovecraft to gain a prominence that augmented his self-esteem. Only a few months after entering the UAPA in early 1914, he was appointed chairman of the Department of Public Criticism, where he had a public forum for supplying painstaking literary advice to the other mem-bers; by 1917 Lovecraft was sufficiently recognized to be elected presi-dent, and in 1920 he became official editor.

It was in the amateur world that Lovecraft found his earliest and clos-est friends and colleagues—such figures as Rheinhart Kleiner, Maurice W. Moe, W. Paul Cook, Alfred Galpin, and James F. Morton. The letters writ-ten to these individuals—all of whom differed significantly in temperament and intellectual focus from Lovecraft, but had many interests in common as well—document Lovecraft's slow maturation from a highly dogmatic thinker and writer, lost in his single-minded devotion to the art and thought of the eighteenth century, into a more nuanced intellect capable of coming to terms with the contemporary world. By the end of Lovecraft's first phase of amateur activity, we see him adopting a pose of cynical so-phistication, appealing not to Pope or Johnson as intellectual mentors but to Oscar Wilde, Baudelaire, and Nietzsche. The radicalism of T. S. Eliot, however, was a bit too much for him, and he condemned *The Waste Land* both in a fiery editorial in his amateur paper, the *Conservative,* and in his ex-quisite parody, "Waste Paper."

By 1920 Lovecraft was tentatively emerging from the shadow of his mother. This too was a subject Lovecraft rarely discussed in letters; but testimony from other sources—notably the account of Clara Hess, a friend and neighbor who saw Lovecraft's mother several times before the break-down that placed her in 1919 in the same insane asylum where her hus-band had died two decades before—gives us some hints of the picture. Still, we can only imagine what it must have been like for Lovecraft to have lived alone with his mother for fifteen years, especially at a time when he should have been attending college and then beginning to work at a job.

Certainly, his mother and his aunts, Lillian D. Clark and Annie E. P. Gamwell, are largely responsible for failing to prod Lovecraft into training for remunerative work, thereby virtually ensuring his subsequent poverty; Lovecraft of course is not free from blame himself, content as he was to remain a kind of "professional amateur." His mother's illness and death in 1921, although it initially stunned Lovecraft, sadly proved a necessary means of liberating him from the physical and psychological prison in which she had placed him.

Grudging as he was to admit it (at least publicly), Lovecraft felt a sense of liberation upon his mother's death. His health began to improve radically, and his previous nervous ailments were sloughed off. He began to travel more—all across New England, then as far west as New York and even Cleveland. With his aunts providing a stable but unobtrusive presence at home, Lovecraft felt at liberty to roam—and to write delightful letters chronicling his wanderings—as far as his slim finances allowed.

Lovecraft frequently admitted that throughout much of his early career he was under the delusion (fostered in part by his mother) that he was a poet. The hundreds of poems he published in the amateur press are certainly well crafted in their rigid, formal way, but they are condemned to aesthetic oblivion because of their imitativeness and their failure to treat issues vitally. Only his satires and his weird poetry retain interest today. Similarly, many of the essays and editorials Lovecraft wrote during his amateur period are crippled by dogmatism, stiff and archaic diction, and superficial or misguided thinking. But what other avenues of expression did Lovecraft have, since he had admitted in 1915 that "I wish that I could write fiction, but it seems almost an impossibility"?[2]

Perhaps we owe Lovecraft's entire fiction-writing career to W. Paul Cook, the amateur publisher who enthusiastically praised the few juvenile tales that survived Lovecraft's 1908 destruction of his fictional work and who encouraged Lovecraft to carry on when the latter resumed story writing in 1917. For the next few years Lovecraft still produced fiction only sporadically; but in late 1919 he discovered the work of the now unjustly neglected Irish fantaisiste Lord Dunsany, then enjoying tremendous popularity and in the midst of an American lecture tour. Lovecraft later came to conclude that the many "Dunsanian fantasies" he produced in 1919–21 were overly imitative, but facets of his own personality do emerge from under their surface. In 1923 the discovery of the great Welsh mystic Arthur Machen cast a powerful influence, but by this time Lovecraft was a sufficiently seasoned writer to be able to absorb Machen's work without having it overshadow his own.

The year 1923 is also significant for the founding of the pulp magazine *Weird Tales*. Readers will have to decide for themselves whether the effect of this magazine—virtually the sole venue for horror fiction during the whole of its long run (1923–54)—upon Lovecraft was beneficial or otherwise. Lovecraft came to regard it negatively, not only because it rejected some of his best work (work that far surpassed the conventional, formula-ridden parameters of pulp fiction) but because the psychological effect of catering, even unconsciously, to *Weird Tales'* standards had made his own later work less subtle and allusive. There is much to be said for Lovecraft's opinion. But in the early years *Weird Tales* was a refreshing influence on Lovecraft, transforming him from a dilettante into something approaching a professional writer. The pinnacle of his early involvement with *Weird Tales* came in 1924, when he was both considered for the editorship of the magazine (he declined the offer) and asked to ghostwrite a tale for Harry Houdini.

Meanwhile Lovecraft's personal life had undergone a radical transformation. It is certainly suggestive that he met his future wife, the Russian Jewish immigrant Sonia Haft Greene, at an amateur convention only six weeks after his mother's death. For one who had purported to scorn "amatory phenomena" in his earlier years (and, indeed, there is every reason to believe that he had never had a relationship with a woman before Sonia), it is remarkable that he believed he could marry a woman whom he had known largely through correspondence. It is one of the great tragedies of Lovecraft studies that Sonia destroyed her letters from Lovecraft; without them, we are at a loss to understand how the two managed to convince themselves that their marriage would be viable.

In any event, the marriage took place in New York on March 3, 1924—and Lovecraft did not bother to notify his aunts of the event until six days later. Did he suspect that they would not approve of this marriage to one who was both a tradeswoman (Sonia was a well-paid executive at a New York hat shop) and not of old New England stock? There is good reason to believe it, although the relative absence of letters from the aunts makes conjecture difficult. Lovecraft himself, as early as his teenage years, had already exhibited ethnocentric beliefs typical of his class and region, and one must come to terms with the fact that he became—and, sadly, remained for the rest of his life—a full-fledged racist. It is the one black mark on what appears to be an otherwise admirable character. How, then, could Lovecraft justify his marriage to a Jew? In his mind, it appears, Sonia was a properly "assimilated" Jew, like his friend Samuel Loveman: she had adopted the mores of the prevailing Anglo-Saxon culture, so that her ethnic background was not an obstacle.

The two years that Lovecraft spent in New York are rightly referred to as an "exile." We know of this period more exhaustively than any other period of Lovecraft's life largely because of his letters—especially the voluminous letters written to his aunts (those to Aunt Lillian alone come to some two hundred thousand words for the years 1924–26), as he first tries to put a brave front on his marriage and move away from home, then reluctantly admits (as he wrote in the story "He") that his "coming to New York was a mistake." Almost at once the couple suffered difficulties, chiefly financial: Sonia had tried to launch her own hat shop, but it failed; Lovecraft was unsuccessful in his desultory attempts to secure literary work, and his later ventures at finding a job—any job, from salesman to hack writer—also failed miserably. By the end of 1924 Sonia had to leave New York to take a position in the midwest; Lovecraft was left alone in a small apartment at 169 Clinton Street, in then decaying Brooklyn Heights, plagued by poverty, mice, and finally the robbery of nearly all his clothes. Under such pressures, even the presence of his many friends and acquaintances—including, for a time, the poet Hart Crane—was not sufficient compensation. Although his New York years were the heyday of the "Kalem Club" (so named because most of the members' last names began with K, L, or M), and although they were the period of his greatest gregariousness and sociability, Lovecraft was acutely miserable. His racism flared to maniacal heights, and his detestation of the gigantism, stridor, and bustle of New York brought him to the verge of a nervous breakdown.

Finally, in March 1926, his aunts summoned him home, releasing him from his exile. Where, exactly, did Sonia fit into these plans? She had thought of opening a store in Boston, but when she proposed to do so in Providence, the aunts put an end to the matter: "the aunts gently but firmly informed me that neither they nor Howard could afford to have Howard's wife work for a living in Providence."[3] The aunts' social standing could not be threatened by a tradeswoman wife for their nephew, and the marriage was essentially over. Lovecraft, for his part, seems content to have sat idly by while his aunts decided his fate. No doubt he wished to resume his life of relative solitude, and he saw nothing wrong with continuing marriage by correspondence; but this was not what Sonia had in mind, and she forced Lovecraft to go through a divorce in 1929.

Lovecraft's return to Providence was ecstatic, and it initiated an unprecedented burst of fiction-writing; in six months he produced two short novels, the landmark story "The Call of Cthulhu" (1926), and other works, including the completion of his treatise "Supernatural Horror in Literature." Lovecraft was home; and because he had a secure base of operations, he could now pursue what had come to be one of his greatest passions—travel. Since 1919 Lovecraft had slowly and tentatively explored the obscurer corners of his native New England in search of antiquarian oases—places like Salem and Marblehead, Massachusetts, where the past lingered almost unchanged to the present. Now he began to go farther afield, and he was enraptured by such locales as Vermont (1927), the rugged rusticity of central Massachusetts (1928), upstate New York with its Dutch survivals (1929), Virginia (1929), the marvelous living museum of antiquity that is Charleston, South Carolina (1930), the forbidding cliffs of Quebec (1930), St. Augustine, Florida, oldest city in the continental United States (1931), and many others. Lovecraft's accounts of these travels—written faithfully to his aunts and also to close friends, and sometimes circulated in carbon-copy typescripts—are among the most remarkable of his correspondence. Beyond their meticulous detail (derived from both guidebooks and travel diaries that Lovecraft kept), their exhaustive charting of the history and topography of the regions he visits, and their piquant, deliberately archaistic diction, it is their heartwarming enthusiasm that makes them imperishable human documents. It is no accident that his single longest literary work, *A Description of the Town of Quebeck* (1930–31), was a travelogue. It was a work that he never attempted to publish: its purpose had been fully served by its mere writing.

It was also in Lovecraft's final decade that he honed his philosophy of life. The depth, detail, and persistence with which Lovecraft grappled with the fundamental issues of human existence go far beyond those of the average creative writer; and though many aspects of his thought were modified over the course of his life as he encountered new evidence, some beliefs persisted. Lovecraft's early grounding in the sciences, especially astronomy, had given him a sense of humanity's inconsequence in the vast vortices of space and time, and had also eliminated any shred of religious belief. It was this "cosmicism" that he sought to express in his most characteristic fictional work. At the same time, however, Lovecraft relied upon his New England heritage as a bulwark against the sense of human futility that might easily come from this "cosmic" perspective, so that he remained socially conservative while being highly progressive intellectually. Lovecraft's return from New York had also affected his aesthetics, and he realized as never before that he was not destined to be a cosmopolitan; instead, he sought to draw literary life from the New England topography and mores of which he was inextricably a part.

Lovecraft was one of those rare creative minds who also probe the theory and practice of their chosen field. For Lovecraft, that field was weird fiction; and even before writing his historical monograph in 1926–27, he had come to evolve a conscious theory of how weird fiction is most effectively written. While the emphasis on the cosmic is perhaps germane only to Lovecraft's own work, his many other remarks make him among the most penetrating theoreticians in this realm. Moreover, his views shifted over the course of years, and in the last decade of his life his theory of weird fiction came very close to the still new genre of science fiction. Lovecraft practiced what he preached, and such of his later stories as *At the Mountains of Madness* (1931) and "The Shadow out of Time" (1934–35) are precise embodiments of his modified position.

One of the most remarkable shifts in Lovecraft's thinking occurred in the 1930s, when his politics altered from extreme conservatism to a moderate socialism. Initially Lovecraft perhaps adopted socialism out of fear that the economic depression of the decade might engender a revolution of the dispossessed masses that would end civilization; but later he understood that society must, for the sake of simple human justice, ensure everyone a place in its fabric, and that unfettered capitalism merely meant the victimization of the weak by the shrewdly cunning and mercenary. Lovecraft's early aristocratic sentiments harmonized with what he came to call his "fascistic socialism," whereby economic wealth would be distributed equitably but political power (specifically, the right to vote) would be restricted to the few who were genuinely capable of exercising it. It is perhaps an impracticable vision in terms of actual political policy, but as a theory it remains compelling.

Generally solitary as Lovecraft was — living first with one aunt and then with the other in small rented quarters in Providence — he established an ever-increasing network of epistolary ties with correspondents all across the country. It is perhaps the highest testimonial to Lovecraft's gifts as a letter writer that many of his associates remained devoted to his memory solely or largely on the basis of their correspondence with him. It is difficult to find a man so universally admired—one about whom his colleagues have so little that is adverse or negative to say—as H. P. Lovecraft. His unfailing generosity, especially of his time and advice; his gentlemanly courtesy, especially to the young or the infirm; and the openness of expression that makes each correspondent feel as if he or she is Lovecraft's best friend—these qualities and more shine through Lovecraft's later correspondence. Even though Lovecraft, toward the end of his life, was plagued increasingly by ill health (he would die at the age of forty-six of intestinal cancer, caused at least in part by a poor diet that was itself the product of severe poverty) and by doubts over the merit of his work, he remained a faithful correspondent to the end: the unfinished document found on his desk upon his death was not a story, a poem, or an essay, but a letter.

Is it, then, a surprise that of the two individuals who would devote much of their life to preserving his work, one had never met Lovecraft, while the other met him on only a few occasions? August Derleth and Donald Wandrei had been introduced to each other by Lovecraft himself; and upon his death they jointly established the firm of Arkham House, initially for the sole purpose of publishing Lovecraft in hard covers. What is more, both men determined immediately not merely to collect Lovecraft's widely scattered fiction and some of his poetry and essays, but also to publish his letters. Although that dream was long deferred through the pressure of other work, lack of finances, and the sheer volume of letters they amassed, it finally did become a reality, and the five-volume *Selected Letters* (1965–76) is, in spite of errors and other drawbacks, a monument. Since that time, other hands have taken a more rigorous approach to the editing of Lovecraft's work, including his letters; but although his fiction has now reached a worldwide audience, those letters remain largely the domain of specialists.

We are therefore gratified to be able to present a wide selection of H. P. Lovecraft's letters, arranged in such a way as to paint a full picture of his life from beginning to end. That picture, as with any writer of consequence, is not merely a chronicle of bare events, but also a reflection of his shifting moods, beliefs, and conceptions of the world. Lovecraft was far from being a recluse, but many of the most dynamic events of his life occurred in his mind; so we have not neglected to supply a sampling of letters and other documents that reflect the evolution of his thought and his creative instincts. If in the end these extracts result in a broader picture of

Lovecraft than has hitherto gained currency—if readers come to believe that Lovecraft was not merely a shudder-coiner but a thinker, a traveler, an observer of national and international affairs, and above all a warm-hearted human being—then the purpose of this volume will have been served.

—S. T. Joshi

David E. Schultz

A Note on the Text

The material in this volume consists of extracts from a few essays by Lovecraft (texts of which are derived from existing manuscripts or early printed appearances) and extracts of many letters. The letters have been secured from two major sources: manuscripts (many of them at the John Hay Library of Brown University and the State Historical Society of Wisconsin at Madison, and a few in private hands) and the so-called "Arkham House transcripts." The transcripts were prepared by Arkham House for use in editing Lovecraft's *Selected Letters;* in many cases the original manuscripts of these letters have not come to light, and in some cases the manuscripts are known to have been destroyed. We have made relatively few alterations in the manuscript letters, occasionally correcting an obvious slip of the pen and writing out Lovecraft's habitual ampersands. We have made more alterations in the transcripts, in cases where there is good reason to believe that the transcriber erred in reading Lovecraft's handwriting.

Few letters are presented in their entirety. We have not placed ellipses at the beginning or end of letters except in cases where our editing has resulted in a sentence fragment; but we have placed ellipses (enclosed in brackets) where we have made cuts or abridgments within a given extract. All other ellipses are Lovecraft's. Occasionally he used more than the conventional three or four periods in an ellipsis, and we have retained this usage to preserve the style of the original documents. We have also preserved other idiosyncratic usages, such as British spelling variants, archaisms or slang, irregular punctuation, and the like. Headnotes preceding the letters help to identify their context and supply other necessary information.

As an epigraph to the volume we have included Lovecraft's "biographical notice" from Edward J. O'Brien's *Best Short Stories of 1928.* The notice, although unsigned, is clearly by Lovecraft, and encapsulates in a remarkably small space the essence of his life and beliefs. As an appendix we have included Lovecraft's most polished autobiographical essay, "Some Notes on a Nonentity," written in 1933.

Names cited frequently in the text (chiefly Lovecraft's colleagues or writers who influenced him significantly) are identified in a glossary of names at the end of the volume. Other names, and other points in the text that require elucidation, are identified in the endnotes. We have not felt the need to overburden the text with notes and commentary, and we believe that most of the extracts are self-explanatory.

Our list of "Sources" identifies the sources for our texts of the letters. In every chapter, each extract is numbered at its beginning, and the numbers correspond to the sequence of letters (or other works) listed in the "Sources." We have appended a list of further reading, supplying information on important editions of works by Lovecraft and significant biographical and critical studies. The literature on Lovecraft has now become immense, and the present list cites only the most significant works.

We are grateful to several individuals who assisted in obtaining or transcribing texts, including Scott David Briggs, Perry Grayson, Derrick Hussey, Chris Jarocha-Ernst, Tim Lonegan, and Judy Montgomery. Other individuals, including Marc A. Michaud and Peter Ruber, have helped in other ways. Any errors that remain are our own.

—S. T. J.

D. E. S.

Lord of a Visible World

LOVECRAFT, HOWARD PHILLIPS. Was born of old Yankee-English stock on August 20, 1890, in Providence, Rhode Island. Has always lived there except for very brief periods. Educated in local schools and privately; ill-health precluding university. Interested early in colour and mystery of things. More youthful products—verse and essays—voluminous, valueless, mostly privately printed. Contributed astronomical articles to press 1906–18. Serious literary efforts now confined to tales of dream-life, strange shadow, and cosmic "outsideness", notwithstanding sceptical rationalism of outlook and keen regard for the sciences. Lives quietly and eventlessly, with classical and antiquarian tastes. Especially fond of atmosphere of colonial New England. Favourite authors—in most intimate personal sense—Poe, Arthur Machen, Lord Dunsany, Walter de la Mare, Algernon Blackwood. Occupation—literary hack work including revision and special editorial jobs. Has contributed macabre fiction to *Weird Tales* regularly since 1923. Conservative in general perspective and method so far as compatible with phantasy in art and mechanistic materialism in philosophy. Lives in Providence, Rhode Island.

—H. P. Lovecraft

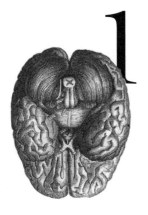

1 Childhood and Adolescence
(1890–1914)

Ancestry

[Lovecraft, sporadically diligent as a genealogist, once found occasion to evaluate both his paternal and his maternal lines in an effort to trace the roots of his own personality. In spite of his Anglophilia he seemed to take greater pride and interest in his maternal line.]

[1]   The whole keynote of my personality, aside from my antiquarianism, is individual revolt against meaningless convention; yet the whole family's branchage behind me is about as solidly conventional a mess as you could well imagine. Any sort of aesthete is rare as a hen's tooth, and intellect doesn't sparkle a bit—but that's to be expected, since I ain't no arc light myself. The overwhelming majority—virtually totality—of my ancestry on both sides is of the staid and stolid country-gentry class, with an abnormally high percentage of *clergymen* droning their amiably well-meaning matins and liturgies across the well-clipt hedges of a subdu'd and commonplace rural mead. I can scare up a full-fledged clerick—the Rev. Francis Fulford, Vicar of Dunsford—in four generations—that is, he is my great-great-grandfather—and by two generations behind him they come up thick and fast. Then on my mother's side, also they rant and

rave—only here they tend to be Puritans and other freaks instead of sober Anglicans. That screechy old Quaker gal hang'd in Boston Common in 1660—Mary Dyer—is among my doubtfully revered progenitrices. Mediocrity seems quite the rule; for the three or four really great lines I touch—Musgrave of Edenhall, Cumberland, Chichester; Carew of Haccombe; Legge, Lord Dartmouth; etc. etc.—are so far back that no trait from them could conceivably have any perceptible share in moulding me. [. . .] In direct male line, I can't get back of the Conquest at all; the family of Lovecroft (early spelling) first appearing in Devonshire, in the valley of the Teign, circa 1450. I can't push my own lineal stem back to 1560 plus or minus, when John Lovecraft (present spelling) of Minster Hall near Newton-Abbot bore the present arms of the family: a chevron, engrailed, Or, between three foxes' heads, erased, Or, on a field Vert. Following his progeny down the line, I don't find a single mark of distinction above the mediocre country-gentry average. Clergymen to burn (though there was no Queen Mary to get it done), just plain squires who probably talked with a dialect almost as broad as their tenants', Captains, Colonels, occasional marriages into old lines but mostly marriages into small-time lines whose charted antecedents don't reach the Domesday Book—that's the bulk of the germ-plasm that made up Grandpa's paternal half. One curious strain is that of Washington—a branch with no discoverable relation to that which emigrated to Virginia and produc'd the arch-rebel. But not a damn thing to indicate a revolt against commonplace unintelligence or a taste for the weird and the cosmic. No philosophers—no artists—no writers—not a cursed soul I could possibly talk to without getting a pain in the neck.

In 1745 we find born a restless egg who probably felt the blind stultification of all this oppressive respectability; for according to common report this Thomas Lovecraft struck out to live where he lived, aided by wine, horses, and the fair. I hope he had a good time, for his legacy to posterity was a general property scattering which shot everything to hell before he croaked—so that he had to sell even his family seat in 1823 . . . . . historick date, on which the Lovecrafts ceased to be gentlemen according to the original and technical definition. Possibly the shock killed the old reprobate, for he himself bumped off three years after that. Out of the wreckage climbed sundry of his numerous lawful progeny—I can't answer for the doubtless numerous rest—including his sixth child and third son Joseph; already married and with six children of his own. This bird Joe, gentlemen, was the great-grandfather of your Grandpaw Tibbald. Casting

around for a possible comeback area, he lit in an evil hour on these re-
volted colonies, whither he transported himself, wife (daughter of the
Vicar of Dunsford), and offspring in the year 1827. Or more exactly, he
meant to settle in still loyal Upper-Canada—the present Ontario—but
found nothing doing, so filtered across the line to the Province of New
York, in whose northern reaches he settled down on an experimental farm
and promptly died, leaving his heirs to worry along as best they might. As
it happened, all of them—John, William, Joseph, George, and Aaron—
and a sister Mary—managed to keep above water; improved in some cases
by advantageous marriages. Of these lines, however, all but two are definitely extinct, and even one of these two probably is. Joseph had a grandson who went west in the 1880's and dropped from sight. And George,
marrying the daughter of a transplanted Allgood of Nunwick, had a son
Winfield—who married into the old Yankee stock of Rhode Island and left
one good-for-nothing descendant to close the family history of these
colonies . . . . . H. P. Lovecraft of Angell Street Grange and Tenbarnes
Manor, author of those numerous works so conspicuously unmention'd in
the annals of fame. [. . .]

What were my maternal strains—and how were they environed during their approximate three centuries in New England? Lumping them, we
find a few points in common. They were, to begin with, wholly local. No
American ancestor of mine (ruling out my whole paternal side as spiritually British) ever lived in any part of America but New England. Narrow-
ing further, they were predominantly the quickly-rebellious strain of
originally-Puritan colonists who came to the Massachusetts-Bay in 1630
and reëmigrated to Rhode Island within the next ten or twenty years. I
have not a single drop of Mayflower-Pilgrim blood—Plymouth being as
remote from my veins as Quebec and South Carolina notwithstanding the
fact that I have never lived in any house from whose roof the former soil of
the Plymouth Colony is not visible—and near enough to count houses
without a telescope. As to origin—most of the lines have an amusing resemblance to just the kind of lines encountered in my paternal ancestry—
giving me a curious accidental homogeneity. Small rural gentry, without
distinction, but nearly all armigerous. Not the meek and pliant stock of the
Pilgrims, nor yet the haughty and expansive stock of Virginia. The Phillips
line here begins with the Rev. George Phillips, son of Christopher Phillips,
Gent., of Rainham St. Martin's in Norfolk, who came on the Arbella in
1630 and settled in Watertown, Mass. From his eldest son Samuel comes

the founder of the Exeter and Andover academies; but I come from his youngest son Michael who emigrated to Newport in 1668. Michael's sons (from two of whom I am descended) crossed the bay and settled in the Narragansett Country, which differed radically from any other part of New England in being divided into rather large patriarchal estates with slaves, large houses, and a non-Puritan Church-of-England civilisation of the Virginian sort. Horse-breeding and dairying were the great industries, Narragansett pacers and cheeses being objects of familiar admiration even in distant countries. The quaint customs of this region would fill books — and have done so . . . . . but the unhappy revolt against His Majesty's lawful authority set it into a decay from which it has never recovered. The youngest children of Narragansett planters generally moved north to smaller farms in the exquisitely idyllic Scituate-Foster country — and there we find my Phillipses after 1750. I have told you of my two pilgrimages to this region — 1926 and 1929 — and of my researches amongst the gravestones there. Life in Foster was conducted on a reduced scale, but never involved dropping from the status of gentry. Money was not free, but children were educated in good academies and reared with a proper regard for pride and taste. My great-grandfather Jeremiah Phillips owned a mill which supplied the neighbouring countryside with grain. My grandfather, moving southward to a small village which he renamed Greene, engaged in lumbering and milling industries and ended by acquiring all the land in and around the village. He built the local hall, founded the local Masonic lodge, saw to the various educational enterprises of the region, and in general reëstablished the magnate-like status of the pre-revolutionary south county; but in 1870 was overtaken by sudden collapse financially — a thing he could have averted by disavowing responsibility for a signed note, but which as a gentleman he refused to evade. This moved the family to Providence, where an happy financial recovery took place; so that I was born into a very comfortable home in the best part of the city — you saw the house on its terrace in 1923, though both it and the locality are not what they were in 1890. Other maternal lines had a very similar history — several having been larger and more important planters in the south county than the Phillipses. The Hazards and Rathbones, I may say without exaggeration, were great houses even in the full Virginian sense — a resemblance obvious even in the old colonial days, when relations between Narragansett and the South were very close. It is no mere caprice which turns my aging fancy toward Charleston. Many a Rhode Islander before the

Revolution went there before me as health declined—so that some Whipple blood still survives there, though not in the male line. It was the congeniality betwixt Narragansett and the South which first exploited Newport as a watering place—the earliest visitors being southern families. Newport, of course, was "the town" frequented by Narragansett planters; Providence being relatively small and crude before the revolution, whilst Newport was a centre of cultivation and the arts. My principal non-Narragansett maternal strains are from the Providence area—Whipple, Field, Clemence, and Mathewson. The Whipples are a Norfolk line who first came to Ipswich, in the Massachusetts-Bay, where one of their branches settled whilst Capt. John Whipple came to Providence and founded the Rhode Island line. The antient Whipple homestead in Ipswich still stands and is used as a museum—a seventeenth century building with an overhang like that of Salem's Seven Gables. In the revolution this family were all damn'd rebels, including the famous privateer Abraham, Capt. Benajah, and my lineal ancestor Capt. Benedict. My ancestor Benjamin Whipple married a daughter of the celebrated Huguenot Gabriel Bernon, who in 1723 founded King's Church (now St. John's) in Providence, but—haw! I caught you there—she is not my ancestress, since he had a second wife Esther Millard from whom I am descended.

Infancy

[The most extensive of Lovecraft's early autobiographical letters is the following account, written to Rheinhart Kleiner on November 16, 1916. It provides a wealth of detail on Lovecraft's first decade of life.]

[2]   I was born on the 20th of August, 1890, at No. 454 (then numbered 194) Angell Street, in the city of Providence. This was the home of my mother's family; my parents' actual residence at the time being in Dorchester, Mass. My father was the son of an Englishman who came from Devonshire to the state of New York in 1847 on account of a loss of fortune. This British grandfather I never saw in person, though he is well known to me through daguerreotypes and photographs. He was the first of his line to adopt a remunerative occupation and American residence, and he remained British in spirit even unto death—even to the extent of a single eyeglass. He made, as I am told, every effort to avoid acquiring an American accent, which is not identical with the speech of cultivated London. My father, his youngest child and only son, was naturally something of an

Englishman himself, though born in Rochester, N.Y. His later residence was in Mt. Vernon, N.Y., with an office in New York City. Still later, after his marriage, he transferred commercial interests to Boston, and lived successively in Dorchester and Auburndale. [. . .]

When I was two years old—or rather, a year and a half old—my parents moved to Auburndale, Mass., sharing a house with a family of the well known poetess, Miss Louise Imogen Guiney, whose verses you have probably seen, and who has been considered one of the foremost poets of the Massachusetts circle. Miss Guiney had been educated in Providence, where she met my mother years before.[1]

At the home of Miss Guiney I probably saw more celebrated persons than I have ever seen since; for her poetical standing is very high. Dr. Oliver Wendell Holmes was a not infrequent caller. And now comes the personal element, for it is there, in Auburndale, amidst the most poetic of poetic auspices, that consciousness first came to my infant mind. I distinctly recall the quiet, shady suburb as I saw it in 1892—and it is a rather curious psychological fact that at this early age I was impressed most of all with the railway bridge and the four-tracked Boston and Albany road which extended beneath it. The trains fascinated me, and to this day I have a love for everything pertaining to railways. (Except the Adamson Law!!) Miss Guiney kept a most extraordinary collection of St. Bernard dogs, all named after authors and poets. A shaggy gentleman by the classic name of Brontë was my particular favourite and companion, being ever in attendance on my chariot as my mother wheeled that vehicle through the streets and avenues. Brontë would permit me to place my fist in his mouth without biting me, and would snarl protectingly if any stranger approached me.

As an infant, I had been restless and prone to cry; now, when able to talk and walk, my temperamental excitability veered in the opposite direction, and I was nicknamed "Little Sunshine" by Mrs. Guiney, mother of the poetess. (Imagine the sour old Conservative being called *"Little Sunshine"!!!!*—Shades of Schopenhauer!!!!!) Mrs. Guiney was a delightfully cultured lady, the widow of a General of Mass. Volunteers, who had carried a bullet in his skull for ten years after the Civil War, when death finally released him from pain. In appearance, I was vastly different then. My hair was yellow, and allowed to curl over my shoulders in ringlets much like those periwigs I am so fond of drawing. This golden mane was another cause of the nickname.

About this time I began to display a precocity which ought to have warned my parents of that mediocre older life which too often follows such an infancy. At the age of two I was a rapid talker, familiar with the alphabet from my blocks and picture-books, and (which will interest you) absolutely *metre-mad!* I could not read, but would repeat any poem of simple sort with unfaltering cadence. Mother Goose was my principal classic, and Miss Guiney would continually make me repeat parts of it; not that my rendition was necessarily notable, but because my age lent uniqueness to the performance. My father, (who was a lover of things military, and who in youth gave up an appointment to West Point only to please his mother) liked me to attain a martial key, and taught me "Sheridan's Ride"[2]—which I declaimed in a manner that brought loud applause—and painful egotism. My nervous utterance was rather well adapted to warlike numbers, and I am told that I put much fire into the lines. My mother innocently helped to swell my self-esteem by recording all my "cute" childish sayings, until I began to make these "naive" remarks *on purpose* to draw attention. (Observe the future Georgian—with his *artificial* wit!!) Miss Guiney would often ask of me: "Whom do you love"? And I would invariably pipe out the stereotyped reply: "Louise Imogen Guiney"! (Today I cannot say as much for her verse—she is too much a disciple of the Browning school, with all its obscurity.) Another "cute" observation and act of mine was to approach my father (whom I barely remember as a handsome figure in black coat and waistcoat and striped grey trousers) and slap him sharply on both knees; crying out, apropos of nothing, "Papa, you look just like a young man"! Since he had not passed his middle thirties, my remark was not exactly incorrect, after all.

Such are the fragments of an early life too far remote for continuous remembrance. In April, 1893, my father was stricken with a complete paralysis resulting from a brain overtaxed with study and business cares. He lived for five years at a hospital, but was never again able to move hand or foot, or to utter a sound.[3] This tragedy dissolved all plans for permanent settlement in Auburndale, and caused the sale of the property recently acquired there. Permanently stricken with grief, my mother took me to the Phillips household, thereby causing me to grow up as a complete Rhode-Islander. At the age of three, my memories crystallize definitely and connectedly for the first time. Both of my maternal grandparents were then living, and my beloved grandfather, Whipple Van Buren Phillips, became the center of my entire universe. A man of culture and extensive travel, he had accumulated a fund of cosmopolitan lore which never ceased to delight me. His acquaintance with all the wonders of Europe, which he had seen at first hand, made me feel almost as if I had seen them myself. It was from him that I acquired my love of Rome. He had loved to muse amidst the ruins of the ancient city, and had brought from Italy a wealth of mosaics, (not the kind that Moe calls my verse!) paintings and other objects d'art whose theme was more often classically *Roman* than *Italian.* He always wore a pair of mosaics in his cuffs for buttons—one of a view of the Coliseum (so *tiny* yet so *faithful*); the other of the Forum. I wear them now—for I still adhere to the old-style round cuff that most have discarded in favour of the modern "link". My grandmother was a serene, quiet lady of the old school, and she did her best to correct my increasingly boorish deportment—for my nervousness made me a very restless and uncontrollable child. She was a devoted student of astronomy, and though she did not personally direct my gaze to the heavens, it was through her library of astronomical books that I first became interested in that direction. My two aunts presented rather a contrast. The elder was (and still is) a devotee of science and literature.[4] She was a potent influence, I think, in turning my fancy toward the classics, while my old love of chemistry also arises from her remarks on that science. She was (though she has ceased to paint now) an artist of great power. When she married Dr. Clark, she proved the means of introducing me to the most substantial classic element of all![5] My other aunt was yet a very young lady when I first began to observe events around me.[6] She was rather a favourite in the younger social set, and brought the principal touch of gayety to a rather conservative household. To the sprightly conversation and repartee of this younger generation, I owe my first lessons in the school of Pope. I could sense the artificiality of the atmosphere, and often strove to ape the airs and affectations of those whom I observed and studied. I extracted not a little celebrity and egotism from my mimicry of various types of callers; particularly one Edward F. Gamwell, who next to my grandfather was my ideal male. I was infinitely delighted when this individual (then a Brown student) decided upon a lasting affiliation with the family.[7] The engagement of my aunt and Mr. Gamwell, and the customary levity of the younger set in their good-natured raillery of the two, imparted to me a curiously worldly cynicism regarding sentimental matters, and forever turned my Muse from the field which you so gracefully adorn.

In 1894 I was able to read fluently, and was a tireless student of the dictionary; never allowing a word to slip by me without ascertaining its

10

meaning. It was then that the mellowed tomes of the family library became my complete world—at once my servants and my masters. I flitted hither and thither amongst them like a fascinated moth, taking supreme joy in the old English volumes of the Lovecrafts, sent to my mother for me when my father was paralysed, since I had become the only male representative of this family. I read everything, understood a little, and imagined more. Grimm's Fairy Tales were my truly representative diet, and I lived mostly in a mediaeval world of imagination. [. . .]

In January, 1896, the death of my grandmother plunged the household into a gloom from which it never fully recovered. The black attire of my mother and aunts terrified and repelled me to such an extent that I would surreptitiously pin bits of bright cloth or paper to their skirts for sheer relief. They had to make a careful survey of their attire before receiving callers or going out! And then it was that my former high spirits received their damper. I began to have nightmares of the most hideous description, peopled with *things* which I called "night-gaunts"—a compound word of my own coinage. I used to draw them after waking (perhaps the idea of these figures came from an edition de luxe of "Paradise Lost" with illustrations by Doré, which I discovered one day in the east parlour.). In dreams they were wont to whirl me through space at a sickening rate of speed, the while fretting and impaling me with their detestable tridents. It is fully fifteen years—aye, more—since I have seen a "night-gaunt", but even now, when half asleep and drifting vaguely along over a sea of childhood thoughts, I feel a thrill of fear [. . .] and instinctively *struggle to keep awake*. That was my one prayer back in '96—each night—to *keep awake* and ward off the night-gaunts!

You will notice that I have made no reference to childish friends and playmates—I had none! The children I knew disliked me, and I disliked them. I was used to adult company and conversation, and despite the fact that I felt shamefully dull beside my elders, I had nothing in common with the infant train. Their romping and shouting puzzled me. I hated mere play and dancing about—in my relaxations I always desired *plot*. My mother once tried to place me in a children's dancing class, but I abhorred the thought. My reply to her suggestion sheds a light on the nature of my bookish browsings in about the year '98. I said: "Nemo fere saltat sobrius, nisi forte insanit!"[8] Which is from Cicero's oration against Catiline. It was in the sombre period of 1896 that I first became a temperance enthusiast. Somewhere I discovered an old copy of John B. Gough's *Sunshine and*

Shadow,[9] and read and re-read it, backward and forward. From that time to this, I have never been at a loss for something to say against liquor! My reading now centred upon classical mythology, to which I had progressed from Grimm. I admired and emulated the poetical quotations so liberally interspersed through the pages of Bulfinch's *Age of Fable*,[10] and in 1897 produced my first formal "poem", entitled "The New Odyssey; or, the Adventures of Ulysses."[11] From 1894 to 1896 I had used only *printed* letters, but I now began to write in script. All this time my spirits were dampened by a vague sensation of impending calamity. I was not blind to a waning of the family fortune, as evidenced by a decrease in the number of servants and closing of the stables. I sadly missed Kelly, the coachman, who was an indisputable authority on all matters pertaining to Hibernian dialect, and who had the forbearance to listen placidly to my laudation of Mother England. By the time of his departure I had acquired a beautiful brogue, which I occasionally aired for the amusement of myself and those about me — particularly Miss Norah _____ (last name forgotten!) who presided over the culinary department. Religious matters likewise fretted me. *I never had the slightest shadow of belief in the supernatural,* but pretended to believe, because it was deemed the proper thing in a Baptist household. Sunday school so much depressed me, that I was soon relieved of that care. Later on my views were tolerated in silence, though not in secrecy. [. . .]

It was in 1898 that I first attempted to attend school. Hitherto it had been deemed unwise to subject so irritable and sensitive a child to discipline of any sort. I entered the highest grade of primary school, but soon found the instruction quite useless, since I had picked up most of the material before. However, I do not regret the venture, since it was in dear old Slater Avenue (alas — to be abandoned next year!) that I made my only childhood friendship — that with Chester and Harold Munroe [. . .].

The Spanish War excited me intensely. For the first time I was in sympathy with those about me; for I sided with the States against a nation which had anciently been England's foe, and whose Armada Drake had destroyed. I longed to participate, but was denied that privilege. It was then that I acquired that admiration for T. R. which still animates me.

By 1899 my poetical outbursts had become quite numerous, one collection being still in my mother's possession. It is a book made of cheap pad paper, bound with pins, and is entitled "Poemata Minora".[12] It contains an ode to the moon, regrets on the passing away of the pagan religion, musings on the downfall of Rome, and such like things!

I had also dabbled much in fiction, delighting mainly in the most exciting and horrible things a child's fancy can conceive of. I enclose an actual manuscript of this period — a short story written at the age of 8, whose conclusion contains a violent death — as did most of my stories. I wonder if you can decipher my childish handwriting? I will also enclose a less dismal tale than "The Secret Cave" — a juvenile attempt at humour entitled "The Little Glass Bottle".[13] These things, as I read them over, reveal to me the fact that my skill in prose was not so great during childhood as I had imagined. We are all prone to overrate our early feats; and I see, in reality, that these 1898 stories were not at all remarkable in structure.

In 1899 a new interest of mine began to gain ascendancy. My predilection for natural science, fostered by my Aunt Lillian, took form in a love of chemistry. A friend of ours is Prof. John Howard Appleton, the venerable professor of chemistry at Brown, and author of many books on the subject. He presented me with his own book for beginners — *The Young Chemist,*[14] and before many months had elapsed, I was deep in experimental research, having a well equipped laboratory in the cellar, which my grandfather had fitted up for me. In March, 1899, I began to publish a chemical daily paper called *The Scientific Gazette,* of which I made four carbon copies for "circulation". How I managed to keep this thing in existence for seven years, as I did, is still a mystery to me. However, it soon degenerated into a weekly!

About 1900 I became a passionate devotee of geography and history, and an intense fanatic on the subject of Antarctic exploration. The Borchgrevink expedition, which had just made a new record in South Polar achievement, greatly stimulated this study. I wrote many fanciful tales about the Antarctic Continent, besides composing "learned" treatises on the real facts. This pursuit of science gave me something of a contempt for art and literature, and my progress in English style was somewhat retarded. I became quite indifferent to verse for a while; using it only in occasional satires. But my prose developed in spite of itself, since my omnivorous reading could not but help it on toward greater fluency.

[Lovecraft elaborates upon his early love of classical antiquity, and its surprising effect upon his early religious sentiments, in the following letter.]

[3]   When I was six my philosophical evolution received its most aesthetically significant impulse — the dawn of Graeco-Roman thought. Always avid for faery lore, I had chanced on Hawthorne's "Wonder Book"

and "Tanglewood Tales", and was enraptured by the Hellenic myths even in their Teutonised form. Then a tiny book in the private library of my elder aunt—the story of the Odyssey in "Harper's Half-Hour Series"—caught my attention. From the opening chapter I was electrified, and by the time I reached the end I was for evermore a Graeco-Roman. My Bagdad name and affiliations disappeared at once,[15] for the magic of silks and colours faded before that of fragrant templed groves, faun-peopled meadows in the twilight, and the blue, beckoning Mediterranean that billowed mysteriously out from Hellas into the reaches of haunting wonder where dwelt Lotophagi and Laestrygonians, where Aeolus kept his winds and Circe her swine, and where in Thrinacian pastures roamed the oxen of radiant Helios. As soon as possible I procured an illustrated edition of Bulfinch's *Age of Fable,* and gave all my time to the reading of the text, in which the true spirit of Hellenism is delightfully preserved, and to the contemplation of the pictures—splendid designs and half-tones of the standard classical statues and paintings of classical subjects. Before long I was fairly familiar with the principal Grecian myths, and had become a constant visitor at the classical art museums of Providence and Boston. I commenced a collection of small plaster casts of the Greek sculptural masterpieces, and learned the Greek alphabet and rudiments of the Latin tongue. I adopted the pseudonym of "Lucius Valerius Messala"—Roman and not Greek, since Rome had a charm all its own for me. My grandfather had travelled observingly through Italy, and delighted me with long firsthand accounts of its beauties and memorials of ancient grandeur. This aesthetic trend had its result in a philosophical way, and prompted my last flickering of religious belief. When about seven or eight I was a genuine pagan, so intoxicated with the beauty of Greece that I acquired a half-sincere belief in the old gods and nature-spirits. I have in literal truth built altars to Pan, Apollo, Diana, and Athena, and have watched for dryads and satyrs in the woods and fields at dusk. Once I firmly thought I beheld some of the sylvan creatures dancing under autumnal oaks; a kind of "religious experience" as true in its way as the subjective ecstasies of any Christian . . . whose unimaginative emotionalism and my unemotional imaginativeness are of equal valuelessness from an intellectual point of view. If such a Christian tell me he has felt the reality of his Jesus or Jahveh, I can reply that I have seen the hoofèd Pan and the sisters of the Hesperian Phaëthusa.

[Lovecraft's early years saw him continually fluctuating between literature and science. His enthusiasm for chemistry is related in the following extract.]

[4]   The science of chemistry, in which I am glad to find you interested, first captivated me in the Year of Our Lord 1898—in a rather peculiar way. With the insatiable curiosity of early childhood, I used to spend hours poring over the pictures in the back of Webster's Unabridged Dictionary—absorbing a miscellaneous variety of ideas. After familiarising myself with antiquities, mediaeval dress and armour, birds, animals, reptiles, fishes, flags of all nations, heraldry, etc. etc., I lit upon the section devoted to "Philosophical and Scientific Instruments", and was veritably hypnotised with it. Chemical apparatus especially attracted me, and I resolved (before knowing a thing about the science!) to have a laboratory. Being a "spoiled child" I had but to ask, and it was mine. I was given a cellar room of good size, and provided by my elder aunt (who had studied chemistry at boarding school) with some simple apparatus and a copy of *The Young Chemist*—a beginner's manual by Prof. John Howard Appleton of Brown—a personal acquaintance. *The Young Chemist* was just the book for me—devoted to easy and instructive experiments—and I was soon deep in its pages. The laboratory "work"—or play—seemed delightful, and despite a few mishaps, explosions, and broken instruments, I got along splendidly. Soon I acquired other books, and began (March 4, 1899) to issue a chemical magazine called *The Scientific Gazette*, which I maintained for eight years. This was, I suppose, my entry to amateur journalism! By 1901 or thereabouts I had a fair knowledge of the principles of chemistry and the details of the inorganic part—about the equivalent of a high-school course, and not including analysis of any kind. Then my fickle fancy turned away to the intensive study of geography, geology, anthropology, and above all *astronomy*, after which came a revival of classicism, latinity, etc. Not until 1906 did chemistry come into my life again. In that year I encountered *physics* in high-school, which reawaked my dormant laboratory instincts, and led me back to the study of matter, its constitution and properties. I increased my chemical library by fully 20 volumes—to say naught of the physics text books I bought—and obtained a plenitude of new instruments. I was now in a smaller house, with a smaller laboratory, but the new room was ample for the purpose. In 1907 I took chemistry in high-school,

but since I knew all the course before, had more fun than instruction in the class room. I left high-school certified in physics and chemistry, and intended to specialise in those subjects at college; but just then my nervous system went to pieces, and I was forced to relinquish all thought of activity. Yet at home I continued my chemical studies, dabbling in a correspondence course which helped me in matters of *analysis* and *organic chemistry,* hitherto neglected by me. But in the mean time literature had been on the increase once more, and I found my interest centreing more and more in old-fashioned scribbling. By 1912 I had practically ceased to be active in chemistry, and have since partially dismantled my laboratory, owing to my mother's nervousness at having deadly poisons, corrosive acids, and potential explosives about the place. One tangible memorial of my hobby remains—a bulky manuscript entitled "A Brief Course in Inorganic Chemistry", by H. P. Lovecraft. 1910.[16] There is also a physical memorial—the third finger of my right hand—whose palm side is permanently scarred by a mighty phosphorus burn sustained in 1907. At the time, the loss of the finger seemed likely, but the skill of my uncle—a physician—saved it. It is still a bit stiff, and aches in cold weather—as no doubt it always will. During the bandage and splint days I had to pick out my verses and articles with my left forefinger only on the typewriter. I am not at all regretful of the time I spent in chemical pursuits, for I have time and again found use for the information I imbibed. I should not feel competent to make philosophical conjectures, were I without at least a moderate knowledge of the laws and properties of matter and energy.

[Aside from studies, Lovecraft fully engaged in the customary activities of carefree boyhood. The following extracts describe his interests in detection, music, and other amusements.]

[5]   As to "Sherlock Holmes"—I used to be infatuated with him! I read every Sherlock Holmes story published, and even organised a *detective agency* when I was thirteen, arrogating to myself the proud pseudonym of S.H. This P[rovidence] D[etective] A[gency]—whose members ranged between nine and fourteen in years, was a most wonderful thing—how many murders and robberies we unravelled! Our headquarters were in a deserted house just out of the thickly settled area, and we there enacted, and "solved", many a gruesome tragedy. I still remember my labours in producing artificial "bloodstains on the floor!!!" But in conformity with

our settled policy of utter candour, I must admit to you that the entire venture was more dramatic than psychological in objects and essence; and that our "deductions" were generally pretty well provided for in advance.

[6]   But I may remark that I, too, was a detective in youth—being a member of the Providence Detective Agency at an age as late as 13! Our force had very rigid regulations, and carried in its pockets a standard working equipment consisting of police whistle, magnifying-glass, electric flashlight, handcuffs, (sometimes plain twine, but "handcuffs" for all that!) tin badge, (I have mine still!!) tape measure, (for footprints) revolver, (mine was the real thing, but Inspector Munroe (aet 12) had a water squirt-pistol while Inspector Upham (aet 10) worried along with a cap-pistol) and copies of all newspaper accounts of desperate criminals at large—plus a paper called *The Detective*, which printed pictures and descriptions of outstanding "wanted" malefactors. Did our pockets bulge and sag with this equipment? I'll say they did!! We also had elaborately prepared "credentials"—certificates attesting our good standing in the agency. Mere scandals we scorned. Nothing short of bank robbers and murderers were good enough for us. We shadowed many desperate-looking customers, and diligently compared their physiognomies with the "mugs" in *The Detective*, yet never made a full-fledged arrest. Ah, me—the good old days!

[7]   My rhythmic tendencies led me into a love of melody, and I was forever whistling and humming in defiance of convention and good breeding. I was so exact in time and tune, and showed such a semi-professional precision and flourish in my crude attempts, that my plea for a violin was granted when I was seven years of age, and I was placed under the instruction of the best violin teacher for children in the city—Mrs. Wilhelm Nauck. For two years I made such progress that Mrs. Nauck was enthusiastic, and declared that I should adopt music as a career—*but,* all this time the tedium of practicing had been wearing shockingly on my always sensitive nervous system. My "career" extended until 1899, its summit being a public recital at which I played a solo from Mozart before an audience of considerable size. Soon after that, my ambition and taste alike collapsed like a house of cards (to use a trite simile). I began to detest classical music, because it had meant so much painful labour to me; and I positively *loathed* the violin! Our physician, knowing my temperament, advised an immediate discontinuance of music lessons, which speedily ensued. Is this not one

of the most typical failures on record? In art, I lacked *talent;* but in music, I lacked *ambition and ability.* Twenty years ago I criticised Verdi and Wagner, and sat rapt with childish adoration at the strains of Beethoven—today I hum and whistle the stuff you despise so much as played on your relative's phonograph, that is, except "nigger laughing songs"!, and a few weeks ago I attended with delight that modern "classic" opera called "Katinka"! If this be not *backwardness* and *dulness,* what *do* you call it? But the climax is yet to come!! Three or four years ago I picked up my little neglected violin, tuned it after purchasing new strings, and thought I would amuse myself with its sound, even though I did no better than a rustic village fiddler. I drew my bow across the strings, when *lo!* I discovered that I had forgotten how to play as much as a single note! *It was as if I had never touched a violin before!!!!*

[8]   When, at the age of 11, I was a member of the Blackstone Military Band, (whose youthful members were all virtuosi on what was called the "zobo"—a brass horn with a membrane at one end, which would transform humming to a delightfully brassy impressiveness!) my almost unique ability to keep time was rewarded by my promotion to the post of drummer. That was a difficult thing, insomuch as I was also a star zobo soloist; but the obstacle was surmounted by the discovery of a small papier-mache zobo at the toy store, which I could grip with my teeth without using my hands. Thus my hands were free for drumming—whilst one foot worked a mechanical triangle-beater and the other worked the cymbals—or rather, a wire (adapted from a second triangle-beater) which crashed down on a single horizontal cymbal and made exactly the right cacophony . . . . much as does the ordinary trap-drummer's single cymbal attached to the bass-drum. I was surely a versatile and simultaneous musician in my day—and on my plane. Had jazz-bands been known at that remote aera, I could certainly have qualified as an ideal general-utility-man—capable of working rattles, cow-bells, and everything else that two hands, two feet, and one mouth could handle. Ah, me—the days that are no more!

Youthful Interests

[A late letter supplies fascinating glimpses of Lovecraft's childhood play activities, both alone and with friends.]

[9]   Having certain fantastic and imaginative interests early (including my perpetual 18th centuryism) tended to give me more new pleasures than

it took away. About the only childish things I disliked were games and other *aimless* activities. Anything with a *coördinated* interest (i.e., something like a *plot* element) gave me the keenest delight. I derived the most extreme pleasure from my toys—of which I had a profuse variety, since our really straitened circumstances date only from 1904. My favourite toys were *very small* ones, which would permit of their arrangement in widely extensive scenes. My mode of play was to devote an entire table-top to a scene, which I would proceed to develop as a broad landscape . . . . helped by occasional trays of earth or clay. I had all sorts of *toy villages* with small wooden or cardboard houses, and by combining several of them would often construct *cities* of considerable extent and intricacy. (Do they make these toy villages now? There were even steepled churches!) Toy trees—of which I had an infinite number—were used with varying effect to form parts of the landscape . . . . even *forests* (or the suggested edges of forests). Certain kinds of blocks made walls and hedges, and I also used blocks in constructing large public buildings. It must be noted that, despite a taste for realism which balked at the obvious exoticism of certain German toys, I cultivated a stoical indifference to the element of *consistent scale* in my designs. I couldn't be over-insistent that all my villages and buildings harmonise in magnitude—so that some of my private houses were undeniably larger than some of my churches and court houses, and so on. This principle applied even more conspicuously to such details as vehicles, human figures, etc. I had to accept what was commonly available, and let my childish imagination exercise a mercifully softening influence. My people were mainly of the lead-soldier type and magnitude—frankly too large for the buildings which they presumably tenanted, but as small as I could get. I accepted some as they were, but had my mother modify many in costume with the aid of knife and paint-brush. Much piquancy was added to my scenes by special toy buildings like windmills, castles, etc. I was always consistent—geographically and chronologically—in setting my landscapes as my infant store of information would allow. Naturally, the majority of scenes would be of the 18th century; although my parallel fascination with railways and street-cars led me to construct large numbers of contemporary landscapes with intricate systems of tin trackage. I had a magnificent repertoire of cars and railway accessories—signals, tunnels, stations, etc.—though this system was admittedly too large in scale for my villages. My mode of play was to construct some scene as fancy—incited by some story or picture—dictated, and then to act out its life for long periods— sometimes a fortnight—making up events of a highly melodramatic cast I went. These events would sometimes cover only a brief span—a war or plague or merely a spirited pageant of travel and commerce and incident leading nowhere—but would sometimes involve long aeons, with visible changes in the landscape and buildings. Cities would fall and be forgotten, and new cities would spring up. Forests would fall or be cut down, and rivers (I had some fine *bridges*) would change their beds. History, of course, suffered in this process; but my data (culled from stories, pictures, questioning of my elders, and a marvellously graphic historic device called "Adams' Synchronological Chart"—which I still have) was of a distinctly juvenile kind and extent. Sometimes I would try to depict actual historic events and scenes—Roman, 18th century, or modern—and sometimes I would make everything up. Horror-plots were frequent, though (oddly enough) I never attempted to construct fantastic or extra-terrestrial scenes. I was too much of an innate realist to care for fantasy in its purest form. Well—I got a great kick out of all this. In about a week or two I'd get fed up on a scene and substitute a new one, though now and then I'd be so attached to one that I'd retain it longer—starting a fresh scene on another table with materials not forming scene #1. There was a kind of intoxication in being lord of a visible world (albeit a miniature one) and determining the flow of its events. I kept this up till I was 11 or 12, despite the parallel growth of literary and scientific interests. I also had a toy theatre—for in those days I took an interest in the drama (I saw my first play at 6, and my first Shakespearian play at 7). Being dissatisfied with the limited array of scenery and characters furnished with it, I used my own characters and made additional cardboard scenery. Of plays, Sheridan's and Shakespeare's were my favourites. I spoke the original lines from the text, clumsily moving the characters in some rough approximation of the action. I always made programmes—

Drury-Lane Theatre
Nov.ʳ 1779
The Company presents a Comedy by Mr.
Sheridan, intitul'd
The Critick;
or, a Tragedy Rehears'd.

But I was by no means solitary, or confined to indoor pleasures. I had a large number of companions, and frequently joined them in outdoor diversions of great variety—generally (if I could so arrange it, for nothing else was so pleasing to me) the acting out of some vivid line of adventure (outlaws, police and criminals, Civil War or other battles, big game hunting, Indians and soldiers, firemen, etc.). We also had a military band, our instruments being those brass horns with membrane discs which gave a cornet-like sound to the voice. Sometimes we played *railway* with express-carts, velocipedes, and a specially-made street-car (based on a packing-box) which I had. Those were great old days. Often our playing would be transferred to the open fields and woods, since the old home was near the edge of the built-up streets and close to a wholly ancient New England countryside. Of this countryside most is gone—engulfed by the paved streets of the expanding city. One marvellous wooded ravine—whose effect on my infant imagination was tremendous—has been wholly filled and obliterated. One section, however—the wooded banks of the Seekonk River, with a tributary ravine like the filled-up one—has remained just as it was; having become a metropolitan park reservation before it had time to decay. Thither I still go nearly every pleasant afternoon in summer, taking my current reading and writing and losing myself in a timeless world at one with the past. Not a visible object is other than as it was in 1900, and sometimes I feel so wafted back that I half-expect to find the adult present a bad dream as I emerge. I half-expect to walk out of the woods into the old, leisurely streets of 1900, with the rattling waggons and smart carriages and little red and green single-truck street-cars (open, with gaily flapping awnings, in summer, but closed—with open platforms—in winter) and sputtering carbon arc-lights (supplemented by surviving gas lamp posts) and red litter-boxes (they're green now) of the period. I always go home (to my birthplace, 454 Angell St.) the same old way, and if dusk be thick, the illusion still persists. The house still stands—as a doctor's office centre —on its high terrace, though the stable perished 2 years ago. After failing fortunes banished our horses and carriages, that stable used to be my personal playhouse. I kept my carts and toy street-car and velocipede and (after 1900) bicycle in the great carriage room . . . where a buggy and a victoria still lingered desolate amidst cobwebs . . . . and used the stall-room as a stage for plays—with the carriage-room for an auditorium and the sliding door for a curtain. The harness-room was my "office"; and the deserted coachman's quarters upstairs—and the great hay-and-vat loft—were the scene of spectral adventures. After my tenth birthday—Aug. 20, 1900—I was an inveterate cyclist, becoming as the years passed almost a wheeled centaur. My bicycles (I used to wear them out so badly that I had 3 in succession) took me all over the neighbouring countryside, and gave me a daily familiarity with rustic landscapes and New England village atmosphere which has always influenced me potently. A frail constitution, however, generally limited my rides to a 15-mile radius. So after all I'd hardly call my youth a wretched one. The fact is, I was actually spoiled—having just about everything I wanted. Many thought I'd turn out to be hopelessly self-centred and recklessly extravagant—though actually I proved able to accommodate myself to greater economies and narrowings of living-scale than even the most pessimistic could have foreseen. Incidentally—I was no such paragon of classical precocity as you seem to have gathered from my early taste for the "Ancient Mariner". Remember that the Doré illustrations (God, how Doré fascinated me! We had and still have his Dante and Milton pictures.) made the edition I read a veritable picture-book. The mind of childhood is a curiously compartmented thing, so that in addition to my love of Grimm, Arabian Nights, Poe, the Greek and Roman myths, and the 18th century poets and essayists, I had a parallel set of utterly commonplace interests—street-cars, houses under construction, Alger, Nick Carter, Henty, and all the customary juvenilia. After 1904 I had a long succession of 22-calibre rifles, and became a fair shot till my eyes played hell with my accuracy. Far from being a prig, I even cultivated considerable toughness when I was first able to attend school continuously. I supplemented the oaths of the 18th century with those of the present, drawing freely upon them whenever milder language would have savoured of softness. I had plenty of foes, but I don't think even the worst ever called me a sissy. I was, in fact, decidedly pugnacious—having a violent and ungovernable temper which the passage of years and a growing sense of the cosmic inevitability of all things has almost totally eradicated. Any affront—especially any reflection on my truthfulness or honour as an 18th century gentleman—roused in me a tremendous fury, and I would always start a fight if an immediate retraction were not furnished. Being of scant physical strength, I did not fare well in these encounters; though I would never ask for their termination. I thought it disgraceful, even in defeat, not to maintain a wholly "you-go-to-hell" attitude until the victor ceased pummelling of his own accord. What I would have done in a fight with lower-class boys who "fight dirty" I don't know, but I was never put to so drastic a test. Occasionally I won fights—aided by my habit of assuming a dramatically ferocious aspect frightening to the nervous . . . . the "by God, I'll kill you!" stuff. Ah, me—the spirit of youth! Now I'm an old man and scarcely ever double up my fists except on paper. [. . .] As for circuses—my early hatred of crowds, plus my ultra-keen sensitiveness to the bad odours of menageries, deterred me from an experience which might have been highly enriching to the imagination. Olfactory evils played such havock with my stomach that (except for such menagerie-going as was needful to a knowledge of natural history) I always shunned any place suspected of harbouring bad odours. In later years a sinus trouble has dulled my sense of smell and removed this attitude. I was also hypersensitive to *sounds*—a pistol shot or firecracker giving me intolerable pain. This caused me to avoid places where loud reports were frequent—though at the same time I tried to acquire through slow gradations a greater hardihood. By the time I was 13 or 14 I could stand an ordinary .32 or .38 pistol shot without too much discomfort, and since then my hearing (like my sense of smell) has mercifully become less acute. Even now, though, I don't like cannonad-ing—and I was under no illusions as to what I would have had to endure aurally had I succeeded in joining the National Guard in 1917. But I ram-ble. The main point is, that I really had a damn good time in childhood—a highly sensitive imaginative life giving me plenty to compensate for any such disadvantages as poor health. One favourite pursuit of mine was seeking out ancient and glamorous street scenes on the hill I now inhabit. (The old home was a mile east of the crest, in a Victorian region) I used to drag my mother all around when I was 4 or 5 and not allowed to be so far from home alone. I hardly knew what I was after, but the centuried houses with their fanlights and knockers and railed steps and small-paned win-dows had a strong and significant effect of some sort on me. This world, I felt, was a different one from the (Victorian) world of French roofs and plate glass and concrete sidewalks and piazzas and open lawns that I was born into. It was a magic, secret world, and it had a *realness* beyond that of the home neighbourhood. It had, I knew, been there long before the home neighbourhood existed—and I felt it would still be there after the other had passed away. Then again, it was just like the Hogarth scenes in the big books in the parlour, and just like the pictures in the coloured books about the Revolution which were given me. It was *familiar*—I had *always* known it—I had *seen it before*—it was *part of me* in a sense that no other scene ever was . . . . . and so I dreamed about it by night and visited it by day when-ever I could. I used to have (as I still do) favourite *vistas*—looking up such and such a street and wondering *what* lay around the curve at the end.

Could I walk into the time of Hogarth and the Revolution if I followed one of those cryptic ways to its unknown end some evening when the twilight was purple and the yellow lamplight flickered up softly behind ancient fan-lights and tiny window-panes? On rainy evenings, when the little old gas lamps (now gone) cast strange reflections on the glistening cobblestones and brick sidewalks, I could almost *see* the figures of yesterday plodding along . . . . cloaks, three-cornered hats, queues losing their powder in the rain . . . . . and I began to dream of myself in those scenes, witnessing tantalising fragments of 18th century daily life that faded too soon into wakefulness. Once I thought I saw a rider galloping madly over the cobbles, whilst all the windows were flung up by staring white-capped housewives and turbaned slaves . . . . . once I saw a troop of the King's men in red coats with muskets and beating drums . . . . were they off to join Shirley or Amherst against the French? God Save the King! . . . . But I loved the ancient fields and farmhouses and stone walls and orchards and deep woods and water-mills and village spires of the countryside, too.

[Another letter outlines the elaborate playground Lovecraft devised for himself and his friends in an adjoining lot.]

[10]   When I was very small, my kingdom was the lot next my birthplace, 454 Angell St. Here were trees, shrubs, and grasses, and here when I was between four and five the coachman built me an immense summer-house all mine own—a somewhat crude yet vastly pleasing affair, with a staircase leading to a flat roof from which in later years I surveyed the skies with my telescope. The floor was Mother Earth herself, for at the time the edifice was constructed I had a definite purpose for it. I was then a railway man, with a vast system of express-carts, wheelbarrows, and the like; plus some immensely ingenious cars made out of packing-cases. I had also a splendid engine made by mounting a sort of queer boiler on a tiny express-wagon. The new building, therefore, must needs be my grand terminal and round-house combined; a mighty shed under which my puffing trains could run, even as the big trains of the outside world ran under the sheds at the old depots in Providence and Boston—depots long since razed to the ground to make way for the Union, Back Bay, and South Stations of today! So the building became in familiar household parlance "The Engine House"—and how I loved it! From the gate of our yard to the Engine House I had a nice track—or path—made and levelled for me; a continuation of the great

railway system formed by the concrete walks in the yard. And here, in supreme bliss, were idled away the days of my youth. As I grew older, I took the road and its buildings more and more under my personal management. I began to make repairs myself, and when I was six I constructed many branch lines. Once I carefully laid track with wooden rails and sleepers—forgetting the trivial detail that I had nothing to run on it! But it looked nice, anyway! Then came changes—one day there was not any coachman to help me, whereat I mourned; but later on I had compensation—the horses and carriages were sold too, so that I had a gorgeous, glorious, titanic, and unbelievable new playhouse—the whole great stable with its immense carriage room, its neat-looking "office", and its vast upstairs, with the colossal (almost scareful) expanse of the grain loft, and the little three-room apartment where the coachman and his wife had lived. All this magnificence was my very own, to do with as I liked! Many were the uses to which I put that stable. The carriage room was now the main terminal of my railway, whilst in other parts were my office, theatre, and other institutions. But the call of the pastoral could not be resisted! Despite my new possession, my interest in the vacant lot and the Engine House was unflagging. One day I decided to alter my scheme, and instead of a railway system my domain became a pastoral countryside. I invited all the boys of the neighbourhood to co-operate in building a little village under the lee of the high board fence, which was in due time accomplished. Many new roads and garden spots were made, and the whole was protected from the Indians (who dwelt somewhere to the north) by a large and impregnable fort with massive earthworks. The boy who suggested that fort and supervised its construction was deeply interested in military things and followed up his hobby. Today he is a Lieutenant-Colonel in the U.S. Army, having attended West Point and served brilliantly as Captain and Major through the World War, being twice wounded. My new village was called "New Anvik", after the Alaskan village of "Anvik", which about that time became known to me through the boys' book "Snow-Shoes and Sledges", by Kirk Munroe. As you see, I then read juvenile matter as well as the classics, and liked it! As the years stole on, my play became more and more dignified; but I could not give up New Anvik. When the grand disaster came, and we moved to this inferior abode, I made a second and more ambitious New Anvik in the vacant lot here. This was my aesthetic masterpiece, for besides a little village of painted huts erected by myself and Chester and Harold Munroe, there was a landscape garden, all of mine own handiwork. I chopped down certain trees and preserved others, laid out paths and gardens, and set at the proper points shrubbery and or- namental urns taken from the old home. My paths were of gravel, bor- dered with stones, and here and there a bit of stone wall or an impressive cairn of my own making added to the picture. Between two trees I made a rustic bench, later duplicating it betwixt two other trees. A large grassy space I levelled and transformed into a Georgian lawn, with a sundial in the centre. Other parts were uneven, and I sought to catch certain sylvan or bower-like effects. The whole was drained by a system of channels ter- minating in a cesspool of my own excavation. Such was the paradise of my adolescent years, and amidst such scenes were many of my early works written. Though by nature indolent, I was never too tired to labour about my estate, attending to the vegetation in summer, and shovelling neat paths in niveous winter. Then I perceived with horror that I was growing too old for pleasure. Ruthless Time had set its fell claw upon me, and I was seven- teen. Big boys do not play in toy houses and mock gardens, so I was obliged to turn over my world in sorrow to another and younger boy who dwelt across the lot from me. And since that time I have not delved in the earth or laid out paths and roads. There is too much wistful memory in such procedure, for the fleeting joy of childhood may never be recaptured. Adulthood is hell.

[Perhaps the most significant intellectual event in Lovecraft's boyhood was his discovery of astronomy. He himself was fully aware of its pro- found effect upon the development of his philosophical thought.]

[11] Hitherto my philosophy had been distinctly juvenile and empiri- cal. It was a revolt from obvious falsities and ugliness, but involved no particular cosmic or ethical theory. In ethical questions I had no analytical interest because I did not realise that they were questions. I accepted Vic- torianism, with consciousness of many prevailing hypocrisies and aside from Sabbatarianism and supernatural matters, without dispute; never having heard of inquiries which reached "beyond good and evil". Though at times interested in reforms, notably prohibition, I was inclined to be bored by ethical casuistry; since I believed conduct to be a matter of taste and breeding, with virtue, delicacy, and truthfulness as symbols of gentil- ity. Of my word and honour I was inordinately proud, and would permit no reflections to be cast upon them. I thought ethics too obvious and com-

monplace to be scientifically discussed, and considered philosophy solely in its relation to truth and beauty. I was, and still am, pagan to the core. Regarding man's place in Nature, and the structure of the universe, I was as yet unawakened. This awakening was to come in the winter of 1902–3, when astronomy asserted its supremacy amongst my studies.

The most poignant sensations of my existence are those of 1896, when I discovered the Hellenic world, and of 1902, when I discovered the myriad suns and worlds of infinite space. Sometimes I think the latter event the greater, for the grandeur of that growing conception of the universe still excites a thrill hardly to be duplicated. I made of astronomy my principal scientific study, obtaining larger and larger telescopes, collecting astronomical books to the number of 61, and writing copiously on the subject in the form of special and monthly articles in the local daily press. As I mentioned in the preceding letter, my intention was to become a professor of astronomy. By my thirteenth birthday I was thoroughly impressed with man's impermanence and insignificance, and by my seventeenth, about which time I did some particularly detailed writing on the subject, I had formed in all essential particulars my present pessimistic cosmic views. The futility of all existence began to impress and oppress me; and my references to human progress, formerly hopeful, began to decline in enthusiasm. Always partial to antiquity, I allowed myself to originate a sort of one-man cult of retrospective suspiration.

[Lovecraft's second attempt at grammar school (1902–3) resulted in the following hilarious incident at the graduation ceremonies.

[12]   In 1902 I again attempted school; and singularly enough, I went to the same old Slater Avenue edifice, which had now acquired a grammar department in addition to the primary grades. Here again I was brought into contact with other children, but my attitude toward them was now different. I had read enough idyllic verse to understand that childhood is a golden age in the life of man; never to be regained when once lost; so I tried to interest myself in the affairs of other boys with some degree of success. I joined the "Slater Avenue Army", whose wars were waged in the neighbouring woods, and though my dramatic suggestions were not always accepted with perfect tolerance, I managed to get along with my "fellow-soliders" fairly well. One of these boys—named Manton Mitchell—later became a *real* soldier; attending West Point and being now a 1st Lieutenant

of the U.S. Infantry. (He was with Pershing's Mexican expedition, but is now home on furlough.) At school I was considered a bad boy, for I would never submit to discipline. When censured by my teacher for disregard of rules, I used to point out to her the essential emptiness of conventionality, in such a satirical way, that her patience must have been quite severely strained; but withal she was remarkably kind, considering my intractable disposition. Her name is Abbie A. Hathaway, called "Abbie" behind her back by the boys. She is now retired on a pension, having been rather elderly even in my time. She still takes an interest in my work, and I chat pleasantly with her (more pleasantly than of yore) whenever I meet her. I managed to excel in studies at Slater Avenue, which perhaps reconciled her to my outrageous deportment. In history classes we used to have thunderous debates, for while "Abbie" was the daughter of a Union veteran, the Munroe boys and I were Confederate sympathizers. How we used to annoy her with our "compositions"—all flaming with love and glorification of the South! [. . .]

On graduation day—in June, 1903—occurred a rather interesting incident. I had affected a great contempt for ceremony of every sort, and had absolutely refused to deliver a "speech" from the platform, according to custom. But after the exercises began, I suddenly resolved to say something after all. I heard so much applause bestowed upon compositions which I felt to be mediocre, that I determined to surpass my fellow scholars by an impromptu address. Accordingly I ceased to pay attention to the speakers, but seized upon pad and pencil, and began to write an essay on the life of Sir William Herschel, the astronomer. It was against all maxims of courtesy to commence scribbling in the midst of a publick ceremony, but I was ever disregardful of the amenities. When I had finished, I quietly stole up to "Abbie's" desk, and informed her in a dictatorial whisper that I would, in spite of my previous refusal, read a paper at the conclusion of the programme. She did not take offense at the eccentric manner in which I prepared my eleventh-hour oration, but announced me at the proper time. I mounted the platform with a sublime scorn of everyone and everything about me, and began in a very condescending and professional manner to address the assembled multitude of parents and children. I employed my best Georgian mode of speech, beginning in this fashion:

"Ladies and gentlemen: I had not thought to trespass upon your time and patience today, but when the Muse impels, it becomes a man but ill to stifle her demand. When I speak of the Muse, I do not mean to say that I am about to inflict my bad verses upon you—far be that from my intention. My Muse this day is Clio, who presides over affairs of history; and my subject, a very revered one to me, is the career of one who rose from the most unfortunate condition of insignificance to the utmost height of deserved eminence—Sir William Herschel, who from an Hanoverian peasant became the greatest astronomer of England, and therefore of the World!"

I think these are nearly the words I used. I kept them long in memory (through egotism) though I have not a copy beside me now. If this version be incorrect, it is because there are not enough long words present. I was a veritable pocket edition of Dr. Johnson for Latinated language. Much to my concern, this offering elicited smiles, rather than attention, from the adult part of my audience; but after I had done, I received a round of applause which well compensated for my trouble, and sent me off the platform with the self-satisfied glow of a triumphant Garrick. Good old Miss Hathaway still relates this anecdote. My selection of Dr. Herschel as a hero for my extemporaneous panegyric, is an index of my latest predilection. Astronomy had seized me in its spell in the winter of 1902–03; and when speaking of the Muses, I should not have mentioned Clio alone, but should have included Urania as well! In the summer of 1903 my mother presented me with a 2½" astronomical telescope, and thenceforward my gaze was ever upward at night. The late Prof. Upton of Brown, a friend of the family, gave me the freedom of the college observatory, (Ladd Observatory) and I came and went there at will on my bicycle. Ladd Observatory tops a considerable eminence about a mile from the house. I used to walk up Doyle Avenue hill with my wheel, but when returning would have a glorious coast down it. So constant were my observations, that my neck became affected by the strain of peering at a difficult angle. It gave me much pain, and resulted in a permanent curvature perceptible today to a close observer. My body has ever been unequal to the demands of an active career.

The Loss of His Birthplace

[The carefree world of Lovecraft's youth abruptly ended when his grandfather died and he and his mother were forced to move from 454 Angell Street. This loss of his birthplace brought Lovecraft, for perhaps the first and last time, to the brink of suicide. Characteristically, he was saved from self-destruction by intellectual curiosity.]

[13]   The one time that I seriously thought of suicide was in and after 1904, when my grandfather died in the midst of business tangles (he was president of a land and irrigation corporation exploiting the Snake River in Idaho, and the total destruction of the dam on which everything depended had caused a frightful situation) and left us all relatively poor. I was (being predominantly geographical-minded) tremendously attached to the old home at 454 Angell St. (now housing 12 physicians' offices — I walk by it still as often as I can) with the grounds and fountain, and stable, but this now had to go . . . . indeed, there had been drastic economies for 5 years before that. My mother and I moved into a 5-room-and-attic flat two squares farther east (598 Angell St., where I dwelt till 1924), and for the first time I knew what a congested, servantless home — with another family in the same house — was. There was a vacant lot next door (although even that was later built up — during my adulthood), which I promptly exploited as a landscape garden and adorned with a village of piano-box houses, but even that failed to assuage my nostalgia. I felt that I had lost my entire adjustment to the cosmos — for what indeed was HPL without the remembered rooms and hallways and hangings and staircases and statuary and paintings [. . .] and yard and walks and cherry-trees and fountain and ivy-grown arch and stable and gardens and all the rest? How could an old man of 14 (and I surely felt that way!) readjust his existence to a skimpy flat and new household programme and inferior outdoor setting in which almost nothing familiar remained? It seemed like a damned futile business to keep on living. No more tutors — high-school next September which would probably be a devilish bore, since one couldn't be as free and easy in high-school as one had been during brief snatches at the neighbourly Slater Ave. school . . . . . . oh, hell! Why not slough off consciousness altogether? The whole life of man and of the planet was a mere cosmic second — so I couldn't be missing much. The *method* was the only trouble. I didn't like messy exits, and dignified ones were hard to find. Really good poisons were hard to get — those in my chemical laboratory (I reëstablished this institution in the basement of the new place) were crude and painful. Bullets were spattery and unreliable. Hanging was ignominious. Daggers were messy unless one could arrange to open a wrist-vein in a bowl of warm water — and even that had its drawbacks despite good Roman precedent. Falls from a cliff were positively vulgar in view of the probable state of the remains. Well — what tempted me most was the warm, shallow, reed-grown Barrington River

down the east shore of the bay. I used to go there on my bicycle and look speculatively at it. (That summer I was always on my bicycle—wishing to be away from home as much as possible, since my abode reminded me of the home I had lost.) How easy it would be to wade out among the rushes and lie face down in the warm water till oblivion came. There would be a certain gurgling or choking unpleasantness at first—but it would soon be over. Then the long, peaceful night of non-existence . . . . what I had enjoyed from the mythical start of eternity till the 20th of August, 1890. More and more I looked at the river on drowsy, sun-golden summer afternoons. I liked to think of the beauty of sun and blue river and green shore and distant white steeple as enfolding me at the last—it would be as if the element of mystical cosmic beauty were dissolving me. And yet certain elements— notably scientific curiosity and a sense of world drama—held me back. Much in the universe baffled me, yet I knew I could pry the answers out of books if I lived and studied longer. Geology, for example. Just *how* did these ancient sediments and stratifications get crystallised and upheaved into granite peaks? Geography—just *what* would Scott and Shackleton and Borchgrevink find in the great white antarctic or their next expeditions . . . . . which I could—if I wished—live to see described? And as to history—as I contemplated an exit without further knowledge I became uncomfortably conscious of what I didn't know. Tantalising gaps existed everywhere. When did people stop speaking Latin and begin to talk Italian and Spanish and French? What on earth ever happened in the black Middle Ages in those parts of the world other than Britain and France (whose story I knew)? What of the vast gulfs of space outside all familiar lands— desert reaches hinted of by Sir John Mandeville and Marco Polo . . . . Tartary, Thibet . . . . . . What of unknown Africa? I knew that many things which were mysteries to me were not such to others. I had not resented my lack of a solution as long as I expected to know *some day*—but now that the idea of *never knowing* presented itself, the circumstance of frustrated curiosity became galling to me. Mathematics, too. Could a gentleman properly die without having demonstrated on paper why the square of the hypotenuse of a right triangle is equal to the sum of the squares of the other two sides? So in the end I decided to postpone my exit till the following summer. I would do a little curiosity-satisfying at first; filling certain gaps of scientific and historical knowledge, and attaining a greater sense of *completeness* before merging with the infinite blackness. Especially would I solve that always-teasing question of how and when "Romans" named *Fabius* Anicius became "Italians" named *Fabio* Anizio. Well—that fall I found high-school a delight and stimulus instead of a bore, and the next spring I resumed publication of the *R.I. Journal of Astronomy*, which I had allowed to lapse. Possibly I would wait till '06 before making my exit . . . . . one could drown in '06 just as well as in '05 or '04! But *new* questions demanding answers were always springing up. First-year *physics* opened problems connected with the nature of visible phenomena and the operation of the universe which my earlier chemistry and astronomy had not even suggested; was it possible that educated men knew things about the basic structure of the cosmos which invalidated all my confidently-held concepts? And god! what a surprise *history* was proving! The whole pageantry of the *Byzantine Empire,* and its hostile connexion with that gorgeous Islam which my early Arabian Nights and my later astronomical studies (cf. terms and names like *azimuth, zenith, Aldebaran, almucantar, nadir, Deneb,* etc.) had made close to me, swept unheralded on my sight—and for the first time I heard of the lost Minoan culture which Sir Arthur Evans was even then busily digging up in Crete. Assyria and Babylonia, too, stood out with greater impressiveness than ever before—and I heard at last of the eternal query of *Easter Island.* What a world! Why, good god, a man might keep busy forever, even in an uncongenial environment, learning new things . . . . pleasantly busy, too, for each new point of satisfied curiosity gave a hell of a kick. Then there was the kick of writing out a mood on paper so that it could be recaptured . . . . I had done some experimenting in fictional structure, and achieved a new level of results with "The Beast in the Cave" (ineffably pompous and Johnsonese—I still have it), which I wrote in April '05. Could it be possible that a poor man without servants or a large house and grounds might get a greater satisfaction from remaining alive and studying and writing than from slipping back to primal nescience and molecular dispersal? The matter was worth considering—at least, the end could go over till '06 . . . . or very possibly, '07. About then I had a nervous breakdown (winter '05–'06) and had to stay out of school for months, and my lack of energy stopped my even thinking about anything. Then the *Providence Tribune* was founded, and I learned that I had a good chance of breaking into *print* at last . . . . contributing monthly astronomical articles just like Prof. Upton's in the *Journal and Bulletin.*[17] One *couldn't* miss a chance like that! Let suicide wait!

[In the end Lovecraft found high school pleasing and entertaining; but the following anecdote shows that he was not above being something of a smart-aleck.]

[14]   As for actual schooldays—I always liked school, although I didn't fit in with the discipline overly well during the fragmentary grammar-school snatches. In high school, however, I never realised there was such a thing as discipline. The teachers—a goodly percentage of them men—took the position that the pupils were near enough to responsible adulthood to be treated as adults, and in return for this compliment the vast majority—including myself—reciprocated by behaving like adults. Naturally we were expected to follow the time-schedule of the school—just as the teach-ers themselves were obliged to—and it was also naturally expected that we were not to shout and jump about the classrooms like infants or puppies. But we didn't regard this as tyrannical discipline because it was obviously reasonable. What school could be conducted otherwise? I don't recall, at high school, any of the senseless and arbitrary little restrictions which irked me at grammar school—and which seem to have existed in your high school. Nor can I cite any instance of disproportionate severity or arrogant authority-parading in the occasional cases of minor rule-infractions due to exuberance. Not all the teachers, of course, were equally well-liked; but there was nothing in my memory amounting to major friction. I really de-tested only one teacher—whom I had in algebra, and who found fault with methods of solving problems, even when correct, if the steps did not agree with his own. He *might* have tried to "ride" me (he especially disliked me because my methods were unorthodox) if I had not brought him up short the first time he became really offensive; but as it was, I was able to force a showdown—a blackboard demonstration of the actual correctness (which he wanted to deny by forestalling proof) of my method. After that a policy of dignified peace—though scarcely of cordiality—prevailed betwixt me and the gentleman. In another case I had a tilt with a history teacher, but made a good friend of him. He asked me what the native races of Europe were, and I told him Caucasian and Mongolian. That last didn't suit him, and he began to tell me that *Asia* was the only home of the Mongol. Then I reminded him of the *Lapps*, and of the original stock, at least, of the Finns, Magyars, and Turks. He was doubtful, but slowly began to see the light; and was afterward the most affable of beings. Another near-tilt was in the

fall of 1906—with a fat old lady English teacher. I had handed in a theme entitled "Can the Moon Be Reached By Man"?[18] And something about it (gawd knows what) led her to question its originality. She said it sounded like a magazine article. Well—chance was with me that day, for I had the ammunition to stage a peach of a tableau. Did I deny the magazine-article charge? Not so! Instead, I calmly informed the lady that the theme was indeed a verbatim parallel of an article which had appeared in a rural weekly only a few days before. I felt sure, I said, that no one could possibly object to the parallelism! Indeed, I added—as the good soul's bewilderment became almost apoplectic—I would be glad to show her the printed article in question! Then, reaching in my pocket, I produced a badly printed cutting from a Rhode Island village paper (which would accept almost anything sent to it). Sure enough—here was the selfsame article. And mixed were the emotions of the honest Mrs. Blake when she perused the heading— CAN THE MOON BE REACHED BY MAN? BY H. P. LOVECRAFT. In studies I was not bad—except for mathematics, which repelled and exhausted me. I passed in these subjects—but just about that. Or rather, it was *algebra* which formed the bugbear. Geometry was not so bad. But the whole thing disappointed me bitterly, for I was then intending to pursue astronomy as a career, and of course advanced *astronomy* is simply a mass of mathematics. That was the first major set-back I ever received—the first time I was ever brought up short against a consciousness of my own limitations. It was clear to me that I hadn't brains enough to be an astronomer —and that was a pill I couldn't swallow with equanimity. But it's just as well to have one's ego deflated early. As for other studies—English rather bored me, because it virtually repeated ground over which my home reading had long ago ranged. Latin and Greek were my delight—although I had a long-standing feud with teachers of the former over pronunciation. My grandfather had previously taught me a great deal of Latin, using the traditional English pronunciation taught in his day, but at school I was expected to follow the "Roman method" which attempts to duplicate the actual pronunciation of the Romans. Instead of *Caesar* (Seezar) I was expected to say "Ky'sar". Cicero became Kikero, Scipio, Skeep'io, and so on. It got on my nerves . . . . . fancy pronouncing *juvenes urbium vicinarum* as *yoo'-way-nace oor-beoom wee-kee-nah'-room!* Ugh! Well—in this case the school won. I had to modify my method, untraditional as the change seemed to me. At least, it was a consolation to reflect that this odd way brought me closer to Immortal Rome itself! But the conflict was never quite settled—and even today I waver between methods, with nigh disastrous results. In Greek I had no quarrel—and didn't get beyond the first six books of Xenophon anyhow. Ancient history I ate up avidly; aided by some previous acquaintance with the subject, and by my abiding love of Rome. Botany was a sort of neutral subject with me. German I frankly disliked. Above all else (except perhaps Latin and Ancient History) I revelled in physics and chemistry—subjects I was also studying at home. I had a small and pretty well equipped basement laboratory of my own, but the chance to use the great school laboratories was a rare delight. All told, I had a pretty good time at high school, and I look back on that period with considerable affection. Alas for the changes of time. Some of the teachers are dead, my physics-chemistry teacher is a lawyer now, and my old principal is in an insane asylum (the one where my young friend Brobst is now a nurse). Eheu fugaces! Well—I live only two squares from old Hope St. High School now, and the building looks pretty much the same. The papers call it an "antiquated fire-trap" these days—though I saw it built in 1897, long before I ever attended it. There's a symbol of senility—the decadence of buildings which one saw rising in one's far-off youth!

"Blank" Period

[The one period of his life that Lovecraft was reluctant to discuss was the five years following what appeared to be a nervous breakdown following his third year of high school. We know only fragmentarily of Lovecraft's life and emotions at this time; but what is clear from several of his remarks is his shame at failing to become a college graduate.]

[15]   In 1908 I was about to enter Brown University, when my health completely gave way—causing the necessary abandonment of my college career. Of my non-university education, I never cease to be ashamed; but I know, at least, that I could not have done differently. I busied myself at home with chemistry, literature, and the like; composing some of the weirdest and darkest fiction ever written by man! I was a close disciple of Poe, and a diligent delver into the regions of the "grotesque and arabesque" to quote his own phrase. It was in this period that I wrote "The Alchemist", my U.A.P.A. credential, which will appear in *The United Amateur* for December.[19] I shunned all human society, deeming myself too much of a failure in life to be seen socially by those who had known me in youth, and had foolishly expected such great things of me. From then to

now, I have been practically unknown save to a very few old acquaintances. I am a complete disappointment, having accomplished absolutely nothing during my 26 futile years of existence. In 1912 my first bit of published *verse* appeared in *The Evening Bulletin*.[20] It is a 62-line satire in the usual heroic couplet, ridiculing a popular movement on the part of the Italians of the Federal Hill slums to change the name of their main street from "Atwells' Avenue" to "Columbus Avenue". I pictured Providence in 2000 A.D., with *all* the English names changed to foreign appellations. This piece received considerable notice of a minor sort, I am told, though I doubt if it had much effect in silencing the Italians' clamour. The idea was so foolish that it probably died of its own weakness.

[16]   Nothing is more unfortunate than a neurotic temperament, and I am just enough inclined that way myself to sympathise deeply with anyone else who suffers from shadowy depressions. Many times in my youth I was so exhausted by the sheer burden of consciousness and mental and physical activity that I had to drop out of school for a greater or lesser period and take a complete rest free from all responsibilities; and when I was 18 I suffered such a breakdown that I had to forego college. In those days I could hardly bear to see or speak to anyone, and liked to shut out the world by pulling down dark shades and using artificial light. I never had any delusions about approaching death, or about the attitude of those around me, but my hypersensitive nerves reacted on my bodily functions to such a degree as to give the appearance of many different physical illnesses.

[17]   Like you I am absolutely devoid of actual friends outside of correspondence. Those whom I knew in youth are all active and successful now—one a Major in the Regular Army, another a lawyer, another an Episcopal clergyman, another a librarian of the R. I. Historical Society, etc., with any number of "rising young businessmen"—if I may employ a "rubber-stamp phrase". With such, a sickly recluse can have little or nothing in common;—their virile success and bustling prosperity but emphasise the melancholy of one whose active career ended at eighteen—if indeed it ever existed in more than a nominal sense. The only persons who could now be real friends, are those who never knew me in my days of high hope and expansive ambition; and who therefore expect no more from me than I am able to furnish. To them, I should exhibit no such ignominious decadence as I must to those who, from early acquaintance, took it for

granted that I would go normally through the university, achieve a profes-
sorship, and by this time be a real person with a recognised place in the social and academic world, instead of a nonentity with absolutely nothing of
real worth to justify existence. The other day, I saw a featured article in *The
New York Tribune* by one whose compositions I used to correct at Hope
Street High School! Could irony be greater? How are the tables turned! I
may only thank the Fates that I am not embittered by the failure which my
invalidism has brought upon me. I do not hate or envy my old acquaintances—I merely wish to sink out of their sight if I cannot shew some
achievements to match theirs. Nor am I like my old friend Dean Swift, embittered with all humanity. I see no cause to blame society or any individual; but simply prefer to have intimacy with those who have never known
me, save at my worst—which is now. I no more visit the Ladd Observatory
or various other attractions of Brown University. Once I expected to
utilise them as a regularly entered student, and some day, perhaps control
some of them as a faculty member. But having known them with this "inside" attitude, I am today unwilling to visit them as a casual outsider and
non-university barbarian and alien.

[Lovecraft emerged from his hermitry in a peculiar way, when he began
reading some of the popular magazines of the day and then wrote letters
to the editor about them; these letters, some of them in verse, were noticed
by a recruiter with the United Amateur Press Association, and Lovecraft
thereby entered the amateur journalism movement.]

[18]   In 1913 I had formed the reprehensible habit of picking up cheap
magazines like *The Argosy* to divert my mind from the tedium of reality.
One of the authors in that periodical so much excited my contempt, that I
wrote a letter to the editor in quaint Queen-Anne prose, satirising the of-
fending novelist. This letter, which was printed in the September number,
aroused a veritable tempest of anger amongst the usual readers of the magazine. I was assailed and reviled by innumerable letters, which appeared in
the editorial department. Among these hostile compositions was a piece of
tetrameter verse by one John Russell, of Tampa, Fla., which had in it so
much native wit, that I resolved to answer it. Accordingly I sent *The Argosy*
a 44-line satire in the manner of Pope's "Dunciad." This was duly printed
in January, 1914, and it created an immense sensation (of hostile character) amongst the *Argosy* readers. The editorial department had nothing but

anti-Lovecraft letters the following month! And then I composed *another* satire, flaying all my tormentors in a stinging pentameter. This, too, was printed, till the storm of fury waxed high. Russell's replies were all rather clever, and well worth answering. Finally I sent Russell a personal communication which led to an ultimate peace—a peace established just in time, for T. N. Metcalf, the editor of *The Argosy* had intimated that the poets' war must soon end, since correspondents were complaining of the prominence of our verses in their beloved magazine. They feared we were usurping all the extra space! So Russell and I officially closed the affair with a composite poem—my part of which was in heroics; his in anapaest. This farewell to *The Argosy* took place in October, 1914, and I have never since beheld that worthy organ of popular literature.

Amateur Journalism
(1914–1921)

A Permanent Amateur

[Lovecraft himself provides a history of the amateur movement in the recruiting pamphlet *United Amateur Journalism:
Exponent of Amateur Journalism* (1915).]

[1]   Amateur journalism, or the composition and circulation
of small, privately printed magazines, is an instructive diversion
which has existed in the United States for over half a century.
In the decade of 1866–1876 this practice first became an organised institution; a short-lived society of amateur journalists, including the now famous publisher, Charles Scribner, having
existed from 1869 to 1874. In 1876 a more lasting society was
formed, which exists to this day as an exponent of light dilet-
tantism. Not until 1895, however, was amateur journalism established as a serious branch of educational endeavour. On
September 2nd of that year, Mr. William H. Greenfield, a gifted
professional author, of Philadelphia, founded *The United Amateur Press Association,* which has grown to be the leader of its
kind, and the representative of amateur journalism in its best
phases throughout the English-speaking world.

     In many respects the word "amateur" fails to do full credit
to amateur journalism and the association which bests represents it. To some minds the term conveys an idea of crudity and

immaturity, yet the United can boast of members and publications whose polish and scholarship are well-nigh impeccable. In considering the adjective "amateur" as applied to the press association, we must adhere to the more basic interpretation, regarding the word as indicating the non-mercenary nature of the membership. Our amateurs write purely for love of their art, without the stultifying influence of commercialism. Many of them are prominent professional authors in the outside world, but their professionalism never creeps into their association work. The atmosphere is wholly fraternal, and courtesy takes the place of currency.

The real essential of amateur journalism and The United Amateur Press Association is the amateur paper or magazine, which somewhat resembles the average high-school or college publication. These journals, varying greatly in size and character, are issued by various members at their own expense; and contain, besides the literary work of their several editors or publishers, contributions from all the many members who do not publish papers of their own. Their columns are open to every person in the association, and it may be said with justice that no one will find it impossible to secure the publication of any literary composition of reasonable brevity. The papers thus published are sent free to all our many members, who constitute a select and highly appreciative reading public. Since each member receives the published work of every other member, many active and brilliant minds are brought into close contact, and questions of every sort—literary, historical, and scientific—are debated both in the press and in personal correspondence. The correspondence of members is one of the most valuable features of the United, for through this medium a great intellectual stimulus, friendly and informal in nature, is afforded. Congenial members are in this way brought together in a lettered companionship, which often grows into life-long friendship; while persons of opposed ideas may mutually gain much breadth of mind by hearing the other side of their respective opinions discussed in a genial manner. In short, the United offers an exceptionally well-proportioned mixture of instruction and fraternal cheer. There are no limits of age, sex, education, position, or locality in this most complete of democracies. Boys and girls of twelve and men and women of sixty, parents and their sons and daughters, college professors and grammar-school pupils, aristocrats and intelligent labourers, Easterners and Westerners, are here given equal advantages; those of greater education helping their cruder brethren until the common fund of culture is as nearly level as it can be in any human organisation. Members are classified according to age; "A" meaning under sixteen, "B" from 16 to 21, and "C" over 21. The advantages offered to those of limited acquirements are immense; many persons having gained practically all their literary polish through membership in the United. A much cherished goal is professional authorship or editorship, and numerous indeed are the United members who have now become recognised authors, poets, editors, and publishers. True, though trite, is the saying that amateur journalism is an actual training school for professional journalism.

[By 1921 Lovecraft, a seven-year veteran of the amateur movement, could look back and reflect upon the mutual benefits derived from the association in one of his earliest autobiographical essays, "What Amateurdom and I Have Done for Each Other."]

[2]   I entered Amateur Journalism late in life—at the age of nearly twenty-four—so that I cannot justly attribute all my education to its influence. This lateness was, however, most emphatically not of my choosing. The instant I heard of amateurdom's existence I became a part of it, and count among my deepest regrets the fact that I did not discover it some seventeen years earlier, when as a youth of seven I put forth my first immortal literary product, "The Adventures of Ulysses; or, The New Odyssey".

Upon joining the United Amateur Press Association I spent the first few months in an attempt to discover just what Amateur Journalism is and just what it is not. My notions had been rather nebulous, and I was not sure whether delight or disillusion awaited me. Actually, I found both; but delight was so much in the majority that I soon realised I was a permanent amateur. That was in 1914. In 1921 I can report unchanged sentiments.

What I have done for Amateur Journalism is probably very slight, but I can at least declare that it represents my best efforts toward coöperating in a cause exceedingly precious to me. As I began to perceive the various elements in the associational sphere, I saw that heterogeneity and conflict were, as in all spheres, the rule. Trying to judge impartially, I concluded that at that particular time the purely literary element stood most in need of support. Fraternalism and good cheer are largely self-sustaining. Politics, in my honest individual opinion, is an evil. What required fostering was the very object which amateurdom professes to hold supreme—aid to the aspiring writer. Accordingly I decided that while sharing in all the general responsibilities of active membership, I would chiefly lend whatever small influence I might have toward the encouraging of mutual literary help.

My chance to do something tangible came sooner than I expected. In the fall of 1914 I was appointed chairman of the Department of Public Criticism in the United, and was thus provided with a bimonthly medium of expression, together with a certain seal of officialdom on my utterances. What I did was to commence a definite campaign for the elevation of the literary standard—a campaign attempting on the one hand a candid and analytical demonstration of prevailing crudities, and on the other hand a tireless flow of suggestions for improvement. I abandoned altogether the policy of praising crude papers and articles because of obscure considerations connected with their standing in amateurdom, and insisted that writers and editors at least choose a goal of urbane correctness. Knowing that such a demand entailed an obligation to help personally, I undertook a fairly extensive amount of private criticism, and offered my services to any person wishing the revision of manuscripts or magazine copy. There were many responses to this offer, and I immediately found myself very busy reconstructing prose and verse and preparing copy for various amateur journals. I met with a certain amount of opposition and made many enemies, but believe that on the whole I may have accomplished some good. The standard of correctness in the United certainly rose, and most of the writers and editors I helped soon began to take pains on their own account; so that my aid became less and less necessary. This, however, is due only in part to my efforts. My successors in the critical bureau have been decidedly better, and the work was at the outset facilitated by a change in recruiting policy, established by others, whereby our new members were drawn from sources involving more extensive previous education.

In other fields I fear I have done all too little for amateur journalism. From 1915 to 1919 I issued an individual paper called *The Conservative*, but circumstances have since forced me to suspend its publication.[1] I have helped in coöperative publishing enterprises, though never with very brilliant results. As official editor of the United this year I am trying to issue a paper of the best quality, but am able to make little headway against the quantitative limitations. I have, I hope, done my share of administrative drudgery both official and unofficial. Despite a distaste for office holding I have accepted various posts in the United whenever my services seemed desirable, and have tried to be useful in substituting for incapacitated officials.[2]

As a writer, the field in which I should like to serve most, I seem to have served least. When I entered amateurdom, I unfortunately possessed the delusion that I could write verse; a delusion which caused me to alienate my readers by means of many long and execrably dull metrical inflictions. An old-fashioned style at present out of favour added to the completeness of my failure. Since emerging from the poetical delusion I have been almost equally unfortunate, for in following my natural inclination toward fantastic and imaginative fiction I have again stumbled upon a thing for which the majority care little. My attempts appear to be received for the most part with either coolness or distaste, though the encouragement of a few critics like W. Paul Cook, James F. Morton, Jr., and Samuel Loveman has more than compensated for the hostility of others. The Cleveland-Chico clique, seeking by ridicule to drive me from the amateur press, is well offset by any one of the gentlemen named. Only time, however, will shew whether or not my effusions possess any value.

Happily, I can be less reserved in stating what amateurdom has done for me. This is a case in which overstatement would be impossible, for Amateur Journalism has provided me with the very world in which I live. Of a nervous and reserved temperament, and cursed with an aspiration which far exceeds my endowments, I am a typical misfit in the larger world of endeavour, and singularly unable to derive enjoyment from ordinary miscellaneous activities. In 1914, when the kindly hand of amateurdom was first extended to me, I was as close to the state of vegetation as any animal well can be—perhaps I might best have been compared to the lowly potato in its secluded and subterranean quiescence. With the advent of the United I obtained a renewed will to live; a renewed sense of existence as other than a superfluous weight; and found a sphere in which I could feel that my efforts were not wholly futile. For the first time I could imagine that my clumsy gropings after art were a little more than faint cries lost in the unlistening void.

What Amateur Journalism has brought me is a circle of persons among whom I am not altogether an alien—persons who possess scholastic leanings, yet who are not as a body so arrogant with achievement that a struggler is frowned upon. In daily life one meets few of these—one's accidental friends are mostly either frankly unliterary or hopelessly "arrived" and academic. The more completely one is absorbed in his aspirations, the more one needs a circle of intellectual kin; so that amateurdom has an unique and perpetual function to fulfil. Today, whatever genuine friends I have are amateur journalists, sympathetic scholars, and writers I should never have known but for the United Amateur Press Association. They alone have furnished me with the incentive to explore broader and newer fields of thought, to ascertain what particular labours are best suited to me, and to give to my writings the care and finish demanded of all work destined for perusal by others than the author.

After all, these remarks form a confession rather than a statement, for they are the record of a most unequal exchange whereby I am the gainer. What I have given Amateur Journalism is regrettably little; what Amateur Journalism has given me is — life itself.

The Providence Amateur Press Club

[One of the first ways in which Lovecraft sought to utilize his skills as tutor was as informal director of a local amateur group, the Providence Amateur Press Club, largely made up of Irish immigrants. Although two issues of the *Providence Amateur* emerged in 1915–16, the group dissolved shortly thereafter.]

[3]   I sincerely hope that you will not be disappointed by the local organisation. As Miss Hoffman[3] has doubtless informed you, the members are recruited from the evening high school, and are scarcely representative of the intellectual life of Providence. Their environment has been distinctly plebeian, and their literary standards should not at this time be criticised too harshly. Most of the members seem very much in earnest, and filled with a sincere thirst for knowledge. I regret very much that I cannot take a more active part in their affairs, and emulate Mr. Moe's work in connection with the Appleton Club;[4] but I am practically a nervous wreck, unable to attend to anything regularly, or to keep definite engagements. The easy irresponsibility of the letter-writing amateur's lot is largely what renders the press association so suitable for me. I have offered to criticise privately all the work of the local members, and to assist them in preparing their credentials for entrance into the U.A.P.A., but they seem rather slow in responding. Since they are as yet almost complete strangers to me, residing in distant and unfamiliar parts of the city, I have not been very closely in touch with them.

Their President, Victor L. Basinet, is a socialist of the extreme type, whose opinions have been formed through contact with the most dangerous labour agitators in the country. He is, however, a man of much native intelligence, and I strongly hope that the influence of the press association may help to modify his conception of society. The Official Editor, John T. Dunn, is a wild Irishman with the usual offensive Popish and anti-English views; but he is of very fair education, and fired by real literary ambition. Of course, there is much frivolity in some of the members, which detracts slightly from the dignity of the meetings. Both Basinet and Dunn are deeply interested in the history of amateur journalism, and I can give assurance that you will have an appreciative audience if you choose to favour them with remarks on that subject.

[4]   I am sorry that modesty caused you to refrain from telling your early experiences in "uplifting the public", for I am sure they must be interesting. My last attempt was in 1914–16, when I laboured with a "literary" club of Micks who dwelt in the dingy "North End" of the city. The brightest of them was an odd bigoted fellow named Dunn, two years older than I. He hated England and was a violent pro-German—and I was foolish enough to waste time trying to convert him—as if an Irishman could reason!! Even after I gave up the club as hopeless, I continued corresponding with this fellow, for he was well-meaning and quite intelligent in his way. But in 1917 came events which caused me to drop him. He took the war very badly, and wrote treasonable letters by the score. When the draft came, he refused to register, and was arrested by government agents. In July he was drafted, but refused to respond to the summons—hence was court-martialled and sentenced to 20 years in the Atlanta Federal Prison—where he still languishes, I presume.[5] I am done with Dunn!

The Conservative

[In 1915 Lovecraft felt bold enough to launch his own paper, The *Conservative*. In its second issue he outlines both its literary and its political orientation, the latter revealing his race prejudice openly.]

[5]   In this, his second issue, The Conservative deems it both proper and necessary to attempt a definition of his journalistic policy, and a forecast of his future endeavours. Though the title of the sheet affords a general index to its basic character, it is nevertheless well to describe and qualify the exact species of conservatism here represented.

That the arts of literature and literary criticism will receive prime attention from The Conservative seems very probable. The increasing use among us of slovenly prose and lame metre, supported and sustained by the light reviewers of the amateur press, demands an active opponent, even though a lone one; and the profound reverence of The Conservative for the polished writers of a more correct age fits him for a task to which his mediocre talent might not otherwise recommend him.

When The Conservative shall have laid down his task, it is his desire that he may be able to employ with justice the closing words of *The Rambler,* who said, over a century and a half ago: "Whatever shall be the final sentence of mankind, I have at least endeavoured to deserve their kindness. I have laboured to refine our language to grammatical purity, and to clear it from colloquial barbarism, licentious idioms, and irregular combinations."[6]

Outside the domain of pure literature, The Conservative will ever be found an enthusiastic champion of total abstinence and prohibition; of moderate, healthy militarism as contrasted with dangerous and unpatriotic peace-preaching; of Pan-Saxonism, or the domination by the English and kindred races over the lesser divisions of mankind; and of constitutional or representative government, as opposed to the pernicious and contemptible false schemes of anarchy and socialism. Though the first-named of these items may superficially appear a rather inappropriate function for a Conservative, it must be remembered, that he who strives against the Hydramonster Rum, strives most to *conserve* his fellow-men.

Amateur Controversies

[Of the many controversies constantly roiling the amateur world, the most severe was the schism in the UAPA as a result of the disputed election of 1912. In a late essay, "A Matter of Uniteds" (1927), Lovecraft seeks to refute disparaging remarks upon his branch of the UAPA made by J. Roy Erford, the head of the other branch.]

[6]   The existence of two Uniteds since 1912 has been so well known a phenomenon that only the very newest members can be deluded by statements such as Mr. Erford makes in his excessive though well-intentioned zeal; but for the sake of these novices it ought to be pointed out that the United duplication is the result of no deliberate creation or imposture on either side. In 1912, at which time the United was living up to its name in spite of more than one previous division, a very hotly contested election took place at the annual convention; the final vote being so close and so

dependent on a technically accurate interpretation of the voting status of many members that no one can say even now with absolute finality which side gained the legal victory. Unfortunately, much recalcitrance was displayed in both camps; and in the end each group of adherents claimed the shade of preference necessary to a decision. Since both parties considered their respective candidates elected as President, each naturally viewed the candidate of the other in the light of an usurper; and in the end a general cleavage occurred, each division realigning its membership and official board in conformity with its conception of who was President, and regarding itself as the authentic continuation of the original society.

Now although I did not join amateurdom until two years after these events, they were still recent enough in my time to make it very plain to me that both sides were equally sincere in their conflicting positions. The branch which I happened to join was that opposed to Mr. Erford's, and I naturally have a bias in its favour; but at no time have I been disposed to brand the other branch as illegal or unjustified, or to do other than regret that continuance of ill-feeling on both sides which makes recombination impossible. Opinionated "die-hards" in either faction are really playing with amusing unconsciousness into the hands of the National when they perpetuate this United division; for with a friendly and coöperative use of half the energy which they spend in calling each other "rebels" and "pro-National traitors" they could undoubtedly reorganise a solid and compact body of literary aspirants which, because of its essential difference of aim from the fraternal National's, would need to fear no competition from that august and archaic body.

[In 1920 Lovecraft attempted to reach out to this other branch of the UAPA and was sharply rebuffed. In response, he wrote the angry editorial "The Pseudo-United."]

[7]   The so-called "United Amateur Press Association of America", which has from time to time favoured our society with amusing displays of puerile animosity, is the result of a political revolt which occurred in 1912 at the La Grande, Oregon, convention. The presidential election on that occasion was a hotly contested one, the candidates being the late Helene Hoffman Cole and one Harry Shepherd of Bellingham, Washington. So close was the result, that considerable examination of ballots had to be made before the victor could be announced; but finally it was determined

to the satisfaction of all impartial observers that the then Miss Hoffman
was safely and lawfully elected. Here the matter should have ended, but
the followers of Mr. Shepherd did not bear the defeat of their candidate
with good grace. Instead of acquiescing and accepting the Hoffman administration—which, by the way, was one of the brightest in our history,
and was extended over a second term—the Shepherdites insisted on pro-
claiming their candidate elected, and withdrew from our activities; para-
doxically calling themselves the "only United" and ostentatiously hailing
the United itself as an "outlaw" or "rebel" association.

Little was gained by this coup d'etat. The most cultivated members
took no part in the secession, and the separatist faction has since maintained its existence only through the support of a few powerful irreconcil-
ables in and near the city of Seattle. Its cultural tone has steadily declined,
until today the majority of its members are of extreme crudity—mostly superficial near-Bolsheviki and soulful plumbers and truck-drivers who are
still at the moralising stage. Their little schoolboy compositions on "Indi-
vidualism", "The Fulfilment of Life", "The Will", "Giving Power to the
Best", and so on, are really touching. One would like to introduce them to
Voltaire, Haeckel, James Branch Cabell, or some other real thinkers! In
material prosperity the intellectual condition is well matched. Official organs are few and far between except when the Erford purse is generously
open, and of the artistic quality of the various publications the less said the
better. Such is the grandiose association which detests us so thoroughly,
yet which we have always suffered to jog along unnoticed, as an always
harmless and sometimes helpful medium for the energies of the very crude.

The present remarks are inspired by the peculiarly insulting manner in
which some of the ungrammatical secessionists have received our amicable
attempts to recruit pseudo-United members for the U.A.P.A. Recognising
that many of the "pseudos" are far from hopeless educationally, we this
year sought to give them the benefits of real amateur journalism, and to
bring them into the United without conflicting in any way with their allegiance to their humbler yet worthy faction. We adopted the very reasonable notion that the world contains room for both associations, each of
which has its own particular object. At first, our overtures seemed to be
met in a rational manner. One very well-meaning Flatbush gentleman,
after asking if he could join the United without the knowledge of his fellows in the pseudo-United, almost decided to affiliate; when conscience—
or the word of a superior officer—caused him to suffer the malady known

as "cold feet" and back out at the last moment, exclaiming in the "reverse English" which has made him a common laughing-stock for five years. [. . .]

Perhaps it is a waste of time to take notice of affairs as trivial as this, but we desire to forestall any remarks from our esteemed contemporaries to the effect that we have been seeking to disrupt a weaker and humbler association. We have borne no malice toward our sometimes peevish "little brother", but have merely tried to give some of its members a chance for improvement. We still think that the pseudo-United has a useful and legitimate place as a primary school to form a stepping-stone to the United, and we hope that its temper will improve as it grows further and further beyond the dominance of its intransigent leaders. Meanwhile we shall do the simplest and most widely acceptable of all things—leave our pseudo-United friends unmolested amidst this native barbarism!

[The broader question of the consolidation of the two major amateur groups, the UAPA and the NAPA, found Lovecraft staunchly opposed. Nevertheless, as early as 1917 he found it prudent to join the NAPA as an ordinary member.]

[8]   Much has been made of the long existence and past career of the "grand old National", and the advocates of Consolidation imagine that the United would consent to a virtual disorganisation merely to secure such a pedigree. But as Thomas Campbell (not Paul J.) remarked over a century ago, "'Tis distance lends enchantment to the view."[7] The National has had as members a considerable number of very accomplished littérateurs, of which the poet Samuel Loveman and the critic Edward Cole are shining examples. But to judge the association by a few men of genius like these is scarcely proper. The National has never more ingenuously confessed its fundamental failing than when referring affectionately to "the small boy with a printing press". This is the much-vaunted grandeur of the National. Not literary, not educational, grandeur, but a record of mere juvenile typographical achievement; a development of the small-boy ideal. While this may be eminently laudable in its way, it is not the kind of grandeur that our United is seeking, and we would certainly hesitate before bartering our own literary traditions for any print-shop record like the National's. At one time the National had the field for itself, and perhaps made more of the educational element than it now does; but the rise of the United, with its increasingly close relations with the high-schools, has overshadowed the

older society in this direction. We have nothing to gain from the "grand old National".

Consolidation, then, would bring us nothing more than a long list of empty names, and an old, boasted title which fails, after all, to do justice to our nobler and more serious aspirations. Let us hope that no further autopsy will be necessary to shew the utter ridiculousness of Consolidation from our point of view. If any shall in future play the part of ghouls above its grave, let them be members of other associations than the United.

[9]   At the repeated solicitation of many persons who declared that my aloofness from the National was a barrier to inter-associational harmony, I sent in an application for membership about a week ago. My connexion, however, will be purely nominal; as I gave the Nationalites very clearly to understand. I have time and strength only for my own association, yet was willing to have my name on the National's list if it would help any. I bear no ill will toward the present Martin administration, which is quite different from the former conditions which so strongly repelled me. There was an unscholarly and blustering quality about certain political rings which I could not help loathing. Daas will be furious at my recognition of the National, but personally, I deemed it best to respond to what seem to be genuinely friendly overtures on the part of the older association. Should the National presume to treat the United with disrespect again, I shall be the first to resent the act. My exhibition of good will is based upon Edward H. Cole's statement that he has induced Graeme Davis to abandon his anti-United campaign. If Davis will be so good, so will I! [8]

Attempted Enlistment

[Lovecraft had joined amateur journalism only a few months before the outbreak of World War I. His ardent Anglophilia led him to excoriate U.S. neutrality in the war; and in spite of his frail health, he wasted no time in attempting to enlist when the U.S. finally entered the war in the spring of 1917.]

[10]   Some time ago, impressed by my entire uselessness in the world, I resolved to attempt enlistment despite my almost invalid condition. I argued that if I chose a regiment soon to depart for France; my sheer nervous force, which is not inconsiderable, might sustain me till a bullet or piece of shrapnel could more conclusively and effectively dispose of me. Accord-

ingly I presented myself at the recruiting station of the R.I. National Guard and applied for entry into whichever unit should first proceed to the front. On account of my lack of technical or special training, I was told that I could not enter the Field Artillery, which leaves first; but was given a blank of application for the Coast Artillery, which will go after a short preliminary period of defence service at one of the forts of Narragansett Bay. The questions asked me were childishly inadequate, and so far as physical requirements are concerned, would have admitted a chronic invalid. The only diseases brought into discussion were specific ailments from which I had never suffered, and of some of which I had scarce ever heard. The medical examination related only to major organic troubles, of which I have none, and I soon found myself (as I thought) a duly enrolled private in the 9th Co. R.I.N.G.! As you may have deduced, I embarked upon this desperate venture without informing my mother; and as you may also have deduced, the sensation created at home was far from slight. In fact, my mother was almost prostrated with the news, since she knew that only by rare chance could a weakling like myself survive the rigorous routine of camp life. Her activities soon brought my military career to a close for the present. It required but a few words from our family physician regarding my nervous condition to annul the enlistment, though the army surgeon declared that such an annulment was highly unusual and almost against the regulations of the service. The fact is, I had really gotten the best of that astute medicus; for without making a single positive misstatement I had effectively concealed the many and varied weaknesses which have virtually blasted my career. Fortune had sided with me in causing no attack of blurred eyesight to come upon me during the physical examination. But my final status is that of a man "Rejected for physical disability." On the appointed day I shall register for conscription, but I presume my services will not be desired. My mother has threatened to go to any lengths, legal or otherwise, if I do not reveal all the ills which unfit me for the army. If I had realised to the full how much she would suffer through my enlistment, I should have been less eager to attempt it; but being of no use to myself it was hard for me to believe I am of use to anyone else. Still, I might have known that mothers are always solicitous of their offspring, no matter how worthless said offspring may happen to be! And so I am still in civil life, scribbling as of old, and looking with envious eye upon the Khaki-clad men who are now so frequently seen upon the streets of the business section and in the cars everywhere. I envy your half-brother his position as a soldier of the N.Y.N.G. During the past week I have been quite prostrated with a cold and with frequent spells of bad vision. Had my enlistment matured successfully, I wonder how I should have kept up! And yet—I will wager that I *would* have kept up some way or other. Now that death is about to become the fashion, I wish that I might meet it in the most approved way, "Somewhere in France". The army doctor pronounced me so sound organically, that I fear I have many weary years to drag out, unless the draft comes to my relief by talking me in spite of medical and maternal protests! *I* shall not protest on mine own account!

[11]   Your experience in the toils of conscription is quite interesting, and reveals a general inefficiency and stupidity on the part of the examiners which is quite the rule throughout the nation. In this city, a *one-eyed* man, exempted by the first doctor, had to pass on to a second physician for full examination—whilst another young man, who had already enlisted in the navy, was called up through a mistake, and subjected to the whole routine before being exempted as a member of his country's forces. I am not sure whether or not I shall undergo examination. The examining physician of my ward is a friend of the family, and thinks that possibly a statement from the National Guard physician who rejected me will be sufficient. The Guard examination was somewhat less clumsy than that which you underwent. It was conducted in an office whose privacy was absolute, and whose floor and temperature were both suitable. The physician who conducted this examination, Maj. Augustus W. Calder, has just been rejected himself by the Federal surgeons as physically unfit. He is receiving the same treatment he finally gave me! If my mother had not interfered, I should certainly have slipped by, and would now be with my company (9th Coast Artillery) at Fort Standish, in Boston Harbour. It would have been an interesting experience, and would have either killed or cured me by this time.

[12]   My questionnaire arrived yesterday, and I discussed it with the head physician of the local draft board—who happens to be a family friend and even a remote relative. I wished, if possible, to place myself in class I, so that I might help in a clerical way as much as I could—as typist, clerk, or something of the sort. But he knew too much of my constitutional ailments, and directed me to class myself in Class V. Div. G.—totally and permanently unfit. This will be later acted upon by himself and his two

associate physicians, but he does not think a reversal very likely; so that I fear whatever service I give the government must be unofficial and strictly voluntary. As he pointed out, my lack of physical endurance would make me a hindrance rather than a help in any work requiring schedule and discipline; also, my manifold weaknesses make me unable to endure any conditions of living except those of a comfortable home. Any work under military auspices would require my presence at camps and various places to which a physician would be loth to consign one of my condition. It is not flattering to be reminded of my utter uselessness twice within the space of six months, but the war is a great exposer of human failings and inefficiency. Had not my mother disturbed my ambitious effort of last May, in which I utilised my absurdly robust-looking exterior as a passport to martial glory in the National Guard, I should now be digging trenches, drilling, and pounding a typewriter at Fort Standish in Boston Harbour, where the 9th Co. R.I. Coast Artillery is placed at present.

Early Philosophical Views

[As Lovecraft gained a wider circle of correspondents in the amateur community, he began to hone his philosophical thought by debates with colleagues whose views differed significantly from his. The following passages on human life, prohibition, religion, and ethics are a sample of the philosophical discussions that fill his early letters.]

[13]   But after all, what is life and its purpose? What right has man arbitrarily to assume his own importance in creation? Science can trace our world to its source; to the moment of its birth from the great solar nebula in the remote past. More — Science can demonstrate that all the planets of our system had a similar origin. Extending the principle to the sidereal heavens, from whose contemplation, indeed, the nebular hypothesis was originally derived, we find the nebular form is the present condition of all creation — a condition which precludes the existence of life. Therefore we are able to comprehend that the human race is but a thing of the moment; that its existence on this planet is extremely recent, as infinity is reckoned; and that its possible existence in all the expanse of illimitable space is but a matter of yesterday. Space and time have always existed and always will exist. This is the only legitimate axiom in all philosophy. And we are able to see that not only humanity but all other forms of organic life as well are mere innovations; unless, perchance, previous and unknown universes have

flourished and perished in the irretrievable recesses of the incomprehensibly remote past. Our human race is only a trivial incident in the history of creation. It is of no more importance in the annals of eternity and infinity than is the child's snow-man in the annals of terrestrial tribes and nations. And more: may not all mankind be a mistake—an abnormal growth—a disease in the system of Nature—an excrescence on the body of infinite progression like a wart on the human hand? Might not the total destruction of humanity, as well as of all animate creation, be a positive *boon* to Nature as a whole? How arrogant of us, creatures of the moment, whose very species is but an experiment of the *Deus Naturae,* to arrogate to ourselves an immortal future and considerable status! How do we know that we have a right to live? Our philosophy is all childishly *subjective*—we imagine that the welfare of our race is the paramount consideration, when as a matter of fact the very existence of the race may be an obstacle to the predestined course of the aggregated universes of infinity! How do we know that that form of atomic and molecular motion called "life" is the highest of all forms? Perhaps the dominant creature—the most rational and God-like of all beings—is an invisible gas! Or perhaps it is a flaming and effulgent mass of molten star-dust. Who can say that men have souls while rocks have none? Perhaps the best thing a man might do is to annihilate himself! But of this we know nothing. We are here on a grain of dust called the Earth, and endowed with a certain imperfect and unhappy consciousness called "life". It is not for us to destroy what the Gods have given; we might err as sadly in one direction as in the other. It is obviously our right and our duty to heed our own ignorance, and to permit Nature to work out her processes without interference from these puny, shadow-haunted centers of unrest which we call our minds. It is our right and our duty to mould the minor manifestations of human character in such a way that the entire race may derive the least amount of pain and misery from the pitiful satire known as "life." Certain evils are beyond redemption, many are capable of amelioration, whilst a very few might possibly be cured. There is such a thing as pleasure and happiness tho' it is experienced by few, and only to be obtained by a career of such strenuous achievement that the majority are denied more than a sip. False, loose pleasures are not happiness at all, and are invariably compensated for by misery, the certain result of wide deviation from the normal. In short, most of us have no hope of happiness, nor should we waste our energy in striving for it, since it is all but unattainable.

[14]   It was the other night my privilege to hear and see a bit of slum reform of a different sort. A speaker belonging to the Prohibition Party and
clad in the vestments of the ecclesiastical rank (Episcopal) had stopped his
motor-car in a publick square, and was holding forth to a great assemblage
of men made up of every rank and condition of society. Gentlemen waiting
for street cars, and riff-raff from the corner saloons, together with every intermediate grade of humanity, were thickly represented. The speaker was
a grey bearded man of fifty-one, who described his early and varied career.
He had begun as a New England farmer's boy, and had soon commenced
to drink in moderation; but after his early youth had become disgusted
with liquor and relinquished the vice voluntarily. Later on he had served as
a sailor aboard a square-rigger, and still later [. . .] as a cowboy all the way
from Montana to Texas. His clerical duties were taken up later on. This
man spoke in a voice marked equally with ease, fluency, dignity, and refinement, and expounded the workings of prohibition in the various states
which have adopted that it [. . .] hath indeed no excuse for existence.
When a sot near his car declared in uncertain tones that beer was a monstrous valuable food, the speaker quietly contrasted the bloated physique
of the heckler with his own spare, wiry strength, remarking without boast-
fulness that no drinking man had ever excelled him either in the rigging of
a brigantine or astride a cow-pony. Without the "aid" of rum he had com-
ported himself with distinction in two of the manliest vocations in American life. It was with admiration that I attended his words, and only the
lateness of the hour induced me to leave the scene before he had completed
his lay sermon.

But scarcely less interesting than the speaker were the dregs of humanity who clustered closest about him. I may say truly, that I have never
before seen so many human derelicts all at once, gathered in one spot. I beheld modifications of human physiognomy which would have startled even
a Hogarth, and abnormal types of gait and bodily carriage which proclaim
with startling vividness man's kinship to the jungle ape. And even in the
open air the stench of whiskey was appalling. To this fiendish poison, I am
certain, the greater part of the squalor I saw is due. Many of these vermin
were obviously not foreigners—I counted at least five American counte-
nances in which a certain vanished decency showed through the red
whiskey bloating. Then I reflected upon the power of wine, and marvelled
how self-respecting persons can imbibe such stuff, or permit it be served

upon their tables. It is the deadliest enemy with which humanity is faced. Not all the European Wars could produce a tenth of the havock occasioned among men by the wretched fluid which responsible governments allow to be sold openly. Looking upon that mob of sodden brutes, my mind's eye pictured a scene of different kind; a table bedecked with spotless linen and glistening silver, surrounded by gentlemen immaculate in evening attire—and in the reddening faces of those gentlemen I could trace the same lines which appeared in full development of the beasts of the crowd. Truly, the effects of liquor are universal, and the shamelessness of man unbounded. How can reform be wrought in the crowd, when supposedly respectable boards groan beneath the goblets of rare old vintages? Is mankind asleep, that its enemy is thus entertained as a bosom friend? But a week or two ago, at a parade held in honour of the returning Rhode Island National Guard, the Chief Executive of this State, Mr. Robert Livingston Beeckman, prominent in New York, Newport, and Providence society, appeared in such an intoxicated condition that he could scarce guide his mount, or retain his seat in the saddle, and he the guardian of the liberties and interests of that Colony carved by the faith, hope, and labour of Roger Williams from the wilderness of savage New-England! I am perhaps an extremist on the subject of prohibition, but I can see no justification whatsoever for the tolerance of such a degrading demon as drink.

[15] Your wonderment 'what I have against religion' reminds me of your recent *Vagrant* essay[9]—which I had the honour of perusing in manuscript some three years ago. To my mind, that essay *misses one point altogether.* Your "agnostic" has neglected to mention the very crux of all agnosticism—namely that the Judaeo-Christian mythology is NOT TRUE. I can see that in your philosophy *truth per se* has so small a place, that you can scarcely realise what it is that Galpin and I are insisting upon. In your mind, MAN is the centre of everything, and his exact conformation to certain regulations of conduct HOWEVER EFFECTED, the only problem in the universe. Your world (if you will pardon my saying so) is *contracted.* All the mental vigour and erudition of the ages fail to disturb your complacent endorsement of empirical doctrines and purely pragmatical notions, because you voluntarily limit your horizon—*excluding certain facts, and certain undeniable mental tendencies of mankind.* In your eyes, man is torn between *only two* influences; the degrading instincts of the savage, and the temperate impulses of the philanthropist. To you, men are of but two

classes—lovers of self and lovers of the race. To you, men have but two types of emotion—self-gratification, to be combated; and altruism, to be fostered. But you, consciously or unconsciously, are leaving out a vast and potent *tertium quid*—making an omission which cannot but interfere with the validity of your philosophical conceptions. You are forgetting a human impulse which, despite its restriction to a relatively small number of men, has all through history proved itself as real and as vital as hunger—as potent as thirst or greed. I need not say that I refer to that simplest yet most exalted attribute of our species—the acute, persistent, unquenchable craving TO KNOW. Do you realise that to many men it makes a vast and profound difference whether or not the things about them are as they appear? Let me use an analogy, since you love concreteness. You recognise a difference between mere pleasure and true happiness. As a consistent theologian, you must chaw this distinction. You point to two men; one a merely frivolous creature, amusing himself by drowning his cares in wine or gaiety; the other a conscientious worker of good, who takes satisfaction in knowing that he is properly adjusted to society and his fellowmen. Both are equally contented, but you will undoubtedly say that only the second man is truly happy. You will say, and rightly, that the joy of the first man is merely mental apathy; and that if ever he should be forced to think about himself and his relation to others around him, he would be acutely dissatisfied—would seek to find his place in life and thereby satisfy the new misgivings which thought aroused in him. But at this point you and other orthodox thinkers find it expedient to "draw a herring across the trail" and turn to other lines of investigation. For the very distinction you draw between empty pleasure and true happiness would by one more step of ratiocination force you to acknowledge the element of the *absolute* whose existence you are so anxious to deny or conceal. In differentiating between pleasure and happiness, you concede that the reality of the source of contentment is a very important thing. Otherwise the serenity of the sensualist and of the saint stand on a level. If effect is all we are to consider, the drunken loafer or the madman who fancies himself a King may be deemed just as blessed as the person whose happiness is founded on actual things. If there be not some virtue in plain TRUTH; then our fair dreams, delusions, and follies, are as much to be esteemed as our sober waking hours and the comforts they bring. If TRUTH amounts to nothing, then we must regard the phantasma of our slumbers just as seriously as the events of our daily lives. Several nights ago I had a strange dream of a strange city—a city of many palaces and gilded domes, lying in a hollow betwixt ranges of grey, horrible hills.[10] There was not a soul in this vast region of stone-paved streets and marble walls and columns, and the numerous statues in the public places were of strange bearded men in robes the like whereof I have never seen before or since. I was, as I said, aware of this city visually. I was in it and around it. But certainly I had no corporeal existence. I saw, it seemed, everything at once; without the limitations of direction. I did not move, but transferred my perception from point to point at will. I occupied no space and had no form. I was only a consciousness, a perceptive presence. I recall a lively curiosity at the scene, and a tormenting struggle to recall its identity; for I felt that I had once known it well, and that if I could remember, I should be carried back to a very remote period—many thousand years, when something vaguely horrible had happened. Once I was almost on the verge of realisation, and was frantic with fear at the prospect, though I did not know what it was that I should recall. But here I awaked—in a very cramped posture and with too much bedclothing for the steadily increasing temperature. I have related this in detail because it impressed me very vividly. This is not a Co[11] romance of reincarnation— you will see that it has no climax or point—but it was very real. I an now trying to recall if I felt any sensation or had any notion of *heat* in the dream. The excessive covering would account for that, if I did. But as a matter of fact, I cannot remember such an impression.

At this point you will ask me whence these stories! I answer—according to your pragmatism that dream was as real as my presence at this table, pen in hand! If the truth or falsity of our beliefs and impressions be immaterial, then I am, or was, actually and indisputably an unbodied spirit hovering over a very singular, very silent, and very ancient city somewhere between grey, dead hills. I thought I was at the time—so what else matters? Do you think that I was just as truly that spirit as I am now H. P. Lovecraft? I do not. "'And there ye ar-re', as Mr. Dooley says."[12]

I recognise a distinction between dream life and real life, between appearances and actualities. I confess to an over-powering desire to know whether I am asleep or awake—whether the environment and laws which affect me are external and permanent, or the transitory products of my own brain. I admit that I am very much interested in the relation I bear to the things about me—the time relation, the space relation, and the causative relation. I desire to know approximately what my life is in terms of history—human, terrestrial, solar, and cosmical; what my magnitude may be in terms of extension,—terrestrial, solar, and cosmical; and above all, what may be my manner of linkage to the general system—in what way, through what agency, and to what extent, the obvious guiding forces of creation act upon me and govern my existence. And if there be any less obvious forces, I desire to know them and their relation to me as well. Foolish, do I hear you say? Undoubtedly! I had better be a consistent pragmatist: get drunk and confine myself to a happy, swinish, contented little world—the gutter—till some policeman's No. 13 boot intrudes upon my philosophic repose. But I *cannot.* Why? Because some well-defined human impulse prompts me to discard the relative for the absolute. You would encourage me as far as the moral stage. You would agree with me that I had better see the world as it is than to forget my woes in the flowing bowl. But because I have a certain *momentum,* and am carried a step further from the merely relative, you frown upon me and declare me to be a queer, unaccountable creature, "immersed . . . . . in the VICIOUS abstractions of philosophy!"

Here, then, is the beginning of my religious or philosophical thought. I have not begun talking about *morality* yet, because I have not reached that point in the argument. *Entity* precedes morality. It is a prerequisite. What am I? What is the nature of the energy about me, and how does it affect me? So far I have seen nothing which could possibly give me the notion that cosmic force is the manifestation of a mind and will like my own infinitely magnified; a potent and purposeful consciousness which deals individually and directly with the miserable denizens of a wretched little flyspeck on the back door of a microscopic universe, and which singles this putrid excrescence out as the one spot whereto to send an onlie-begotten Son, whose mission is to redeem those accursed flyspeck-inhabiting lice which we call human beings—bah!! Pardon the "bah!" I feel several "bahs!", but out of courtesy I only say one. But it is all so very childish. I cannot help taking exception to a philosophy which would force this rubbish down my throat. 'What have I against religion?' That is what I have against it! (Do not mistake me—I have a great deal *for* it as well. I do *not* 'deny it a place in the life of the world'. I am coming to this about twenty or thirty pages farther on!!)

Now let us view *morality*—which despite your preconceived classification and identification has nothing to do with any particular form of religion. Morality is the adjustment of matter to its environment—the natural arrangement of molecules. More especially it may be considered as dealing with organic molecules. Conventionally it is the science of reconciling the animal *homo* (more or less) *sapiens* to the forces and conditions with which he is surrounded. It is linked with religion only so far as the natural elements it deals with are deified and personified. Morality antedated the Christian religion, and has many times risen superior to co-existent religions. It has powerful support from very non-religious human impulses. Personally, I am intensely moral and intensely irreligious. My morality can be traced to two distinct sources, scientific and aesthetic. My love of truth is outraged by the flagrant disturbance of sociological relations involved in so-called "wrong"; whilst my aesthetic sense is outraged and disgusted with the violations of taste and harmony thereupon attendant. But to me the question presents no ground for connection with the grovelling instinct of religion. However—you may exclude me from the argument, if you will. I *am* unduly secluded though unavoidably so. We will deal only with materials which may presumably lie within my feeble reach. Only one more touch of ego. I am *not* at all passive or indifferent in my zeal for a high morality. But I cannot consider morality the essence of religion as you seem to. In discussing religion, the whole fabric must bear examination before the uses or purposes are considered. We must investigate the cause as well as alleged effects if we are to define the relation between the two, and the reality of the former. And more, granting that the phenomenon of faith is indeed the true cause of the observed moral effects; the absolute basis of that phenomenon remains to be examined. The issue between theists and atheists is certainly not, as you seem to think, the mere question of whether religion is useful or detrimental. In your intensely pragmatical mind, this question stands paramount—to such an extent that you presented no other subject of discussion in your very clever *Vagrant* article. But the "agnostic" of your essay must have been a very utilitarian agnostic (that such "utilitarian Agnostics" do exist, I will no deny. *Vide* any issue of *The Truthseeker!* But are they typical?)! What the honest thinker wishes to know, has nothing to do with complex human conduct. He simply demands a scientific *explanation* of the things he sees. His only animus toward the church concerns its deliberate inculcation of demonstrable untruths in the community. This is human nature. No matter how white a lie may be—no matter how much good it may do—we are always more or less disgusted by its diffusion. The honest agnostic regards the church with respect for what it has done in the direction of virtue. He even supports it if he is magnanimous, and he certainly does nothing to impair whatever public usefulness it may possess. But in private, he would be more than a mere mortal if he were able to suppress a certain abstract resentment, or to curb the feeling of humour and so-called irreverence which inevitably arises from the contemplation of pious fraud, howsoever high-minded and benevolent.

The good effects of Christianity are neither to be denied, nor lightly esteemed, though candidly I will admit that I think them overrated.

[16]   I hope that your recent state is merely one of transition from the idealism of youth to the realism of middle life, when the thinker realises that there is no such thing as ideal happiness and justice, and ceases to strive after illusions so empty and unreal. Solid bourgeois contentment — with the settled conviction that wild pleasures are too rare, elusive, and transitory to be worth seeking — is the best state of mind to be in. One should come to realise that all life is merely a comedy of vain desire, wherein those who strive are the clowns, and those who calmly and dispassionately watch are the fortunate ones who can laugh at the antics of the strivers. The utter emptiness of all the recognised goals of human endeavour is to the detached spectator deliciously apparent — the tomb yawns and grins so ironically! Whatever bliss we can gain, is from watching the farce, removing ourselves from the strife by not expecting more than we receive, and revelling in that world of the unreal which our imagination creates for us. To enjoy tranquillity, and to promote tranquillity in others, is the most enduring of delights. Such was the doctrine of Epicurus, the leading ethical philosopher of the world. If one's interest in life wanes, let him turn to the succour of others in a like plight, and some grounds for interest will be observed to return. About the time I joined the United I was none too fond of existence. I was 23 years of age, and realised that my infirmities would withhold me from success in the world at large. Feeling like a cipher, I felt that I might well be erased. But later I realised that even success is empty. Failure though I be, I shall reach a level with the greatest — and the smallest — in the damp earth or on the final pyre. And I saw that in the interim trivialities are not to be despised. Success is a relative thing — and the victory of a boy at marbles is equal to the victory of an Octavius at Actium when measured by the scale of cosmic infinity. So I turned

to observe other mediocre and handicapped persons about me, and found pleasure in increasing the happiness of those who could be helped by such encouraging words or critical services as I am capable of furnishing. That I have been able to cheer here and there an aged man, an infirm old lady, a dull youth, or a person deprived by circumstances of education; affords to me a sense of being not altogether useless, which almost forms a substitute for the real success I shall never know. What matter if none hear of my labours, or if those labours touch only the afflicted and the mediocre? Surely it is well that the happiness of the unfortunate be made as great as possible; and he who is kind, helpful, and patient, with his fellow-sufferers, adds as truly to the world's combined fund of tranquillity as he who, with greater endowments, promotes the birth of empires, or advances the knowledge and civilisation of mankind. Thus no man of philosophical cast, however circumscribed by poverty or retarded by ailment, need feel himself superfluous so long as he holds the power to improve the spirits of others. [. . .] There is a vast satisfaction in alleviating the misfortunes of another. When I am able to bring a smile of gratitude to the vacuous face of a *Crowley* or the childish visage of a *Tryout Smith*,[13] I am impressed with my own ability to do such a thing; and have thereby the better opinion of myself. And I can feel some share of their pleasure, since as a fellow-struggler I am able to appreciate their limitations. The secret of true contentment, I am convinc'd, lies in the achievement of the *cosmical* point of view; whereby the most cruel distinctions betwixt great and small things are shewn to be merely apparent and unreal. The next philosophical step is to acquire the impersonal attitude—to divest oneself of egocentrick consciousness, and assume the role of a spectator at the comedy of man. Thus depersonalised, one may roam through all history and all legend with imagination as a guide; enjoying the pleasant things of life without experiencing the anguish of participation. If lonely in his own life, the dreamer may find company at the tables of Will's or Button's, or may join the embattled hosts of some shadowy monarch who defends with fabulous sword the gates of his gorgeous and unheard-of capital, which rises among the gold and diamond mountains beyond the Milky Way. To the impersonal dreamer belongs all infinity—he is lord of the universe and taster of all the beauties of the stars. As for the future—what is sweeter than *oblivion*, which the humblest of us may share with the Kings of all the ages, and even with the gods themselves?

Aryan Supremacy

[Lovecraft was not shy in uttering—both in private correspondence and in a few published amateur essays—his notions of Aryan supremacy. The following passage makes clear that many of Lovecraft's views were developed as a result of the conservative and racially homogeneous environment of his native Providence.]

[17]   I hardly wonder that my racial ideas seem bigoted to one born and reared in the vicinity of cosmopolitan New York, but you may better understand my repulsion to the Jew when I tell you that until I was fourteen years old I do not believe I ever spoke to one or saw one knowingly. My section of the city is what is known as the "East Side" (nothing like New York's "East Side"!!!) and it is separated from the rest of the town by the precipitous slope of College Hill, at the top of which is Brown University. In this whole locality, there are scarcely two or three families who are not of original Yankee Rhode Island stock—the place is as solidly Anglo-American as it was 200 years ago. Over on the "West Side", it is very cosmopolitan, but the East Side child might as well be in the heart of Old England so far as racial environment is concerned. Slater Avenue school was near my home, and the only non-Saxons were niggers whose parents work for our families or cart our ashes, and who consequently know their place. Imagine, then, my feeling on entering high-school and being confronted with the offscourings of Judaea! True, some of the Jews were intelligent; in fact there were some very brilliant scholars among them; but how could a child used to other children like himself find anything in common with hook-nosed, swarthy, guttural-voiced aliens? Repulsion was instinctive—I never denied the mental capacity of the Jew; in fact I admire the race and its early history at a distance; but association with them was intolerable. Just as some otherwise normal men hate the sight or presence of a cat, so have I hated the presence of a Jew. Then, all apart from this instinctive feeling, I very soon formed a conviction that the Oriental mind is but ill adapted to mingle with the Aryan mind—that the glory of Israel is by itself. Oil and water are both desirable, but they will not mix. And the more I study the question, the more firmly am I convinced that the one supreme race is the Teuton. Observe the condition in the British Isles. The English are wholly Teutonic, and therefore dominant. The southern Scotch and Eastern Irish are also of that blood—they certainly surpass their fellows to

the north and west. The Welsh, who have no Teutonic blood, are of little account. Had it not been for the Teutonic infusion at the beginning of the Dark Ages, southern Europe would have been lost. Who were these early "French" kings and heroes that founded French civilisation? Teutons, to a man! It was the Teutonic might of Charles Martel that drove the Saracen Semite out of Gaul. Who were the Normans? Teutons of the North. It is pitiful to me to hear apostles of equality pipe out that other races can equal this foremost of all—this successor to the Roman race in power and virility.

Metrical Mechanic

[Lovecraft wrote hundreds of poems during his amateur career, but few of them are of any note. He was severely hampered by antiquated notions of poetic technique, and he was well aware that all he sought to do in poetry was to transfer himself psychologically into the eighteenth century he loved.]

[18]   Through Mr. Daas, I learn that you would 'like to see me get away from the heroic couplet, and see what I could do in other forms'. I fear that it is quite beyond me thus to leave a form of expression on which I seized almost by instinct, and in which nearly all my rhythmical efforts are cast. As the strength of Antaeus depended on his contact with Mother Earth, so does any possible merit in my verses depend on their execution in this regular and time-honoured measure. Take the form away, and nothing remains. I have no real poetic ability, and all that saves my verse from utter worthlessness is the care which I bestow on its metrical construction.

I am really a relic left over from Queen Anne's age. I do not know how it came about, but from the time of my earliest recollection, I have seemed to fall into the mental habits of two centuries ago. My constitutional feebleness kept me from regular attendance at school, so that I acquired what little knowledge I possess from a rather indiscriminate perusal of the volumes of the family library. Curiously enough, I never felt at home save with the writers of the late seventeenth and early eighteenth centuries. Longfellow, Tennyson, and Browning were aliens; Dryden, Addison, and Pope were intimate friends. My classical knowledge was confined to Latin, a fact which still further bound me to a period whose inspiration was in everything more Latin than Greek. In this manner my style was formed; not as conscious archaism, but as though I had actually been born in 1690 instead of 1890. Every image, every turn of expression, every word, which

I acquired, was of the artificial, regular, definite, Queen Anne type, so you can readily perceive how vague, over-familiar, abrupt, and amorphous, modern poetry must appear to me. My literary appreciation begins with Dryden, and ends with Goldsmith and Dr. Johnson.

Now I am perfectly aware that this is no more than downright perverted taste. I know as well as any man that the beauties of poetry lie not in the tinsel of flowing metre, or the veneer of epigrammatical couplets; but in the real richness of images, delicacy of imagination, and keenness of perception, which are independent of outward form or superficial brilliancy; yet I were false and hypocritical, should I not admit my actual preference for the old resounding decasyllabics. Verily, I ought to be wearing a powdered wig and knee-breeches. I have written in iambic octosyllabics like those of Swift, in decasyllabic quatrains, as in Gray's "Elegy", in the old ballad metre of Chevy-Chase, in blank verse like Young's and Thomson's, and even in anapaests like those in Beattie's "Hermit", but only in the formal couplet of Dryden and Pope can I really express myself. Once I privately tried imitations of modern poets, but turned away in distaste. Their vocabulary and technic alike seem utterly strange to an ancient like myself.

[A letter of 1929 maintains—quite unjustly—that Lovecraft's imitative habit extended even to his prose fiction.]

[19]   In my metrical novitiate I was, alas, a chronic and inveterate mimic; allowing my antiquarian tendencies to get the better of my abstract poetic feeling. As a result, the whole purpose of my writing soon became distorted —till at length I wrote only as a means of re-creating around me the atmosphere of my 18th century favourites. Self-expression as such sank out of sight, and my sole test of excellence was the degree with which I approached the style of Mr. Pope, Dr. Young, Mr. Thomson, Mr. Addison, Mr. Tickell, Mr. Parnell, Dr. Goldsmith, Dr. Johnson, and so on. My verse lost every vestige of originality and sincerity, its only care being to reproduce the typical forms and sentiments of the Georgian scene amidst which it was supposed to be produced. Language, vocabulary, ideas, imagery— everything succumbed to my one intense purpose of thinking and dreaming myself back into that world of periwigs and long s's which for some odd reason seemed to me the normal world. Thus was formed a habit of imitativeness which I can never wholly shake off. Even when I break away, it is generally only through imitating something else! There are my "Poe"

pieces and my "Dunsany" pieces—but alas—where are any *Lovecraft* pieces? Only in some of my more realistic fictional *prose* do I shew any signs of developing, at this late date, a style of my own—though some have been so good as to say that my epistles have a certain originality within the limits of the 18th century tradition; as Cowper's differ from Walpole's, or Gray's from Swift's. In verse, I have cheated myself of a style by copying the styles of others. Now of course I am an extreme case, but what has harmed me greatly might easily harm everyone a little, in proportion to the extent they practiced the imitative principle. Therefore I invariably warn all bards—in the slang of the day—to *be themselves;* saying what they wish to say as they wish to say it, and allowing the masters to influence them only indirectly— broadening their sensitivenesses and capacities for imaginative experience rather than affecting their habits of utterance.

Early Writings: Fiction

[Although Lovecraft did not know it at the time, fiction would become his chief avenue of self-expression. In a long letter written in January 1920 to the correspondence group the Gallomo, Lovecraft supplies hints as to the progress of his fiction writing from 1917 up to his discovery of Lord Dunsany in late 1919.]

[20]   T'anks fer de remarks on "Dagon", kid! I rather liked that thing myself. It was written in 1917, and is the second tale I wrote after resuming my fictional pen after a nine years' lapse. I think I told youse ginks that I quit writing fiction in 1908, despairing of my ability to shape anything with the grace of a Poe. I went over all my old MSS., bade most of them a last farewell, and saved out only two—"The Beast in the Cave", written in April, 1905, when I was 14 years and 7 months old, and "The Alchemist", which I had just finished. Thereafter I sent in "The Alchemist" for a credential;[14] thinking that in an immature organisation stories might be better appreciated than verse or essay matter. I never expected to see that published, but later the chance came, and I tinkered with it a while, preparing the slightly revised version which appeared in 1916. So far I had never thought of resuming my old pastime. But then I chanced to send Culinarius[15] "The Alchemist", and he immediately told me that fiction is my one and only province! Mildly amused, I sent him the "Beast", which he snapped up as though it were worth printing. My stock of tales was now quite exhausted, but Cook kept urging me to improve my supposed gift for

weird tales, so I decided to revive the old atmosphere. For a long time I was too indolent to do anything, but one June day in 1917 I was walking through Swan Point Cemetery with my aunt and saw a crumbling tomb-stone with a skull and crossbones dimly traced upon its slaty surface; the date, 1711, still plainly visible. It set me thinking. Here was a link with my favourite aera of periwigs—the body of a man who had worn a full-bottom'd wig and had perhaps read the original sheets of *The Spectator.* Here lay a man who had lived in Mr. Addison's day, and who might easily have seen Mr. Dryden had he been in the right part of London at the right time! Why could I not talk with him, and enter more intimately into the life of my chosen age? What had left his body, that it could no longer converse with me? I looked long at that grave, and the night after I returned home I began my first story of the new series—"The Tomb". My narrative pen was very rusty—believe me, boys, very rusty indeed! To drop back into the forms of fiction was exceeding hard after nine quiescent years, and I feared that the result would be the limit of absurdity. But the spell of the grue-some was upon me, and I finally hammered out the hideous tale of Jervas Dudley. At last—a Poe again! Honestly, I was afraid to send the deuced thing to Cook—especially afraid because he had himself just begun to write stories again after an eleven year lapse, and said he had lost all his talent. I really felt that the new attempt was inferior both to the "Beast" and "Alchemist". Meanwhile I had been reading Poe again—for about the ten millionth time. The new or rather revived mood was hard to dismiss, and after limbering up my style a bit with practice work I perpetrated "Dagon" in August. To me it seemed better than "The Tomb"—smoother, less halting and angular. I felt that my practice had done me a bit of good. Meanwhile Cook paid me a personal call—in September. We talked about everything under the sun, and in observing some little rusticities and ple-beianisms in his dress and demeanour, I lost some of my awe for his fic-tional greatness. Before he bade me a reluctant farewell, I had placed the manuscript of "The Tomb" in his hands—not being quite ready to part with "Dagon", which I was still polishing in places. With eagerness I awaited Cook's verdict on my revived art—and fancy my delight when he wrote enthusiastically, saying my new tale immeasurably surpassed all my juvenile attempts, and declaring he would print it in his de luxe MONAD-NOCK at some indefinite future date![16] Tickled, I at once began work on "Psychopompos"—as yet unable to cast off my beloved heroicks alto-gether, even in fiction. Duties pressed, and I worked slowly. "Psychopompos"

was abandoned midway, and not resumed till the summer of 1918, when I
sent it to Cook and received a glowing acknowledgment.[17] My egotism was
now becoming almost Galpinian again, and I hustled with a new yarn—
"Polaris"—which you fellers saw before anyone else. That really was an
important milestone in muh brilliant career—for its unconscious resemblance to the work of Dunsany is all that finally led to my acquaintance
with that then unknown source of inspiration. My next job was more mechanical.[18] A singular dream had led me to start a nameless story about a
terrible forest, a sinister beach, and a blue, ominous sea. After writing one
paragraph I was stalled, but happened to send it to Mrs. Jordan. Fancy my
surprise when the poetess replied that she had had a precisely similar
dream, which, however, went further. In her dream a piece of the shore
had broken off, carrying her out into the sea. A green meadow had loomed
up on the left hand side, and horrible entities seemed to be hiding among
the trees of the awful forest behind her. The piece of earth on which she
was drifting was slowly crumbling away, yet this form of death seemed
preferable to that which the forest things would have inflicted. And then
she heard the sound of a distant waterfall and noted a kind of singing in the
green meadow—at which she awaked. It must have been quite some
dream, for she drew a map of it and suggested that I write a story around
it. After a little consideration I decided that this dream made my own proposed story a back number, so I abandoned my plan and used my original
opening paragraph in the new story. Just as I was speculating how I
should infuse a little life and drama into the rather vague fragment, my
mother broke down, and I partially broke down as a result of the shock.
For two months I did nothing—in fact, I can hardly remember what I even
thought during those two months—I know I managed to perform some imperative amateur work mechanically and half-consciously, including a critical report or two. When I emerged, I decided to add piquancy to the tale
by having it descend from the sky in an aerolite—as Galba[19] knows, for I
sent the thing to him. I accordingly prepared an introduction in very prosaic newspaper style, adding the tale itself in a hectic Poe-like vein—
having it supposed to be the narrative of an ancient Greek philosopher
who had escaped from the earth and landed on some other planet—but
who found reason to regret his rashness. As it turned out, it is practically
my own work all through, but on account of the Jordanian dream-skeleton
I felt obliged to concede collaboration, so labelled it "By Elizabeth Neville
Berkeley and Lewis Theobald, Jun." I sent it to Cook, who will soon print

it.[20] Then came "Beyond the Wall of Sleep"—written spontaneously after reading an account of some Catskill Mountain degenerates in a N. Y. TRIBUNE article on the New York State Constabulary.[21] By this time I was beginning to hear Dunsanian urgings, but I paid them scant attention. My next—"Juan Romero"—was written merely as a reaction from copying a dull yarn by Phil Mac.[22] He had made such a commonplace adventure yarn from such a richly significant setting, that I yearned to shew what ought to be done with such a setting. Youze gazinks have seen both Mac's and my yarns. And then, having been told so often that my "Polaris" was exactly like Dunsany, I idly began to read "A Dreamer's Tales"! The rest is history—or would be if I amounted to anything.

Discovery of Lord Dunsany

[There is no question that Lovecraft's discovery of the work of Lord Dunsany gave his fiction a tremendous impetus. After reading Dunsany in September 1919, he solidified his devotion to the Irish writer by seeing him in person the next month in Boston, as Dunsany was engaging in an extensive American lecture tour. Imitations of Dunsany's work emerged from Lovecraft's pen shortly thereafter.]

[21] It interests me to hear of your first perusal of "A Dreamer's Tales". Mine was in the fall of 1919, when I had never read anything of Dunsany's, though knowing of him by reputation. The book had been recommended to me by one whose judgment I did not highly esteem,[23] and it was with some dubiousness that I began reading "Poltarnees—Beholder of Ocean". The first paragraph arrested me as with an electric shock, and I had not read two pages before I became a Dunsany devotee for life. It was such a discovery as I shall never experience again, for I am too old for such emotional effects now. Thank Pegāna I came across Dunsany when I did!

[22] At 7:00 a party consisting of Miss H., her aunt, young Lee, and L. Theobald set out for the great event. Arriving early at the Copley-Plaza, we obtained front seats; so that during the address I sat directly opposite the speaker, not ten feet from him. Dunsany entered late, accompanied and introduced by Prof. George Baker of Harvard. He is of Galpinian build— 6 ft. 2 in. in height, and very slender. His face is fair and pleasing, though marred by a slight moustache. In manner he is boyish and a trifle awkward; and his smile is winning and infectious. His hair is light brown. His

voice is mellow and cultivated, and very clearly British. He pronounces *were* as *wair*; etc. Dunsany first touched upon his ideals and methods; then hitched a chair up to his reading table, seated himself, crossed his long legs, and commenced reading his short play, "The Queen's Enemies." This is based very obviously upon the anecdote of Nitocris in the second book of Herodotus; but Dunsany averred that the had purposely avoided reading details or even learning the names of the characters in the story, for fear his original imaginative work on the play might be hampered or impaired. I advise you to read it for yourself—it is in "Plays of Gods and Men", which every well-regulated library has or ought to have on the shelves. Later Dunsany read selections from other works of his, including a masterly burlesque on his own style—"Why the Milkman Shudders when he Sees the Dawn".[24] As he read this, he could not repress his own smiles and incipient chuckles! The audience was large, select, and appreciative; and after the lecture Dunsany was encircled by autograph-seekers. Egged on by her aunt, Miss Hamlet almost mustered up courage enough to ask for an autograph, but weakened at the last moment. [. . .] For mine own part, I did not seek a signature; for I detest fawning upon the great. Dunsany himself has written a piece ("Fame and the Poet", in the August *Atlantic*) which shews his contempt for the flatterers of genius. To some of those with whom he shook hands, Dunsany remarked that he had a severe headache. I could sympathise; for although I had stood the day of unusual exertion remarkably well, my poor cranium was pounding and reeling most lamentably— the pain having begun about half way through the lecture. Still, I was able to keep up and navigate my course through the maze of now disarranged chairs in the vast ballroom where the address was delivered. We saw Dunsany enter his cab and drive off; then repaired to the nearest white post for my South Stationward car. Of course, I could have taken the Prov. train at the adjacent Back Bay, but I hate that bleak barn, and wished to get in the train as soon as it was made up; ensconsing myself in a seat and beginning to read Dunsany's "The Gods of Pegāna", which Miss H. had kindly lent me. The H.'s invited me to stay all night, but I am a home-seeking soul and the hour was not late. So, after promising to call again—though I may never be able to do so—I boarded a car for the subway, and after one change reached the station and the 11:00 train. Opening the book, I was dead to the world and forgot my headache till the brakeman's cry of "*Pawtucket!*" reminded me of home—and of *P. D. S.!*[25] I donned my overcoat in time to alight at Providence at 12:35—and damn it all, I missed the last

Swan Point car home! (12:40) but I took the 1:10 Red Bridge car, and finally made #598 at 1:30—exhausted but not prostrated. The nervous reaction was less than I expected—I was able to get down the next evening and buy a *Boston Transcript* with an (unsatisfactory!) account of the lecture. Altogether it was a most remarkable and highly enjoyable experience for me in these latter days of valetudinarian retirement. I had not been in Boston before since Jan. 1916—and not in Cambridge since *1910*. To see and hear a favourite author is something rare indeed for one whose favourites lie so largely in the past!

[23] As you infer, "The White Ship" is in part influenced by my new Dunsanian studies. There are many highly effective points in Dunsany's style, and any writer of imaginative prose will be the better for having read him. I have filed recommendations for *all* his works at the local publick library, and have met with favourable responses. Today I go down to obtain the very latest Dunsany book—just published—"Unhappy Far-Off Things", which I first saw advertised in the November *Atlantic*. Recently I read "Time and the Gods", which is not only highly interesting but richly philosophical. You surely must read Dunsany—in places his work is pure poetry despite the prose medium.

[A late letter, written to the budding fantaisiste Fritz Leiber in 1936, shows a far more nuanced appreciation of Dunsany than the starry-eyed devotion of Lovecraft's earlier years.]

[24] Dunsany has a peculiar appeal for me. Casual and tenuous though any one of his fantastic flights may seem, the massed effect of his whole cycle of theogony, myth, legend, fable, hero-epic and dream-chronicle on my consciousness is that of a most potent and particular sort of cosmic liberation. When I first encountered him (through "A Dreamer's Tales") in 1919 he seemed like a sort of gate to enchanted worlds of childhood dream, and his temporary influence on my own literary attempts (vide "Celephaïs", "The Doom That Came to Sarnath", "The Quest of Iranon", "The White Ship", etc.) was enormous. Indeed, my own mode of expression almost lost itself for a time amidst a wave of imitated Dunsanianism. There seemed to me to be in Dunsany certain poetic adumbrations of the cosmic lacking elsewhere. I may have read some of them in myself, but am sure that a goodly number must have been there to start with. Dunsany knows

a certain type of dream and longing and vague out-reaching natural to the Nordic mind and shaped in childhood by the early folklore and literary impressions afforded by our culture—the Germanic fairy-tale, the Celtic legend, the Biblical myth, the Arabian-Nightish Orientale, the Graeco-Roman epic, and so on. This vision or longing or out-reaching he is able to crystallise in terms of certain elements drawn from all these simple and familiar sources, and the result has an odd universal magic which few can deny. The philosophy behind his work is essentially that of the finer minds of our age—a cosmic disillusion plus a desperate effort to retain those fragments of wonder and myth of significance, direction, and purpose which intellectual progress and absorption in material things alike tend to strip away. Of course Dunsany is uneven, and his later work (despite the different sort of charm in "The Curse of the Wise Woman") cannot be compared with his early productions. As he gained in age and sophistication, he lost in freshness and simplicity. He was ashamed to be uncritically naive, and began to step aside from his tales and visibly smile at them even as they unfolded. Instead of remaining what the true fantaisiste must be—a child in a child's world of dream—he became anxious to show that he was really an adult good-naturedly pretending to be a child in a child's world. This hardening-up began to show, I think, in "The Book of Wonder"—say around 1910. It was very perceptible in "The Last Book of Wonder"—though it did not creep into the plays so soon. A decade later it relaxed slightly in the novels "Chronicles of Rodriguez" and "The King of Elfland's Daughter", but it shews at its worst in the "Jorkens" tripe. Alas that no writer can ever keep up to the level of his best! When I think of Dunsany, it is in terms of "The Gods of the Mountain", "Bethmoora", "Poltarnees, Beholder of Ocean", "The City of Never", "The Fall of Babbulkund", "In the Land of Time", and "Idle Days on the Yann".[26]

Dreams

[Lovecraft's remarkable career as a dreamer began at the age of five, when he had terrible visions of "night-gaunts" as a result of the gloom enveloping his family upon his grandmother's death. In the early years of his fiction-writing career, Lovecraft experienced a number of terrifying dreams that in many cases he wove directly into his stories.]

[25]   Before quitting the subject of Loveman and horror stories, I must relate the frightful dream I had the night after I received S.L.'s latest letter.

We have lately been discussing weird tales at length, and he has recommended several hair-raising books to me; so that I was in the mood to connect him with any thought of hideousness or supernatural terror. I do not recall how this dream began, or what it was really all about. There remains in my mind only one damnably blood-curdling fragment whose ending haunts me yet.[27]

We were, for some terrible yet unknown reason, in a very strange and very ancient cemetery—which I could not identify. I suppose no Wisconsinite can picture such a thing—but we have them in New-England; horrible old places where the slate stones are graven with odd letters and grotesque designs such as a skull and crossbones. In some of these places one can walk a long way without coming upon any grave less than an hundred and fifty years old. Some day, when Cook issues that promised *MONADNOCK,* you will see my tale "The Tomb", which was inspired by one of these places. Such was the scene of my dream—a hideous hollow whose surface was covered with a coarse, repulsive sort of long grass, above which peeped the shocking stones and markers of decaying slate. In a hillside were several tombs whose facades were in the last stages of decrepitude. I had an odd idea that no living thing had trodden that ground for many centuries till Loveman and I arrived. It was very late in the night—probably in the small hours, since a waning crescent moon had attained considerable height in the east. Loveman carried, slung over his shoulder, a portable telephone outfit; whilst I bore two spades. We proceeded directly to a flat sepulchre near the centre of the horrible place, and began to clear away the moss-grown earth which had been washed down upon it by the rains of innumerable years. Loveman, in the dream, looked exactly like the snapshots of himself which he has sent me—a large, robust young man, not the least Semitic in features (albeit dark), and very handsome save for a pair of protruding ears. We did not speak as he laid down his telephone outfit, took a shovel, and helped me clear away the earth and weeds. We both seemed very much impressed with something—almost awestruck. At last we completed these preliminaries, and Loveman stepped back to survey the sepulchre. He seemed to know exactly what he was about to do, and I also had an idea—though I cannot now remember what it was! All I recall is that we were following up some idea which Loveman had gained as the result of extensive reading in some old rare books, of which he possessed the only existing copies. (Loveman, you may know, has a vast library of rare first editions and other treasures precious to the bibliophile's heart.)

After some mental estimates, Loveman took up his shovel again, and using it as a lever, sought to pry up a certain slab which formed the top of the sepulchre. He did not succeed, so I approached and helped him with my own shovel. Finally we loosened the stone, lifted it with our combined strength, and heaved it away. Beneath was a black passageway with a flight of stone steps; but so horrible were the miasmic vapours which poured up from the pit, that we stepped back for a while without making further observations. Then Loveman picked up the telephone output and began to uncoil the wire — speaking for the first time as he did so.

"I'm really sorry", he said in a mellow, pleasant voice; cultivated, and not very deep, "to have to ask you to stay above ground, but I couldn't answer for the consequences if you were to go down with me. Honestly, I doubt if anyone with a nervous system like yours could see it through. You can't imagine what I shall have to see and do — not even from what the book said and from what I have told you — and I don't think anyone without ironclad nerves could ever go down and come out of that place alive and sane. At any rate, this is no place for anybody who can't pass an army physical examination. I discovered this thing, and I am responsible in a way for anyone who goes with me — so I would not for a thousand dollars let you take the risk. But I'll keep you informed of every move I make by the telephone — you see I've enough wire to reach to the centre of the earth and back!"

I argued with him, but he replied that if I did not agree, he would call the thing off and get another fellow-explorer — he mentioned a "Dr. Burke," a name altogether unfamiliar to me. He added, that it would be of no use for me to descend alone, since he was sole possessor of the real key to the affair. Finally I assented, and seated myself upon a marble bench close by the open grave, telephone in hand. He produced an electric lantern, prepared the telephone wire for unreeling, and disappeared down the damp stone steps, the insulated wire rustling as it uncoiled. For a moment I kept track of the glow of his lantern, but suddenly it faded out, as if there were a turn in the stone staircase. Then all was still. After this came a period of dull fear and anxious waiting. The crescent moon climbed higher, and the mist or fog about the hollow seemed to thicken. Everything was horribly damp and bedewed, and I thought I saw an owl flitting somewhere in the shadows. Then a clicking sounded in the telephone receiver.

"Lovecraft — I think I'm finding it" — the words came in a tense, excited tone. Then a brief pause, followed by more words in a tone of ineffable awe and horror.

"God, Lovecraft! *If you could see what I am seeing!*" I now asked in great excitement what had happened. Loveman answered in a trembling voice:

"I can't tell you—I don't dare—I never dreamed of *this*—I can't tell—It's enough to unseat any mind————wait————what's this?" Then a pause, a clicking in the receiver, and a sort of despairing groan. Speech again—

"Lovecraft—for God's sake—it's all up—Beat it! *Beat it!* Don't lose a second!" I was now thoroughly alarmed, and frantically asked Loveman to tell what the matter was. He replied only "Never mind! Hurry!" Then I felt a sort of offence through my fear—it irked me that anyone should assume that I would be willing to desert a companion in peril. I disregarded his advice and told him I was coming down to his aid. But he cried:

"Don't be a fool—it's too late—there's no use—nothing you or anyone can do now." He seemed calmer—with a terrible, resigned calm, as if he had met and recognised an inevitable, inescapable doom. Yet he was obviously anxious that I should escape some unknown peril.

"For God's sake get out of this, if you can find the way! I'm not joking—So long, Lovecraft, won't see you again—God! Beat it! *Beat it!*" As he shrieked out the last words, his tone was a frenzied crescendo. I have tried to recall the wording as nearly as possible, but I cannot reproduce the tone. There followed a long—hideously long—period of silence. I tried to move to assist Loveman, but was absolutely paralysed. The slightest motion was an impossibility. I could speak, however, and kept calling excitedly into the telephone—"Loveman! Loveman! What is it? What's the trouble?" But he did not reply. And then came the unbelievably frightful thing—the awful, unexplainable, almost unmentionable thing. I have said that Loveman was now silent, but after a vast interval of terrified waiting another clicking came into the receiver. I called "Loveman—are you there?" And in reply came a *voice*—a thing which I cannot describe by any words I know. Shall I say that it was hollow—very deep—fluid—gelatinous—indefinitely distant—unearthly—guttural—thick? What shall I say? In that telephone I heard it; heard it as I sat on a marble bench in that very ancient unknown cemetery with the crumbling stones and tombs and long grass and dampness and the owl and the waning crescent moon. Up from the sepulchre it came, and this is what it said:

"YOU FOOL, LOVEMAN IS DEAD!"

Well, that's the whole damn thing! I fainted in the dream, and the next I knew I was awake—and with a prize headache! I don't know yet what it was all about—what on (or under) earth we were looking for, or what that hideous voice at the last was supposed to be. I have read of ghouls—mould shades—but hell—the headache I had was worse than the dream! Loveman will laugh when I tell him about that dream! In due time, I intend to weave this picture into a story, as I wove another dream-picture into "The Doom that Came to Sarnath". I wonder, though, if I have a right to claim authorship of things I dream? I hate to take credit, when I did not really think out the picture with my own conscious wits. Yet if I do not take credit, who'n Heaven *will* I give credit tuh? Coleridge claimed "Kubla Khan", so I guess I'll claim the thing an' let it go at that. But believe muh, that was *some* dream!

[26]   Speaking of the "Carter" story, I have lately had another odd dream—especially singular because in it I possessed another personality— a personality just as definite and vivid as the Lovecraft personality which characterises my waking hours.[28]

My name was Dr. Eben Spencer, and I was dressing before a mirror in my own room, in the house where I was born in a small village (name missing) of northern New York State. It was the first time I had donned civilian clothes in three years, for I was an army surgeon with the rank of 1st Lieut. I seemed to be home on a furlough—slightly wounded. On the wall was a calendar reading "FRIDAY, JULY 8, 1864". I was very glad to be in regular attire again, though my suit was not a new one, but one left over from 1861. After carefully tying my stock, I donned my coat and hat, took a cane from a rack downstairs, and sallied forth upon the village street. Soon a very young man of my acquaintance came up to me with an air of anxiety and began to speak in guarded accents. He wished me to go with him to his brother—my professional colleague Dr. Chester—whose actions were greatly alarming him. I, having been his best friend, might have some influence in getting him to speak freely—for surely he had much to tell. The doctor had for the past two years been conducting secret experiments in a laboratory in the attic of his home, and beyond that locked door he would admit no one but himself. Sickening odours were often detected near that door . . . and odd sounds were at times not absent. The doctor was aging rapidly; lines of care—and of something else—were creeping into his dark, thin face, and his hair was rapidly going grey. He would remain in that locked room for dangerously long intervals without food, and seemed uncannily saturnine. All questioning from the younger brother was met with scorn or rage—with perhaps a little uneasiness; so the brother was much worried, and stopped me on the street for advice and aid. I went with him to the Chester house—a white structure of two stories and attic in a pretty yard with a picket fence. It was in a quiet side street, where peace seemed to abide despite the trying nature of the times. In the darkened parlour, where I waited for some time, was a marble-topped table, much haircloth furniture, and several pleasing whatnots covered with pebbles, curios, and bric-a-brac. Soon Dr. Chester came down—and *he had aged*. He greeted me with a saturnine smile, and I began to question him, as tactfully as I could, about his strange actions. At first he was rather defiant and insulting—he said with a sort of leer, "Better not ask, Spencer! Better not ask!" Then when I grew persistent (for by this time I was interested on my own account) he changed abruptly and snapped out, "Well, if you must know, come up!" Up two flights of stairs we plodded, and stood before the locked door. Dr. Chester opened it, *and there was an odour*. I entered after him, young Chester bringing up the rear. The room was low but spacious in area, and had been divided into two parts by an oddly incongruous red plush portiere. In the half next the door was a dissecting table, many bookcases, and several imposing cabinets of chemical and surgical instruments. Young Chester and I remained here, whilst the doctor went behind the curtain. Soon he emerged, bearing on a large glass slab what appeared to be a human arm, neatly severed just below the elbow. It was damp, gelatinous, and bluish-white, and the fingers were without nails. "Well, Spencer," said Dr. Chester sneeringly, "I suppose you've had a good deal of amputation practice in the army. What do you think, professionally, of this job?" I had seen clearly that this was not a human arm, and said sarcastically, "You are a better sculptor than doctor, Chester. This is not the arm of any living thing." And Chester replied in a tone that made my blood congeal, *"Not yet, Spencer, not yet!"* Then he disappeared again behind the portiere and emerged once more, bringing another and slightly larger arm. Both were left arms. I felt sure that I was on the brink of a great revelation, and awaited with impatience the tantalisingly deliberate motions of my sinister colleague. "This is only the beginning, Spencer," he said as he went behind the curtain for the third time. *"Watch the curtain!"* And now ends the fictionally available part of my dream, for the residue is grotesque anticlimax. I have said that I was in civilian clothes for the first time since '61—and naturally I was rather self-conscious. As I waited for the final revelation I caught sight of my reflection in the glass door of an instrument case, and discovered that my very carefully tied stock was awry. Moving to a long mirror, I sought to adjust it, but the black bow proved hard to fashion artistically, and then the whole scene began to fade—and damn the luck! I awaked in the distressful year of 1920, with the personality of H. P. Lovecraft restored! I have never seen Dr. Chester, or his young brother, or that village, since. I do not know what village it was. I never heard the name of Eben Spencer before or since. Some dream! If that happened to Co, he would be duly seeking a supernatural explanation; but I prefer actual analysis. The cause of the whole is clear—I had a few days before laid out Mrs. Shelley's "Frankenstein" for re-reading. As to details—Ambrose Bierce supplied the Civil War atmosphere, no doubt; whilst it is easy to trace in Dr. *Chester* and his brother—facially, I mean—the likenesses of my boyhood friends *Chester* and Harold Munroe; those brothers of whom I spoke in one of my ancient KLEICOMOLOES. I am not sleeping much this week, but last night I had a promising fragment of a dream that was cut short by premature awakening. I was alone in a black space, when suddenly, ahead of me, there arose out of some hidden pit a huge, white-robed man with a bald head and long snowy beard. Across his shoulders was slung the corpse of a younger man—cleanshaven, and grizzled of hair, and clad in a similar robe.[29] A sound as of rushing wind or a roaring furnace accompanied this spectacular ascent—an ascent which seemed accompanied by some occult species of levitation. When I awaked, I had an idea for a story—but queerly enough, the idea had nothing to do with the dream!

[27]   Last night I had a brief but typical dream. I was standing on the East Providence shore of the Seekonk River, about three quarters of a mile south of the foot of Angell Street, at some unearthly nocturnal hour. The tide was flowing out *horribly*—exposing parts of the river-bed never before exposed to human sight. Many persons lined the banks, looking at the receding waters and occasionally glancing at the sky. Suddenly a blinding flare—reddish in hue—appeared high in the southwestern sky; and *something* descended to earth in a cloud of smoke, striking the Providence shore near the Red Bridge—about an eighth of a mile south on Angell Street. The watchers on the banks screamed in horror—"*It* has come—*It* has

come at last!"—and fled away into the deserted streets. But I ran toward the bridge instead of away; for I was more curious than afraid. When I reached it I saw hordes of terror-stricken people in hastily donned clothing fleeing across from the Providence side as from a city accursed by the gods. There were pedestrians, many of them falling by the way, and vehicles of all sorts. Electric cars—the old small cars unused in Providence for six years—were running in close procession—eastward away from the city on both of the double tracks. Their motormen were frantic, and small collisions were numerous. By this time the river-bed was fully exposed—only the deep channel filled with water like a serpentine stream of death flowing through a pestilential plain in Tartarus. Suddenly a glare appeared in the West, and I saw the dominant landmark of the Providence horizon—the dome of the Central Congregational Church, silhouetted weirdly against a background of red. And then, *silently*, that dome abruptly caved in and fell out of sight in a thousand fragments. And from the fleeing populace arose such a cry as only the damn'd utter—and I waked up, confound the luck, with the very deuce of a headache!

Did I tell you in my last letter about my dreams (1) of the ancient house in the marsh, and the staircase that had no end, (2) of the mediaeval castle with the sleeping men-at-arms, and the battle on the plain between the archers of England and the *things* with yellow tabards over their armour, who vanished when their leader was unhelmeted and found to have *no head inside the empty helm,* and (3) of the street car that went by night over a route that had been dismantled for six years, and that lost five hours in climbing College Hill, finally plunging off the earth into a star-strown abyss and ending up in the sand-heaped streets of a ruined city *which had been under the sea?* Those were *some* dreams, believe your Grandpa Theobald!! I tell all these to the Kidlet, and he thinks them rather unusual—as does Mo also, who receives carbon copies. Oh—and one other dream![30] I was in a museum somewhere down town in Providence, (there ain't no sech place!) trying to sell the curator a bas-relief which *I* had just fashioned from clay. He asked me if I were crazy, attempting to sell him something *modern* when the museum was devoted to antiquities? He seemed an old and very learned man, and smiled kindly. I replied to him in words which I remember *precisely*. "This," I said, "was fashioned in my dreams; and the dreams of man are older than brooding Egypt or the contemplative Sphinx or garden-girdled Babylon." The curator now bade me shew him my bas-relief, which I did gladly. Its design was that of a procession of Egyptian priests. As I shewed the sculpture, the old man's manner changed suddenly. His amusement gave way to vague *terror* — I can even now see his blue eyes bulging from beneath his snow-white brows — and he said slowly, softly, and distinctly — "WHO ARE YOU?" I can reproduce the awe and impressiveness of his low voice only in capitals. I replied very prosaically — "My name is Lovecraft — H. P. Lovecraft — grandson of Whipple V. Phillips." I fancied a man of his age could place my grandfather better than he could place me. But he answered impatiently, "No! No! — *before that!*" I answered that I recalled no other identity save in dreams. Then the aged curator offered me a high price for the Thing I had made from clay, but I refused it; for intuition told me that he meant to *destroy* it, whereas I wished it hung upon the wall of the museum. Then he asked me *how much* I would take for the bas-relief; and I jocularly replied, having now no mind to part with it, *"One million pounds sterling."* (Currency mixed!) To my amazement the old man did not laugh. He seemed perplexed, dazed, and frightened. Then he said in a quavering tone: "Call again in a week, please. I will consult with the directors of the corporation." This is the end — although I did not awake here. At this point the dream changed to one of drifting down a stagnant river betwixt high basalt cliffs, and wondering why I drifted; *since the water had no motion, and there was no breath of wind in the awful SILENCE.* This pair of dreams occurred in the middle of an afternoon when I paused in my work from nervous exhaustion and rested my head on my arm on the table before me. I am coming to a stage where I doze off like this very frequently — it helps me keep up and accomplish more than usual. As mere yarns, these jumbled fantasies would be hardly worth notice; but being bona fide dreams, they are rather picturesque. It gives one a sense of weird, fantastic, and unearthly *experience* to have *seen* these strange sights apparently with the visual eye. I have dreamed like this ever since I was old enough to remember dreams, and probably shall till I descend to Avernus. My dreams are just as vivid as in youth, but no more so. Among my best remembered visions are those of the awful cliffs, peaks, and abysses — hideous bleak rock and loathsome blackness — over which I was borne in the clutch of black winged daemons to which I gave the original name of "night-gaunts", at the age of six! Verily, I have travelled to strange places which are not upon the earth or any known planet. I have been a rider of comets, and a brother to the nebulae.

[28]   "Nyarlathotep"[31] is a nightmare—an actual phantasm of my own, with the first paragraph written *before I fully awaked*. I have been feeling execrably of late—whole weeks have passed without relief from headache and dizziness, and for a long time three hours was my utmost limit for continuous work. (I seem better now.) Added to my steady ills was an unaccustomed ocular trouble which prevented me from reading fine print—a curious tugging of nerves and muscles which rather startled me during the weeks it persisted. Amidst this gloom came the nightmare of nightmares— the most realistic and horrible I have experienced since the age of ten— whose stark hideousness and ghastly oppressiveness I could but feebly mirror in my written phantasy. It occurred after midnight as I lay on the couch exhausted after a tussle with the "poetry" of that damned fool Bush.[32] The first phase was a general sense of undefined apprehension— vague terror which appeared universal. I seemed to be seated in my chair clad in my old grey dressing-gown, reading a letter from Samuel Loveman. The letter was unbelievably realistic—thin, 8½ × 13 paper, violet ink signature, and all—and its contents seemed portentous. The dream-Loveman wrote:

"Don't fail to see Nyarlathotep if he comes to Providence. He is horrible— horrible beyond anything you can imagine—but wonderful. He haunts one for hours afterward. I am still shuddering at what he showed."

I had never heard the name NYARLATHOTEP before, but seemed to understand the allusion. Nyarlathotep was a kind of itinerant showman or lecturer who held forth in publick halls and aroused widespread fear and discussion with his exhibitions. These exhibitions consisted of two parts— first, a horrible—possibly prophetic—cinema reel; and later some extraordinary experiments with scientific and electrical apparatus. As I received the letter, I seemed to recall that Nyarlathotep was already in Providence; and that he was the cause of the shocking fear which brooded over all the people. I seemed to remember that persons had whispered to me in awe of his horrors, and warned me not to go near him. But Loveman's dream-letter decided me, and I began to dress for a trip down town to see Nyarlathotep. The details are quite vivid—I had trouble tying my cravat— but the indescribable terror overshadowed all else. As I left the house I saw throngs of men plodding through the night, all whispering affrightedly and bound in one direction. I fell in with them, afraid yet eager to see and hear the great, the obscure, the unutterable Nyarlathotep. After that the dream followed the course of the enclosed story almost exactly, save that it did not go quite so far. It ended a moment after I was drawn into the black yawning abyss between the snows, and whirled tempestuously about in a vortex with shadows that once were men! I added the macabre conclusion for the sake of climactic effect and literary finish. As I was drawn into the abyss I emitted a resounding shriek (I thought it must have been audible, but my aunt says it was not) and the picture ceased. I was in great pain—forehead pounding and ears ringing—but I had only one automatic impulse—to *write*, and preserve the atmosphere of unparalleled fright; and before I knew it I had pulled on the light and was scribbling desperately. Of what I was writing I had very little idea, and after a time I desisted and bathed my head. When fully awake I remembered all the incidents but had lost the exquisite thrill of fear—the actual sensation of the presence of the hideous unknown. Looking at what I had written I was astonished by its coherence. It comprises the first paragraph of the enclosed manuscript, only three words having been changed. I wish I could have continued in the same subconscious state, for although I went on immediately, the primal thrill was lost, and the terror had become a matter of conscious artistic creation. Still, the tale ought to hold a shiver or two for sensitive readers, and Loveman (the real waking Loveman!) was effusively laudatory when he beheld it. Altogether, that nightmare was *some* dream, believe me!

Amatory Phenomena

[Although Lovecraft appears to have elicited the admiration of several women in the amateur movement, he claimed lofty disdain of "amatory phenomena" and remained a resolute bachelor until his sudden elopement in 1924.]

[29] Of course, I am unfamiliar with amatory phenomena save through cursory reading. I always assumed that one waited till he encountered some nymph who seemed radically different to him from the rest of her sex, and without whom he felt he could no longer exist. Then, I fancied, he commenced to lay siege to her heart in businesslike fashion, not desisting till either he won her for life, or was blighted by rejection. Of seeking affection for affection's sake—without any one special fair creature in mind—I was quite ignorant! Pardon, I pray you, the dulness of one but imperfectly instructed in the details of Paphian emotion.

[30]   Your brief for the defence in the case of Κόσμος versus Ἔρος is admirably eloquent, but I am not to be moved by any such idealist as R. W. Emerson or his master Πλάτων! Eroticism belongs to a lower order of instincts, and is an animal rather than nobly human quality. For evolved man—the apex of organic progress on the earth—what branch of reflection is more fitting than that which occupies only his higher and exclusively human faculties? The primal savage or ape merely looks about his native forest to find a mate; the exalted Aryan should lift his eyes to the worlds of space and consider his relation to infinity!! So much for the high-sounding argument. Really, I suppose my opinion is determined by the much simpler fact that I chance to have vastly more imagination then emotion. About romance and affection I never have felt the slightest interest; whereas the sky, with its tale of eternities past and to come, and its gorgeous panoply of whirling universes, has always held me enthralled. And in truth, is this not the natural attitude of an analytical mind? What is a beauteous nymph? Carbon, hydrogen, oxygen, nitrogen, a dash or two of phosphorus and other elements—all to decay soon. But what is *the cosmos?* What is the secret of time, space, and the things that lie beyond time and space? What sinister forces hurl through the black incurious aether these titanic globes of living flame, and the insect-peopled worlds that hover about them? Here—here, at last, is something worthy of the interest of enlightened mankind!!! The veil hangs tantalisingly—what lies on the other side?

Illness and Death of Lovecraft's Mother

[Lovecraft's carefree life as a professional amateur was jarringly interrupted by the illness of his mother. We can only speculate on the psychological effects of living alone with his mother for fifteen years (1904–19), especially as in her later years she began to display increasing signs of mental abnormality. Her illness and eventual death were stunning blows to Lovecraft.]

[31]   My mother, feeling no better here, has gone on a visit to my elder aunt for purposes of complete rest; leaving my younger aunt as autocrat of this dwelling. My aunt does splendidly—but you above all others can imagine the effect of maternal illness and absence. I cannot eat, nor can I stay up long at a time. Pen-writing or typewriting nearly drives me insane. But my nervous system seems to find its vent in feverish and incessant

scribbling with a pencil. I have written a great deal, though perhaps the results shew the effects of my condition. I am assured, however, that my mother's state is not dangerous; that the apparent stomach trouble is neurotic and not organic. She writes optimistic letters each day, and I try to make my replies equally optimistic; though I do not find it possible to "cheer up", eat, and go out, as she encourages me to do. Such infirmity and absence on her part is so *unprecedented*, that it cannot but depress me, despite the brightest bulletins of her physician—whom, by the way, she writes that she is now well enough to dismiss.

[32]   My mother, showing no signs of recovery, has gone to a hospital, where she is receiving the most expert care which medical science can afford. I strongly hope the change will benefit her. It has a good chance to do so, since many features of diet and regimen which the physicians are prescribing, are directly opposite to those prescribed by the previous practitioner. She herself seems satisfied with the treatment, and is more optimistic than at any time for a month before. My own energy is spasmodic. For days at a time I can do nothing—but I wrote an entire March critical report[33] one evening recently, and I am this morning able to write letters after having been up all night.

[33]   I wish I could report equal improvement in my mother's case, but her condition is distressingly stationary. She has now gone to the best sanitarium in this state, where every curative agency known to science, and every phase of expert nursing, care, and diet, may be hers. Her sojourn there, however, will have to be of great duration; and I am obliged to look forward to a long and dreary interval wherein home will be but half a home for want of its dominant figure. The prospect is not a pleasing one; but I shall be thankful if any procedure, however protracted, can restore my mother to normal or nearly normal health. My nerve strain seems now to be manifesting itself in my vision—I am frequently dizzy, and cannot read or write long without a blurring of sight or a severe headache. Existence seems of little value, and I wish it might terminate!

[34]   The death of my mother on May 24 gave me an extreme nervous shock, and I find concentration and continuous endeavour quite impossible. I am, of course, supremely unemotional; and do not weep or indulge in any of the lugubrious demonstrations of the vulgar—but the psychological

effect of so vast and unexpected a disaster is none the less considerable, and I cannot sleep much, or labour with any particular spirit or success.

Despite my mother's nervous illness and presence at a sanitarium for two years, the fatal malady was entirely different and unconnected—a digestive trouble of sudden appearance which necessitated an operation. No grave result was apprehended till the very day before death, but it then became evident that only a strong constitution could cause survival. Never strong or vigorous, my mother was unable to recover. The result is the cause of wide and profound sorrow, although to my mother it was only a relief from nervous suffering. For two years she had wished for little else— just as I myself wish for oblivion. Like me, she was an agnostic with no belief in immortality, and wished for death all the more because it meant peace and not an eternity of boresome consciousness. For my part, I do not think I shall wait for a natural death; since there is no longer any particular reason why I should exist. During my mother's lifetime I was aware that voluntary euthanasia on my part would cause her distress, but it is now possible for me to regulate the term of my existence with the assurance that my end would cause no one more than a passing annoyance—of course my aunts are infinitely considerate and solicitous, but the death of a nephew is seldom a momentous event. Possibly I shall find enough interesting things to read and study to warrant my hanging on indefinitely, but I do not intend to endure boredom beyond a certain limit. It is better to be as one was in the eternity before he was born. My mother was, in all probability, the only person who thoroughly understood me, with the possible exception of Alfred Galpin. She was a person of unusual charm and force of character, accomplished in literature and the fine arts; a French scholar, musician, and painter in oils. I shall not again be likely to meet with a mind so thoroughly admirable.

[35] Psychologically I am conscious of a vastly increased aimlessness and inability to be interested in events; a phenomenon due partly to the fact that much of my former interest in things lay in discussing them with my mother and securing her views and approval. This bereavement decentralises existence—my sphere no longer possesses a nucleus, since there is now no one person especially interested in what I do or whether I be alive or dead. However, the inevitability of such disasters renders tears and clamorous lamentation not only futile but puerile and vulgar as well. My mother has secured exactly what she most desired—complete oblivion and

non-existence, — so that grief must needs be for oneself rather than for her. I am as active as possible — quite so in amateurdom — and externally appear as usual; since I never display emotion, but prefer to be calm or slightly satirical. For some time I was unable to dress or be about — the shock affected my throat and motor nerves so that I could not eat much, or stand and walk with ease; but even then I was free from all emotional displays. As I continued to stagnate in dressing-gown and slippers — increasingly active with the pen, but inert physically — my aunts endeavoured to arouse me to some variation of the indoor monotony, and insisted that I respond to an invitation which I had received a month before, to visit an exceedingly learned and brilliant new United member — Miss M. A. Little, A. B., A. M., a former college professor now starting as a professional author — in Hampstead, N. H., near Haverhill, Mass. This I finally did, as you already know from the postcard mailed at the latter place.

3 Expanding Horizons
(1921–1924)

Romance with Sonia

[The bachelor who had no experience of amatory phenomena
found himself inexorably drawn to the Russian immigrant
Sonia H. Greene; and the following passages make clear that
she was the moving force that led to their marriage less than
three years after their first meeting at the NAPA convention
in July 1921.]

[1]   Your voluble friend, the generous Mme. Greenevsky,
announceth that she will be in Providence for two days at the
end of the present week; and I can but hope that the lethal boredom of our archaic and provincial atmosphere may not asphyxiate her United activity altogether. It's a safe bet it won't, for
just as I predicted, my boy Alfredus hath become her cherished
idol; and will serve admirably as an anchor. He has told her the
sad, sad story of his whole life, and his mother will be lucky if
she does not kidnap him some day. Also, she hath told him that
I am egotistical from reading Nietzsche—which disturbeth me
not in the least. Anybody can call me anything he damn pleases
if he will give fifty sinkers to the organ fund and issue a United
paper as good as the RAINBOW promises to be![1] It would
take more than one siren to lure my chee-ild away from his own
adopted Grandpa! And besides—so volatile a Slav means the

---

censure no more than the taffy. Bless her heart, if she hasn't just sent Grandpa a beauteous gift, in the form of a copy of Shaw's new play, "Back to Methuselah"! I hope she didn't think I was hinting for the amateurs to keep my library supplied when I mentioned your "Vathek" gift! But one thing Mme. Greenevna says quite desolates me—she avers that her fair and frivolous offspring is not to be captivated by the charms of any highbrow, not even the otherwise irresistible Bolingbroke! To think that the St. Johnly magic should fail, even in one case! Gad's blood, if any daughter of mine refused to pay homage to the graces of a Clynor,[2] I'd disown the wench! Had I two daughters, I would have no sons-in-law but thou and Galpinius! Try being jazzy and lowbrow, my boy, and sport a flashier cane, and you may yet win the giddy fair! By the way—I have just returned proofs of my RAINBOW article, which is a melange of cynical aphorisms culled from two letters of mine.[3] Whoever was the printer knoweth his business, for errors were monstrous few. The R. will evidently be quite some paper—pictures 'n' everything. Surely Mrs. G. is the find of the present year amateurically.

[2]   As to my social programme—you have doubtless heard part of it already from the Mme. Greenevsky, whose Providence visit formed half of it. This volatile and beneficent personage arrived in Providence's sylvan shades on the afternoon of Sunday, Sept. 4, obtaining Theobald Manor on the telephone and thus notifying Grandpa, who forthwith proceeded to the Crown Hotel—amateurdom's official headquarters in this village. I have been to the Crown only thrice—in 1914 to see W. B. Stoddard, in 1920 to see the incomparable St. John, and in 1921 to see Mme. G.—an amateur mission in each case. Arriving at the Crown about 3:15 p.m., I paused only to snap the fair with my V. P. Kodak [. . .] and proceeded at once to show the quiet sights of Providence with the assurance born of practice on you and Daas. Though rather fearing that our tame and uneventful scenic pedestrianism would pall upon so effervescent a visitor, I repeated the familiar tour up the hill, to Prospect Terrace, and by the new Queen-Anne manor house where you and I snapped each other in the courtyard. This time the gate was closed, so I merely snapped the gable end as it stood majestic in the gold of afternoon's sunlight—a vivid bit of the old days re-created for the sight of a generation too stupid to appreciate it. Thence the route extended to Angell Street, and up the north side of that not unbeauteous thoroughfare to #598. Mme. G. appeared pleased with the

aspect of this section with its detached residences, neat lawns, and abundant foliage, and even expressed admiration for the Colonial style of architecture — though not that intense admiration which can arise only from an unmixed Anglo-American heritage. She admired the classic beauty of the lines — I admire the whole atmosphere and spirit with the fervour which comes from a mind shaped by 1400 years of English heredity, and from a taste centreing primarily in the age of swords and periwigs. God Save King George the Third!

Finally #598 was reached, and the visitor was introduced to the present regent of these domains — my elder aunt. Both seemed delighted with each other, and my aunt has ever since been eloquent in her praise of Mme. G., whose ideas, speech, manner, aspect, and even attire impressed her with the greatest of favourableness. In truth, this visit has materially heightened my aunt's respect for amateurdom — an institution whose extreme democracy and occasional heterogeneity have at times made it necessary for me to apologise for it. [. . .] At length the meeting adjourned, and Mme. G. generously invited both my aunt and myself to dinner at the Crown. Having had a noon meal, (we eat but twice daily) we were not ready for another; so my aunt had to decline, whilst I went along and consumed only a cup of coffee and portion of chocolate ice-cream. Mme. G. [. . .] preferred to make the return trip another scenic walk. This time I showed her the southern and really antique residential district where I took you, though preceding the display with a glimpse of the neo-Colonial Orchard Avenue, where we photographed each other in 1919. Mme. G. seemed to like the antique and solemn hush of the venerable streets, and the Georgian dignity of the old mansions on Power Street — including the Brown residence where Gen. Washington was entertained in August 1790. She also liked the cloistral hush of the Brown University campus, especially the inner quadrangle; where in the deserted twilight there seemed to brood the spirit of the dead generations. Thereafter a descent of College Hill was made, and the visitor did not fail to grasp the sensation of anticlimax involved in the abrupt transition from the ancient to the garishly modern. The soul of Providence broods upon the antique hill — below there is only a third-rate copy of New York. The Crown Tavern regained, there followed a meal spiced with philosophy — the latter revolving round a letter to Mme. Gr. from my boy,[4] which I was permitted to peruse. With her he adopts a vein slightly different from that he uses toward his Grandpas Mocrates and Tibaldus; being careful to show off his superior mind and varied erudition in a series of polished epigrams, curt cynicisms, and (I must admit despite a Grandparent's pride) modernistic affectations of prose style. He must, at all costs, be deem'd a young man of the world! The repast completed, I could think of no diversion more original than mine own hackneyed mode of killing a Sabbath Eve—the trite old band concert at Roger Williams Park. It was rather late for going thither, but some of the tunes were yet unplayed; so the trip was made. Mme. G., who does not care what she does with her spare cash, hired a horseless hackney-coach on the outbound voyage; though condescending to use the plebeian tramway on the return trip. After a brief final session of philosophical discussion in the lobby of the Crown—which recalled the Kleiner-Morton-Theobald session at the Brunswick on July 5–6[5]—the meeting disbanded till the morrow; and Grandpa sought his domestick hearth once more.

Postero die the session re-convened at the Crown at 1 p.m. with three delegates present—Mme. G. having invited both my aunt and myself thither for a noon repast. Her generosity is, in sooth, quite unbounded; bespeaking a mind deserving of the highest commendation and respect. The repast being over, all adjourned to the R. I. School of Design; whose museum and Pendleton House (which we visited in 1919) were apparently of great interest to the distinguished visitor. Thereafter a return to #598 by tram-car was made, and the residue of the afternoon was spent in the examination of old amateur papers. As the hour of six approached, some haste was exercised in seeking the train scheduled to depart Manhattan-ward shortly after that hour. Finally it was seen that only extreme haste would enable Mme. G. to obtain the desiderate choo-choos, hence a hectic rush to the Crown, and an excited hackney-coach trip to the station, ensued. At last the line of railway-carriages was discovered in time, and a more than obliging brakeman assigned his important passenger a seat in a carriage devoid of fellow-travellers—which he announced to the world as "reserved for a special party!" Conversation held sway until the slow motion of the train indicated a start, whereupon Grandpa alighted and journeyed home. The event was assuredly a felicitous one, marred only by the absence of Randolph St. John, who was more than frequently alluded to. Mme. G. is certainly a person of the most admirable qualities, whose generous and kindly cast of mind is by no means feigned, and whose intelligence and devotion to art merit the sincerest approbation. The volatility incidental to a Continental and non-Aryan heritage should not blind the analytical observer to the solid work and genuine cultivation which underlie it. This amiable and philanthropic personage is certainly due to make the greatest stir in amateurdom of any recent recruit; for unlike the majority, she takes the institution seriously enough to put real cash into it, and (so far) sees in its activities an actual branch of intellectual and aesthetic endeavour. Her latest idea is to have a sort of convention of freaks and exotics in New York during the holidays; inviting for two weeks such provincial sages as Loveman, The Chee-ild, and poor Grandpa Theobald! Only a sincere enthusiast could thus think of uprooting such outland fixtures from their respective native heaths! The practicability of such an enterprise may well be questioned—the fare from Appleton or Madison to N. Y. must be a young fortune—but if it could occur it would certainly be some convention! Damn me if I wouldn't give ten years of my declining life to see that little divvle Alfredus; to gaze one moment upon the flower-like face of my chee-ild, from whom the woild has crooly kep' me apart all these long y'ars! If the Kid should really come, I'd get to N. Y. if I had to go on foot and return in an ambulance! However—such titanic migrations are not likely to occur; and I fancy that the holidays will find the outland sages still chained to their hearthstones. N. Y. is rather an ambitious trip for an old gentleman whose limit is so far Hampstead, N. H., and whose sole immediate plan extends no farther than Athol, Mass.

[3]   Your new friend Mme. Greenevsky is livening up the social programme hereabouts. She is representing her firm at Magnolia, Mass., an ultra-fashionable watering-place on the coast near Gloucester, an hour's ride northeast from Boston; and Sunday she blew into Providentia for the afternoon and evening. For friendliness and generosity she sure beats hell—she is so stuck on my younger aunt Mrs. Gamwell, that she's trying to get her to come to N.Y. and permanently share her abode! And strange to say, my aunt likes her immensely despite a racial and social chasm which she doesn't often bridge. Gawd! Even the dowagers are getting democratic in these decadent days! But damme if Mme. Greene ain't a good sort, after all. She is trying to get the whole bally family to visit her in Magnolia, and failing to do that, is insisting that the old gent accept an invitation for a week or two beginning July 1st. An absolutely free trip, mind ya. [. . .] Lawd knows it's a helluva imposition—I decline as many times as courtesy permitted—but if she is determined to blow de coin, it ain't no business of mine to stop her! I gave ample warning, too, what an infernal bore the old man's senile prattle would get to be after a few days! So unless sumpun

new toins up, I'll soon have Magnolian material for another forty paged *Molo.* From wot I 'ears, de scenery had orta be good for about twenty pages—cliffs, chasms, 'n' ever'thin'. Last Sunday Mme. Greene hit Providence at one-forty-five. My younger aunt and I were at the dee-po to meet her, but she missed us and went on a wild-goose-chase in a taxi up to the house and back! When she finally did heave in sight, my aunt took her to the Crown Hotel for eats (they're as bad as Kleiner!) and put one over on her by paying the check herself! Thereafter occurred a triangular walk to the house, a five-hour session of quadrangular discussion in which the three females got so far away from literature that Grandpa dropped out now and then for an old-gentlemanly nap, more *eats* (gawdelpus!) around nine p.m., and finally a walk back to the deep-o with Grandpa as the sole local guide. This jaunt terminated in a watery grave. The day was dubious, and Mme. Greene had borrowed an umbrella. About half way down town the overhead sprinklers started, and sail was hoisted. I had no sunshade of me own, for I hate such devices like the devil. All would have been well had the one existing contraption been of sturdy timber—but! Just at the foot of the hill—some five squares from the dee-po—the celestial nimbi began to unload their aqueous cargo in earnest, and the damn portable Pantheon-dome dissolved into its constituent molecules like Ol' Doc Holmes' uni-equine vehicle; the umbrellian debris was cast into the nearest convenient gutter! Without being totally dissolved, the navigators finally reached port ten or fifteen minutes before train-time; and the only way I could stop Mme. Greene from hiring a taxi to cart my remains home for identification was to point out that not all the streams of Pater Oceanus could make me wetter than I was! My 1921 straw hat and 1918 summer suit sure were objects which Triton would have delighted to drape with fraternal seaweed. Mme. Greene had a wonderfully opportune cloak—but as for her hat—it's damn lucky she's in the millinery business! That lid'll never unfold its flowers to the summer sun again. And as I left the station on me 'omeward way—behold! The bally rain, having done its worst, had stopped! Mme. Greene sure had some visit—beginning with a false-alarm taxi ride and ending with a flood.

Travels

[The "convention of freaks and exotics in New York" did indeed occur in April 1922, and Lovecraft chronicles in detail his first impressions of the metropolis.]

[4]   On April 1, in response to Mrs. Greene's repeated inducements, Loveman had hit N. Y. in quest of a commercial situation. Finding his hostess absent, he was so depressed that he almost went home immediately; but a local friend persuaded him to wait at an hotel. April 3 Mrs. Greene reached home and found the disconsolate one on her doorstep, as it were. She succeeded in slightly cheering him up, but not in getting him a job; and by the next evening he was about to depart in tenebrous discouragement. Mrs. Greene had turned her entire flat over to him, stopping at a neighbour's herself, but not even that super-hospitality seemed likely to hold him. Then, since the bard had done me the undeserv'd honour of wishing I were there, Mrs. Greene called me up on the long-distance as an expedient for cheering her guest. You can imagine my ecstatic delight at hearing at last the actual voice of the poet I had admired for seven years—and to whom I had written commendatory verses before I knew whether he was living or dead![6] It was a great conversation, but I never expected to *see* the celebrity at the other end. He was resolved to go home at once! But Morton and Kleiner, with whom he was in touch, added their voices; and he decided to tarry "one more day". On the evening of the 5th I was called up by the assembled Loveman-Greene-Morton-Kleiner forces and invited to join them. The later presence of my kid protege Frank Belknap Long Jr. was promised, and Loveman said he would stay in N.Y. only on condition that I came. It was the suddenness and unexpectedness which finally turned the trick. I accepted, packed a valise, and on the following sunny morning caught the ten-six for New York.

I spent the five-hour journey reading Dunsany and peering at way-stations. New-London is a dingy little burg—a Victorian relic. New-Haven seems alert and metropolitan from the station angle. Ditto for Bridgeport. Shortly before three p.m., the train reached the lofty and colossal Harlem River viaduct (Only by chance did I secure the unique panorama—because the train was a Washington, D.C. express. Ordinary N.Y. trains go by a tamer route and into the Grand Central Station), and I saw for the first time the Cyclopean outlines of New-York. It was a mystical sight in the gold sun of late afternoon; a dream-thing of faint grey, outlined against a sky of faint grey smoke. City and sky were so alike that one could hardly be sure that there was a city—that the fancied towers and pinnacles were not the merest illusions. It was ten miles away, approximately—that is, the skyscraper region was. Actually, the train had crossed to Long Island, there to move south till a tunnel should take it under the East River and the streets of Manhattan to the Pennsylvania Station.

The station was reached on time, and I was supposed to be met by Loveman and Mrs. Greene; but by some mishap in calculation the reception committee had become lost in the mazes of the vast terminal. I waited a while, then made a scientific search which finally unearthed Mrs. Greene. Loveman had returned to Brooklyn in discouragement! By means of subway and taxi, we beat Loveman to 259 Parkside—meeting him just as he ascended the steps. Some meeting! Loveman is all right and then some! Absurdly as Mrs. Greene overpraises most persons, I doubt if there is any vital inaccuracy in even the wildest of her Lovemanic rhapsodies and dithyrambs. A great boy, Samuel! [. . .]

To resume the history of the voyage—after a long Lovemanico-Theobaldian session, during which I read my latest hell-beater "Hypnos" and received the flattering verdict that it's the best thing I ever wrote; Mrs. Greene returned from town, whither she had gone unnoticed during the two-Love introductory whirl of words, and took both guests to dinner at a neighbouring refectory. Nothing as sensational as the Pfister orgy—just broiled chicken with modest concomitants which I cannot recall in Mocratic detail—but a neat and quietly tasteful meal in surroundings of the same description. Upon our return to 259 we were soon privileged to hail the well-beloved Klei, emancipated from diurnal toil and vespertine nourishment. Then followed another whirl of words, which lasted till one a.m.—long after Mrs. Greene had been turned out of her own house and home for the night. The *Lokleilo* trio wrote a joint epistle to our kidlet friend in Madison, chinned some more, and then dispersed. Klei hit the trail, and Lolo hit the hay—Samuelus, good ol' scout, insisted that the less hardy and less easily somnolent Theobald take the only available bedchamber whilst he dumped down on the parlour couch—which is convertible into a bed or bedlet of a sort. I couldn't make him alternate—damn generous cuss—and I hadn't the heart to tell him I didn't sleep much anyway!

Friday dawned successfully, and all hands proceeded to the Manhattan section. Loveman and I took an omnibus up 5th Ave. to the Metropolitan Museum of Art, where we spent the entire day. Some day! For us were the sinister wonders of Ægyptus—we entered the nighted tomb of antique Perneb, transferred stone by stone from its age-long habitat beside the cryptical Nilus (in another place we saw the actual mummy of a priest of 2700 B.C.—the actual uncovered face, brown and withered, and the actual clawlike hands of a holy man who lived 4600 years ago!). For us were likewise the glories of fulgent Hellas—we found a young athlete's head (original—fifth century B.C.) so beautiful that the poetic Lovemanos went quite wild, purchased a half dozen postcard pictures of it, and chose it as the illustration for his "Hermaphrodite". Nor were the obscure secrets of dark Etruria absent—we saw a chariot, sixth century B.C., which might well have borne some warlike Lucume, Arnus, or Lars Porsenna. Paintings there were in abundance—by old masters and new—and many of these afforded us the keenest aesthetick gratification. But for me the supreme thrill—not only of the museums but of all New-York—came from the majestick memorials of mine own classical spirit-home—S.P.Q.R. Roma. I felt Rome the moment I entered the Musaeum—the main hall is like a gigantick atrium, with the effect enhanced by an heroick (Roman original) statue of the Imperator Gallienus silhouetted against the archway leading to the southerly wing. How different is a Greek like Lovemanos from a Roman like Theobaldus! He worshipped every statue of Hellenick beauty, whilst I tingled with exaltation at every eagle-nosed, gesturing effigy of a Roman consul or imperator! The summit of all grandeur was the great model of the Parthenon, built by M. Vipsanius Agrippa, three times consul, during the principate of our divine lord Octavianus Augustus. *Ave, Marce, bene fecisti!* The present model, restored by Charles Chipiez, shows the magnificent edifice at the height of its glory; with the exquisite frieze and statuary which once adorned and surmounted it. The exterior is awe-inspiring—but when one stoops and enters!!! The head of the spectator of the interior comes well above the floor level, in a large circular aperture provided for such rubbernecking. The effect is that of being in the temple itself, for the smallness of the walls and dome seems but natural to an eye in the centre of a floor so vast. I raised my head to shut off the disillusioning aperture and wooden rim—raised my hand and gazed at tier on tier of mounting Corinthian columns; niche on niche of heroic statues of gods and deified Augusti; vistas of marble beauty and sublimity, and a gold-inlaid dome that is the wonder and glory of the world, and whispered of even by the remote Parthians beyond the Euphrates, and the Germans and Sarmatians beyond the Rhine and Danube. I gazed, intoxicated with the mounting pride of a civis Romanus—a patrician of the Lolii Pagani and the Valerii Messalae—gazed at the supernal grandeur and loveliness which was Rome's might and proud splendour expressed and crystallised in lines of titanic sweep and more than martial grace. And as I gazed I sneered at the trifling arts and pleasures of the Greeks, and spat upon the grey dream of dim centuries of cursed superstition and effeminacy to come after our Roman world should die of weariness and barbarian blood; — superstition and effeminacy bred of some of the Syrian cults which infest the slums of the Suburra and trans-Tiber regions. [. . .]

After the Museum we went down to Madison Square on omnibus — as far as it went — and feet, and took a surface car (a common ornery closed car of the vintage of about 1895, just like a small town car except that its trolley was on the bottom instead of on top, running in a slot to the Avernian caves much like the gripper of an antique cable-car) down Broadway to the tall building section. The cloud-piercers certainly present a sight fairly unique, but that was not what we went for. We were bound for 206 and George Julian Houtain.[7] His office is a cramped dump on the ninth floor of a building which the neighbouring Woolworth tower quite dwarfs, but there was nothing cramped about G. Julian's laugh! Same old side-shaker! [. . .] We got back to Parkside safely, and Loveman heaved a sigh of relief when he found that Mrs. Greene could amicably survive the shock of learning that we had not only been to Houtain's, but had made a dinner engagement at his house for the next evening.

> Now sound the clarions and awake the drums,
> For matchless *Morton* in his chariot comes![8]

Just as we were about 0.75 through an excellent dinner prepared by Mme. Greene, good ol' woollybean blew in to bear us off to a stupid musicale on which his honest heart was set. It was at the home of an ex-member of the United — one Adeline E. Leiser — and most of the local amateurs, including our benign hostess, were none too enthusiastic about it because they had not been invited. It didn't sound very inviting (pardon paronomasia) to Loveman and me, but we'd do damn near anything for good old Jim. [. . .]

[. . .] We went — and kept awake through the whole programme of bourgeois Victorianism at the lyre. One of the singers could almost have sung if provided with a real song, whilst a yellow-haired young man resembling a truck-driver did noble service with a French horn in warding off the ever-present peril of obvious nodding. The best thing came from Mortonius — a pair of dramatic recitations of which the second was the famed mad scene by "Monk" Lewis — the "I-am-not-mad-but-soon-shall-be" thing. James F. reeled it off splendidly, ending in a shriek and a fall to the floor. He has a great reputation for this performance in B. P. C.[9] circles—it is the inevitable Morton encore. The triangular walk back to Parkside—Lovemanus-Mortonius-Theobaldus—was the best part of the evening; a literary symposium with the Elizabethan dramatists as chief ingredient. Morton left us at the door, and when we got in we found a note from Mme. Greene saying she would not be there next morning and telling us to get our own breakfast. (N. B. Loveman got the breakfast.)

Saturday was sightseeing day—and who could ask for a better guide than our—good ol' Klei? We met—Loveman-Theobald, Mortonius, and Klei, in front of the Woolworth Building, after the two Loves had indulged in a tour of old bookstalls in Vesey-Street. (I picked up some good Poe-iana) The assembled clan's first move was up—clean up to the top of N.Y.! It costs half a ducat per rube, and is worth it. Loveman was dizzy, but your grandpa wasn't—gawd knows how hard I worked when I was ten years old to conquer my native tendency to dizziness from altitudes! I walked on high railway trestles, and hell knows what not! But I digress. All Manhattan, Brooklyn, and Jersey City lay below, outspread like a map—in fact, I told Mortonious that the city-planners had done an excellent job in making the place almost as good as the map in my Hammond Atlas at home.

At length descending, we set out for the studio of Louis Keila, where rest in imperishable marble (plaster) the sculptured (modelled) features of our James Ferdinand. [. . .] After Keila, bookstalls. Everybody right tew hum, even if it was in bustling and remote Novum-Eboracum. Then a d. store and some post–1919 hootch, (coca-colas for Klei and Sam, orange phosphate for Theobaldus) and the subway for the financial district. In the sub. we saw Houtain's *Home Brew* on sale, and I picked up a copy with sophisticated nonchalance and pointed out my name and work . . . . . Reg'lar author'n' ever'thin' . . . . . Then we came to the surface on Old New-York— the financial district and heart of the town in Dutch and early British days. Wall St. was the old North boundary—it enclosed a village beside which Appleton would be a metropolis and even Elroy a great city. Trinity Church represents the Britannic period at its best—I saluted it—not the ecclesiastical mockery but the symbol of Royal dominion. Here we got some skyscraper vistas which enabled me to echo very faintly Klei's worship of his native burg. Now came the subway again—to Brooklyn. A stranger can tell when he is under the river (it's really a *strait*, not a "river") by the pressure on his ear-drums—the tube is very deep. When we came up for air we were in the City of Churches, [. . .] and proceeded to a hash joint to satisfy Klei's gastric pangs. [. . .] Next we hit the old residential district, which is the world's only replica of Boston's Back Bay. For a cent I'd have taken oath I was in Beacon-Street with the Charles peeping betwixt the brick mansions. At Montague St. we found an abandoned garden and broken flight of steps which set both the poets off mooning—you may hear the echoes in some amateur journal. But the big thing was Manhattan Bridge and the view of the New-York skyline there obtained. Right there I surrendered to Klei about the beauties of his home town. Out of the waters it rose at twilight; cold, proud, and beautiful; an Eastern city of wonder whose brothers the mountains are. It was not like any city of earth, for above purple mists rose towers, spires, and pyramids which one may only dream of in opiate lands beyond the Oxus; bloomed flower-like and delicate; the bridges up which fairies walk to the sky; the visions of giants that play with the clouds. Only Dunsany could fashion its equal, and he in dreams only. And as I gazed upon this gorgeous phantom sight I said to the wise men about me, "Behold the beauty of earth, which is mineral, titanic, and frore; even as a palace of ice by the ultimate boreal pole, which hath nothing of man it. For this was the world born, and the contemplative moon. And as insects unseen and unsung have reared in warm seas the loveliness that is coral, branching and glorious; so have insects called men, a little seen and a little sung, reared to the sky these pinnacles of breathing stone. Let us be patient. Not long will insects swarm upon earth, but long will stand the beauty whose creation was their task. And when the world is ice and the heavens are dim, and the jest called life long-forgotten; then will rubescent stars drink from these unvocal flowers of stone the joy and loveliness that were made for the delight of stars."[10]

[. . .] Sunday morning Loveman and I explored Prospect Park, fed the squirrels, and talked literature. At noon I did some kodak shooting, during which process there dawned upon us the new infant celebrity who was to form our principal focus of interest during the entire residue of the sojourn—

FRANK BELKNAP LONG, JR.

Long, whose phantasies you have doubtless read (I believe you once mistook one for Theobaldian stuff!) is an exquisite boy of twenty who hardly looks fifteen. He is dark and slight, with a busy wealth of almost black hair and a delicate, beautiful face still a stranger to the gillette. I think he likes the tiny collection of lip-hairs—about six on one side and five on the other—which may with assiduous care some day help to enhance his genuine resemblance to his chief idol—Edgar Allan Poe. Long is a sartorial triumph from spats to Fedora—he will undoubtedly carry a cane some day—and affects a mode subtly suggesting the Poe and the poet. But dost fancy I am describing a vapid dude? Fergit it, 'bo! The kid's a baby wonder—a secondary Galpinius—all wool and a yard wide! A scholar; a fantaisiste; a prose-poet; a sincere and intelligent disciple of Poe, Baudelaire, and the French decadents. He is as modest as Loveman himself, and the years seem likely to develop amazing gifts in him. I may be partial, because he flattered me by informing me that he always carries my picture in his pocket book (!!), but I don't think so. Loveman shares my view, and even our lofty little Galba person is beginning to take notice of him. Long is a cynic and a deist of the Voltaire type—he will be a materialist before he is through college. He attends N. Y. University, but is now out because of his convalescence from last winter's appendicitis operations. His life was despaired of, and he is still in bandages. He cannot walk swiftly yet, and has to retire each night at nine p.m.

At dinner—about one-thirty—were Loveman, Theobald, Long, Mme. Greene, and the latter's flapper offspring, yclept Florence—a pert, spoiled, and ultra-independent infant rather more hard-boiled of visage than her benignant mater. Trough-exercise was no sooner completed than a sizeable gang began to assemble—for this Sabbath had been appointed as the proper season for a fairly representative Blue Pencil conclave to do honor to the divine Lovemanus. [. . .]

The gathering, from which Mortonius had to be absent on account of a lecture, dispersed at twilight; whereupon Mme. Greene, who cannot keep still for two consecutive seconds, piloted Loveman and me through Prospect Park, which we had already explored. Upon returning to 259, Mortonius was discovered on the doorstep; and his amiability met with so haughty a reception that my Anglo-Saxon pride rebelled! I took him under my own thoroughly British wing, and let the foreigners shift for themselves during the residue of the evening; which included supper (how these birds do *eat!*) and a trip down to see the famed "White Way" and some of its denizens all lit up. The illumination is unique and extensive, but neither superlatively impressive nor in any sense truly artistic. At the elevated station at 6th Ave. and 42nd St. I lost my fellow Anglo-Saxon, whose home is far to the north in the semi-African jungles of Harlem; and the depleted party was haled to a swell eatery where the waiters hardly speak English and have no spots on their immaculate shirt-fronts. Eating again—my gawd! What are their stomachs made of! Our hostess ordered a strawberry concoction probably closely akin to what she handed you at the Ppffister—and of which I was able to partake only because I had made the preceding meal a matter of urbane evasion.

Thereafter once again to Parkside via subway—then more or less oblivion. It was hard work persuading Loveman to remain in N.Y. all this time, but perfect team-work did it. He saw that he could get no position, though Mme. Greene tried with frantic generosity to secure one for him— even unto the last moment.

Monday was Long-Poe day. Dinner at Long's, then as large an expedition as possible to the Poe cottage at Fordham—on the mainland north of Manhattan, but within the present limits of the vast municipality. Loveman and I started out early and went to the Public Library, later taking a Riverside Drive omnibus and reaching the Long apartment at eleven-thirty. The Greene flat is of much elegance on a small scale, but the Long menage *really* "belongs". It is a sumptuous place at the corner of 100th St. and West End Ave.—one alights from the 'bus at a picturesque landing stage at 100th and Riv. Drive, a point embellished by a firemen's memorial having the most beautifully tasteless and anachronistic bas-reliefs. Loveman and I are agreed on one thing—that all really great sculptural art died utterly with the Hellenic period. Long's pater is a dentist—a genial fellow of fifty-three who looks as though the numerals ought to be read the other way around. It is from him that Frank Jr.—called "Belknap" by his doting parents—gets his youthfulness. Long Sr. has a thick shock of black hair without a touch of grey, and on his boyish face is not a solitary line. During the war they used to hold him up for his draft registration card! Mrs. Long is very cultivated, and takes vast interest in her lone chick's achievements. She sometimes calls him "dear" and "darling" right afore comp'ny—and he bears it bravely though without noticeable pleasure. He's some boy! Young Belknap, by the way, loathes and abhors his native New-York—he says it is sordid and oppressive, and that he only really lives when up in Maine for the summer. Even Atlantic City, whither they frequently go, is not agrestic enough for this delicious little Melibeus!

Dinner at the Long's is a very formal institution—all the approved courses in rigidly proper order from fruit down through soup, meat, salad, etc. etc. to an appropriately proper dessert. Woe to the maid who mixes the menu or transposes the courses—one such blunder did occur on this occasion, and Mrs. Long was careful to inform us that the services of the culpable ancilla would terminate with the week! The delights of the Long household are enhanced by two parrots and an exquisite "coon" cat from Maine—a sumptuous creature with silky mane who answers to the simple title of "Felis", bestowed by his affectionate young master. My coming *Conservative* will contain a prose-poem by Kid Belknap, inspired by "Felis".[11] About dessert time good old James F. blew in—and Samuelus had to blow out, summoned by a last fruitless business call on the telephone. This delayed the Fordham party—we waited till Loveman called up from the city to tell us whether he could come or not. He couldn't, so Jim, Belknap, and Grandpa started off alone—the first one hundred percent Aryan, Anglo-Saxon gang to get together during the entire "convention"! GOD SAVE THE KING. We, the dominant British stock who founded this system of colonies, started north to pick up young Keil,[12] who lives at the top of a young Woolworth building in Fordham—a baby Bunker Hill Monument without an elevator, whose interminable stairs were too much for our little Longlet. Finally we got up, but found Paul Livingston out. His ma and kid sister brought forth some weak lemonade and stale cookies, (*eating* again, after that Long orgy!) and finally the missing youth appeared. Thereupon the quartette, still one hundred per-cent Aryan, sallied forth for a Bronx omnibus—and Poe.

We arrived at the cottage just too late to get in, but the exterior was an eyeful. Prior to 1913 it was a disgrace—rented to any old tenant and altered beyond recognition. In the above year it was purchased by a memorial association, moved out of the path of the ever-encroaching apartment-house wave to a safe spot in a park, and restored to its 1844–49 aspect. Even the *grounds*, as shewn in prints of the Poe period, were re-created— walks and trees. Today it is a thing to stir the pulses. Fordham is now hopelessly fused into the solid mass of elevateds, apartment-house cliffs, busses, and boulevards which is New-York. But in Poe's day it was a village of magical charm, with verdant arcades, purling brooks, and fragrant sylvan lanes leading to quaint and antique Highbridge—a favourite haunt of the great one. You will realise what beauty has been destroyed by the fiendishly gnawing city when you reflect that the sketch "Landor's Cottage" was partially inspired by the author's own humble, rented home.

We had a date to meet Klei on the Pub. Libe steps at six-thirty, so soon bade adieu to the place of beautiful memories. Keil had to go home, and Long's health would not allow him to be in on the evening jaunt, but the latter kid was so anxious to see Loveman again that he rode down town with us on the elevated, only to ride back again after he had paid his respects to the Divine Syrian—to say naught of the ever-genial Klei. It was not certain that Loveman could be held another day—I could not get him to promise till late that night! After Long's departure—more *eating!* An automatic beanery in a basement—gorge and guzzle—bah! But after a while we pried Klei loose from his trough and set him at the head of a guiding party. We walked in pairs—Klei-Lo ahead, Loveman-Morton behind—so that my detachment reminded me of the good old Kleiner visits in Providence. Mme. Greene may have told you that Klei has rather retrograded through intimacy with Houtain—but that is only superficially true. If I had him in Providence for a week I could bring back the old Kleiner . . . . . he admitted to Loveman and me that he sometimes wishes he had never left his old dream-world. A good old boy, Klei! Our course lay down 5th Ave. to Washington-Square—once the centre of fashionable society under George III, but now very decadent. The "Greenwich Village" nuts have been there and departed—and there is a slight prospect of at least a partial rehabilitation to ancient glory. There is a Roman arch there, under which I walked with pride of a patrician triumphator. We sat on a bench in this clearing for nearly an hour, discussing all manner of learned things. Then the hour of a Writers' Club meeting drew near. Klei and Jim both belong, but the former funked. J. Ferd had to go because he had a speech to deliver. Some orator! This was our final adieu, for Loveman had intimated that if he stayed another day he wanted the company only of Long and myself—why the especial choice, only de lawd knows.

Klei, now at the head of a triangular expedition with the same personnel as Saturday's, proceeded to lead us into the slums; with "Chinatown" as an ulterior objective. My gawd—what a filthy dump! I thought Providence had slums, and antique Bostonium as well; but damn me if I ever saw anything like the sprawling sty-atmosphere of N.Y.'s lower East Side. We walked—at my suggestion—in the middle of the street, for contact with the heterogeneous sidewalk denizens, spilled out of their bulging brick kennels as if by a spawning beyond the capacity of the places, was not by any means to be sought. At times, though, we struck peculiarly deserted areas—these swine have instinctive swarming movements, no doubt, which no ordinary biologist can fathom. Gawd knows what they are—Jew, Italian, separate or mixed, with possible touches of residual aboriginal Irish and exotic hints of the Far East—a bastard mess of stewing mongrel flesh without intellect, repellent to eye, nose, and imagination—would to heaven a kindly gust of cyanogen could asphyxiate the whole gigantic abortion, end the misery, and clean out the place. The streets, even in the centre, are filthy with old papers and vegetable debris—probably the street-cleaners dislike to soil their white uniforms by visiting such infernos.

And then Chinatown appeared. Here cleanliness reigned, for certain enterprising rubberneck-wagon owners use it as a sort of seat of local colour—they have fake opium joints which they point out as the real thing. Doyers St., the main thoroughfare, is narrow and crooked. It is fascinatingly Oriental, and Loveman rhapsodised on the evil faces of the natives. Probably it was only the usual low-caste physiognomy of the coolie type which so thrilled him—but bless me! let the poets find thrills where they can!

We emerged on the Bowery, and proceeded to cross Manhattan Bridge to Brooklyn. Here we saw the city skyline electrically illumined, but it did not equal that flower-like, fairy-like vision in the twilight, when softly golden pinnacles reached up to consort with the first stars of evening. Loveman and I were damn near dead with tramping, but I refused to show it. Morton had called me the most nonchalant and imperturbable person he had ever seen, whose cynical poise could not be shaken even by a River Beach rollercoasting thunderbolt, so I resolved to justify his flattery or die standing and jesting. How Klei stands such tramping about, only the local small gods of the city can reveal. By the time we reached a homeward subway I was ready to write a joint two-Love elegy.

Tuesday morning—last full day—found me a pretty drowsy customer. I went out and purchased a much-needed new collar, and returned to rest in the deserted flat whilst Loveman and Mme. Greene went about their respective Metropolitan affairs. I had arranged to meet Loveman at the Pub. Libe at noon—but eheu! I got to sleep and was nearly an hour late! We went to Long's again for dinner, and found an entire change of dietetic programme just as elaborate as the first spread. They do that sort of thing right along—as would we all, no doubt, if we had the dough! I can recall traces of it in mine own household in extreme youth, ere chill penury had got in his most repressive work. After the ordeal we fared northward again to the shrine of the only vital force which America has yet contributed to the general current of world-literature. The day, like all the others of the trip, was delightfully and unseasonably hot—which sustained my tropic-loving bulk wonderfully.

At Fordham—thank Pegāna—we found the Poe cottage open, and forthwith entered a small world of magic. Poor Poe, a creature of poverty driven from pillar to post in hired houses and with no stable, ancestral furniture, left very little with which to embellish the interior; but his own desk is there, and the chair in which he wrote "Annabel Lee", and the bed on which his wife died. The rest of the furniture was chosen from among the semi-antiques in strict accordance with the known styles of the period and the various accounts in letters of, to, and about Poe and his home. It is believed to represent with fair accuracy the actual furniture of the cottage during Poe's occupancy. Our friend Burton Rascoe, late of the *Chitrib* and now of the *N.Y. Tribune*, recently made a bonehead play in writing up the cottage—he spoke of 'Poe's taste in furniture', as though the stuff were really his. There are several Poe busts, a couple of awkward stuffed ravens, and some good Poe portraits. There are specimens of his handwriting and a lock of his hair. The atmosphere grows on one and finally grips one—it is so terribly vivid—the 'forties recalled in every sombre detail. The pitiful poverty shows—something sombre broods over the place. I seemed to feel unseen bat-wings brush my cheek as I passed through a bare, cramped corridor . . . . . the house is so pathetically small . . . . . and such hideous things have been written there. Such was the home of the man to whom I probably owe every genuine artistic impulse and method I possess. My master—the great original whose titanic powers I can so feebly seek to copy . . . . . Edgar Allan Poe.

It was deuced hard to break away, but it hadda be did. We hit the elevated in an effort to get to the Museum of Natural History, but lo! Our little native N.Y. guide Belknap got the wrong train and landed us on the east instead of the west side of Central Park! Damn! Having arranged to meet Mme. Greene at 57th St., we had no time to cross over, but consoled ourselves by strolling slowly down town beside the delectable *rus in urbe*. It was early spring—and some early flowers were in bloom. Magnolias were white, and there were other flowering shrubs as delicate as a Japanese print. A shower sprang up, and we sought the shelter of the porch of a magnificent mansion. Then it cleared in the west—the sun shone golden, and a rainbow appeared in the east. (Loveman looked for it in the WEST—haw! Poetic soul doesn't give scientific accuracy!)

We met Mme. Greene in front of her lid shop, and after a ceremonious farewell kid Long hiked for the northbound elevated. Too bad he wasn't able to keep with us — but he has to be careful of his convalescent anatomy. When he is better, he and Mortonius will be great pals — Jim Ferd has a vast paternal admiration for his unusual qualities. Meanwhile he is getting more closely in touch with the United — Loveman, Galpin, and Theobald. Great Kid, we'll say! After the adieu the residual triad hiked to a cafe of semi-subterranean altitude on 49th St., where the lavish Mme. Greene made what appeared to be a sturdy effort to buy the place out. Actually, I suppose it was what they call their regular dinner, Italian-style, — but I'd like to see the human being who could eat it all! I wonder what they do with the inevitable residuum? Chicken, spaghetti, and other things were included — damn me if I can remember. The order of courses had no relation to Anglo-Saxon dining customs, and gawd knows I didn't try to tackle half of 'em. When we broke away it was to attend a performance, in the 49th St. Theatre, of that rather well known Muscovite melange of cleverly dippy vaudeville called the "Chauve Souris" and managed by a comical fattish cuss of long speeches and short English named HIKITA БАλIЕВ (since the limit of your linguistick attainment is Assyrian cuneiform, I'll translate it — Nikita Balieff.) It was a balmy sort of mess in spots, but pretty damn good at that. The star act was a company of ginks dressed up with inimitable cleverness as *wooden soldiers*. Their musical drill was sure some knockout — it brought down the house. Take it from me — in a couple years ham companies 'll be tryin' to put over that act in every tank town on the small-time circuit! It's a bird, and no mistake! When the show let out, darn the luck, it was raining again, but not all the aqueous wrath of the sky could dampen the spirits of the irrepressible Mme. Greene — so she led the docile guests to a Russian restaurant (*eats* again — bah!) on thirtysomething street. We trifled lightly with cake and coffee, and finally hit the Parkside trail. After Mme. Greene's departure Loveman and I finished valise-packing and prepared to snatch a bit of rest before our simultaneous embarkation for opposite points on the morrow. He gave me some books to remember him by — good boy!

Wednesday we were up betimes, and guided by Mme. Greene to the Grand Central Station via the underground. It's quite a dee-po, but not so artistic as the Pennsylvania — or, for that matter, as the Union Station in Worcester. But it beats by a mile anything in Boston or Providence. My train left for the East at eight-thirty-three a.m.; Loveman's for the West at eight-forty-five. Mine was N.Y.N.H.S.H.; his was N.Y.C. & H.R. Mme. Greene bade the twain a joint farewell when the time arrived for her to hit 57th St. and work; and thereafter Lovemanus and I discoursed in the manner of a Greek and a Roman about to part in brotherly amity. Then train time approached. I got a good seat and slept all the way home, so that the next sight I recall was our own marble-domed R.I. State House, the habitat of an equally marble-domed legislature. Loveman had a trying trip— noisy fellow-passengers, wakefulness, and ennui generally. His trip was also over twice as long as mine. At one-twenty, I was on Providence soil, whilst he didn't hit Cleveland till midnight. I'll say it was some trip. Whilst it lasted I kept up very well, though not sleeping much. Afterward I did very little but sleep—I'm hardly over it yet! But it was worth it.

[In August and September Lovecraft undertook his most ambitious excursion to date, traveling all the way to Cleveland to visit Alfred Galpin and Samuel Loveman (and such of Loveman's associates as the bookseller George Kirk and the young poet Hart Crane), then returning to New York for an extended visit with Sonia Greene and other friends.]

[5]   Saturday, at six-thirty p.m., I boarded the "Lake Shore Limited" at the Grand Central, and was soon whirling up the Hudson amidst the resplendent Palisades and Catskills.

I had expected to seem rather clumsy and inexperienced in sleeping-car procedure—I had an upper berth, and knew nothing of the technique —but by a judicious combination of guess-work, deduction, and observation I managed to "get by" without drawing the least bit of notice to my ignorance. I dressed and undressed in my berth—some feat!

Having rested surprisingly well, I awaked in Pennsylvania and settled down to await the momentous Clevelandic arrival. The train was one and one-half hours late, but at ten-thirty (or I should say, *nine-thirty,* since Cleveland does not use daylight time) the suburban 105th St. station was reached. Meanwhile I had been intensely interested in watching the Ohio landscape from the window. It is quite unlike—and inferior to— New-England, having vast level stretches, sparser vegetation and foliage, and different types of architecture. (Flatter roofs, etc.) The villages are insufferably dismal—like "Main St." They have no ancient features, and totally lack the mellow charm and scenery which make New-England villages so delightful. I was glad that my destination was a large city!

At ten-thirty I alighted from the train, and immediately perceived a lank, altitudinous, hatless form loping cordially toward me. Mutual recognition? I'll say so! The Kid is *exactly* like those recent Madison pictures, and he says I am exactly like my own snapshots. Some meeting! I exclaimed spontaneously—"So this is my Son Alfredus!" And he responded, "It sure is!" We shook hands till paralysis threatened to set in, and then began to talk an incessant stream. Are we congenial? I'll tell the world! The Kid is utterly delightful—exactly the same as he is on paper, and as fascinating a companion as Harold Munroe into the bargain. We have not been out of each other's sight a second since we met, except when sleeping, and it will certainly be a melancholy event when I have to bid him *au revoir* on the fifteenth at midnight. At that hour he goes to Mackinac to join his father in a sail around the Great Lakes, whilst I go to New-York. After our ecstasy of greetings, Alfredus guided me to a neat and inexpensive lunch counter (where we have since taken most of our humble but excellent meals). The blessed child insisted not only on paying for his Grandpa's refreshments, but on carrying the old gentleman's heavy valise as well. Some boy! Subsequently we proceeded to our joint hangout—9231 Birchdale—which is just around the corner from Loveman's house. The neighbourhood is very good, and the cottage very pleasant. My room is diagonally across a hall from my grandson's. We rise about noon, eat twice a day, and retire after midnight—a routine forming a sort of cross betwixt normalcy and Theobaldism. This is A. G.'s ordinary schedule when not in school. After Saturday Alfredus and I will be sole masters of the house—the family is going away for a week, leaving us in undisturbed possession. Probably we shall sing and shout to our heart's content—and dance clog dances in the parlour if we want to! But we shan't break any windows or spit tobacco on the floor. Heigho—but this is the life!

After settling down at 9231, we proceeded around the corner to Loveman's place—The Lonore Apartments—which is an excellent place. S. L. was on hand, looking ten years younger and ten times more cheerful than last April, and full of flattering compliments for the Old Gentleman. His mother, a kindly and excellent person, and his genial brother—with the automobile—were on hand, and presently took us for a ride of sightseeing. Loveman's room is a veritable museum—filled with antiques and books of rare vintage. His devotion to all the arts is well attested by a profusion of art books and an unrivalled collection of classical records for the phonograph. Before he and Alfredus are through with me, I shall probably be half-civilised—they feed me large doses of art, music, and literature. The automobile ride gave me a chance to become familiar with Cleveland and its suburbs—it is a rather attractive city whose chief characteristic is *breadth* in parts and entirely alike. The streets are very broad, houses set far back from sidewalks, and the whole spread out over an immense area. Despite a population of about a million, (it is the fifth city of the U.S.) there are no subways or elevateds; and the atmosphere of provincialism subtly lingers. The climate is not as good as that of the East. In the daytime the heat is actually oppressive—even to *me* (!!!)—and one drinks glass after glass of water. Not till the evening breeze comes in from Lake Erie is there a clearing of the general discomfort and stickiness. I am glad I brought along an ample shirt supply—much of which is now in the capable Mongolian hands of one Sam Lee on Superior St., for purposes of rejuvenation . . . . . . Sunday evening we met the rare book dealer George Kirk—a friend of Loveman's—and the quartette of us explored the excellent Cleveland Art Museum in Wade Park.

Monday morning Alfredus and I loafed around Loveman's room—looking at rare books and pictures, and hearing phonograph records. We saw the hideous drawings of Loveman's friend Clark Ashton Smith—grotesque, unutterable things,—and I took some over here for subsequent study. [. . .] Did you ever see anything more ghoulish? Smith is a genius, beyond a doubt.[13] [. . .] Monday afternoon Galpin and I went out to the suburbs to see George Kirk, who showed us an infinity of rare books and plates, and who has a delectable black angora cat named "Hodge" (after Dr. Johnson's) which sat in my lap and purred all through the visit. Later Kirk, Galpin, and I took a long scenic walk through "Forest Hills"—the Rockefeller Estate, which is used as a public park. The scenery is very beautiful, and quite transported the Westerners, though it is not nearly so attractive as Quinsnicket. We are going again some time *by moonlight*. Monday evening Loveman, Galpin, and I went to the Public Library and watched a thunderstorm gather, burst, and fade away. There are very few long rains in Cleveland—storms are short and sudden.

Tuesday we called on Loveman in the book shop where he works—a very inviting place. Later we read in Rockefeller Park, and in the evening Loveman organised a party to see the most lavish cinema show in town—a party consisting of himself, a friend named Baldwin, Kirk, young Wheeler, Galpin, and myself. It is odd to see a really sumptuous and artistic theatre devoted to moving pictures—but such is Cleveland.

Meanwhile a strange transformation had taken place in the aspect of Grandfather Theobald! That I had become tanned and thinner, was only to be expected—but who could have expected the rest? Moved by the oppressive heat, and by the constant and rejuvenating companionship of youth, I proceeded to imitate my grandson in the following details:

(a) I left off my vest and bought a belt—a fine new kind with my initial on the buckle; which has no perforations, but adjusts to *any* circumference.

(b) I bought some *soft* collars (yes, really!) and have worn them continuously.

(c) I commenced going *hatless* like A. G.—using a hat only on formal occasions.

Can you picture me vestless, hatless, soft-collared, and belted, ambling about with a boy of twenty, as if I were no older? I will have Alfredus take a snap shot to prove it! One can be free and easy in a provincial city—when I hit New York again I shall resume the solemn manner and sedate vestments befitting my advanced years, but for the present I have cast aside the eleven years which separate me from His Imperial Kidship! The face is doing finely,[14] and I am altogether free from melancholy—positively cheerful, in fact. What I need in order to be cheerful is the constant company of youthful and congenial literary persons.

[6]   As for the kind of time I am having—it is simply great! I have just the incentive I need to keep me active and free from melancholy, and I look so well that I doubt if any Providence person would know me by sight! I have no headaches or depressed spells—in short, I am for the time being really alive and in good health and spirits. The companionship of youth and artistic taste is what keeps one going! The programme of the past few days is much like that of the days previously chronicled, but last night was rather unusual. We held a meeting here of all the members of Loveman's literary circle, at which the conversation covered every branch of aesthetics. I have often spoken of "Allston flattery", but the Cleveland article is more enthusiastic still! It gave me a novel sensation to be "lionised" so much beyond my deserts by men as able as the painter Sommer,[15] Loveman, Galpin, etc. I met some new figures—Crane the poet, Lazare,[16] an ambitious literary student now in the army, and a delightful young fellow

named Carroll Lawrence, who writes weird stories and wants to see all of mine. Loveman persuaded me to deliver my scene from "Richard III", and it was received with surprising applause — just as if I could really act! All the circle say they like my stories — which duly inflates me with pride. I am learning to appreciate music — Galpin has given me a record of a Chopin Nocturne, played by De Pachmann, which was especially potent in evoking imaginative images — here's hoping I don't break it on the way home. Tonight Galpin, Crane, I, and a fellow I have not met are going to a concert held in the art museum building. Great days!!

I am sorry you miss me — though much flattered that you should do so! I wish that you and A E P G could be here — this city is much more intellectually alive than Providence, where all artistic manifestations are confined to artificial and quasi-Victorian society groups. (But don't tell A E P G that I concede any point of superiority to a non-Providential city!) My money is holding out amazingly, because both Galpin and Loveman, to say nothing of Kirk, insist on playing the host with unlimited generosity wherever we go. However — all Paradises must eventually be lost, so that before many weeks I shall indeed be stagnating in accustomed hibernation. I shall get to N.Y. Wednesday or Thursday — depending on whether or not I take the Niagara Falls trip — and after a reasonable period of metropolitan sightseeing will again hit the homeward trail. After so ample and varied a glimpse of the outside world I certainly ought to have some material for literary production during the quiet months!

[7]   As to my recent programme — I believe the last chronicle left off Saturday, Sept. 16, with a hasty exterior P.S. telling of the afternoon's trip with Kleiner, Belknap, and Morton. That evening Kleiner and I investigated the principal antiquity of this section — the old Dutch Reformed Church — and were well repaid for our quest. Parkside Avenue, be it known, is not part of the original town of Brencklin — or Brookland — or Brooklyn — as the Long Island metropolis is variously known, but is a remnant of the early Dutch village of *Flatbush*, which was engulfed about a quarter of a century ago by the expansion of the great city. Most of the original village edifices have long been destroyed, and replaced by blocks of shops and apartment houses; but some benign fate has preserved the ancient village church, whose ivy-twined belfry and spire still dominate the local skyline. This venerable congregation was founded in 1654 by the honest and simple Holland burghers who settled the region. In 1698 a

second and more elegant church replaced the original structure—British rule had brought prosperity, yet the villagers still adhered to their Dutch speech and manners. Then, in about three-quarters of a century, came the lamented rebellion of the colonies, with the unfortunate victory of the rebels and the secession of all His Majesty's Dominions south of Canada. Alas! Time passed; and in 1796, under the newly-welded government of the United-States, the worthy Flatbush burghers built a third and still more substantial church on the ancient site—the graceful structure of Georgian outlines which stands to this day. But though they adopted the artistic architecture of the conquering Saxon, they themselves remained unalterably Dutch. Around the old pile is a hoary churchyard, with interments dating from about 1730 to the middle of the nineteenth century. Nearly all the stones bear inscriptions and epitaphs in the Dutch language—beginning with the characteristic "Hier lygen", which analogy makes quite easily recognisable to the devotee of English graveyards. Up to about 1815 or 1820 the Dutch tongue predominates. Here and there an English inscription tells of a family looking forward to the changing order of things; and now and then an English *name* reveals the beginning of that gradual intermarriage which has today completely fused the Dutch and English colonists into one native stock—a stock, alas, now menaced in its turn by the appalling tidal wave of modern inferior immigration. As I viewed this village churchyard in the autumn twilight, the city seemed to fade from sight, and give place to the Netherland town of long ago. In fancy I saw the cottages of the simple Dutchmen, their small-paned windows lighted one by one as evening stole over the harvest-fields. And I reflected upon the vanity of mankind, which seeks even after death a tawdry fame in carven stone and marble. Here were slabs chiselled with care, that all the world might know the virtues—real or fictitious—of those who sleep beneath; slabs designed for the eyes of the future, yet through fate's triumphant irony couched in a fading speech which today no passer-by can read! So, too, may be the pompous legends which adorn our own sepulchres and mausolea—transient hieroglyphics which succeeding ages and succeeding races of conquerors will labour in vain to decipher. Sic transit gloria mundi! This ancient churchyard is, in a sense, a discovery of my own; since none of the local amateurs had ever visited it, or so much as suspected that any Dutch cemetery remained in the country. Kleiner and I have since examined it again—also in the twilight, when small birds flew down in great numbers out of the sky and pecked at the ancient grave-earth as if imbibing some hideous species of nourishment. I would like to have understood the mocking chatter of those birds, as they hopped about on the graves of forgotten burghers, or flew to shelter beneath the shadowy eaves of that old and ivied church . . . . . . From one of the crumbling gravestones—dated 1747—I chipped a small piece to carry away. It lies before me as I write—and ought to suggest some sort of a horror-story. I must some night place it beneath my pillow as I sleep . . . . who can say what *thing* might not come out of the centuried earth to exact vengeance for his desecrated tomb? And should it come, who can say what it might not resemble? At midnight, in many antique burying-grounds, shadows steal terribly about; shadows in periwigs and three-cornered hats, and tattered, mouldy knee-breeches that flap about crumbling bones. They have no voices, but sometimes do hideous deeds *silently.*[17]

[In December 1922 Lovecraft visited antiquarian sites in Salem, where he heard of a better-preserved haven of antiquity, the town of Marblehead. His sight of it seemed the culmination of his longing for the past.]

[8]   On Monday I departed, but so fired with the spirit of antient research that I went not home but to Salem, in the same province, for a solitary tour of observation and discovery. The result was an aesthetick and historicall orgy of delight such as I never before experienc'd; for truly, I had not dream'd so much of the *seventeenth* century still remain'd for the contemplation of the studious. Salem, as I may mention in case you have seen it not, retains whole streets and squares scarce alter'd since the reign of George the Third; with an impressive array of mansions built by the rich merchants whose ships traded in the Indies, China, and Japan. There is, besides, a surprising profusion of houses built as far back as Charles the First's time, the age of Cromwell's treason, the aera of the glorious Restoration, and King William the Third's reign; strange sinister edifices in whose queerly pitch'd roofs and diamond pan'd windows lurk a profusion of weird suggestions. I visited the *Old Witch House,* said to have been inhabited by Rev. Roger Williams before his coming to Providence-Plantations, and investigated the several scenes pertaining to the late ingenious Mr. Hawthorne, including his birthplace, and the house of Seven Gables, where I was shewn a secret staircase and permitted to ascend it. The Essex Institute is a Museum of universal celebrity, which I abundantly enjoy'd; and I did not quit the town without resolving to visit it repeatedly in vari-

ous seasons, and to become saturated with that air of pleasing antiquity which is its particular property and chief pride. Salem, in truth, hath inherited from its past a dignity which for ever keeps it above the absurdity of a common rustick town.

But not even from Salem did I go directly home; for whilst conversing with natives there, I had learnt of the neighbouring fishing port of *Marblehead*, whose antique quaintness was particularly recommended to me. Taking a stage-coach thither, I was presently borne into the most marvellous region I had ever dream'd of, and furnish'd with the most powerful single aesthetic impression I have receiv'd in years.

Even now it is difficult for me to believe that Marblehead exists, save in some phantasticall dream. It is so contrary to everything usually observable in this age, and so exactly conform'd to the habitual fabrick of my nocturnal visions, that my whole visit partook of the aethereal character scarce compatible with reality. This place was settled in King Charles the First's time, by fishermen of French and English blood from the channel islands. Its Town House, in the town-square, was finish'd in 1727, and by 1770 most of the land was well built up with plain but substantial houses. The ground is very hilly, and the streets were made crooked and narrow, so that when finish'd, the town had gain'd much of the eccentrick aspect of such antient Gothick towns as Nuremburg, in Bavaria, where the eye beholds small buildings heap'd about at all angles and all levels like an infant's blocks, and topp'd with a pleasing labyrinth of sharp gables, tall spires, and glittering vanes. Marblehead, indeed, was the scene of many romantick incidents; one of which concern'd Sir H: Frankland of Frankland-Hall, and was writ of by Dr. Holmes the poet. Over all the rest of the scene tower'd a hill on which the rude forefathers of the hamlet were laid to rest; and which was in consequence nam'd Old Burying Hill. In subsequent years a newer part of the village rose across the bay, and became almost as great a watering-place as Bath or Brightelmstone. But the conservative temper of the old villagers excluded such invasions of their settled district, and produced the greatest modern miracle that hath ever met my gaze. That miracle is simply this: *that at the present moment the Georgian Marblehead of 1770 stands intact and unchanged!* I do not exaggerate. It is with calm assurance that I insist, that Gen. Washington could tomorrow ride horseback down the long street nam'd for him without the least sensation of strangeness. Wires are few and inconspicuous. Tramway rails look like deep ruts. Costumes are not marked in the twilight. And on every hand stretch the endless rows of houses built betwixt 1640 and 1780—some even with overhanging gables—whilst both to north and south loom hills cover'd with crazy streets and alleys that Hogarth might have known and portray'd, had he but crossed the ocean to discover them. It is a dream— a grotesque and unbelievable anachronism—an artist's or antiquarian's fancy stept out of his brain and fixt to earth for publick inspection. It *is* the 18th century. There are no modern shops or theatres, and no cinema show that I cou'd discover. The railway is so remote from the town-square, that its existence is forgotten. The shops have small windows, and the men are very old. Time passes softly and slowly there.

I came to Marblehead in the twilight, and gazed long upon its hoary magick. I threaded the tortuous, precipitous streets, some of which an horse can scarce climb, and in which two waggons cannot pass. I talked with old men and revell'd in old scenes, and climb'd pantingly over the crusted cliffs of snow to the windswept height where cold winds blew over desolate roofs and evil birds hovered over a bleak, deserted, frozen tarn. And atop all was the peak; Old Burying Hill, where the dark headstones clawed up thro' the virgin snow like the decay'd fingernails of some gi- gantick corpse.

Immemorial pinnacle of fabulous antiquity! As evening came I look'd down at the quiet village where the lights came out one by one; at the calm contemplative chimney-pots and antique gables silhouetted against the west; at the glimmering small-paned windows; at the silent and unillu- mined fort frowning formidably over the snug harbour where it hath frown'd since 1742, when 'twas put up for defence against the French King's frigates. Shades of the past! How compleatly, O Mater Novanglia, am I moulded of thy venerable flesh and as one with thy century'd soul! God Save His Majesty, George the Third, and preserve his Province of the Massachusetts-Bay!

My return to the Providence-Plantations was accomplisht without any events more untoward than a delay of three hours occasion'd by a railway wreck at Readville; but I can never again have any considerable part in the thoughts of this decaying aera. *I have look'd upon Marblehead, and have walk'd waking in the streets of the 18th century.* And he who hath done that, can never more be a modern.[18]

[9]   God! Shall I ever forget my first stupefying glimpse of MARBLE- HEAD'S huddled and archaic roofs under the snow in the delirious sunset

glory of four p.m., Dec. 17, 1922!!! I did not know until an hour before that I should ever behold such a place as Marblehead, and I did not know *until that moment itself* the full extent of the wonder I was to behold. I account that instant—about 4:05 to 4:10 p.m., Dec. 17, 1922—the most powerful single emotional climax experienced during my nearly forty years of existence. In a flash all the past of New England—all the past of Old England—all the past of Anglo-Saxondom and the Western World—swept over me and identified me with the stupendous totality of all things in such a way as it never did before and never will again. That was the high tide of my life. I was thirty-two then—and since that hour there has been merely a recession to senile tameness; merely a striving to recapture the wonders of revelation and intimation and cosmic identification which that sight brought.

Philosophical Development

[In the early 1920s Lovecraft came upon a series of new intellectual discoveries that affected his philosophical thought. His earlier readings of Nietzsche were now augmented by studies of Sigmund Freud and Einstein. Meanwhile, in politics he announced himself as a staunch supporter of Mussolini's fascism.]

[10]   Altogether, Kant is one whose name might be quite readily commenced with a lower-case "c". His value in stimulating thought and advancing philosophy need not be questioned, but in matters of detail he is simply an empty and exaggerated name—one of those figures who receive accretions of blind adulation until they become mere magic words—mystical abracadabras of classical tradition whose revered mouthings and dialectics would evaporate if examined without the deafness and blindness of irrational veneration. As sequels to Kant, I sincerely trust that you will read Schopenhauer and Nietzsche, in the other named; following these with the most modern rational work—"Modern Science and Materialism", by Hugh Elliot, (1919). To emerge from the artificial fog of empty, resonant, mystical words without a single real idea behind them, into the clear light of minds with actual conceptions, is a tonic to the intellect. Lest you fancy that I am making an idol of Nietzsche as others do of Kant, let me state clearly that I do not swallow him whole. His ethical system is a joke—or a poet's dream, which amounts to the same thing. It is in his method, and his account of the basic origin and actual relation of existing ideas and

standards, which make him the master figure of the modern age and founder of unvarnished sincerity in philosophic thought. It is impossible to understand philosophy without Nietzsche—as Mencken says; like him or not, you cannot escape him.

Dr. Sigmund Freud of Vienna, whose system of psycho-analysis I have begun to investigate, will probably prove the end of idealistic thought. In details, I think he has his limitations; and I am inclined to accept the modifications of Adler,[19] who in placing the ego above the eros makes a scientific return to the position which Nietzsche assumed for wholly philosphical reasons. But to Freud is due the credit of discovering the basic principles of one dominating motive behind all psychological processes; establishing inductively what Nietzsche established deductively—the selfish, individual *wille zur macht* which is the only driving force in the organic world.

As I grow older, I lose much of the prejudice and shallow enthusiasm for empirical and accepted traditions which retarded my progress toward realism in earlier years. I have today not a single well-defined wish save to die or to learn facts. This position makes me eminently receptive, for a new idea no longer meets with any conflict from old ideas—I can change my theories as often as valid evidence is changed, or as my judgment improves through exercise in the province of philosophical reflection. I am, I hope, now a complete machine without disturbing and biassing volition; a machine for the reception and classification of ideas and the construction of theories. As such, I may say that the obsoleteness of religion and idealism as systems of enlightened thought is impressed upon me with redoubled force. If any thing is true, it is that these beliefs are soon to be finally extinct until some cataclysm shall wipe out civilisation and inaugurate a new Dark Age of myth and ignorance.

[11]   Anent the Fascist problem—assuredly we approach it from radically different directions. Galpinius and I have been discussing democracy a lot lately, and we agree that it is a false idol—a mere catchword and illusion of inferior classes, visionaries, and dying civilizations. Life has no ultimate values, and our proximate values can be little more than what we like to see or possess. "Right" and "wrong" are primitive conceptions which cannot endure the test of cold science. Now Galpin and I maintain that, logically, a man of taste should prefer such things as favour strong and

advanced men at the expense of the herd. Of what use is it to please the herd? They are simply coarse animals—for all that is admirable in man is the artificial product of special breeding. We advocate the preservation of conditions favourable to the growth of beautiful things—imposing palaces, beautiful cities, elegant literature, reposeful art and music, and a physically select human type such as only luxury and a pure racial strain can produce. Thus we oppose democracy, if only because it would retard the development of a handsome Nordic breed. We realise that all conceptions of justice and ethics are mere prejudices and illusions—there is no earthly reason why the masses should not be kept down for the benefit of the strong, since every man is for himself in the last analysis. We regard the rise of democratic ideals as a sign of cultural old age and decay, and deem it a compliment to such men as Mussolini when they are said to be "XVth century types." We are proud to be definitely *reactionary,* since only by a bold repudiation of the "liberal" pose and the "progress" illusion can we get the sort of authoritative social and political control which alone produces things which make life worth living. We admire the old German Empire, for it was a force so strong that it almost conquered all the combined forces of the rest of the world. Personally, my objection to Germany in the late war was that it formed a menace to our English Empire—an Empire so lamentably split in 1775–83, and so regrettably weakened by effeminate ideas of liberty. My wish was that we English reunite into one irresistible power and establish an hegemony of the globe in true Roman fashion. Neither we nor Germany will ever be really strong till we have unified imperial control.

Our modern worship of empty ideals is ludicrous. What does the condition of the rabble matter? All we need to do is to keep it as quiet as we can. What is more important, is to perpetuate those things of beauty which are of real value because involving actual sense-impressions rather than vapid theories. "Equality" is a joke—but a great abbey or cathedral, covered with moss, is a poignant reality. It is for us to safeguard and preserve the conditions which produce great abbeys, and palaces, and picturesque walled towns, and vivid sky-lines of steeples and domes, and luxurious tapestries, and fascinating books, paintings, and statuary, and colossal organs and noble music, and dramatic deeds on embattled fields . . . *these are all there is of life;* take them away and we have nothing which a man of taste or spirit would care to live for. Take them away and our poets have nothing to sing—our dreamers have nothing to dream about. The blood of a million men is well shed in producing one glorious legend which thrills posterity . . . and it is not at all important *why* it was shed. A coat of arms won in a crusade is worth a thousand slavering compliments bandied about amongst a rabble.

Reform? Pish! We do not *want* reform! What would the world be without its scarlet and purple evil! Drama is born of conflict and violence . . . god! shall we ever be such women as to prefer the emasculate piping of an arbitrator to the lusty battle-cry of a blue-eyed, blond-bearded warrior! The one sound power in the world is the power of a hairy muscular right arm!

Yah! How I spit upon this rotten age with its feeble comforts and thwarted energies—its Freuds and Wilsons, Augustines and Heliogabali,—rabbles and perversions! What these swine with their scruples and problems, changes and rebellions, need, is a long draught of blood from a foeman's skull on the battlements of a mountain fortalice! We need fewer harps and viols, and more drums and brasses. The answer to jazz is the wild dance of the war-like conqueror! Don't complain of the youth's high-powered motor-car unless you can give him an horse and armour and send him to conquer the domains of the neighbouring kings! Modern life—my gawd! I don't wonder that literature is going to hell or chaos! What is there to write about now? Before we have *literature* we must have *life*—bold, colourful, primitive, and picturesque. We must change a George V for a Richard Coeur de Lion—a *Plantagenet!*

Of course, all talk of reviving real and vigorous life is a pipe dream. Our civilisation, like all its predecessors, is nearing the end of its rope; so that all we can sensibly do is to throw a little sand on the toboggan. And I think that the Fascisti movement is the best sand-box we have yet seen. True, it overrides technical *law*, but *not until that law has justly forfeited the tolerance of sensible men.* Democratic government is rabble whim. More important than any legalistic formality, are certain traditions woven inextricably into the finer part of the race; and these *must* be preserved, by *any* means at hand—legal or illegal. Freedom of press and speech *sound* well— but these vague principles cannot be allowed to interfere with the fight of a race for the values which are its only solid possessions. In fine—today certain nations need certain policies; and they need them so badly that we can't afford to complain of any means they use in getting them. I don't give a damn how the Fascisti got in power, but I take off my hat to them if they have preserved for Italy the life that built up her palaces and towers, bridges and monuments, arts and letters. These fruits of civilisation are all that count.

What we must do is to shake off our encumbering illusions and false values—banishing sonorous platitudes in a civilised realisation that the only things of value in the world are those which promote beauty, colour, interest and heightened sensation. The one great crusade worthy of an enlightened man is that directed against whatever impoverishes imagination, wonder, sensation, dramatic life, and the appreciation of beauty. Nothing else matters. And not even this really matters in the great void, but it is amusing to play a little in the sun before the blind universe dispassionately pulverises us again into that primordial nothingness from whence it moulded us for a second's sport.

[12]   I have no opinions—I believe in nothing—but assume for the time whatever opinion amuses me or is opposite to that of the person or persons present. Ho, hum! My cynicism and scepticism are increasing, and from an entirely new cause—the Einstein theory. The latest eclipse observations seem to place this system among the facts which cannot be dismissed, and assumedly it removes the last hold which reality or the universe can have on the independent mind. All is chance, accident, and ephemeral illusion— a fly may be greater than Arcturus, and Durfee Hill may surpass Mount Everest—assuming them to be removed from the present planet and differently environed in the continuum of space-time. There are no values in all infinity—the least idea that there are is the supreme mockery of all. All the cosmos is a jest, and fit to be treated only as a jest, and one thing is as true as another. I believe everything and nothing—for all is chaos, always has been, and always will be. Ease, amusement—these are the only relative qualities fit to be classed as values.

Literary Development

[As Lovecraft's philosophical vision expanded, so too did the range of his fiction. In 1923 he received a new impetus with the founding of *Weird Tales*, the first pulp magazine devoted exclusively to horror fiction. In his cover letter to the first editor of *Weird Tales*, Edwin Baird, Lovecraft deliberately did everything he could to get his stories rejected — referring to his noncommercial attitude, pointing out that some of the stories had been previously rejected, and casting aspersions on the magazine itself. Nevertheless, the tales were accepted.]

[13]   Having a habit of writing weird, macabre, and fantastic stories for my own amusement, I have largely been simultaneously hounded by nearly a dozen well-meaning friends into deciding to submit a few of these Gothic horrors to your newly founded periodical. The decision is herewith carried out. Enclosed are five tales written between 1917 and 1923.[20]

Of these the first two are probably the best. If they be unsatisfactory, the rest need not be read. . . . "The Statement of Randolph Carter" is, in the main, an actual dream experienced on the night of December 21–22, 1919; the characters being myself (Randolph Carter) and my friend, Samuel Loveman, the poet and editor of *Twenty-One Letters of Ambrose Bierce.*

I have no idea that these things will be found suitable, for I pay no attention to the demands of commercial writing. My object is such pleasure as I can obtain from the creation of certain bizarre pictures, situations, or atmospheric effects; and the only reader I hold in mind is myself.

My models are invariably the older writers, especially Poe, who has been my favourite literary figure since early childhood. Should any miracle impel you to consider the publication of my tales, I have but one condition to offer; and that is that no excisions be made. If the tale cannot be printed as written, down to the very last semicolon and comma, it must gracefully accept rejection. Excision by others is probably one reason why no living American author has a real prose style. . . . But I am probably safe, for my MSS. are not likely to win your consideration. "Dagon" has been rejected by _____ _____,[21] to which I sent it under external compulsion — much as I am sending you the enclosed. This magazine sent me a beautifully tinted and commendably impersonal rejection slip. . . .

I like *Weird Tales* very much, though I have seen only the April number. Most of the stories, of course, are more or less commercial — or should I say conventional? — in technique, but they all have an enjoyable angle. "Beyond the Door" by Paul Suter, seems to me the most truly touched with the elusive quality of original genius — though "A Square of Canvas", by Anthony M. Rud,[22] would be a close second if not so reminiscent in denouement of Balzac's "Le Chef d'Oeuvre Inconnu" — as I recall it across a lapse of years, without a copy at hand. However, one doesn't expect a very deep thrill in this sophisticated and tradesman-minded age. Arthur Machen is the only living man I know of who can stir truly profound and spiritual horror.

[A later letter to Baird enunciates Lovecraft's theories of weird fiction.]

[14]   And here is another horror for your approval or rejection. This thing—whose long title you can shorten to "The Late Arthur Jermyn" if the original presents typographical problems—was written about two years ago. Its origin is rather curious—and far removed from the atmosphere it suggests. Somebody had been harassing me into reading some work of the iconoclastic moderns—these young chaps who pry behind exteriors and unveil nasty hidden motives and secret stigmata—and I had nearly fallen asleep over the tame backstairs gossip of Anderson's *Winesburg, Ohio*. The sainted Sherwood, as you know, laid bare the dark area which many whited village lives concealed; and it occurred to me that I, in my weirder medium, could probably devise some secret behind a man's ancestry which would make the worst of Anderson's disclosures sound like the annual report of a Sabbath school. Hence Arthur Jermyn. Most of those who have seen the MS. profess themselves properly horrified—all, in fact, except one chap who has travelled in Rhodesia, and declares himself bound by ties of the purest and most undaunted affection to all the denizens, negro and simian alike, of the Dark Continent.

Popular authors do not and apparently cannot appreciate the fact that true art is obtainable only by rejecting normality and conventionality in toto, and approaching a theme purged utterly of any usual or preconceived point of view. Wild and "different" as they may consider their quasi-weird products, it remains a fact that the bizarrerie is on the surface alone; and that basically they reiterate the same old conventional values and motives and perspectives. Good and evil, teleological illusion, sugary sentiment, anthropocentric psychology—the usual superficial stock in trade, and all shot through with the eternal and inescapable commonplace. Take a werewolf story, for instance—who ever wrote a story from the point of view of the wolf, and sympathising strongly with the devil to whom he has sold himself? Who ever wrote a story from the point of view that man is a blemish on the cosmos, who ought to be eradicated? As an example—a young man I know lately told me that he means to write a story about a scientist who wishes to dominate the earth, and who to accomplish his ends trains and overdevelops germs (à la Anthony Rud's "Ooze"),[23] and leads on armies of them in the manner of the Egyptian plagues. I told him that although this theme has promise, it is made utterly commonplace by assigning the scientist a normal motive. There is nothing outré about wanting to conquer the earth; Alexander, Napoleon, and Wilhelm II wanted to do that. Instead, I told my friend, he should conceive a man with a morbid, frantic, shuddering hatred of the life-principle itself, who wishes to extirpate from the planet every trace of biological organism, animal and vegetable alike, including himself. That would be tolerably original. But after all, originality lies within the author. One can't write a weird story of real power without perfect psychological detachment from the human scene, and a magic prism of imagination which suffuses theme and style alike with that grotesquerie and disquieting distortion characteristic of morbid vision. Only a cynic can create horror—for behind every masterpiece of the sort must reside a driving daemonic force that despises the human race and its illusions, and longs to pull them to pieces and mock them.

[In a letter to Frank Belknap Long, Lovecraft discusses his masterful short story "The Rats in the Walls" (1923) in detail, in particular the climactic scene where the protagonist, Walter Delapore, descends the evolutionary scale and utters cries in a succession of languages culminating in apelike gibberish.]

[15]   About the anthropological background of "The Rats"—undoubtedly you are right, although all deductions concerning primitive man are too nebulous to permit of dogmatism of any sort. No line betwixt "human" and "non-human" organisms is possible, for all animate Nature is one—with differences only in degree; never in kind. There are many elephants more human than many Bantu niggers. I know that the tendency is to give a separate classification to the Neanderthal-Piltdown-Heidelberg type using the flashy word "Eoanthropus"—but in truth this creature was probably as much a man as a gorilla. Many anthropologists have detected both negroid and gorilla resemblances in these "dawn" skulls, and to my mind it's a safe bet that they were exceedingly low, hairy negroes existing perhaps 400,000 years ago and having perhaps the rudiments of a guttural language. Certainly, it is not extravagant to imagine the existence of a sort of sadistic cult amongst such beasts, which might later develop into a formal satanism. It is all the more horrible to imagine such a thing, on account of the intima-

tions of extraphysical malignancy in such a thought. Indeed, I think that certain traits in many lower animals suggest, to the mind whose imagination is not dulled by scientific literalism, the beginnings of activities horrible to contemplate in evolved mankind. As for details—the Cro-Magnon is too high a type to present definite horror per se. He was not inferior to savages now existing. And it is by no means established that the Eoanthropoi are not the ancestors of *any* "homines sapientes" if one includes negroes in that category. Klaatsch held the Neanderthal man to be indisputably human, and closely allied to the negro-gorilla stock. We of the Caucasian race are probably descended from other ape-stock—that is we have no negro-gorilla ancestors, but go back through other apes to a common simian stock of great primitiveness—yet that means relatively little in an ultimate sense. We have had ancestors just as bestial, if at present undiscovered—and so far as any story is concerned, it is a cultural rather than physical lineage implied . . . Eoanthropus, Celt, Roman, Teuton . . . so that Delapore's spectacular atavism is largely *spiritual*. Weird tales have the privilege of including mythological ideas. And now one final fling—I deny that the Java pithecanthropus has been conclusively levelled down to the biological altitude of living apes.

But in any case, these obscure matters have very little bearing on weird art. It is enough to visualise in hazy outline a thing half ape and half man—clearer definition not only fails to enhance the illusion, but actually tends to destroy it. Don't believe all the scientific smart alecks tell you, Sonny! Tomorrow they'll be contradicting all they tell you today—for in truth the best they ever can do is guess.

That bit of gibberish which immediately followed the atavistic Latin was *not* pithecanthropoid. The first actual ape-cry was the "*ungl*". What the intermediate jargon is, is *perfectly good Celtic*—a bit of venomously vituperative phraseology which a certain small boy ought to know; because his grandpa, instead of consulting a professor to get a Celtic phrase, found a ready-made one so apt that he lifted it bodily from "The Sin-Eater", by Fiona McLeod, in the volume of "Best Psychic Stories" which Sonny himself generously sent![24] I thought you'd note that at once—but youth hath a crowded memory. Anyhow, the only objection to the phrase is that it's *Gaelic* instead of *Cymric* as the south-of-England locale demands. But as—with anthropology—details don't count. Nobody will ever stop to note the difference.[25]

It will interest you to observe the professional rejection of this piece by

R. H. Davis, Esq. of the Munsey Co., to whom I sent it at the insistence of my adopted son Eddy.[26] You will note that the contention of Leeds appears to be justify'd; since Davis, tho' admitting it hath some merit, holds it too horrible for the tender sensibilities of a delicately nurtured publick. Leetle Bairdie is become a very great friend of mine, and designs to publish my efforts with much regularity. I will enclose an epistle of his, which please return. He hath since accepted "Arthur Jermyn", and I am not without hopes for "Hypnos" and "The Rats in the Walls", which I am this day sending him.

[The pinnacle of Lovecraft's early involvement with *Weird Tales* occurred when owner J. C. Henneberger commissioned him to ghostwrite a story for the celebrated magician Harry Houdini. The result—titled by Lovecraft "Under the Pyramids" and published as "Imprisoned with the Pharaohs"—is a surprisingly creditable performance, given its artificial genesis.]

[16]   Yes, Child, WEIRD TALES is certainly shovin' a lot of work at your aged Grandsire! Entire new job—to rewrite a strange narrative which the magician Houdini related orally to Henneberger; a narrative to be amplified and formulated, and to appear as a collaborated product— "By Houdini and H. P. Lovecraft."[27] Henneberger demanded a telegraphed reply as to whether or not I'd accept the job, and promises INSTANT PAY on delivery! I wired him an affirmative, and am now at work familiarising myself with the geographical details of the Cairo-Gizeh locality where the alleged adventure is set—especially with the singular subterranean place betwixt the Sphinx and the second pyramid known as "Campbell's Tomb".

It seems that once Houdini was in Cairo with his wife on a non-professional pleasure trip, when his Arab guide became involved in a street fight with another Arab. In accordance with custom, the natives decided to fight it out that night on the top of the Great Pyramid; and Houdini's guide, knowing of the magician's interest in exotic oddities, invited him to go along with his party of seconds and supporters. Houdini did, and saw a tame fistic encounter followed by an equally mechanical reconciliation. There was something off-colour and rehearsed about it all, and the wizard was hardly surprised when suddenly the frame-up was revealed, and he found himself bound and gagged by the two Arabs who had faked the combat. It had all been prearranged—the natives had heard of him as a mighty wizard of the West, and were determined to test his powers in a land where wizards had once ruled supreme. Without ceremony they took him to an aperture in the roof of the Temple of the Pharaohs (Campbell's Tomb) where a sheer drop of fifty-three feet brings one to the floor of the nighted crypt which has but one normal entrance—a winding passage very far from this well-like opening. Producing a long rope, they lowered him into this abode of darkness and death and left him there without means of ascent—bound and gagged amidst the kingly dead, and ignorant of how to find the real exit. Hours later he staggered out of that real exit; free, yet shaken to the core with some hideous experience about which he hesitates to talk.[28] It will be my job to invent that incident, and give it my most macabre touches. As yet, I don't know how far I can go, since from a specimen Houdini story which Henneberger sent me I judge that the magician tries to pass off these Munchausens as real adventures. He's supremely egotistical, as one can see at a glance. But in any case, I guess I can weave in some pretty shocking things . . . unsuspected lower caverns, a burning light amidst the balsam'd dead, or a terrible fate for the Arab guides who sought to frighten Our Hero. Maybe they can rig up as mummies to scare Houdini, and as such enter the crypt themselves . . . afterward being found dead with clawlike marks about their throats which could not possibly have been made by the hands of Houdini. The more latitude Houdini allows me, the better yarn I can evolve—I'm asking Henneberger to get me as much as possible from the versatile showman.

4

Marriage and Exile
(1924–1926)

Elopement

[Perhaps the most remarkable letter Lovecraft ever wrote was to his elder aunt, Lillian D. Clark, on March 9, 1924, six days after he had married Sonia H. Greene in New York. In this letter Lovecraft unwittingly suggests that marrying Sonia was merely a welcome alternative to boredom and suicide.]

[1]   I need not say how glad I was to receive your delightful letter and the accompanying matter. But pray don't feel lonesome, since you are most certainly coming right along hither yourself! Bless my old bones! Dost fancy the Old Gentleman would transfer the family seat without sending for his first-born daughter? You will feel better and more active here—I wish you could behold Grandpa this week, getting up regularly in the daytime, hustling briskly about, and even being able to replace a vast amount of facial tweezer technique with honest, simple, and rapid gilletting. And all this with a prospect of regular literary work—my first real job—in the offing!

Meanwhile—and here prepare for revolutionary news—there is no need to worry about my securing an adequate room, or being well taken care of (doddering patriarch that I am) until you arrive. 259 Parkside is pretty homelike with the fine Colonial secretary cleared out and devoted to my use, and will be still more so when all my things—and yourself—reach here.

By this time the drift of this ponderous epistle will have begun to make itself clear. The selection of 259 Parkside as a *permanent* residence, rallying-point, and successor to 454 and 598 is in truth the only maturely logical and thoroughly common-sense solution of the problem created when finance disrupts the Old Homestead and forces aged Theobald to "give over" his listless midnight mooning and helpless hermitage for a more active life.

That more active life, to one of my temperament, demands many things which I could dispense with when drifting sleepily and inertly along, shunning a world which exhausted and disgusted me, and having no goal but a phial of cyanide when my money should give out. I had formerly meant to follow this latter course, and was fully prepared to seek oblivion whenever cash should fail or sheer ennui grow too much for me; when suddenly, nearly three years ago, our benevolent angel S.H.G. stepped into my circle of consciousness and began to combat that idea with the opposite one of effort, and the enjoyment of life through the rewards which effort will bring.

At the time, this doctrine seemed to me singularly impracticable; for how could I ever maintain—or even begin—a programme of activity and achievement when engulfed by the uninspiring seclusion surviving from a weak and nerve-racked childhood and youth? How, I wondered, could anyone so sensitive to environment ever keep up and apply himself to a career of genuine labour without the constant stimulus of vigorous, understanding, and sympathetic literary companionship—the companionship which adds to an enlivening energy the rarer and more potent boon of perfect psychological comprehension?

Such were my reflections—reflections all the more marked when Magnolia, N.Y., etc. showed me how marvellously I actually did rally in response to companionship of the right kind; companionship which I saw no way of securing permanently as the incentive to an active life, and which therefore only seemed to emphasise the difficulty of breaking away from the tentacles of ingrained inertia and oblivion-seeking.

But meanwhile—egotistical as it sounds to relate it—it began to be apparent that I was not alone in finding psychological solitude more or less of a handicap. A detailed intellectual and aesthetic acquaintance since 1921, and a three-months visit in 1922 wherein congeniality was tested and found perfect in an infinity of ways, furnished abundant proof not only that S.H.G. is the most inspiring and encouraging influence which could possibly be brought to bear on me, but that she herself had begun to find me more congenial than anyone else, and had come to depend to a great extent on my correspondence and conversation for mental contentment and artistic and philosophical enjoyment. Being, like me, highly individualised; she found average minds only a source of grating and discomfort, and average people only a bore to escape from—so that in our letters and discussions we were assuming more and more the position of two detached and dissenting secessionists from the bourgeois *milieu;* a source of encouragement to each other, but fatigued to depression by the stolid grey surface of commonplaceness on all sides and relieved only by such isolated points of light as Sonny Belknap, Mortonius, Loveman, Alfredus, Kleiner, and the like.

S.H.G. was not tardy, I believe, in mentioning to you and A.E.P.G. sundry phases of her side of this mutual indispensability; but as a follower of the unsentimental tradition, reluctant to be spoofed about a matter which was truly more rationally psychological than sentimental, I was naturally more conservative in giving estimates of my side—although of course I freely extolled the revivifying effects of my Magnolia and Parkside visits, and of S.H.G.'s various visits to the Providence or Eastern New-England area.

With a congeniality so preponderant, and having such a vital bearing on the progress, activity, and contentment of those concerned, one might well wonder why some permanent programme of propinquity was not arranged over a year and a half ago. Radical events, however, do not develop hastily; no matter how sudden their conscious and immediate planning, or their final occurrence, may seem to be. You know Theobaldian reserve, Theobaldian conservatism, and Theobaldian adherence to the old order of things until some *deus ex machina* roughly descends to override all indecision and precipitate an abrupt turn of affairs. In this case finance, pessimistic weighing of all life against cyanidic oblivion, sheer inertia, reticence, and a blind clinging to the hibernatory past as represented by uncommercial daytime sleeping at 598, all united to maintain a listless *status-quo.* Then dawned the inevitable need of doing something definite— the need to "get up and get" industrially, or to make good my ancient plan of shuffling off to a Swan Point subterranean repose. The old sleep was over, and unless I wished to face a new and voluntarily eternal sleep I must

secure the settled and bracing environment which can electrify a fat, ambi-
tionless, and drowsing senile shuffler into a real man and professionally capable entity.

New York! Of course! Where else can one be alive when he has no vitality of his own and needs the magic spur of external inducement to active
life and effective toil? And Parkside? Seemingly sudden, yet where else
should one go when that is the seat of the greatest encouragement, inspiration, and congeniality? A "room" somewhere might be all very well—but
how stupid to accept clumsy makeshifts when a real *home* was waiting,
with all the care, kindred taste, regard, and incentives for waging the battle of life that a weary, sensitive, and otherwise spiritless Old Gentleman
might wish? Of course there is always the financial question—bogie of the
bourgeois—which naturally deferred any suggestions of mine till it was rationally laid to rest amidst the full, free, logical, and sanely un-attitudinized
discussion which preceded the move. Parkside was there, and would be
paid for just the same whether or not shared by the aged Theobald. That
same Theobald, moreover, would come not as a burden but as the filler of a
lonely void and the bearer of aesthetic and intellectual congeniality to one
who had not found this quality in others. More still—and this was his own
point—he would of course contribute to the common fund as much as he
safely could . . . and easily as much as he would otherwise pay for a "room";
adopting a more responsible basis when warranted by substantial earnings. In short—for artificial prides and hackneyed notions was substituted
the rare and revered principle of comfortable adjustment and intelligent
co-operation.

At this point—or earlier—or a minute later—you will no doubt ask
why I did not mention this entire matter before. S.H.G. herself was anxious to do so, and if possible to have both you and A.E.P.G. present at the
event about to be described. But here again appeared Old Theobald's hatred of sentimental spoofing, and of that agonisingly indecisive "talking
over" which radical steps always prompt among mortals, yet which really
exceeds the fullest necessary quota of sober and analytical appraisal and
debate. Wandering discussion, incredulous exclamations, sighs of "I never
would have thought it", and all that sort of thing are infinitely exhausting
to a sensitive personality after calm reason has had its leisurely reflection
and expression, and made its logical decision. It hardly seemed to me that,
in view of my well-known temperament, anyone could feel even slightly
hurt by a decisive and dramatic gesture sweeping away the barnacles of

timidity and of blindly reactionary holding-back. The step, once well considered, was for each an individualistic one; and the news will be broken to the amateur circle only after this more important message has been completed. Even Little Belknap yet remains to be called up by his Old Grandpa!

So, epochal and stupefying as it sounds, (pray don't faint, or I shall feel that all the preceding paragraphs of artistic preamble have gone for naught!) the unbelievable is a reality. Old Theobald is a householder at last, and (hold in readiness the smelling-salts) a bona-fide partner with that most inspiring, congenial, tasteful, intelligent, solicitous, and devoted of mortals and co-workers, S.H.G., in the venerable and truly classical institution of Holy Matrimony!

(RECESS FOR RECOVERY OF POISE)

Yes, my daughter, the Old Gentleman has brought you a new mother at last! Gradual and sudden at once . . . for backed as it was by a mature evolution of years, and long dreamed of vaguely, academically, and objectively as a possibility for some remote future, the imminent certainly scarcely crystallised till the final week; when the actual "brass tacks" of moving and settling came up with a coldly realistic insistence not to be denied.

After the cataclysmic springing of the *idea*, the *events* cannot but be somewhat anticlimactic to relate—yet it were barbarous to frustrate the natural demands of human curiosity.

I missed the 10:09 train Sunday, but got the 11:09, and after a pleasing journey blew into the Grand Central (instead of the Pennsylvania as planned . . . . . I sent a corrective telegram) at 3:40 p.m.; there met by S.H.G. We at once proceeded to 259, where Miss Tucker of *The Reading Lamp* was a guest, and there the whole programme and future were zestfully discussed with an intensely interested and sympathetic auditor. Miss T. is of old Baltimore stock, and is a figure of much influence in N.Y. literary circles. (Sample of her stationery enclosed.) She has taken a most keen liking to S.H.G.L., and will do anything she can to promote the progress of all connected with that prepossessing deity. She believes that my stories, and my essays as exemplified by letters to S.H., are of singular merit; and is considering most seriously their publication in book form. Meanwhile she has every expectation of getting me a job in some publishing house—a job which my newly-acquired helpmate will see that I reach each morning punctually and in good order. The chicken dinner was superb—as all S.H. dinners are—and I was not too fatigued by the week's efforts to appreciate it. Post-prandial discussion was congenial and appropriate, and included Miss Tucker's interested and not altogether unamused perusal of Friend Henneberger's epistles. [. . .]

The following morning—the eventful *third of March*—all three started out for a busy day . . . . busy? Believe an Old Married Man! The morning was spent at the *Reading Lamp* office, where Miss T. got some idea of what I can do at various literary tasks. Then S.H. and I went to a Dago joint in thirty-somethingth street and absorbed a fine *spaghetti* dinner. After that— and here note the dawn of decisive events—we beat it by subway to the Brooklyn borough hall, where we took out a marriage license with all the cool nonchalance and easy *savoir faire* of old campaigners . . . . . migosh! but you'd ought to have saw me! Brigham Young annexing his 27th, or King Solomon starting in on the second thousand, had nothing on me for languid fluency and casual conversation! The bimbo that handed out the papers has been to Providence, and is quite an admirer of Waterman St. . . . . . . which he knew by location but not by name.

Then for the ring! S.H. having discovered that plain gold bands are old stuff, we gave the once-over to some rather more contemporary baubles of kindred import. Through business connexions S.H. obtained some reduced quotations at a small shop, and (although she first selected a white gold trifle of inexpensive aspect) I induced her to blow in eighty-five fish for something worth one hundred fifty—platinum with twenty-four diamond chips—whose expense I shall defray (as befits an arrogant and masterful spouse) from my next Hennebergian influx. Yes—there was a nifty li'l' case, and everything!

We now prepared for the historic spectacle of the execution; wishing to face Fate sprucely and jauntily, and die game! S.H. patronised a mani-cure in order that the eighty-five-berry-worth-one-hundred-fifty finger-hoop might be lived up to, and I condescended to get both a haircut and a shoe-shine. Then, having reconvened, we hopped a taxi (real sports— don't care how much they spend!) and proceeded to the *Place de la Guillo-tine.*

And what was the place? A hades of a question to ask an old British Colonial ever faithful to His Majesty, King George the Third! Where was it that Richard, Lord Howe, Admiral of His Majesty's fleet, worshipped from 1776 to 1783—and where H.R.H. the Prince of Wales (later the Prince Regent and finally King George IV) was a communicant whilst a midshipman with the fleet? Where, indeed, can one find most strongly Old Theobald's traditional and mythological background—a background intensified by the marriage of his parents in Boston's venerable St. Paul's? (1820) Yes—of course you guess'd it! St. Paul's Chapel, Broadway and Vesey Sts., built in 1766, and like the Providence 1st Baptist design'd after St. Martin's-in-the-Fields! GOD SAVE THE KING! (Booklet under separate cover.)

In the Church St. parsonage we hunted up the resident curate, Father George Benson Cox, who upon inspecting the licence was more than willing to perform the soldering process. Having brought no retinue of our own, we availed ourselves of the ecclesiastical force for purposes of witnessing—a force represented in this performance by one Joseph Gorman and one Joseph G. Armstrong, who I'll bet is the old boy's grandson although I didn't ask him. With actors thus arranged, the show went off without a hitch. Outside, the ancient burying ground and graceful Wren steeple; within, the glittering cross and traditional vestments of the priest —colourful legacies of OLD ENGLAND'S gentle legendry and ceremonial expression. The full service was read; and in the aesthetically histrionic spirit of one to whom elder custom, however intellectually empty, is sacred, I went through the various motions with a stately assurance which had the stamp of antiquarian appreciation if not of pious sanctity. S.H., needless to say, did the same—and with an additional grace. Then fees, thanks, congratulations, inspections of Colonial pictures in Father Cox's study, and farewells! Two are one. Another bears the name of Lovecraft. A new household is founded!

We had intended to depart for Philadelphia at once, but the fatigue of the preceding heavy programme prompted us to defer this melilunar pilgrimage till the morrow. On that day we notified some of S.H.'s nonamateur friends of the change, and received their ecstatic congratulations; good Mrs. Moran, down-the-hall neighbour and mother of the stamp-collecting and erstwhile cat-owning boy, being especially delighted. The name "Greene" on the door directory and mail box was suitably transmuted to "Lovecraft", and the *nouveau regime* in general given a visible and appropriate recognition. Incidentally—mail, express, and freight destined for this domicile need no longer be "in care of" anybody! Anything addressed to "H. P. Lovecraft" or (miraculous and unpredictable appellation)

"Mrs. H. P. Lovecraft" will henceforward reach its recipient without additional formalities.

Tuesday afternoon we did get started for Philadelphia, leaving from the magnificently Roman Pennsylvania Station which I missed the Sunday before by missing the 10:09 Wash'n Express. Of the details of the trip, and of the unique personality of sprawling and antique Philadelphia, I shall say more in the travelogue with which I shall answer A.E.P.G.'s appreciated letter. Here, lest I bore you with a superposition of treatise upon treatise, I will simply outline the salient itinerary. Arriving at the Quaker City at six p.m., we stopped at the Robert Morris hotel—a new but reasonably inexpensive hostelry which performs the marvel of harmoniously combining a Gothic exterior with a Colonial interior. Signing the register "Mr. and Mrs." was easy despite total inexperience! Being obliged to get some typing done instantly,[1] we finished the evening at the only public stenographer's office in town which was then open—that at the Hotel Vendig, where for a dollar we obtained the use of a Royal machine for three hours. S.H. dictated whilst I typed—a marvellous way of speeding up copying, and one which I shall constantly use in future, since my partner expresses a willingness amounting to eagerness so far as her share of the toil is concerned. She has the absolutely unique gift of being able to read the careless scrawl of my rough manuscripts—no matter how cryptically and involvedly interlined!

The next day we "saw Philadelphia right" in the double trip of the Royal Blue Line rubberneck wagon. (Vide enclosure). Of that more anon—but I may here remark that the town of William Penn is one of the most distinctive and interesting I have ever seen, (tho' dull to inhabit continuously) and one which we must inspect more minutely later on. It is only two hours from N.Y., hence can hardly be called inaccessible. You have seen the cards—and you will see the travelogue soon. I send under separate cover a complete Independence Hall set, from which you may gain at least a fair idea of that noted edifice's magnificent colonial interior. That evening we had to do typing again at the Vendig—truly, a most practical and industrious honeymoon—and late at night we returned to N.Y., putting in the remaining days writing; since on Monday S.H.'s vacation will be over, whilst I myself (incredible as it may sound) may have to be ready for business engagements of one sort or another.

Such is the epic, down to date! Could any Fate for Old Theobald be better? I await with eagerness the congratulations I know you and

A.E.P.G. will extend, and only wish you were both here now to observe the new menage, and to see Grandpa up brightly every day and amazingly free from facial trouble. The latter improvement is almost *miraculous* — I have had no severe probings and comparatively few pullings; the vast majority of hairs coming naturally to the surface and causing so little trouble that I can retain them and reduce most of the question to a short genuine shave every other day. Really, astounding as it appears, I honestly believe that the face will form scarcely any handicap to my future industrial efforts, as I had feared it would before migrating. Please send the tin box with all my Gillette blades — for I am now able to put them to a very good and cheerfully optimistic use!

My general health is ideal. S.H.'s cooking, as you know already from me and from A.E.P.G., is the last word in perfection as regards both palate and digestion. She even makes *edible* bran muffins! She is also a fresh-air specialist, and as great an insister on carefulness and remedies as you are with the camphor discoids already she has deluged me with a nose and mouth wash, and has made me heal with vaseline the cracked lip which was open all winter — to say nothing of the place where I skinned my shin slipping downstairs that time last week — when I tripp'd on a trip to the attic. And — *mirabile dictu* — she is at least *trying* to make me stick to the Walter Camp exercises known as the "Daily Dozen"! The headache prescription came safely, and I shall get a bottle of my Old Reliable — although so far I haven't had a headache since the wearing off of the one induced by the Houdini-Henneberger rush. Decidedly, Old Theobald is alive as he was never alive before!

Job Prospects

[Although the couple initially seemed well-off financially, Sonia's failure to establish her own hat shop, conjoined with Lovecraft's inability to secure work as a writer or editor, resulted in severely straitened circumstances. By July Lovecraft was forced to look for a job — any job — including even one so unsuited to him as a salesman for a collection agency. His account of his job-hunting attempts makes for poignant reading.]

[2]   I trust that my occasional cards have helped to dispel the impression which my extended epistolary silence may have created, that Grandpa Theobald is altogether dead and buried! Truth to tell, the death and burial

are only partial, and occasioned by the bustle and strain of the industrial quest which tense finances have served to accelerate. The non-materialisation of sundry literary prospects, coupled with the somewhat disastrous collapse of S.H.'s independent millinery venture, has created something of a shortage in the exchequer; so that it seemed advisable for me to investigate whatever commercial prospects of any kind might offer themselves—but the results thereof to date have been conspicuously negative. Positions of every kind seem virtually unattainable to persons without experience, and the enclosed matter—representing only part of the total attempts made—tells the tale of a quest which has so far failed to pay for the ink and shoe-leather consumed. What came nearest to materialisation was the Newark venture—whose interesting amplitude has led me to devote a separate envelope to it. As you will note, it began by my answering an attractive advertisement and receiving an attractive reply. I telephoned to Newark immediately upon receiving the first Ott letter, and made an appointment for the next day—Wednesday, July 23. The opening proved to be for canvassing salesmen to introduce the service of the Creditors' National Clearing House, a Boston firm with a Newark branch, whose specialty (vide enclosed sales approach as revised by me) is the collection of slightly overdue accounts before they develop into bad debts. The sales manager, Mr. Ott, seemed to welcome my affiliation; and although there was no salary—only a commission on sales, with a prospect of a permanent district position if a certain amount of business was done in three months—I decided to give the thing a trial . . . especially since all other positions seemed unattainable. Accordingly I took home contracts, application for bond, and the like, and the next day returned to Newark, where I presented the filled-out blanks and received a briefcase full of selling material which I was to study before reporting for final details at a salesmen's meeting Saturday morning. The situation, on investigation, seemed clear; so much so that I revised the main line of approach (vide enclosed) in order to marshal the facts effectively. On Saturday the 26th I attended the salesmen's meeting, absorbed points from veteran salesmen, and was introduced to the head of the Newark branch, a crude but well-meaning fellow named William J. Bristol, who seems to display traces of a Levantine heritage. My revised version of the "selling talk" created something of a sensation in a mild way, and I had the satisfaction of hearing myself mentioned at the meeting—when Mr. Ott announced to the assembled multitude that my text was to be adopted thereafter as the regular sales formula of the house! But the actual struggle began on Monday, when I set out to canvass among whole-salers whose names, as per Ott's suggestion, I had culled from a telephone business directory. One of the enclosed documents—the rough draught of my day's report to Ott—tells the salient features of this fruitless and ex-hausting day. Much energy spent, but nothing gained. By the time fatigue supervened to cut the labour short, I had reached a pretty definite opinion that I lack the magnetism, or brass, or whatever wizardry it may be, which forms the essential part of an effective canvasser. But, having been told by a veteran that retailers are easier than wholesalers, I returned to the fray on Wednesday, after my joints and muscles had progressed somewhat on the road to retained normalcy. This time I covered the main business dis-trict of Brooklyn, but with results scarcely better than before. The dealers were more courteous, but not a whit more inclined to discussion. Only two—an optician and a tailor—cared so much as to hear the distinctive features of the collection service or to have printed matter left with them. Obviously, I was not progressing very rapidly toward the nonchalant and insolent successfulness of the born canvasser! On Thursday—yesterday— I (together with one other novice, a dashing and prepossessing young ex-officer in the A.E.F. named Edward Hutchings) had an appointment to meet the head of the branch in Manhattan, and to be taken around on a specimen canvassing tour with an expert, so that subtle points of experi-enced salesmanship might be picked up. The meeting-point was the Fulton St. entrance of the Hudson Tubes (about which A.E.P.G. can tell you), and Hutchings and I were promptly on hand at the designated hour—nine-thirty a.m. He had had slightly better success than I, but was very dissatis-fied with his progress and intimated the likelihood of his early resignation. Our conferee—Bristol and a breezy veteran salesman named De Kay— were over half an hour late; but treated us to a free open car ride up Broad-way to the New York sub-branch—the office of a Mr. D. Costa, who takes orders from the Newark territorial headquarters. There many details were discussed, but the "roughneck" nature of the proposition became more and more evident—especially since it developed that most successful canvass-ing lies among the so-called "needle trades"—i.e., garment industries which are almost wholly in the hands of the most impossible sort of per-sons. The party then split for the specimen tours; De Kay taking Hutch-ings and Bristol taking me. I had not walked far when my guide became very candid about the tone of the business, and admitted that a gentleman born and bred has very little chance for success in such lines of canvassing

salesmanship . . . where one must either be miraculously magnetic and cap-
tivating, or else so boorish and callous that he can transcend every rule of
tasteful conduct and push conversation on bored, hostile, and unwilling
victims. I will own that I was marvellously relieved to be able to resign my
arduous burthen without serving the week's notice which had been stipu-
lated in the contract—and I was still further pleased at the deference and
cordiality which honest Bristol displayed. For no sooner was the canvassing proposition out of the way, than he began to tell me something of his future plans, and to intimate that he may be able to co-operate with me quite
extensively some time in revisory and other ways. He is (though he asked
me not to mention it) dissatisfied with his present managership, and anxious to re-enter the insurance business, where his main experience lies.
When he does that, he said, he may be able to offer me some proposition of
really feasible nature; for in such a case he would need the assistance of a
gentleman . . . his own crudity being painfully in his consciousness, and
forming in his opinion a serious handicap to his success in higher lines of
commercial endeavour. As a beginning, he is having me revise (or rather,
write completely from oral hints) a letter of application for a general
agency or district managership, which he means to send in duplicate to all
the principal insurance companies of the country. With this approach in
faultless rhetoric, he relies on his practical knowledge of the business to
plead his cause after he has secured an audience with whatever powers
may be. Here's wishing him success—his plight is a bit pathetic, taking into
account the ceaseless struggle between unlimited ambition and a crudity of
which he does not share David V. Bush's idyllic unconsciousness. He
wants to improve his speech and oratory as well as his written style—but
for this I have referred him to a better authority than myself—none other
than good old Morton, who is a graduate and former instructor of the
Curry School of Expression in Boston. Heigho—it's a great life! I enclose
the application letter I have prepared for Bristol. No use—if I have any
forte, it's in the line of writing and revision. The best sort of position I'll
ever get is one which employs my pen—and I trust in Time and the Gods
to put such an opening in my path!

Yes, so far as finance is concerned, we have no bonanzas today! As I
said, the independent millinery venture turned out badly; and S.H. has had
great difficulty in finding another regular affiliation. A couple of weeks ago
she was engaged by a large and prominent firm in 57th Street, the Bruck-
Weiss Millinery, whose head is a dour, capricious, and uncultivated

woman with more ability than conscientiousness. The salary was to be sixty dollars per week and the duties of great variety and importance. One of the first acts of the firm was to request from S.H. a list of all her tried and true customers, and a form letter to be sent to all of them, telling of the new affiliation and urging them to transfer their patronage to the establishment. This did not impress S.H. very favourably, but she nevertheless complied; furnishing a letter of admirable point and taste, which the firm was glad enough to adopt, multigraph, and distribute to those whom S.H. had listed. But lo! Only yesterday S.H. was notified that on account of slack trade she is to have a vacation for the next two weeks—a device, she is certain, for severing the connexion altogether, although the final dismissal will not come at once, but will arrive tardily and sneakily by letter or over the telephone. The "game", apparently, was to extract the list of names and the letter—wherefore S.H. was hired despite the fact that the sales force was evidently large enough before. Now that the desiderate matter is obtained, the victim may look out for herself! Such is modern business, as practiced by the rising and exotic commercial oligarchy of bad manners and vacant background into whose hands the apparel trade of this colourful and heterogeneous metropolis hath fallen! The immediate results for this household are alarming enough. Unless something arrives from somewhere, the overdue instalments on the Bryn Mawr property will furnish a pretty complication indeed[2]—whilst as to immediate rent, grocery bills, and the like . . . . one may only bow ceremoniously to Pegāna's gods. We have considered cheaper living quarters; though of course as long as I decide to retain my own life, my books, furniture, and heirlooms will be with me. Mariano's semi-annual cheque arrived this morning, and I shall proceed with proper caution to its cashing and dispersal.[3] Meanwhile my economy is something to admire . . . if I do say it myself! I never spent so little in my life before, and am soundly laying the foundations of a strong and miserly character. When I do get gold, I shall be like Old Gaspard in the Chimes of Normandy, and keep it in leathern bags to take out now and then for admiration; letting it clink through my fingers and through my unkempt hair . . . if I have any of the latter left. Better be sure to keep me supplied with that hair tonic, lest I have to spin my future doubloons and pieces of eight on a glabrous and reluctant hemisphere! But avaunt, dull care! Let me drown my worries in watered ink, or the clatter of Remington keys.

[Another bootless attempt at remunerative work involved, of all things, the writing of advertising copy. This too came to nothing, although some specimens of copy written by Lovecraft at this time survive.]

[3]   The work in this Yesley establishment is simple, consisting wholly of writing up complimentary articles descriptive of striking business ventures or outstanding mercantile and professional personalities; each article to be about 1¼ to 1½ double-spaced typed pages in length. This writing is all from facts supplied—"leads", as they call them, culled from press notices or advertising matter. Sometimes the writer digs up his own leads by scanning the press and picking up all the catalogues that come his way—or even watching the streets for new shops and building enterprises as they appear one by one—but generally, if he is a novice at business, he is content to write up the leads which his more commercially minded colleagues have previously selected and catalogued. His article, when done, is sent to the office; and unless too bad to be accepted is taken out by a trained salesman to the person or company whereof it treats. This salesman, after giving the interested party a chance to revise, urges the latter to order a quantity of the magazines mentioning him—for advertising purposes; and if he succeeds, (as he does in a surprising number of cases, since the sales force is a very expert one) the writer of the article receives 10% of the sum paid by the purchaser—amounts varying from $1.50 to over $30.00 according to the extent of the order. Thus with good luck and some ability there is here an excellent hack field for the pure writer—with trained business men to attend to the commercial details at both ends; the lead-finding at the start and the salesmanship at the finish. All that one needs is fluency and some inventiveness, plus a sense of language sufficient to capture the particular sort of atmosphere needed for each type of subject. Most of the men connected with the venture make very tolerable livings despite the commission rather than salary basis; and experts like Kamin's relative or connexion Fenton net over fifty dollars per week. Leeds is now making enough to float him but for the enormous past debts hanging over his head. A few writers work in the office, but still more do their writing at home— not only in New York, but in other cities whence they communicate by mail. Many make it a part-time venture, picking up extra cash as a sideline to other industrial endeavours. All told, it is a *speculation,* with time instead of money as the commodity staked. One writes a certain number of

articles; knowing that *all* may not "take", yet feeling sure that enough will be marketed to make up for the "false alarms" and bring a tidy sum each week—not even sums but averaging a decent amount over any considerable stretch of time as fat weeks compensate for the lean. Belknap and I have talked this proposition over with Leeds before—having ourselves in mind—and he had said he would put us in touch with some work as soon as the enterprise was really under way. This is its first week, and behold! Pure chance, working through a wholly different channel, introduces it to Loveman before Leeds has a chance to meet us! But there is no question of crowding—the field is vast; and once started, Yesley (pronounced Yez'ley) can't get enough writers! Leeds and Kamin, as I have intimated, are urging Loveman to stick; but only the gods know what he will do—or for that matter has done—since last I saw him at the meeting yesterday evening! It may be, of course, that a real poet lacks the needed command of incisive business language, or the prose fluency essential to profitable quantity production where rapid hack work is demanded. [. . .]

[. . .] At the last, he and Leeds and I had talked very seriously about the Yesley writing venture; and when I rode down town with Leeds I continued the conversation, getting more and more workable details from his kindly and willing lips. So keen on the trail of industrial facts did I become, indeed, that I broke my anti-loafing rule and had coffee with him at a restaurant near his hotel; absorbing the general "hang" of his proposition and learning exactly what I would and wouldn't be expected to do if I definitely decided to go in for it and "play the market" for real money with some of my new and hard-won time, energy, and independence. He agreed to shew me the ropes thoroughly, and see that my articles (which need not be signed) receive proper sales treatment; and predicted that I ought to stand as good a chance at making money as himself or anybody else who has proved he can do it. And so I told him I would tackle the thing—and he means to send me my first assignment in a week or two, when he can get together the leads best suited to me (real estate, largely) and find the right models for imitation among his old magazines. Of course, I am no longer moved or excited over any outlook of this sort. I know all these business vistas turn very swiftly to mirages before one's eyes, and make one kick oneself for any naive enthusiasm one may have shewn in advance. But it is at least no crime to indulge in frankly fantastic speculation, and I can see myself—in an imaginatively fictional way—with an actual income and possible future for the first time in my life.

[Lovecraft finally secured paying work in March 1926, although it was only temporary. It involved nothing less august than addressing envelopes for Samuel Loveman's bookshop.]

[4]   This is a sort of farewell to the world for a period of perhaps several weeks—the result of a modest but feasible and welcome *money-making* scheme. It seems that Loveman's bookselling firm need the temporary services of an envelope-addresser to help in mailing their catalogues; and since I was able to do such rapid and effective work in connexion with Kirk's catalogues, I am resolved to try my hand at the present venture. It will be very confining, involving regular hours at the establishment each day beginning at 9 a.m., but it will *not* be *mentally* exacting—having a purely mechanical cast and leaving my faculties free for whatever creative work they can accomplish. There are about 10,000 catalogues to be sent out, so that the work may last several weeks at (Loveman thinks) $17.50 per week. I shall use this matter as an excuse to abandon much correspondence; for if I thus sacrifice the major portion of each day, I certainly intend to have the leisure residue *purely and simply for myself*—my own personal reading and literary composition. I shall, too, indulge in at least two and perhaps three wholly recreational extravagances which I shall deem justified in view of the inconvenience with which I purchase them—(a) a $3.00 Philadelphia excursion, (b) a $5.00 Washington excursion, and (c) possibly a Roman terra-cotta head from that marvellous sale at the Metropolitan Museum. The addressing would seem to begin Monday at 9 a.m., but I shall of course reap no financial returns till the following Saturday. I'll let you know later how it turns out—and whether anything arises at the last moment to nullify the entire design.

Dieting

[With Sonia having departed for the Midwest at the end of 1924, Lovecraft resumed a kind of bachelor's existence; and one of the first things he was able to do was to control his diet, losing fifty pounds in a few weeks.]

[5]   But my most spectacular feat of the season is *reducing*. You knew how fat I was in 1923, and how bitterly I resented the circumstance. In 1924 I grew even worse, till finally I had to adopt a #16 collar! During the

combined period of my wife's hospital sojourn and my Philadelphia trip, I had the opportunity of regulating my own diet for the first time in my entire career—eating just as much as I wanted, rather than as much as someone else thought I ought to have. Upon the close of this period I had thinned perceptibly, returning to a 15¾ collar . . . . I don't know how much I lost, for after passing the 193 mark on the upward course a year before, I had refused to mount a pair of scales! During the winter I kept a sterner guard of my diet, and managed not to regain the tonnage I had lost—and then, when in January I became absolute autocrat of my breakfast, dinner, and supper table, I flung my hat in the air—or ring—and started reducing *in earnest!!* And oh, Boy!!! what results! D'ya know, I didn't ever need to be fat at all! It was all the result of acquiescing spinelessly in the dicta of one's solicitous family! How the pounds flew! I helped the course along by exercise and outdoor walks, and every time my friends saw me they were either pleased or frightened at the startling shrinkage. Fortunately I had not been fat for so many years that the skin suffered radical distension. Instead, it shrunk neatly along with the tissue beneath, leaving a firm surface and simply restoring the lost outlines of 1915 and before. And what a story the scales and my clothing told! The latter had to be thoroughly re-tailored, whilst every week I bought smaller and smaller collars. It was dramatic—breathless—sensational—this reclamation of a decade-lost statue from the vile mud which had so long encrusted it! As you may imagine, my wife protested fearfully at what seemed an alarming decline. I received long scolding letters from my aunts, and was lectured severely by Mrs. Long every time I went up to see Little Belknap. But I knew what I was doing, and kept on like grim death. I had simply changed my dietetic standard to the normal, and—as I hope—permanently broken the fat-accumulating tendency. When I had condensed to my old pre-war figure, I ceased to apply the extremes of my method—yet not only did I escape a subsequent increase, but have even lost nine additional pounds—this last without even trying. I now publickly avow my personal mastery of my diet, and do not permit my wife to feed me in excess of it. If you were to meet me on the street tomorrow you would not know me except from the very earliest pictures you ever saw—the story is told by figures like these: weight, *146 lbs.;* waist with shirt and underclothing on, *30* inches; collar (and a loose fit at that) 14¾. And I mean to stay that way a long, long while! Here is a snapshot of Little Belknap and me, taken a month ago when my weight was 154. Some difference from the old porpoise you saw a couple of years ago, eh?

[Lovecraft's dieting was intimately related to his severe poverty. In the following two extracts, written to his aunt, he appears to boast of his frugality in meals; but his aunt must have expressed alarm at his parsimonious diet, and like a schoolboy he tries to maintain that he really is eating healthfully.]

[6]   Diet and walking are the stuff—which reminds me that tonight I've begun my home dining programme, having spent *30¢* for a lot of food which ought to last about *3* meals:

1 loaf bread	0.06	
1 medium can beans	0.14	I obtained this at the
¼ lb cheese	0.10	James Butler chain
		stores—like our
Total	0.30	Mayflowers.

The beans I'll heat on the sterno, keeping the residue in a cup covered with a saucer. Yes—I'm getting to be a highly efficient housekeeper, and you can bet that any steep bills won't be in the direction of the larder!

[7]   As to my dietary programme—bosh! I *am* eating enough! Just you take a medium-sized loaf of bread, cut it in four equal parts, and add to each of these ¼ can (medium) Heinz beans and a goodly chunk of cheese. If the result isn't a full-sized, healthy day's quota of fodder for an Old Gentleman, I'll resign from the League of Nations' dietary committee!! It only costs 8¢—but don't let that prejudice you! It's good sound food, and many vigorous Chinamen live on vastly less. Of course, from time to time I'll vary the "meat course" by getting something instead of beans—canned spaghetti, beef stew, corned beef, etc. etc. etc.—and once in a while I'll add a dessert of cookies or some such thing. Fruit, also, is conceivable. Likewise, I shall probably get a restaurant meal once or twice a week as the occasion dictates—at Johnson's or the Automat—which may cost 25¢ or so. It would cost more to get a bread box from storage than to buy another—so I did the latter, obtaining for 75¢ a fine square white-enamell'd box with hinged lid and clasp. I keep it on the shelf of the alcove, out of reach of rodent marauders. [. . .]

[. . .] bless my soul, but you-all mustn't be frightened at Grandpa's dietary programme!! Hang it all, but I *do* eat enough! All one really needs for a meal is some highly nutritious base, containing all the various food elements—proteids, vitamines, carbohydrates, etc.—in their proper balance—plus some tasty auxiliary to make it palatable—though of course it is all the better if the auxiliary can itself be of food value. In my case, the auxiliary *does* happen to be highly nourishing—being usually either baked beans or cheese or both. And incidentally—I often **do** get cocoa or chocolate instead of coffee when the gang tank up at their numerous one-arm filling stations. Enough is as good as a feast, and I certainly get enough—enough to feed a normal frame, but not such a gross excess as to build an additional burden of useless adipose tissue which is itself a debilitating drag and consumer of valuable energy. Let me assure you that I feel twice as well as when I was weighing in the vicinity of 200! As to feeding up before my trip—Great God! if you could see the engulfing plethora of needless nutriment which S II has been stuffing down me during her sojourn here!! Twice a day to—and beyond—my capacity; pressed beef, sliced ham, bread, American and Swiss cheese, cake, lemonade, buns, cup puddings, (of her own manufacture—she brought along eight, in one of those utensils of connected cups) etc. etc. etc.—indeed, I'll be shot if I don't wonder how in Pegāna's name I can get on my new 15 collars any more! Tonight I'm expected to get some spaghetti with the gang at the Downing St. Italian restaurant, (in Greenwich-Village—the place they have the playful tiger-kittens) but I vow, I've not a cubic millimetre of additional ventral space to spare!

The Kalem Club

[Lovecraft's New York period saw the heyday of his informal group of literary friends, named the Kalem Club because the last names of the initial group of members all began with K, L, or M. Lovecraft was the only married man of the group, but he behaved as a virtual bachelor by engaging in all-night feats of exploration and fervent discussions in cafeterias or in the various members' homes. On several occasions in late 1924 Lovecraft encountered Hart Crane, who had moved to New York from Cleveland.]

[8]   We begin on my birthday, which I spent at the machine as you already know. The next day, Aug. 21, was likewise spent at home with pen in

hand; but in the evening something started which indeed merits ample record! The Boys met at Kirk's, and a royal good time was had by all. Leeds bought a copy of that Little Old New York book—the first I had seen—and the talk ran much on antiquarian matters. At 1:30 a.m. the meeting broke up, and we all started out—including our genial host, who resolved to walk as far as the farthest-walking of his guests. We dropped Morton and McNeil at the 104th St. elevated station, (Belknap being in Atlantic City) and Kleiner at the 103d street subway kiosk. That left Leeds, Kirk, and Grandpa Theobald as the surviving pedestrians. Down Broadway we walked, admiring the architecture and planning explorations. At Columbus Circle we turned into 8th Avenue, obtaining at an all-night orangeade booth the bottles of Private Stock which I later shipped to my daughters. Gay atmosphere! At 49th Street we dropped Leeds at his new hotel—the Ray—to which he had just moved from the Cort across the street. Then, cleared for action and with the evening yet young before us, Kirk and I resolved to "do" the Colonial town. Having a receptive audience, I proposed to show off the local Georgian antiquities as they should be shewn! We continued down Eighth Avenue with an air of expectancy. Hitherto we had encountered nothing colonial, since with rare exceptions all the town above 14th street dates from the 19th century or later. Around the twenties we saw an old house or two—survivors from the one-time Chelsea Village—but the "real stuff" burst upon us just below Fourteenth, where Eighth Avenue melts into ancient Hudson St. at a crossroads as quaint and old-world as that Soho view I am enclosing. This marks, of course, the entrance into Greenwich-Village; and is made still more interesting by the park-like triangular breathing space called Abingdon Square. Brick colonial houses were now numerous, and I pointed out to Kirk in the early morning stillness the characteristic features of the leading types of N.Y. colonial doorways. From Hudson we turned into Grove, where some splendidly preserved colonial specimens occur; and from there we entered the grilled iron gate of Grove Court, (ask A E P G about it) a delicious 18th century byway where bits of garden and occasional restored doorways lend an atmosphere which only a poet could describe. It is out of the vulgar world, and part of the fabric of tranquil and lovely dream. The flowers were sweet in the stillness, and graceful grey cats lent a touch of mingled beauty and eeriness. Thence we repaired to Gay Street (see former letter), whose curving unworldliness captivated Kirk, and afterward we crossed to Patchin and Milligan Places, and the nameless inner place of which I have already told you. If these ancient spots were fascinating in the busy hours of twilight, fancy their utter and poignant charm in the sinister hours before dawn, when only cats, criminals, astronomers, and poetic antiquarians roam the waking world! Kirk went into raptures, seeing them for the first time; and I, though I had seen them before, was not far behind in enthusiasm. Truly, we had cast the modern and visible world aside, and were sporting through the centuries with the spirit of timeless antiquity! From this section—the "Jefferson Market" section of Greenwich Village,—we proceeded to that congeries of lanes known as the "Minettas" [. . .] where night brought a thousand charms I had never anticipated. All the Italian squalor was faded into shadow, and I could fancy spotless periwigs and sedan chairs under the wan, waning half moon that struggled above the lines of antique gables. We explored some cryptical inner courts which I had never seen before, and where black recesses and bits of archaic moonlit wall formed pictures worthy of any etcher. From these we sought the broad colonial expanse of Varick Street, where endless rows of 18th century dormer windows and occasional gambrel roofs give an unrivalled mass picture of the New York known to Hamilton and Washington. At a small restaurant we stopt for a cup of coffee—it was near dawn now, but our spirits were yet fresh! The street lamps were still burning when we turned into ancient Charlton Street—best preserved of all the colonial thoroughfares, where spotless paint and gleaming knockers suggest the neat prosperity as well as the artistic inclinations of the Georgian householders. More raptures—and the dawn was grey when we entered Prince Street, crossed Broadway, and paused at the pitifully decrepit house where James Monroe died. This, one might fancy, was enough for any trip; but the fever of the explorer was upon us, so forgetting the hour we turned south toward the Brooklyn Bridge section, alternating between Mott and Mulberry streets in order to observe as many ancient houses as possible. This section was farm land in colonial times, so that all the old houses are farmhouses—crowded amidst the unending brick squalor of a populous slum. At Chatham Square we saw the ancient cemetery, and presently turned toward the picturesque antiquities of Patavia and Cherry Streets. In the latter narrow hilly way we found many wonders, including a marvellous hidden court where burns a venerable diamond-shaped lamp—the only one I have seen in N.Y. except the one in Milligan Place. Later ascending to Franklin Square, we passed under the piers of Brooklyn Bridge, observing the old sugar-house where rebel prisoners were confined from 1776 to 1783, (original house torn down, but one of the windows incorporated into the new building) and discovering a magnificent colonial section around Vandewater and New Chambers Streets—where gambrel roofs, curving iron railings, and all the appurtenances of the past abound. We now went down Pearl Street to Hanover Square and Fraunces' Tavern, incidentally drinking in the colonial houses and cross-street waterfront vistas which loomed along the way. After that we crossed Broadway to the west waterfront, noting the venerable edifices on every hand, and remarking especially the Planters' Hotel—the colonial building which Poe inhabited in its seedy old age—and Tom's Chop House, which has been open continuously since 1797. Of course we meditated in Trinity and St. Paul's churchyards, and admired the Georgian beauty of St. Paul's—both facade and steeple. Then, as a climax, we approached the City Hall (1812); whose classic beauty is immortal. The rosy dawn had broken whilst we were on Pearl Street, gilding the steeples of the Brooklyn shore across the glittering water. By the time we reached the city hall it was bright morning, and we gazed at the sun-splendid pinnacles of the Woolworth Building as seen through the arch of the Municipal building. This was the culmination. Glancing at the fine unfinished courthouse whose classic lines are apparently going to be spoiled by some tawdry addition above the pediment, we sought our respective home stations—parting at a little before eight by St. Paul's colonial clock. [. . .]

[. . .] The next day—Friday the 19th—I did some Henneberger work, and at 4:30 p.m. welcomed Loveman. He was feeling rather weak, however, so that he slept in the morris-chair most of the time, whilst I continued to work. After dinner he felt much better—perhaps due to the quinine which he purchased and took—and I accompanied him to his room in Columbia Heights, where I met the redoubtable Crane, a little ruddier, a little puffier, and slightly more moustached than when I saw him in Cleveland two years ago. Crane, whatever his limitations, is a thorough aesthete; and I had some enjoyable conversation with him. His room is in excellent taste, with a few paintings by William Sommer (that elderly eccentric whom I described when I visited Cleveland), a choice collection of modern books, and some splendid small objets d'art of which a carven Buddha and an exquisitely carved Chinese ivory box are the high spots. Loveman's room is at the other end of the hall, with an outlook over the East River and a stupendous panorama of the Manhattan skyline. I nearly swooned with aesthetic exaltation when I beheld the panorama—the evening scene with innumerable lights in the skyscrapers, shimmering reflections and bobbing ship lights on the water, and at the extreme left and right, the flaming Statue of Liberty and the scintillant arc of the Brooklyn Bridge, respectively. But even this was not exactly the climax. That came when we went out on the flat roof (Crane and Loveman are on the fourth and top story) and saw the thing in all its unlimited and unglassed magnificence. It was something mightier than the dreams of old-world legend—a constellation of infernal majesty—a poem in Babylonian fire! No wonder Dunsany waxed rhapsodic about it when he saw it for the first time . . . . it is beyond the description of any but him! Added to the weird lights are the weird sounds of the port, where the traffick of all the world comes to a focus. Fog-horns, ships' bells, the creak of distant windlasses . . . . . visions of far shores of Ind, where bright-plumed birds are roused to song by the incense of strange garden-girt pagodas, and gaudy-robed camel-drivers barter before sandalwood taverns with deep-voiced sailors having the sea's mystery in their eyes. Silks and spices, curiously-wrought ornaments of Bengal gold, and gods and elephants strangely carven of jade and carnelian. Ah, me! Would that I could express the magick of the scene! Crane is writing a long poem on Brooklyn Bridge in a modern medium, which may some time be printed in the Dial.[4]

[9]   After dinner we walked down to the Brooklyn Heights section to call on his friend Hart Crane in Columbia Heights, with whom he had stopped till he moved up to Kirk's in 106th St., Manhattan. The walk was very lovely—downhill from the heights on which the Brooklyn Museum stands, and with many a sunset vista of old houses and far spires. We reached the heights in the deep twilight, when the aërial skyline across the river had a charm peculiar to the hour—a perfect silhouette effect, since it was too dark for surface definition, yet too light to allow the contours to become merged into the black recesses of engulfing night. We found Crane in and sober—but boasting over the two-day spree he had just slept off, during which he had been picked up dead drunk from the street in Greenwich Village by the eminent modernist poet E. E. Cummings—whom he knows well—and put in a homeward taxi. Poor Crane! I hope he'll sober up with the years, for there's really good stuff and a bit of genius in him. He is a genuine poet of a sort, and his excellent taste is reflected in the choice objets d'art with which he has surrounded himself. I would give much for a certain Chinese ivory box of his, with panels exquisitely carved into deli-

cate pastoral scenes in high relief—every detail of landscape and foliage standing out with that absolute beauty and maturely assured perfection for which the best Chinese art is distinguished. After some conversation we all went out for a scenic walk through the ancient narrow hill streets that wind about the Brooklyn shore. There is a dark charm in this decaying waterfront, and the culmination of our tour was the poor old Fulton Ferry, which we reached about 9 o'clock, in the best season to enjoy the flaming arc of Brooklyn Bridge in conjunction with the constellation of Manhattan lights across the river, and the glimmering beacons of slow-moving shipping on the lapping tides. When I was last there—in 1922 with Kleiner—the old ferry was still running, and the pensive wooden statue of Robert Fulton was looking down on the scene of decline from his niche in the front of the floridly Victorian ferry-house. Now even these things are gone. The ferry made its last trip on the 19th of last January, and the statue has vanished—presumably to adorn some museum—leaving a gapingly empty niche to brood over the spectacle of desolation. Thence we returned to Crane's, threading more old streets, and incidentally looking up rooms for Loveman in Columbia Heights. There was one splendidly large room for $10.00 per week in an impressive brick mansion of the Rutherford B. Hayes period—presided over by an aged Mrs. Grey, who has seen better days. Loveman, however, didn't take it; and if I could afford that much rent I'd snap it up tomorrow. I can't, though—and I think I'll get in touch with Crane and ask him about the smaller $5.00-per-wk. rooms which he was likewise recommending to Samuelus.

[By May 1925 Lovecraft was beginning to weary of the endless round of socializing; and he sought by various means to reserve some time for himself and his writing.]

[10]   The hour was two p.m., and Kirk was ready for an afternoon of empty dawdling around bookstalls and cafeterias—already he had proposed some coffee at the Sheridan Square place [. . .] since the Downing Street joint is weak on that beverage—but what do you suppose Grandpa did? I'll tell you! The old gentleman made exceedingly polite excuses, bowed low, and took the underground stage-coach home—straight home, James!—where he sat tight reading and writing all the rest of the day, retired at night, and arose on the morrow to tuck his books under his arm and start for a solitary open-air day in nearby Fort Greene Park. There, on

a bench against a secluded verdant slope, I read continuously all day; stopping only at twilight, when I wended my homeward way, pausing at John's spaghetti place for my usual Sunday dinner of meat balls and spaghetti, vanilla ice cream, and coffee. Incidentally—not many doors away, on the other side of Willoughby St., I found a restaurant which specialises in home-baked beans. It was closed on Sunday, but I shall try it some time soon. Beans, fifteen cents, with pork, twenty cents. With Frankfort sausages, twenty-five cents. Yes—here is a place which will repay investigation!

After dinner I laid in some supplies at the cheapest place open on Sunday, thence proceeding home—where I took one of our 454 dining-room chairs and went "out" for the evening—to my alcove with a pile of books! A knock came at the door—but I was not there. Windows and door-cracks show'd no light. Whose business whither I had gone? And so till bedtime, when I quietly turned in, awaking Monday noon and resuming my reading and writing. Having supplies, I didn't go out or dress, but when evening came I decided it wouldn't be politic to be "out" again. Two nights in succession would seem odd *at first,* though that will come very soon when the gang's habit is weakened a trifle more. Thus I let the light show—and surely enough, Loveman called. Now grasp the subtle work! I was cordial—but in slippers and dressing-gown, and with room not picked up. I apologised, but introduced no new or personal topics. With the sight of my writing all heaped about me, and with the burthen of conversation all thrown on him, my guest did not loll in the morris-chair by the hour as usual; but shortly adjourned to Kirk's den—though not without a promise to call on his way down. Another half-hour passes, and still I write. Now come Kirk's three familiar taps on the radiator pipe—to which I have to respond, since he knows I'm home. But my response is slow, and when I arrive I am cordial but not inventive of conversation. Another half-hour and Loveman leaves—with perfect cordiality—whilst Kirk puts himself in line for a favour—a thing I am particularly glad to grant him, since he has virtually forced so many substantial courtesies upon me. He, it appears, had also been loafing about—or working about—in his dressing-gown, and was greatly in want of a meal yet reluctant to bother to dress. Now I too was about to dine, so with the utmost hospitality I invited him down, treated him to A and P spaghetti, cheese, bread, and vanilla wafers off my best blue china, and bade him a courtly adieu almost immediately afterward—for he too felt the inadvisability of lingering in view of the obvious

air of preoccupation about the place. All this while I had been lightly and
banteringly alluding to my literary reform, both to Kirk and to Loveman;
and speaking of the solid work ahead of me. Thus it was easy to capture the
morrow by taking the initiative about when I would meet them again —
saying that I would see them at the regular Boys' meeting *Wednesday*, and
thus virtually exempting Tuesday. By this step, I could be sure of a quiet
Tuesday night WITHOUT retiring to the alcove.

[Everett McNeil's death in late 1929 inspired Lovecraft to wax reminiscent both about the naive author of boys' novels and about his experiences with the Kalems.]

[11]   It is an infernal shame that he couldn't have had a longer period of
emancipation from Hell's-Kitchen squalor at the close of his career. The
N.Y. terrain will never seem the same to the gang without him, for his
naive, characteristic note was so inextricably woven into our folklore. He
forms a vital part of that first, fresh, fantastically marvellous impression of
the metropolis which I receiv'd before familiarity bred disgust — that elusive, ecstatically mystical impression of exotick giganticism and Dunsanian strangeness and seethingly monstrous vitality which I picked up in
1922, before I knew it too well . . . . . . Cyclopean phantom-pinnacles flowering in violet mist, surging vortices of alien life coursing from wonder-
hidden springs in Samarcand and Carthage and Babylon and Ægyptus,
breathless sunset vistas of weird architecture and unknown landscape
glimpsed from bizarrely balustraded plazas and tiers of titan terraces, glittering twilights that thickened into cryptic ceilings of darkness pressing
low over lanes and vaults of unearthly phosphorescence, and the vast, low-
lying flat lands and salt marshes of Southern Brooklyn; where old Dutch
cottages reared their curved gables, and old Dutch winds stirred the
sedges along sluggish inlets brooding gray and shadowy and out of reach
of the long red rays of hazy setting suns. And I remember when good old
Mac display'd Hell's Kitchen to Little Belknap and me — a first glimpse for
both of us. Morbid nightmare aisles of odorous Abaddon-labyrinths and
Phlegethontic shores — accursed hashish-dreams of endless brick walls
bulging and bursting with viscous abominations and staring insanely with
bleared, geometrical patterns of windows — confused rivers of elemental,
simian life with half-Nordic faces twisted and grotesque in the evil flare of
bonfires set to signal the nameless gods of dark stars — sinister pigeon-

breeders on the flat roofs of unclean teocallis, sending out birds of space with blasphemous messages for the black, elder gods of the cosmic void— death and menace behind furtive doors—frightened policemen in pairs —fumes of hellish brews concocted in obscene crypts—49th St.—11th Ave.—47th St.—10th Ave.—9th Ave. elevated—and through it all the little white-hair'd guide plodding naively along with his head in a simpler, older, lovelier, and not very possible world . . . . . a sunny, hazy world of Wisconsin farm-days and green shores of romantick boy-adventure and Utopian lands of fixt, uncomplex standards and values . . . . . good old Mac! When will there ever be another like him?

Robbed!

[To add insult to injury, in late May 1925 Lovecraft was robbed of all but one of his suits, along with other property belonging to Sonia and to Samuel Loveman. Although initially stunned, Lovecraft could in a few days find a kind of sardonic humor in the incident.]

[12]   I hate to add bad news—but I might as well tell you what I discovered on going to get my clothes to mail this letter. Prepare yourself for something of a shock—there may be a reversal and better news later after I get in touch with Mrs. Burns and possibly the police.

The bad news is this—that while I slept, (for it couldn't have been while I was in the alcove, on account of the sounds I'd have instantly heard) my dressing-alcove was entered, either through the door to the next room or through my door by someone having a key; and *all* my suits except the thin blue, my Flatbush overcoat, a wicker suitcase of S.H.'s, Loveman's radio material, and I know not what else, have been stolen. One circumstance—the position of a long rod in the alcove—makes me suspect the youths now inhabiting the next room, or else persons working through that room in their absence. This has occurred since Sunday morning, for at that time—as you know from my bulletin to A.E.P.G.—I tried on the newly fixed trousers . . . . . alas! shall I ever see them again? Now I haven't been out of the house since, or even out of the room except to the bathroom. Nor could it have occurred, conceivably, whilst I was in the wash alcove. It must have happened whilst I slept—roughly, between six a.m. and eight-thirty p.m. Sunday, eight a.m. and three-thirty p.m. Monday, or nine p.m. and one-thirty a.m. (just now) Monday-Tuesday. I don't think it would serve any useful purpose to create a disturbance now, but I shall

dress and be ready for a busy day today—alas for my programme of retirement! Nothing in the outer room appears to have been touched. The
thieves were apparently professionals, knowing what was salable material.
For example, they stole the newest overcoat and no other. They omitted
the blue suit, no doubt, because it was hanging on a chair in the outer
room.

I can't yet accustom myself to the shock—to the grim truth that I
haven't a suit of clothes to my back save the thin, blue summer one. What
I shall ever do if the property isn't recovered, Heaven alone knows! And
after all this boxing! I can't get along on one thin suit—at least, I don't see
how I can—and that near the final stage of disintegration. It certainly is a
devilish mess, and I hope to Pegāna that I can recover the stuff. Unless I
do—may the Gods assist me! I fear I shall have to draw some cash or
something—I wear my things so long that it wouldn't be an extravagance
to begin the accumulation of another stock of four suits—one good summer, and one good winter at first, and later another winter to allow of alternate wear—for the coming decade if I live that long. But then—my only
really fresh-looking overcoat is gone, so what's the use? Tough luck!
Here's hoping I do recover my property. No—upon my word, I don't know
what to do next, with only one thin suit to my name. I suppose I must simply wear an overcoat on cool days, and wait for the gods to wake me up
from the nightmare of my destitution. And—changing the phase of the
subject—what shall I ever say to poor Loveman about his radio parts?
Their value, I fear, is close to a hundred dollars! And I thought I was doing
him a favour by storing them! His Fawcett books and paintings haven't
been touched.

Well—I'll seal this, and if anything new develops I'll add it on the envelope. I could curse the atmosphere blue! Just as I had decided to try to
look more respectable by keeping my clothes in good order, here comes
this blasted, infernal thunderbolt to deprive me of the battery of four suits
and one really decent overcoat needed as a minimum of neat appearance.
To Hades with everything!

Now I'll dress—scant worry about what to choose this time—and
swear at the walls till somebody is up to swear at. Damnation!

[13]   Thanks prodigiously for the sympathy on the recent disaster—but
don't let it worry you! Never waste emotion on the other fellow's plight—
if any expressiveness is needed, I can furnish enough cuss-words to fill the

suppressed part of a censored dictionary of synonymes! Yah! If I were writing a primer at the moment I'd cut out the A B C's altogether, and start in with a really vital and graphic letter—in double-size, heavy-faced, capitalised, italic form! Yes—it takes real rhetoric to expound the sensation of one suddenly stript of raiment which formed not only a tasteful adornment of the present, but a relique of former youth and a legacy of past ages amounting—in the case of the older garments—to the virtual sentimental equivalent of an heirloom! Alas for the robes of my infancy, perennial in their bloom, and now cut off—or snatched off—in the finest flowering of their first few decades! They knew the slender youth of old, and expanded to accommodate the portly citizen of middle life—aye, and condensed again to shroud the wizened shanks of old age! And now they are gone— gone—and the grey, bent wearer still lives to bemoan his nudity; gathering around his lean sides as best he may the strands of his long white beard to serve him in the office of a garment!

Yes—it certainly was quite an affair! Of course the quasi-partitional door *ought* to have been bolted and barred—and will be now that the damage is comfortably over. Loveman's pangs at his radio loss were mitigated by his joy at the fact that none of his Edgar Fawcett books was touched; but even so, he's in a position to condole with me through really subjective sympathy! He still owes $20.00 for the instalment purchase of a thing he no longer possesses, and when he reported the loss to the company in the course of finding out the serial number of the machine, the clerk seemed to suspect him of some dodge to evade payment until he reiterated his determination to come across to the very final farthing! It's a hard world! The detective, an affable, competent-looking person with the brisk voice and steely-blue eyes which belong with the part, avowed his intention of doing his very best; taking from me a minute description of each missing garment, and eliciting a thorough picture of the fugitive appropriators from Mrs. Burns—who is the only one able to identify them. What he can do has not yet appeared . . . . . . but hope and faith, the platitudinarians and fundamenentalists tell us, are the twin cornerstones of orderly society! As I've just written A E P G, I really don't know the established custom of endowing the authorities with gratuities in cases of success; but I seem to have read things about passing around cigars and the like. The graceful gesture is always important. As for me—your advice is exactly what my own judgment has dictated; to wait a reasonable time and keep the home folks posted. The whole business is the most damnable sort of a blow at a time when I was mustering up the forces of optimism, industry, and re-asserted individuality—but even at that, I guess the above-mentioned forces in combination are enough to give the new hydra-head a safely fractured skull. Granted a room, leisure, a book, a bathrobe, a pen, and a stack of paper, there's life left in the old man yet! But I wish to Pete those pesky pillagers had staged their Macheath act before I lavished so much cash on the pressing and repair of those suits! Let us take stock of what we have and haven't:

YES, WE HAVE NO	OTHER	BUT WE DO HAVE
new Flatbush overcoat 1924	ABSTRACTIONS	1918 thin blue suit
old 1914 thick suit	S H's wicker	1909 light overcoat
newer 1921 " "	suit case	1917 " "
newest 1923 thin grey suit	Loveman's	1915 winter overcoat
TODAY	radio set	moth-eaten odd flannel
		trousers—grey
		odd grey skeleton coat—
		shapeless
		straw hat—clean and
		shapely
		newly renovated felt hat
		old brown felt hat for
		rainy days
		all gloves, ties, and linen
		all shoes and rubbers and
		slippers
		STILL

Why, yes—item for item, the "still-haves" certainly do make a cheerfully impressive list—if one naively trains oneself to look at things that way. And of course the most important fact of all is that the corsairs didn't cruise into the main room at all, thus leaving unmolested the books, pictures, and other cherished objects which are—far more than any garments could be—my very life itself.

[Lovecraft set about promptly finding the most economical ways to replenish his depleted wardrobe and to purchase other necessities for his

solitary existence. Some of the letters of this period become rather maniacal in their dwelling on minute particulars of his shopping ventures, but
they are still leavened with self-deprecating humor, as the following
lengthy passage reveals.]

[14]   And now [. . .] I will proceed to the gorgeous chronicle of shopping
triumphs which I was going to send you anyway tonight—whether or not
I heard from you. Let us begin (for I may as well weave in the diary also)
with the Perfection heater which I was starting out to get yesterday afternoon when last I wrote. Though I had been advised to go to Macy's, I
thought I might as well start nearer home—especially since there is a very
high-grade hardware store just around the block in Court St.; a dignified
old place with real Yankee clerks, remaining from the time when the neighbourhood was a first-class and undecayed business street. Thither I
went—and found the place a veritable headquarters for Perfection stoves!
There were two sizes, one $5.49 and the other $6.20, of which I chose the
latter because of its greater oil capacity. This is undoubtedly the one you
have seen at $7.00—reputed to hold a gallon, tho' not quite doing so unless
one crowds the tank a bit perilously . . . which I don't. The obliging clerk
had a brand new stove uncrated for me in the cellar, and after bringing it
up, instructed me in whatever points were not included in the generous
and accurate card of minute directions—about the oil gauge, etc. His advice coincided with yours except that he insisted that no *mat* or *tray* is necessary. The tank, being filled and wiped elsewhere, (I shall always do it in
the alcove when I get a light there—now I do it on a pile of newspapers in
the room proper) never drips, whilst the base and legs never become hot.
And since it does not always stand in the same spot, it is not likely to wear
a hole in the carpet very soon. Accordingly I have not yet obtained this article—tho' I will if your experience and observation indicate its extreme
desirability. So far the contraption seems most delightfully cleanly and
practical—and I followed all your advice in starting it, even tho' your latest
bulletin did not arrive till I had begun operations. The printed instructions,
you see, agreed with you. I see that the top has a damper to open when the
stove is used for heating vessels, and note what you say about keeping
water there. I have not yet resorted to this expedient, because I dislike the
looks of a saucepan in a gentleman's study, and doubt if the hygienic advantage can be so *very* vast. But I may come to it yet if I can find a sufficiently aesthetick bowl capable of enduring the blaze. What I *shall* use the

stove-top for is the preparation of *hot dinners*.[5] No more cold beans and spaghetti for me—and today I bought a canned goulash-and-macaroni dinner for 35¢, which will make me two piping hot meals. In winter I dare keep the second half in a Mason Jar till the next day. You know what these complete canned dinners are—remember when we got the beef stew? The grocery in Clinton St. under the Taormina restaurant keeps a prodigious variety, (beef and lamb stew, goulash, boiled dinner, frankfurt and beans, kidney stew, etc. etc. etc.) and I shall be a consistent patron throughout the winter. The *variety* prevents that turning of the palate which beans and canned spaghetti (cold) produced early this autumn. 35¢ for 2 meals means 17½ cents a meal—and adding 5¢ for bread and cookies, the sum (22½¢) is not at all formidable as such things go. *Goulash* is brazed beef covered with a highly seasoned sauce—an Hungarian dish very popular in restaurants, and a prodigious favourite of mine. You may recall my ordering it at the St. Regis one evening last winter. I'll let you know how this canned edition of it tastes when I use the one I've just obtained. But returning to my store purchase . . . Since the shop was only a block from this door, I decided to carry the stove myself and avoid the delay of delivery; hence had it safely beside my desk in less than half an hour after my super-envelope postscript to you. The afternoon was still open, and I debated whether to go down and look over the Mackinac or embark on that quest of a Leedsian cheap suit which the welfare of my splendid acquisition seemed almost to force on me. Daily wear had already done much to blunt those knife-edge knee creases, and I could only groan at thinking of what the months of constant friction would inflict on those elbows and that seat—for in this weather the use of the thin blue has become impossible, and the new triumph[6] was doomed to take the brunt of daily knockabout wear—"hiking" and around the house—unless I could find a $5.00 or $10.00 alternative covering like Leeds' emergency outfit. Of course, I meant to take my time and employ all the patience in the world, for that is the only way to obtain a real *bargain*. What I had done in the realm of a good suit I resolved to do in the realm of emergency covering—and to find some remnant or odd and end at no price at all and with no fine material at all, but which might nevertheless surpass Leeds' $5.00 suit in having at least the cut and colour of a gentleman's garment. Leeds' thing roughly fits him, and wears excellently—but its texture and style are frankly impossible. It is a constant humiliation to him, but he was forced to buy in haste without widely looking around, since his former suit was actually falling to pieces at the time of the purchase. As he told me, one must in seeking such a thing look for one or the other of two types of garment: manufacturer's remnants, which one finds only by chance at sales, and staple workmen's suits, which are in stock all the time and one of which he was obliged to get. The centre for all such junk is 14th St and 7th Ave., rather near where Kirk lives now, and in this section I planned to look (after a preliminary Brooklyn survey) until I found a really *decent* looking rag or had to give up. I *wouldn't* be seen in publick with an outfit like Leeds'—and in case of finding nothing I decided to see what I could do in matching my suit with some cheap, coarse trousers for "hikes", house, and rainy days. These would be better than nothing, for it is always the trousers that get the worst of things. Anything to prevent the instant ruination of what ought to be a best suit for dignified wear to the Longs', the museum, and such places as give a shabby person a sense of embarrassment. Well, as I say, I debated whether I'd haunt the waterfront or go on this perhaps hopeless quest. At first I decided on the waterfront, but was deterred by the raw, cold blasts that swept up State St. as I turned down it. So, reversing my direction, I headed up Fulton St. and Flatbush Ave. on a slightly modified search for that alchemic goal of all the ages—something for nothing!

Brooklyn was a flat failure. There were no "cheap joints" in the sense my present condition required, and I'll vow the $20.00 things they displayed were about as bad as Leeds' $5.00 catastrophe! At the same time I enjoyed myself tremendously—and for this reason: that *every* salesman I interviewed mistook my new suit for an expensive made-to-order product of a first-class tailor. As one man they remarked upon the choice quality of the goods, and deprecatingly expressed fears that their humble products were not well calculated to meet the taste of a man accustomed to such a manner of dressing. It was, as the cant phrase runs, "pretty rich"; and I could not bear to shatter their peace of mind and sense of congruity by telling them that the radiantly aristocratic ensemble had cost me but 25 plunks! It confirms my original belief that I have secured a very rare bargain, and further confirms my belief in my own taste where clothing is concerned. You'll recall my saying how I pounced on that suit the minute I saw its fabric and cut (before I discovered it was only 2-button)—and in general I think I have developed an eye for the difference between the clothing a gentleman wears and that which a gentleman doesn't. What has sharpened this sense is the constant sight of these accursed filthy rabbles that infest the N.Y. streets, and whose clothing presents such systematic differences from the normal clothing of real people along Angell St. and in Butler Ave. or Elmgrove Ave. cars that the eye comes to feel a tremendous homesickness and to pounce avidly on any gentleman whose clothes are proper and tasteful and suggestive of Blackstone Boulevard rather than Borough Hall or Hell's Kitchen. Belknap wears the right sort, and so does Kirk. Loveman usually does, tho' his taste is not perfect. But Morton, Kleiner, Leeds, and McNeil are frankly impossible. And so, pining for the sight of a Swan Point car full of regular men, I have resolved to dress like Butler Ave. or not at all. Confound it, I'll be either in good Providence taste or in a bally bathrobe!! Certain lapel cuts, textures, and fits tell the story. It amuses me to see how some of these flashy young 'boobs' and foreigners spend fortunes on various kinds of expensive clothes which they regard as evidences of meritorious taste, but which in reality are their absolute social and aesthetick damnation—being little short of placards shrieking in bold letters: *"I am an ignorant peasant"*, *"I am a mongrel gutter-rat"*, or *"I am a tasteless and unsophisticated yokel."* And yet perhaps these creatures are not, after all, seeking to conform to the absolute artistic standard of gentlefolk. Possibly their object is entirely different; involving a recognition of their non-membership in the cultivated part of the community, and a desire simply to dress in accordance with the frankly different standard of their own candidly acknowledged type and class—as a Breton or Catalan peasant affects the grotesque finery of his kind, regardless of the attire of general European society. Sonny and I have frequently discussed the possible rise of a definite American plebeian costume, and we think we can already see evidences of it. Its present visible signs are tight, waist-fitting coats, with narrow lapels and buttons near together; extremely low-cut waistcoats, approximating evening waistcoats and probably derived from the rabble's ignorant admiration of the dress-suited heroes of their favourite cinemas; and exotick and effeminate "pastel" tones of colour—purple, lavender, and the like. The whole general trend of this growing peasant garb is toward the conspicuous and the feminine—infallible marks of a decadent slave-stock as opposed to the classically subdued and loosely but finely hung garments characteristic of a genuinely refined and wholesomely masculine ruling or conquering class or race-stock. The phenomenon, as Belknap noted even before I reminded him, is a perfect parallel of the degradation of the virile Roman stock into the fussy gaudinesses of the Byzantine mob. Eventually, as the whole civilisation decays, this artistic corruption will spread to the upper classes as well as the herd; but for the present it is possible to divide clothing pretty clearly into what gentlemen wear and what they don't. Better far to wear the frayed and tattered rags of something with taste, than to sport the newest and freshest plebeianism and decadence. But sententious reflection hath taken me far from my diary! I was saying that the Brooklyn dealers, whilst having nothing of Leedsian cheapness, all pleased me by confirming my taste and exalting my new suit—a thing, by the way, they would never have done had they known it was ready-made; since *clothiers* as apart from *tailors* pursue a policy of deadly rivalry and mutual derogation. How assiduously I concealed the label on the inside coat-pocket! I enclose a couple of the cards they were all so anxious to give me—souvenirs of the professional regard commanded by the truly well-drest man! Well—having exhausted Brooklyn, I descended to the depths, and took the subway for the 14th St-7th Ave. colony. Pegāna, what a gauntlet to run! Indescribable scum pulling one into holes in the wall where flamboyant monstrosities ululate their impossibility beneath price-cards of $4.95, $7.50, $10.00, $12.50, $15.00, $17.00, $18.00 ..... puffy rat-eyed vermin hurling taunts when one does not buy and airing spleen in dialects so mercifully broken that white men can't understand them ..... crazinesses in cloth hanging in fantastic attitudes and displaying unheard-of anomalies—before Heaven I vow that despite the horrors I've seen *on* people, I never saw the like of these fungous freaks *off* people! Perhaps the human form inside a suit fills it out to some semblance of Nature—certainly these empty nightmares swinging in the winds like gallows-birds had nothing of Nature in them! Once I came on a shop that handled remnants, and saw some very tolerable things which I would have barely consented to wear—but none that were of my size were of the desired winter weight. Once, again, I saw something in a "bargain basement" that caused my heart to flutter .... but found it was *second-hand*, and fled!

And now approaches the moment of a success so miraculous that I cannot believe it without looking down at the garment I am wearing. For I am saved, by all the Powers that be! Saved, and restored to my pre-robbery four-suit status by a "find" so titanic that I need have no trepidation in shewing my "alternative covering" to the four winds and all the world! Safe on its shoulders ready for the museum or the Longs' is my cherished triumph, (whose trousers I shall now have pressed after their week of hard and steady wear) whilst on my aged form as I sprawl carelessly about is a garment of dark, rich brown (sample enclosed—if your memory is good you will recall that it is closely similar to my winter suit of *just 20 years ago*—my heavy brown of 1905, which was the first suit I ever bought at the Outlet) whose weight and cut are exactly the same as those of my best suit, (for I have a *best* suit now!) whose fit is *perfect*, whose general aspect is *exactly* the same as that of all my usual clothes, (*nothing* off-colour or indicative of cheapness) which has (as if in answer to the one probable objection of cheap goods which the salesman so volubly denied) *two pairs of trousers*, and which—to come to a fitting climax at last—cost me (with the extra trousers) just **$11.95!!!**

Look at the sample and see if you believe it! Look also at the snap-shot which I will later have taken of myself in it! The point is, that it is really a gentleman's garment in design, material, and fit; which will enable me to wear it to ordinary meetings and on the street as well as on "hikes" and around the house, thus saving the "triumph" and conclusively removing the need of getting another good suit a year from now. Of course I don't know how it will wear—but even that matter is of minor importance in view of the extra trousers. The remnant salesman claimed it was a Rogers-Peet suit—or one originally designed for that firm and later sidetracked and shopworn—but since it lacks a label I reserve my right to be healthily sceptical on that point.

As for details of acquisition—these are singularly undramatick. I had come upon merely another one of the myriad sales of misfits and left-overs in 14ᵗʰ St, and had donned about a dozen coats of varying degrees of impossibility, when I suddenly knew that I was suited. The coat was a limp rag; crushed, dusty, twisted, and out-of-press, but I saw that cut, fabric, and fit were just right. There was no mistaking it. Other coats I might have worn on rough trips under the spur of necessity,—all in the great cause of saving the "triumph"—but here was the sort of thing I might conceivably *choose* in buying a good suit; a garment of my own general style and atmosphere, (despite the now unavoidable 2-buttonism) sober and aristocratic, and suggesting a mellow background which not even its mussed and distorted condition or its pauperish price (for this was a *$9.95* sale) could obscure to my now trained eye. The suggestion of 'pattern' or *mixture* (for there is no *pattern* beyond the blend of dark shades as you may see it) which the sample displays, is scarcely noticeable in the broad surfaces of the fabric as a whole; the massed effect being a plain dark brown even more in my style than my only other brown suit of 20 years ago—which had a definite stripe. The coat was a 42; but chancing to run small, fitted me to perfection except where the neck was crushed—and I could easily envisage the rectification of this feature. The salesman was doubtful of matching it with trousers, since of the three pairs he had (there was no other coat and vest) one was too big and two were too small. He was selling the extra ones separately at $4.00, and trusting to luck and the tailor to piece out a suit when the coat sold. Well—I let him shew me other things; crinkly and repulsive fabrics, crude cuts, and shapeless things with coarsely sewed edges, as well as fairly decent things which were too thin or didn't fit; but eventually I brought him back to this one. He wanted me to take the too-small trousers and have them let out rather than the too-big ones and have them taken in; but I balked, since I saw that the former would in any case have to sit low on the hips instead of coming high as mine always do. Here a dispute threatened to intervene, and (although I *would* have taken the suit anyway) I signified my unwillingness to accept the garment unless the roomy trousers were included. He, on his part, evinced a corresponding reluctance to include those trousers; when suddenly there appeared what was probably his original plan, but which was really just as agreeable to me as to him. He would, he said, include the larger trousers if I would also buy the smaller ones as an extra pair—"two-trouser suits" being quite the thing now, as you know. Good Oriental guile, but I had not read the Arabian Nights in my youth for nothing. "Season, O excellent Hafiz," I said, (in effect) "the price of good enterprise with the salt of philosophy, and reflect that he sells most amongst the merchants of Bagdad's bazaars who most bounteously meets the purses of the caravans from Ormas and Samarcand and Bokhara. I have come far across the Golden Sands; my camels are weary and my drachmae of Indian gold are nearly spent. I must away to the caravanserai at the Bab-El-Tilism except I be well suited; for I am in no mind for a bad bargan, and my camel-drivers clamour to be free to royster in the taverns beyond the Mosque of Almansor. Hei! I have no thirst for your extra breeches. I should not know what to do with them. Think you I am like my camels, or yonder donkey pulled by the water-boy, that I have four legs to be clothed? Why should I give you four pieces of gold for that which I do not wish? Turban of the Prophet! It were better fitting that I buy no garments at all, but give my few coins to the poor and make the pilgrimage to Holy Mecca's Kaaba Stone, that my grandsons in Samarcand may bless my beard and call me an Hadji! It is not thus that the merchants of Balsarah and Damascus rob an aged pilgrim—consider what generosity is due to venerable years, and what generosity will sell that which else would not be sold! But fie! I am not without pity for a worthy merchant. Let us say that you are poor, and saddled with that which none will buy. I will be generous, and pour the balsam of compassion on the wounds of indigence. Your robes I will buy, and the extra breeches too—if for those breeches you will demand but less. Perhaps my son can wear them, for he is small and slim. Hear, merchant! To the jaws of avarice I offer the meat of compromise—take these *two* pieces of gold for the breeches and I will buy your garments, even tho' they be worn and dusty and altogether unfit save to sell at a loss to the brown coral-traders from the Indian Sea!" And so it went—suit $9.95, extra trousers $2.00! The tailor at once measured me, and when I returned the next day I found everything absolutely perfect except the larger trousers, which were too long, but which were capably shortened to exact perfection whilst I waited. The coat was utterly perfect without alteration; hugging my collar tightly, and bearing no mark of its former crushed condition; whilst the vest became neat and trim with the first fixing. The larger trousers are very loose in the seat, but not at all baggy; and of course the coat comes far below any place where the bagginess would be manifest. The smaller trousers, despite my objection, really hang excellently; and the vest meets them with safety and to spare even when they are at their lowest. I shall divide wear betwixt the two pairs of trousers, thus avoiding the holy seats of the two stolen garments; whose repeated repair cost me so much trouble and expense, as you'll recall. The smaller ones shall be devoted to roughest purposes—country walks, rainy days, and around the house—whilst the larger ones will serve for those middling occasions like ordinary meetings or library trips when I can't be my toughest, yet oughtn't to be wearing the "triumph" out. Of course I don't know how long the cloth will last—but it's a safe bet that I get a good $11.95 value out of the outfit! Really, when you see the snapshot you'll understand how surprised I am at my good luck. [. . .] The fact is, that whereas two weeks ago I almost despaired of getting *one* good suit for $35.00, I have for about that very sum obtained not only a superlatively fine garment which arouses the marked and favourable comment of experts, but *another* whose outward aspect is every inch as good as that of any suit (except the "prize", and perhaps my 1904 and 1912 grey mixed suits) I have ever owned—and this with *two trousers*. I can't yet account for the excellence of design in so cheap a thing—it is *exactly* correct, even in the smallest matters of lapels or buttons on the sleeves, whereas virtually all the other 14th St. junk bore obvious and visible crudities, and marks of the plebeian in design. The suit has, to all appearances, those intangible refinements of outline and composition which cheap suits *never* have—and at the moment, while it is fresh, I'd willingly wear it anywhere. Whatever be its material in point of wear, and whatever be the cause of its appearance in a $9.95 sale, it was certainly cut to a very aristocratic pattern having absolutely nothing in common with the shape and style of cheap suits as sold at $5.00 to $18.00 in 14th St. Naturally, I don't believe the Rogers-Peet legend; but I think it may possibly be a stray $22.50 suit from one of those chain manufacturers who assiduously copy the best models—like the "Richmond Clothes" of Cleveland, where Loveman obtained his present delightful bargain.

Well—such is which! In my prime I could never have gotten so excited over clothes, but exile and old age make trifles dear to me. With my nervous hatred of slovenly and plebeian dressing, and after the maddening robbery which threatened to reduce *me* to exactly the thing I hate, you'll admit that apparel became very legitimately a "touchy" subject with me till such a time as I might again possess the four suits necessary for balanced dressing both in summer and in winter. But all things pass—and after one more letter descriptive of the reaction of the gang to my "alternative covering" I shall cease for evermore to discuss or think of suits. A gentleman should be always attired in good taste, but he should never be actively conscious of his clothes. They should be to him integral outgrowths of his personality and aesthetick sense; matters of course, and never artificial bedizenments to be flaunted. They become an active issue only when they disappear and leave one stranded—and now I have my four again and am good for another ten years if I live that long.

Clinton Street and Red Hook

[A year after leaving New York, Lovecraft reminisced about his disastrous Clinton Street experience.]

[15]   Naturally I would have shunned a lodging which seemed to savour of coarseness, but here again unusual conditions conspired to deceive me. I still think that none but a seer and prophet could have escaped error, and that the house had until almost that precise time been of the quality I thought I had found. My guess is that its decay had just set in, owing to the spread of the Syrian fringe (all unsuspected by me) beyond Atlantic Avenue. The man having my room before me was a N.Y.U. professor, and there was still in the house a splendid young chap who knew people that I

knew in Providence. The landlady was a refined-looking woman with two prepossessing youths as sons, and with a British accent of such absolutely authentic caste that there can have been no mistake about her tale of better days—the usual thing—and her claim of being the daughter of a cultivated Anglican vicar in Ireland, educated in a private school in England. Poor old Mrs. Burns! Only later was I to learn of her shrewish tongue, desperate household negligence, miserly watchfulness of lights and unwatchfulness of repairs, and reckless indifference to the class of lodger she admitted! I think her decadence must have been a gradual one—probably she wanted good lodgers, for she seemed naively impressed with the traditions which my books and furniture and effects seemed to imply, and vowed that they gave her wistful memories of her childhood home at the vicarage in Ireland; but she must have stopped asking references when the sinking of the neighbourhood made the house harder and harder to fill with people of the right sort. I was soon disillusioned—and with what a thud! Voices came from the next room—and *what* voices! Of course poor Mrs. Burns apologised for these particular roomers, of whom she said she was very anxious to get rid—but when I began to see some of the other anthropological types in the hallway my cynicism began to mount. Friends who came to see me—better versed in Brooklyn ways than I, for my metropolitan residence had been confined to the quiet section of Flatbush—were quicker than I to see and tell me what a wretched hole I had crawled into; but by that time I was all settled, and with my desperate finances the idea of a removal was quite impossible. I had only moved twice before in all my life, and was en-camped amongst all my effects—for such is my ingrained domesticity that I could not live anywhere without my own household objects around me— the furniture my childhood knew, the books my ancestors read, and the pictures my mother and grandmother and aunt painted. The presence of all these things at the edge of Red Hook was really almost humorous, (al-though Dr. Love across the street was no doubt equally surrounded by his cherished hereditary things) and visitors not infrequently commented on the virtual transition from one world to another implied in the simple act of stepping within my door. Outside—Red Hook. Inside—Providence, R.I.! For it has always been Providence wherever I have been, and must always remain so. That is the valuable lesson I extracted from my asinine metro-politan experiment—a lesson which will teach me not to separate the spiritual from the geographical Providence again. But at the outset I was deluded. Comically enough, I even persuaded a friend—George Kirk, formerly of Cleveland—to take the room above mine, and for several months we had the mild amusement of telegraphing on the steam-pipes— for one quickly falls into boorish ways in a boorish milieu. Kirk held out uncomplainingly till May; when, having fewer non-portable chattels than I, he betook himself to gay Manhattan. But laden as I was, I stuck; hence came to know that squalid world as few white men have ever known it. The sounds in the hall! The faces glimpsed on the stairs! The mice in the partitions! The fleeting touches of intangible horror from spheres and cycles outside time. Once a *Syrian* had the room next to mine and played eldritch and whining monotones on a strange bagpipe which made me dream ghoulish and incredible things of crypts under Bagdad and limitless corridors of Eblis beneath the moon-cursed ruins of Istakhar. I never *saw* this man, and my privilege to imagine him in any shape I chose lent glamour to his weird pneumatic cacophonies. In my vision he always wore a turban and long robe of pale figured silk, and had a right eye plucked out because it had looked upon something in a tomb at night which no eye may look upon and live. In truth, I never saw with actual sight the majority of my fellow-lodgers. I only *heard them* loathsomely—and sometimes glimpsed faces of sinister decadence in the hall. There was an old Turk under me, who used to get letters with outré stamps from the Levant. Alexander D. Messayeh—Messayeh—what a name from the *Arabian Nights!* I suppose the praenomen implied a Greek strain—those Near-East spawn are hopelessly mongrelised, and belong for the most part to the Orthodox Greek Church. And what scraps of old papers with Arabic lettering did one find about the house! Some times, going out at sunset, I would vow to myself that gold minarets glistened against the flaming skyline where the church-towers were! "We take the Golden Road to Samarcand!"[7] My tailor was a Syrian named Habib, and around the corner in Atlantic Ave. were Syrian shops with strange goods and delicacies. Once Kirk and I visited the Cairo Garden, where subtle incense evoked mirages of clustered bulbous domes and city-gates of alabaster, and fat, swarthy minstrels plucked meaninglessly at Eastern lutes whilst tenebrous and unpotable "coffee" (I use the nomenclature of faith, not of analysis or proof) was served in small curious cups without handles. It was a queer enough setting, and one which no person of my acquaintance can yet parallel—though our venerable fellow-gangster McNeil (author of boys' books) was at that time living in the roaring slums of Hell's Kitchen, (W. 49th St. Manhattan—a wild but rather colourless slum without mystery or the memories of fallen grandeur) and

Vrest Orton is even now experimenting with life at a Settlement-Workers' headquarters in the Italian (but far from Florentinely resplendent) turmoil of East 105th St. The keynote of the whole setting—house, neighbourhood, and shop, was that of loathsome and insidious decay; masked just enough by the reliques of former splendour and beauty to add terror and mystery and the fascination of crawling motion to a deadness and dinginess otherwise static and prosaic. I conceived the idea that the great brownstone house was a malignly sentient thing—a dead, vampire creature which sucked something out of those within it and implanted in them the seeds of some horrible and immaterial psychic growth. Every closed door seemed to hide some brooding crime—or blasphemy too deep to form a crime in the crude and superficial calendar of earth. I never quite learned the exact topography of that rambling and enormous house. How to get to my room, and to Kirk's room when he was there, and to the landlady's quarters to pay my rent or ask in vain for heat until I bought an oil stove of my own—these things I knew, but there were wings and corridors I never traversed; doors to rear and abutting halls and stairways that I never saw opened. I know there were rooms above ground without windows, and was at liberty to guess what might lie below ground. There lay a pall of darkness and secrecy upon that house—it subtly discouraged from first to last one's inclination to speak aloud, and at times one felt a faint miasmal tangibility in the circumambient air. The great high rooms had something of the mausolean in their crumbling stateliness, and in the halls at night one always had to be sure the great, white flamboyant Corinthian pilasters never moved just the least bit. Something unwholesome—something furtive—something vast lying subterrenely in obnoxious slumber—that was the soul of 169 Clinton St. at the edge of Red Hook, and in my great northwest corner room "The Horror at Red Hook" was written. It is nearly a full year ago that I left it without a pang to come home to my own—to the clean, white, and ancient New England that bred me, and whose hills and woods and steeples are the food and essence of my soul—and as the year has passed the squalid old Brooklyn setting has become less and less of an active outrage and horror and more and more a grotesque and even fascinating legend. The ruffled dignity of thinking I have dwelt in such a place gives ground to a dreamy doubt of my ever having been actually there— the episode becomes a tale told in the third person, and the realities are decked in a glittering mantle of myth. At this distance I am almost glad the mishap occurred—for it gave a touch of colour to a life otherwise tame, conventional, and uneventful, and made me better able to appreciate the slum chapters in many vital works of literature—high among them, Machen's autobiographical volumes, wherein are told that dreamer's struggles with squalor and poverty in late-Victorian London. I shall certainly write about 169 Clinton St. some day—and the tale will be one to chill the reader's blood. And if somewhere in the wide world there light upon it the sinful eyes of the two young men who stole my clothing from the alcove, they will so thank Mercurius (who presides over the craft of thieves) for their timely deliverance from such a peril that they may, as a votive offering, make restitution of what they took—in which case I trust they will add a cash balance to compensate for wear and tear on the apparel since May 1925!

Travels

[As a means of bolstering his spirit after repeated failures at securing a job and other disappointments, Lovecraft undertook increasingly ambitious—and usually solitary—explorations of the New York area, seeking antiquarian oases to counterbalance the grating modernity of the metropolis. One of the most delightful spots he discovered was Elizabeth, New Jersey, which he visited in October 1924 and which immediately inspired a memorable tale.]

[16]   Friday the 10th, in accordance with a plan of long standing which a chance editorial in the *Times* (enc.) brought to fruition, I started out on a tour of exploration whose focus was the antient colonial city of Elizabethtown, (now call'd Elizabeth) in the Province of New-Jersey. I went by way of Staten Island, taking the ferry from the Battery to St. George, and at that point taking the trolley line across the north shore of the island through antique Port Richmond to the old Elizabethtown ferry, where in 1780 His Majesty's forces under Sir Henry Clinton crossed on a temporary pontoon bridge in their attempt to capture the town. I had been to Port Richmond before—with Kleiner two years ago, when I wrote you about the 1783 church under which a brook flows, and behind which is a hellish neglected graveyard. This time I did not stop to see these things, but kept on the car and changed from side to side to watch the antiquities which loomed on every hand. And how abundant those antiquities were! Shabby, dilapidated houses along the waterfront and on every grassy hillock, with here and there a village-like cluster leading inland. Their type is very local

and distinctive, and markt by a great prevalence of pillared facades—with porch and Dutch curved roof join'd by great rows of square or classic columns extending up two stories as in the late southern plantation-houses. This arrangement exists not only in the spacious mansions, but with equal frequency in the humbler houses, where it possesses a certain touch of subtle incongruity. A touch of the sinister is supply'd by the paint-lessness and *extreme* decrepitude of most of these places, some of which are uninhabited and lonely on their sparsely turfed sand banks. The whole effect is bleak and a bit terrifying—I shall never forget the hideously gnarled and grotesque willow trees, and the little steep lanes leading up forbidding hillsides. At last the ferry was reached, and I went across to the dingy wharf at Elizabethport. This is now a Polish slum, and lacking all knowledge of the city I had to take a car to the business centre to procure maps, guides, pictures, historic matter, and the like. At last, having rolled from pillar to post—stationery store, public library, and newspaper office—I managed to accumulate a fine array of data, including the historical guide booklet of which I sent you a duplicate. Thus armed, I did some quick studying; and finally proceeded to follow the routes prescribed by the booklet. Night fell all too soon, but there was a great moon; and I continued my quest in the spectral night. Never will I forget the sunset as it came upon me that day—I was on a scarcely used part of the old Essex and Middlesex turnpike, a road yet unpaved, and lined with the great elms and tiny colonial cottages that Genl. Washington knew. To the west strecht the open fields and the primeval forest, and down over that haunted expanse sank the great solar disc in a riot of flame and glamour, painting the sky with a thousand streamers of weird and unimagined wildness long after the glowing edge had vanished beneath the trees and the hills. I returned to Brooklyn via steam-train, Hudson Tubes, and subway in the late evening, but returned the first thing on the following day—anxious to study the town at leisure by sunlight, and with the background of geographical and historical knowledge which I had so extemporaneously acquired. On that second day I went both ways by the Staten Island and ferry route—which has vast inexpensiveness, to say nothing of vast picturesqueness, to recommend it.

Elizabethtown, as you already know from the book, was founded in 1664 and well built up at an early date, both with small houses and with mansions of taste and opulence. The largest and oldest part of the town is a little over a mile inland, on the narrow and curving Elizabeth river, and is reached from the ferry by an ancient road—King's Highway, now comprising Elizabeth Ave. and First Ave.—which is older than the town itself, having been laid out by the Dutch to communicate betwixt New-Amsterdam and the settlements in Delaware.

Landing at the ferry house, one walks a trifle south to King's Highway and commences the march inland—fancying oneself, perchance, part of a spectral column of His Majesty's invading troops under Clinton or Kuyphausen. Not far from the shore, in front of a branch library, is a boundary stone of 1694, which at once establishes connexions with the past which one is seeking.

Approaching the town by the gently curving road, we see more and more colonial houses; till at last, near Union Square, they become delightfully prevalent. At that point the highway bends considerably, dipping straight down to the gentle valley where the old town nestles through the ages. Straight ahead on the skyline looms the tall, slender steeple of the old Presbyterian Church—still the dominant feature of the city's silhouette—and all around it cluster the ancient gambrel roofs of the forefathers—good old English roofs, for Elizabethtown was never Dutch—wrapt in the blue haze of distance which is akin to elfin magick. Down we march to the main street—Broad—where still the houses of the past are thickly sprinkled. As we approach the First Church we perceive what a marvellous place it is—standing in the front yard and looking north we have on our left the great facade and mighty spire—magnificent later Georgian work—and beside and beyond it the ancient churchyard with crumbling brownstone slabs (instead of slate, as in N.E.) dating back to the sixteen-hundreds, long before the present edifice was built. Here sleep the fathers—their stones of varying workmanship, their names variously spelt. Crane, Craine, Hetfield, Hatfield, Hindes, Ogden—and so on. In the rear are willow trees and grassy banks and impressive tombs. Clad in mellow ivy is the old brick church, which was built in 1784 on the site of one burnt in 1780. To the north winds crooked old Broad street, still studded with colonial gambrels, though some of the ancient houses have been raised like those of our own South Main St. to permit of modern shops beneath. Adjoining the churchyard is the new parish house—brick, and on such severe colonial lines that it might well be deem'd contemporary with the church. All vistas beckon us, but we choose the southward road, across the quaint stone bridge which spans the narrow, winding river. And what a river! Down to its sloping banks of grass and moss stretch the yards of the most ancient houses, gay with the tangles of old-fashion'd gardens, and grim with the great snakelike willows that bend out from the shore and lean far over the tranquil stream. Sime or Doré[8] would revel in the sight—as did I in my humbler and unproductive fashion. Beyond the bridge the land sinks to the east and rises to the west. I chose the latter course, where Washington St. meanders up betwixt incredibly archaic houses to a striking crest where colonial gables brood on every corner, and a great many-dormered gambrel-roofer silhouettes itself boldly against the polychrome sunset as a background in full keeping with the spirit of the place. Climbing this hill, it is well to follow Washington St. as it bends south to join the ancient Essex and Middlesex turnpike, passing another Georgian church and finally reaching the open country. Most of this country is now doomed by prospective real-estate developments, but one may still enjoy it as one cuts across the newly laid out and still houseless Bayway to Rahway Ave., an old-time road—part of the original King's Highway—on which are many mansions of noble refugees from France, chief among which is the "Old Chateau" of the Jouets, an impressive stone building in the middle Georgian manner, with two great wings. It is well here to turn north toward the town again, noting such alluring landmarks as the old De Hart house, perched on its high terrace and still displaying the airs and graces of 1766.

One now returns down the hill—eastward past the great gambrel-roofer and antediluvian chimneys by the river—and crosses Broad St., following the curving line of Pearl past many an archaic rooftree and garden, and past the old bridge to Elizabeth Ave., which spans another bend of the sinuous river. Pearl St. finally curves south, where it used to end among the marshes, though it is now being cut through to an entirely new factory district. At the old foot of the street, close to the open fields, stands the ancient Hatfield house, (1667) peaked and gabled in the earliest pre-Georgian manner, and probably forming today the oldest house in Elizabethtown if not in all New Jersey. You have probably read about it in the book—though I must warn you that the quaint well-sweep has vanished during the iconoclastic decade since 1914, when the little guide was printed. It is now interesting to retrace one's steps to the bridge at the bend in Pearl St., cross to Elizabeth Ave., and examine the ancient houses in the streets, lanes, and hidden courts nearby. The "old fort" in Thompson's Lane was built in 1734, and is still in good condition—a long brick house of plain lines—today inhabited entirely by niggers! The Andrew Joline house, built in 1735, is wholly hidden from the street by shops, but stands in a spectral courtyard, with its back on the river bank. And on the northeast corner of Bridge St. and Elizabeth Ave. is a terrible old house—a hellish place where night-black deeds must have been done in the early seventeen-hundreds—with a blackish unpainted surface, unnaturally steep roof, and an outside flight of steps leading to the second story, suffocatingly embowered in a tangle of ivy so dense that one cannot but imagine it accursed or corpse-fed. It reminded me of the Babbitt house in Benefit St., which as you recall made me write those lines entitled "The House" in 1920. Later its image came up again with renewed vividness, finally causing me to write a new horror story with its scene in Providence and with the Babbitt house as its basis. It is called "The Shunned House", and I finished it last Sunday night.

[17]   Being at last possess'd of a spare moment, I take my pen in hand to acquaint you with the particulars of my late delightful visit to the Federal City of Washington, and the adjacent parts of Virginia. Tho' my time of observation was short, I endeavour'd to employ it to the best advantage; so that I feel certain of having procur'd a very fair notion of the antient region I travers'd. [. . .]

And so I emerg'd from under the Roman arch and beheld the city. The morning sun was high and brilliant, and the summerish air told me at once that I had at last set foot in that gentle Old South of which I have so often dream'd. Green and white were omnipresent—springtime leaves and grass, and delectable expanses of aethereal cherry-blossoms; which latter, indeed, were past their greatest profusion, and beginning to be replac'd by the gay and multi-colour'd flowers of the many gardens. The town, brooding quietly in the Sabbath radiance despite the herds of sightseers unloos'd upon it, does not at first impress one. The Monument is so distant, the sky so vacant of tall buildings, and the ground so devoted to parks, malls, and wide spaces, that one cannot gather the sense of compact and active life which one usually associates with large cities. Then, too, near the station are certain temporarily undeveloped tracts, and a plenitude of large, low buildings which—though having an elderly and colonial aspect—are really only the temporary lath-and-cement structures put up in war-time to house the excess of special government workers. I saw the capitol dome looming importantly through the delicate verdure of young foliage, and was on every hand conscious of a note of leisure and reposefulness at once bespeaking the austral milieu. Now came stamps—bought at a post office next the station where a grandly cloistral air animated an interior of vast size and drowsily ornate dimness—and a matutinal meal, snatched at a modest refectory but little suggestive of background and glamour. Supplies on board, we[9] set out with buoyant step for the Capitol; observing as we went the temporary war buildings, which on closer inspection display'd some highly attractive Georgian characteristicks. The general landskip was still unimpressive, tho' a peculiar atmospherick quality induc'd a sense of mild exaltation—perhaps thro' aesthetick channels, since the sky was bluer, the foliage greener, the flowers gayer, and the marble structures whiter, than such things seem in the North. We did not omit noticing the Library of Congress, which fail'd to captivate us, or the House and Senate buildings; and once in a while a vista wou'd open up and enhance our impression of semi-rural spaciousness and freshness, whilst the charm of the low skyline grew on us each moment. At last, after traversing a delectable bit of park, we reacht the Capitol on its commanding elevation, and began to circumnavigate it till we attain'd that central and original portion whose corner-stone was laid by Genl. Washington, with Masonick ceremonies, in 1793, whose north wing was first occupy'd in 1800, and whose south wing was completed in 1811, under the architectural superintendence of Latrobe, designer of the United States Bank at Philadelphia and of the Popish cathedral at Baltimore. The central or connecting part, as all know, was erected after the burning of the city in 1814 during the war, and modell'd from the plans of the mighty Boston architect Charles Bulfinch, who to his native city was a veritable Christopher Wren, and whose crowning work is the golden-domed Boston State House on Beacon Hill, put up in 1795. The original Capitol building—central portion with dome, and the two wings—was finisht in 1827; the two extensions being added during the 'fifties. The present dome, as most are aware, is not the first dome; but a replacement, of stronger material, completed in 1865. As I gaz'd upon this gigantick construction, I cou'd not but compare it with other similar buildings I have seen; and I will confess that some of its rivals did not suffer by the estimate. For perfect artistry of form, delicacy of detail, and purity of material, it cannot compare with our own modern Rhode-Island State House; and I am certain no true Providence man can help feeling pride when he reflects that its superior constantly looms majestick and marmoreal over his native place, giving background and dignity to Exchange-Place and Market-Square, and forming a magnificent focus for the upper end of Narragansett Bay. God Save His Majesty's Province of Rhode-Island

and Providence-Plantations! The original part of the Capitol is *painted*, notwithstanding its ostensibly marble material; and a recent rumour hints at a century-old "graft" whereby an inferior stone was substituted. But let it not be thought that the building is unimpressive. Seen at a distance, the whole ensemble with dome and extensions is a stupendously noble thing, and one rejoices that it shares with the Washington Monument the distinction of being prominently visible from nearly every point in the city.

Having survey'd the celebrated structure to our full satisfaction, we descended from the elevation to the lower level of the town, following a convenient flight of steps that ran through garden-like terraces with fringing boughs. Below us lay the spreading city with venerable roofs and spires, wide park spaces, multifarious statues, and snatches of far background where the superbly slender Monument and Greek-souled Lincoln Memorial loomed white against the still more distant fragments of gleaming Potomac and templed Virginia hills. Behind and above towered the Capitol we had left, doubly majestick in the citadel-like environment furnisht by our point of view. Soon we had attain'd the bottom lands, where there burst freshly upon us the vernal charm of the place and season — the cleanness and vitality and village calm, precious things which more northerly cities seem to lose when they atchieve corresponding importance. The people, too, were infinitely less repulsive and mongrel than the crowds of New-York and its neighbours; so that the entire scene held a dreamlike glamour which titillated the spirit and made one question his own awakeness. Magnolias were in bloom, and with the fading cherry-blossoms help'd to give the air a zest and fragrance hard to describe and impossible to duplicate.

After a turn or two around the flower-fring'd paths by the Grant statue in the Publick Gardens, we proceeded to Pennsylvania Avenue and walkt along that thoroughfare toward the White House, noting as we went the many antient houses — late 18th or early 19th century — which are mostly of brick, and which have the same general outline and window-and-door arrangement as the corresponding class of colonial houses in New-York and Philadelphia — i.e., narrow facade, door at one side, symmetrically placed windows, and a pert pair of dormers jutting from a slant roof of average pitch. Doorways are seldom elaborate — the finest classick specimens, I feel, are to be found in New-England — but are often very tasteful. They are somewhat like those of Philadelphia, and do not resemble New-York doorways at all. Occasionally one sees a slanting cellar door projecting outward from the front of a house in the Philadelphia fashion—and another Philadelphia trait is the arched passageway in a solidly blocked house, leading to a garden or courtyard in the rear. Besides these distinctly urban types set solidly, there are all manner of other colonial patterns—village homes of almost farmhouse cast, more pronouncedly rectangular in facade, of brick or wood, with flaring lintels above the windows and slant roofs with or without dormers. I did not see many of the definitely Southern-Colonial type, or yet of the gambrel-roof design; both of these modes having largely vanisht before the construction of the city. Some of the more rural types, set in their own verdant and shady yards, impart a deliciously provincial tone to the town; and even the Victorian buildings scatter'd about have a certain suggestion of lazy refinement and artistick repose which accords with the major spirit of the scene. The great breadth and general level quality of the streets may subtract a bit from what would otherwise be Marbleheadish picturesqueness, but really adds something to the atmosphere of indolent Southern fascination. The bulk of the city is not—intrinsically and aesthetically—to be call'd strictly *beautiful*. It is too genteelly shabby for that—too heterogeneous in design, with Victorian jostling Georgian, and tiny wooden cottages tuck'd now and then betwixt incipient modern office buildings. But charm and personality it certainly does have; and those attributes grow on one powerfully during every minute of his sojourn, till he is finally won over as an ardent devotee. One hates to leave the restful spot when one has not a New-England to return to.

Writings

[Lovecraft did not manage much creative writing during his two years in New York: only five stories and a few poems. On several occasions he discusses "The Horror at Red Hook," one of the grimmest of his tales set in New York.]

[18]   I like a tale to be told as directly and impersonally as possible, from an angle of utter and absolute detachment. Which reminds me that I have just finished a new attempt at fiction—the story I told you I would write, with Brooklyn as a setting. The title is "The Horror at Red Hook", and it deals with hideous cult-practices behind the gangs of noisy young loafers whose essential mystery has impressed me so much. The tale is rather long and rambling, and I don't think it is very good; but it represents at least an

attempt to extract horror from an atmosphere to which you deny any qualities save vulgar commonplaceness.

[19]   No — I've never read any of the jargon of formal "occultism", since I have always thought that weird writing is more effective if it avoids the hackneyed superstitious and popular cult formulae. I am, indeed, an absolute materialist so far as actual belief goes; with not a shred of credence in any form of supernaturalism — religion, spiritualism, transcendentalism, metempsychosis, or immortality. It may be, though, that I could get the germs of some good ideas from the current patter of the psychic lunatic fringe; and I have frequently thought of getting some of the junk sold at an occultists book shop in 46th St. The trouble is, that it costs too damned much for me in my present state. How much is the brochure you have just been reading? If any of these crack-brained cults have free booklets and "literature" with suggestive descriptive matter, I wouldn't mind having my name on their "sucker lists". The idea that black magic exists in secret today, or that hellish antique rites still survive in obscurity, is one that I have used and shall use again. When you see my new tale "The Horror at Red Hook", you will see what I make of the idea in connexion with the gangs of young loafers and herds of evil-looking foreigners that one sees everywhere in New York.

I have a nest of devil-worshippers and devotees of Lilith in one of the squalid Brooklyn neighbourhoods, and describe the marvels and horrors that ensued when these ignorant inheritors of hideous ceremonies found a learned and initiated man to lead them. I bedeck my tale with incantations copied from the "Magic" article in the 9th edition of the *Britannica,* but I'd like to draw on less obvious sources if I knew of the right reservoirs to tap. Do you know of any good works on magic and dark mysteries which might furnish fitting ideas and formulae? For example — are there any good translations of any mediaeval necromancers with directions for raising spirits, invoking Lucifer, and all that sort of thing? One hears of lots of names — Albertus Magnus, Eliphas Levi, Nicholas Flamel — etc., but most of us are appallingly ignorant of them. I know I am — but fancy you must be better informed. Don't go to any trouble, but some time I'd be infinitely grateful for a more or less brief list of magical books — ancient and mediaeval preferred — in English or English translations.

[In the following extract Lovecraft speaks of "He," another powerful tale of New York. Interestingly, he had to leave the city and go to Elizabeth in order to write the story.]

[20]   At Hanover-Square, seat of the best British gentry before the Revolution, I lifted my hat in honour of King George the Third; then passing on by the Queen's Head Tavern—Fraunces', that is—to those regions of Battery Park where one or two colonial mansions yet linger. It was now five o' the morning, and I had so fully thrown off melancholy by my free and antique voyage, that I felt exactly in the humour for writing. The clouds were dissolving, and another day was done. Should I drag it away in New-York, and lose the keenness of my mood, or keep on in my dash for liberty—gaining fresh strength as I kicked aside the irritating fetters of the usual? The sea was before me—the clean, salt harbour beyond which lay a white man's country—and a Staten Island ferry rode at anchor. Who, possessed of any imagination whatsoever, could pause for an instant? So I planked down my nickel, boarded the ship, and in a few moments was riding the billows under a dawn-paling sky. Whither bound? The New-Englandish soul within me suggested the nearest substitute,—ancient Elizabethtown—so upon my landing in the grey twilight I took the proper trolley and rode in ecstasy past seashores and hills turning pink and gold with the sunrise. At the Elizabethtown ferry I saw the burnished copper disc of the sun gleaming gloriously on the waters, and by 7 a.m. I was in the central district of the village, gravely saluting the old colonial spire that towers—as you will remember—above the shady churchyard. At a small shop I bought a dime composition book; and having a pencil and pencil-sharpener (in a case, which S H gave me) in my pocket, proceeded to select a site for literary creation. Scott Park—the triangular space we passed in going to look at those rooms in East Jersey St.—was the place I chose; and there, pleasantly intoxicated by the wealth of delicate un-metropolitan greenery and the yellow and white colonialism of the gambrel-roofed Scott house, I settled myself for work. Ideas welled up unbidden, as never before for years, and the sunny actual scene soon blended into the purple and red of a hellish midnight tale—a tale of cryptical horrors among tangles of antediluvian alleys in Greenwich Village—wherein I wove not a little poetick description, and the abiding terror of him who comes to New-York as to a faery flower of stone and marble, yet finds only a verminous corpse—a

dead city of squinting alienage with nothing in common either with its own past or with the background of America in general. I named it "He", and had it nearly done by three, when my Leeds-Loveman engagement called me back to Babylon.

[In late 1925 W. Paul Cook asked Lovecraft to write a history of weird fiction for his planned amateur magazine, the *Recluse*. The task of researching and writing this treatise—"Supernatural Horror in Literature"—lent a certain discipline to Lovecraft's aimless life in New York.]

[21]   With my rotten memory I lose the details of half the stuff I read in six months' or a year's time, so that in order to give any kind of intelligent comment on the high spots I selected, I had to give said spots a thorough re-reading. Thus I'd get as far as "Otranto", and then have to rake the damn thing out and see what the plot really was. Ditto the "Old English Baron". And when I came to "Melmoth" I carefully went over the two anthology fragments which constitute all I can get of it—it's a joke to consider the rhapsodies I've indulged in without having ever perused the opus as a whole! "Vathek" and the "Episodes" came in for another once-over, and night before last I did "Wuthering Heights" again from kiver to kiver.[10] Ere long—as soon as I can get a fresh batch of correspondence out of the way—I'm going to give your Bulwer-Lytton favourites another chance to amuse and instruct me. Yes—all told, Grandpa's a pretty busy old gentleman—though at that I'm only on page twenty of the bally manuscript. It'll be a young book when I'm through with it and Culinarius will greatly lament that sentence of his—"there is absolutely no limit as to length."

[22]   This course of reading and writing I am going through for the Cook article is excellent mental discipline, and a fine gesture of demarcation betwixt my aimless, lost existence of the past year or two and the resumed Providence-like hermitage amidst which I hope to grind out some tales worth writing. In the first place, it furnishes an admirable excuse for my absenting myself from engagements—breaking the social ties, as it were, that chained me too closely to the gang. In the second place, it exercises my literary inventiveness and prose style. And in the third place, it restores my mind to its natural field of bookish seclusion and accelerates my speed and retentiveness in reading to something like their old Providence standard. This article done—as it will be in two or three weeks—I shall devote

myself to the composition of more stories to submit to Weird Tales—that magazine now having but four of mine awaiting publication.

Jews and Foreigners

[Perhaps not surprisingly, Lovecraft's racism came to the fore during his trying time in New York. Both African Americans and Jews bore the brunt of his vicious remarks.]

[23] The next day—Saturday the 4th—said to be a provincial holiday in these parts—I was up in the early afternoon and accompanied S H on an excursion to a place neither had previously visited—Pelham Bay Park, high up in the Bronx in the shore opposite Long Island. We had often heard of it, and the fact that the B.P.C.'s next meeting will be a picnic near there had called our attention to it afresh. So we went—taking the East Side Subway and changing at 125th St. It took an hour to get there; and since the train was uncrowded, we formed the highest expectations of the rural solitudes we were about to discover. Then came the end of the line— and disillusion. My Pete in Pegāna, but what crowds! And that is not the worst . . . . for upon my most solemn oath, I'll be shot if three out of every four persons—nay, full nine out of every ten—weren't flabby, pungent, grinning, chattering **niggers**! Help! It seems that the direct communication of this park with the ever thickening Harlem black belt has brought its inevitable result, and that a once lovely soundside park is from now on to be given over to Georgia camp-meetings and outings of the African Methodist Episcopal Church. Mah lawdy, but dey was some swell high-yaller spo'ts paradifyin' roun' dat afternoon! Wilted by the sight, we did no more than take a side path to the shore and back and reënter the subway for the long homeward ride—waiting to find a train not too reminiscent of the packed hold of one of John Brown's Providence merchantmen on the middle passage from the Guinea coast to Antigua or the Barbadoes.

[24] The so-called Jews of today are either Carthaginians or squat yellow Mongoloids from Central Asia, and the so-called Christians are healthy Aryan pagans who have adopted the external forms of a faith whose original flabbiness would disgust them. The day of belief as a significant factor is past—now we heed only the biological and cultural heritage of a stock as an index of its place. The mass of contemporary Jews are hopeless as far as America is concerned. They are the product of alien

blood, and inherit alien ideals, impulses, and emotions which forever pre-
clude the possibility of wholesale assimilation. It is not a matter of being
orderly citizens and caring for their poor—the question is more profound
than can be dealt with in superficial formulae, and vast harm is done by
those idealists who encourage belief in a coalescence which never can be.
The fact is, that an Asiatic stock broken and dragged through the dirt for
untold centuries cannot possibly meet a proud, play-loving, warlike
Nordic race on an emotional parity. They may want to meet, but they
can't—their inmost feelings and perspectives are antipodal. Neither stock
can feel at ease when confronted by the other, and Joseph Pennell the
artist only speaks the unvarnished truth when he alludes in his recent
memoirs to "the vague, unformulated dislike of a Jew felt instinctively by
every properly constituted person of my generation". East versus West—
they can talk for aeons without either's knowing what the other really
means. On our side there is a shuddering physical repugnance to most Semitic types, and when we try to be tolerant we are merely blind or hypocritical. Two elements so discordant can never build up one society—no
feeling of real linkage can exist where so vast a disparity of ancestral memories is concerned—so that wherever the Wandering Jew wanders, he will
have to content himself with his own society till he disappears or is killed
off in some sudden outburst of mad physical loathing on our part. I've easily felt able to slaughter a score or two when jammed in a N.Y. subway
train. Superior Semites—especially those of rural heritage or of the Portugese stock typified by the Newport Touros and Mendezes of colonial
times—can be assimilated *one by one* by the dominant Aryan when they
sever all ties of association and memory with the mass of organised Jewry.
But this process is necessarily slow and restricted, and has no bearing at all
on the problem of the alien mass. That mass must evolve its own aristocracy and live its own separate life, for the Asiatic and European cultures
can never meet in common social intercourse. No member of the one, in
good standing, can have any social dealings with the opposite body. The
line is clearly drawn, and in New York may yet evolve into a new colour-
line, for there the problem assumes its most hideous form as loathsome Asiatic hordes trail their dirty carcasses over streets where white men once
moved, and air their odious presence and twisted visages and stunted
forms till we shall be driven either to murder them or emigrate ourselves,
or be carried shrieking to the madhouse. Indeed, the real problem may be
said to exist nowhere but in New York, for only there is the displacement

of regular people so hellishly marked. It is not good for a proud, light-skinned Nordic to be cast away alone amongst squat, squint-eyed jabberers with coarse ways and alien emotions whom his deepest cell-tissue hates and loathes as the mammal hates and loathes the reptile, with an instinct as old as history—and the decline of New York as an American city will be the inevitable result. Meanwhile all one can do is to avoid personal contact with the intruding fabric—ugh! they make one feel ill-at-ease, as though one's shoes pinched, or as though one had on prickly woollen underwear. Experience has taught the remnants of the American people what they never thought of when the first idealists opened the gates to scum—that there is no such thing as the assimilation of a stock whose relation to our own history is so slight, whose basic emotions are so antithetical to ours, and whose physical aspect is so loathsome to normal members of our species. Such is New York's blight. Our own New England problem, though less violently repellent on the surface, is yet of discouraging magnitude; for where New York is swamped with Asiatics, our own streets are flooded with scarcely less undesirable Latins—low-grade Southern Italians and Portugese, and the clamorous plague of French-Canadians. These elements will form a separate Roman Catholic culture hostile to our own, joining with the Irish—who in a highly unassimilated state, are the pest of Boston. Many of these stocks could be assimilated—such as the Nordic Irish of Eastern Ireland and such of the French-Canadians as are of Norman extraction—but the process will be very slow. Meanwhile separation and mutual hostility must continue, though there is much less of that shuddering, maddening physical aversion which makes New York a hell to a sensitive Nordic. New England is by far the best place for a white man to live, and some of the northern parts are still astonishingly American. One could dwell very comfortably in Portsmouth N.H. Outside the N.Y. and N.E. belt other racial and cultural problems occur. The hideous peasant Poles of New Jersey and Pennsylvania are absolutely unassimilable save by the thinnest trickling stream, whilst the Mexicans—half to three-quarters Indian—form a tough morsel in the Southwest. The Indians themselves are very self-effacing and unobtrusive where they still remain—and the nigger is of course an altogether different matter involving altogether different principles and methods. In general, America has made a fine mess of its population, and will pay for it in tears amidst a premature rottenness unless something is done extremely soon.

Impending Return

[Finally, in the latter half of 1925 and into 1926, Lovecraft's aunts began to consider his return to Providence. A startling prelude to the discussion comes in August 1925, when Lovecraft defends himself against the notion that he is excessively tied to his possessions, maintaining that they alone are keeping him from a breakdown.]

[25]   Yes—on paper it is easy to say that "possessions are a burden", and that it is wisest to have nothing, but merely to live in a valise or trunk . . . . and so on . . . . fine theory indeed! But in actual fact it all depends on the person. Each individual's reason for living is different . . . i.e., to each individual there is some one thing or group of things which form the focus of all his interests and nucleus of all his emotions; and without which the mere process of survival not only means nothing whatsoever, but is often an intolerable load and anguish. Those to whom old associations and possessions do not form this single interest and life-necessity, may well sermonise on the folly of "slavery to worldly goods"—so long as they do not try to enforce their doctrines on others. They are lucky—chance has been kind to them! But to others who are so constituted as to require tangible links with their background, it is useless to preach such ideals and hypotheses. Nature has given their nervous systems other needs; and to advise them to burn their goods for freedom's sake is as silly as to advise them to cut off their legs in order to escape the burden of buying trousers. It so happens that I am unable to take pleasure or interest in anything but a mental re-creation of other and better days—for in sooth, I see no possibility of ever encountering a really congenial milieu or living among civilised people with old Yankee historic memories again—so in order to avoid the madness which leads to violence and suicide I must cling to the few shreds of old days and old ways which are left to me. Therefore no one need expect me to discard the ponderous furniture and paintings and clocks and books which help to keep 454 always in my dreams. When they go, I shall go, for they are all that make it possible for me to open my eyes in the morning or look forward to another day of consciousness without screaming in sheer desperation and pounding the walls and floor in a frenzied clamour to be waked up out of the nightmare of "reality" and my own room in Providence. Yes—such sensitivenesses of temperament are very inconvenient when one has no money—but it's easier to criticise than to cure them. When a poor fool possessing them allows himself to get exiled and

sidetracked through temporarily false perspective and ignorance of the world, the only thing to do is to let him cling to his pathetic scraps as long as he can hold them. They are life for him.

[The first significant mention of Lovecraft's return comes in December 1925, and the implication is that his aunts are urging Lovecraft simply to abandon Sonia and come home. Although greatly tempted, Lovecraft demurs, noting that Sonia's conduct has been exemplary.]

[26]   As for the matter of permanent locations—bless my soul! but S H would only too gladly coöperate in establishing me wherever my mind would be most tranquil and effective! What I meant by 'a threat of having to return to N.Y.' was the matter of industrial opportunity, as exemplified in the Paterson possibility; [11] for in my lean financial state almost any remunerative opening would constitute something which I could not with any degree of good sense or propriety refuse. Now if I were still in N.Y., I could perhaps bear such a thing with philosophical resignation; but if I were back home, I could not possibly contemplate the prospect of leaving again. Once in New England, I must be able to stick there—thenceforward scanning Boston or Providence or Salem or Portsmouth for openings, rather than having my eyes on Manhattan or Brooklyn or Paterson or such distant and unfamiliar realms. I may remark, incidentally, that the Paterson matter stands exactly as before. The work on the museum building is held up, and until then all expansion is in abeyance—Morton being meanwhile instructed to hold small displays and exhibitions in the library building. But, he says, the work will almost certainly begin in the spring; and at that time an assistant will almost certainly be required—so there one is! I could stand the prospect (for the work itself would be congenial) if I had not meanwhile had sight of a real white man's country—but if I once saw New England again, with her hilly streets leading down to the sea, and her avenues of ancient elms, and her clustered gambrel roofs, and her white steeples rising over centuried churchyards, I could nevermore bring myself to venture outside her confines. S H's attitude on all such matters is so kindly and magnanimous that any design of permanent isolation on my part would seem little short of barbaric, and wholly contrary to the principles of taste which impel one to recognise and revere a devotion of the most unselfish quality and uncommon intensity. I have never beheld a more admirable attitude of disinterested and solicitous regard; in which each

financial shortcoming of mine is accepted and condoned as soon as it is proved inevitable, and in which acquiescence is extended even to my statements (as determined by my observation of the effect of varying conditions on my nerves) that the one *essential* ingredient of my life is a certain amount of quiet and freedom or creative literary composition—to be snatched whether or not I am otherwise employed, and whether or not it conflicts with that schedule of early hours and regularity which a more simply industrial regime stamps as normal. A devotion which can accept this combination of incompetence and aesthetic selfishness without a murmur, contrary tho' it must be to all expectations originally entertained; is assuredly a phenomenon so rare, and so akin to the historic quality of saintliness, that no one with the least sense of artistic proportion could possibly meet it with other than the keenest reciprocal esteem, respect, admiration, and affection—as indeed it was met at first, when manifested under less trying circumstances and with far less comprehension of the chronicle of failure stretching ahead. It is one of the marks of an old-fashion'd gentleman, as distinguished from the herd of crude and careless moderns, that he recognises his harmonious relation to the pattern in which Fate has set him, and never ceases to live up as fully as he may to such aesthetic responsibilities as may arise from his previous decisions. Ineffective and injudicious I may be, but I trust I may never be inartistic or ill-bred in my course of conduct. Harsh or sudden revolts and repudiations are alien to an Englishman of taste; and when one's profoundest admiration, deference, and regard are elicited by the conditions one encounters, it is not difficult to follow that conservative course which all the canons of art and all the precepts of gentle breeding map out as the only proper one. But to turn from abstractions to the concrete—S H fully endorses my design of an ultimate return to New England, and herself intends to seek industrial openings in the Boston district after a time—tho' for the present this second Cleveland position seems to present great advantages and to offer conditions which are unusually congenial for a thing of the sort. The remuneration is not great, but the prospects of advancement are considerable; and the prevailing spirit of fairness and forbearance shewn alike by management and employees is an incalculable relief after the nerve-racking friction of the former position—with flashy upstart scum as employers. (although even there the *employees* were tolerable) This Halle establishment is the leading department-store of Cleveland; perhaps equivalent to our Shepard's. And so you may be assured that only the Paterson possibility holds me in New York.

The slightest chance of a position in New England would being me home at any minute with a haste almost comical to a spectator; and indeed, the definite disappearance of a Paterson possibility would cause me to migrate anyhow—to secure quarters near Boston and begin a systematic hunt for work through *Transcript* advertisements much (tho' I hope not as vainly!) as I hunted in New York through *Times* advertisements during the first year. In Boston, indeed, I might be able to put more inward heart (tho' I certainly could put no more patience and diligence!) into the quest; for there would be around me a world to which I bear at least some semblance of relation, instead of the alien desert that is the Gotham of today.

[Finally, in late March 1926, the return had become a reality. Lovecraft could scarcely contain his enthusiasm. Another letter, written a few days later, responded to the aunts' suggestion that he go to Boston or Cambridge because of increased opportunities for literary work there; and it was at this time that Lovecraft made his celebrated remark, "I am Providence."]

[27]   And now about your invitation. Hooray!! Long live the State of Rhode-Island and Providence-Plantations!!! But I'm past the *visiting*-point. Even if my physique is flourishing, my nerves are a mess—and I *could never board a train away from Providence toward New York again.* If I went to East Greenwich or Wickford I'd have to use trolleys—or busses in the case of Wickford, since the poor old Sea View has failed. I'm not eager for ignominious returns via the smaller orifice of the trumpet; but if you and AEPG think it's perfectly dignified for me to slip unobtrusively back toward civilisation and Waterman St., I'm sure I couldn't think of anything else logical for one who is an integral part of Rhode Island earth. Only last night I dreamed of Foster. If I ever use my brain, I guess it'll have to be in R.I.—though I might stand the Boston area if any imperative business fixed me there. But as to details—I'm all in favour of letting you and A E P G do *all* the planning, if you don't mind, and of sending my things ahead of me. When *I* land in person, I want my address to be *115 Waterman St.* Your plan for the little apartment is so ideal that I can't do anything save blister my palms applauding—and once I'm in it, I'll certainly hustle like the devil with writing to see if I can make enough to assure it permanence. I'll trust you to do all the arranging—you know how big the room at 169 is, and exactly what's in it; and can easily see that the new quarters come up to space

requirements. There's no hurry—just wait till all is well, then hire your space and *let me know!* Packing will be a deuce of a job—but with a new lease of life at stake I shall have the energy of a daemon! I'll hire Kirk and his boy to pack my books, and will consult with the Excelsior Warehouses about other delicate things. Had I better wait till some Providence moving man has his van in N.Y. before arranging for any large shipments? All this can extend over weeks if necessary—I shall be perfectly content to camp out here amidst diminishing possessions. Only one thing I must have *now*, and that is a *couch*. I *will not* have a *bed* in my room, for it must be primarily a pleasant study as now. I am now used to sleeping on a narrow couch, (I never *open* the one here when alone) and wish a cheap specimen of the same (it needn't be an unfolding one—just a slim single steel-frame device) to precede me to the new place. Then I will dress it with green blanket, afghans, and pillows as I do this one here. If there are no alcoves to conceal dressing apparatus, I must have a cheap Japanese screen. Otherwise I am all right. I hate to think of the expense—but I'll cut out the Philadelphia and Washington trips I had planned, and will postpone any Salem, Marblehead, and Portsmouth jubilations till my purse may have had a chance to recuperate. Quinsnicket shall be my longest excursion for a time, and walks to Blackstone Park will cost even less. My library card expires on the 17th of next month, but I'll get it renewed, and with the address changed from 598. My stack permit has already expired—but good old William E. Foster has been tolerant of lapses before. When the last load goes, I'll send change-of-address cards to Providence and Brooklyn post-offices, and to the Journal and Bulletin—also to the editor of the United and National Amateurs. Then—being tolerably well disposed of so far as my effects are concerned, I shall amble around myself—the least important part of the business. When I hit town the fact that I've been away will be only a sort of vague nightmare.

[28]   Now about migrations—there is no question of disillusion involved. I don't expect to live in a seventh heaven of happiness anywhere, and only want to drag out my last few days in some quiet backwater where the general environment isn't too obtrusively offensive. There is no question of illusion or disillusion about Providence—I know what it is, and have never mentally dwelt anywhere else. When I look up from my work it is Angell St. I see outside the windows, and when I think of going out to buy anything it is Westminster St. that comes to my eyes until objective realism

painstakingly corrects the image. I have no emotional as apart from intellectual conviction that I am not in Providence this moment—indeed, psychologically speaking, I *am* and always will be there. Whenever I hear a whistle in the night I always think it is some boat on the bay, or some train down at the Bristol Depot.

But as I have said before; if all hands think Boston or Cambridge a more appropriate haven, I am not disposed to pit against their judgments an opinion from a mind whose ghastly rashness and idiocy of 1924 brought about the New York move. I could certainly work well in Cambridge, and the general atmosphere there is—apart from the single detail of early personal associations—of course even closer to my particular cast of mind than is Providence. Naturally, since Providence is a commercial port whilst Cambridge is a cultural centre, the latter would be expected to fit a literarily inclined person much better—and the only reason it would not, is that I am essentially a recluse who will have very little to do with people wherever he may be. I think that most people only make me nervous—that only by accident, and in extremely small quantities, would I ever be likely to come across people who wouldn't. It makes no difference how well they mean or how cordial they are—they simply get on my nerves unless they chance to represent a peculiarly similar combination of tastes, experiences, and heritages; as, for instance, Belknap chances to do. To all intents and purposes I am more naturally isolated from mankind than Nathaniel Hawthorne himself, who dwelt alone in the midst of crowds, and whom Salem knew only after he died. Therefore, it may be taken as axiomatic that the people of a place matter absolutely nothing to me except as components of the general landscape and scenery. Let me have normal American faces in the streets to give the aspect of home and a white man's country, and I ask no more of featherless bipeds. My life lies not among *people* but among *scenes*—my local affections are not personal, but topographical and architectural. No one in Providence—family aside—has any especial bond of interest with me, but for that matter no one in Cambridge or anywhere else has, either. The question is that of which roofs and chimneys and doorways and trees and street vistas I love the best; which hills and woods, which roads and meadows, which farmhouses and views of distant white steeples in green valleys. I am always an outsider—to all scenes and all people—but outsiders have their sentimental preferences in visual environment. I will be dogmatic only to the extent of saying that it is *New England* I *must* have—in some form or other. Providence is part of me — I *am* Providence — but as I review the *new* impressions which have impinged upon me since birth, I think the greatest single emotion — and the most permanent one as concerns consequences to my inner life and imagination — I have ever experienced was my first sight of *Marblehead* in the golden glamour of late afternoon under the snow on December 17, 1922. That thrill has lasted as nothing else has — a visible climax and symbol of the lifelong mysterious tie which binds my soul to ancient things and ancient places. But I was not born in Marblehead, and I did not live all the best days of my life there — although the place (in common with Salem, Portsmouth, and all old New England scenes) gives me at times an intensely poignant illusory sensation of having done so in the period around 1750–1760. Providence is my home, and there I shall end my days if I can do so with any semblance of peace, dignity, or appropriateness. Industrially, I suppose Cambridge has more openings — in fact, Orton has promised to speak a good word for me with Boston publishers, whilst only last week I asked Mrs. Miniter for exact particulars of the occasional proof-reading she used to do for Ginn and Co. at their plant in Cambridgeport. But Providence would always be at the back of my head as a goal to be worked toward — an ultimate Paradise to be regain'd at last.

5 Homecoming
(1926–1930)

Paradise Regain'd

[Lovecraft's letter to Frank Belknap Long recounting his return to Providence after two dreadful years in New York must also rank among the jewels of his correspondence. He also recounts settling into a small but comfortable apartment with his aunt Lillian at 10 Barnes Street.]

[1]   And now Grandpa will tell you—all of you boys—about his return to normalcy and his awakening from the queer dream about being away from home. As supplementary material I send three items in care of Belknap, but design'd for the equal attention of all—a folder of modern Providence, a set of cards of historick Providence, and a newspaper extract describing and illustrating our splendid new art museum—whose opening was deferr'd till last week, as if to allow the Old Gentleman to get home in ample time to be in at the start.

Well—to begin with—back in the dream period Grandpa has some notion of having boarded a train somewhere. A blur of stations follow'd, and all at once there came a sight which presaged a return to the world of reality—an old-fashion'd wall of tumbled stone betwixt rolling meadows! Memory! Broken threads! But see! A little white farmhouse amidst green hills! A village steeple beyond a distant crest! A square wooden Georgian building on an eminence! Who am I? What am I? Where am I? I—a corpse—once lived, and here are the signs of a resurrection! The year? It must be 1923–24 . . . . and the place . . . . look! The old familiar billboards! Packer's Tar Soap! Gorton's Codfish! GOD, I AM ALIVE! And this is Home! Novanglia Æterna! Novanglia Caput Mundi! His Majesty's Province of Connecticut, which on the East adjoins the Centre of Civilisation! A sense of rushing through chartless corridors seized me, and I saw dates dancing in aether—1923—1924—1925—1926—1925—1924—1923—crash! Two years to the bad, but who the hell gives a damn? 1923 ends—1926 begins! Even the spring had delay'd so that I might see it break over Novanglia's antient hills! What does a blind spot or two in one's existence matter? America has lost New York to the mongrels, but the sun shines just as brightly over Providence and Portsmouth and Salem and Marblehead—I have lost 1924 and 1925, but the dawn of vernal 1926 is just as lovely as I view it from Rhodinsular windows! After all, a fantaisiste ought to like a little shaking-up or abnormality in chronology and geography—New York was a nightmare, and I have already form'd a most delightful picture of the gang as meeting in various colonial Providence homes! As time passes, my selective imagination will form an idealised picture of those things in N.Y. which were really beautiful—the skyline, the sunsets over Central Park, the Pantheon model in the Museum, the Japanese Garden in the Bklyn. Museum grounds, etc.—and they will stand out apart from the Babylonish squalor and parvenu garishness of a dead city, as delectable bits seen through an old-fashion'd stereoscope in some beautifully Victorian but fascinatingly familiar old high-ceiled parlour with Rogers groups and bearskin rugs, in the heart of a real Providence home. Now that I am learning to write 1926 instead of 1923 all will go on very much as usual—I, an essential Providentian, will die as I was born—and Brooklyn will take its place beside Cleveland, Washington, Philadelphia, and other distant towns which I have briefly visited. Well—the train sped on, and I experienced silent convulsions of joy in returning step by step to a waking and tri-dimensional life. New Haven—New London—and then quaint *Mystic,* with its colonial hillside and landlocked cove. Then at last a still subtler magick fill'd the air—nobler roofs and steeples, with the train rushing airily above them on its lofty viaduct—*Westerly*—in His Majesty's Province of RHODE-ISLAND AND PROVIDENCE-PLANTATIONS! GOD SAVE THE KING!! Intoxication follow'd—Kingston—East Greenwich with its steep Georgian alleys climbing up from the railway—Apponaug and its ancient roofs—Auburn—just outside the city limits—I fumble with bags and wraps in a desperate effort to appear calm—THEN—a delirious marble dome outside the window—a hissing of air brakes—a slackening of speed—surges of ecstasy and dropping of clouds from my eyes and mind—HOME—UNION STATION—*PROVIDENCE!!!!*[1] Something snapped—and everything unreal fell away. There was no more excitement; no sense of strangeness, and no perception of the lapse of time since last I stood on that holy ground. Of disillusion, or of disparity betwixt expectation and fulfilment, there was not the faintest microscopic suggestion, because the wildly improbable notion of ever having been away had utterly receded into the gulfs of fantasy and dream. What I had seen in sleep every night since I left it, now stood before me in prosaic reality—precisely the same, line for line, detail for detail, proportion for proportion. Simply, I was home—and home was just as it had always been since I was born there thirty-six years ago. There *is* no other place for me. My world is Providence. We now took a taxicab for the house in Barnes St.—an ancient colonial neighbourhood I had always known—and were soon greeting my aunts and the faithful negress Delilah, whom they had hired to straighten things out. Then followed a resumption of real life as I had dropped it two years ago—the life of a settled American gentleman in his ancestral environment. [. . .]

As for the place—I have a fine large ground-floor room (a former dining-room with fireplace) and kitchenette alcove in a spacious brown Victorian wooden house of the 1880 period—a house, curiously enough, built by some friends of my own family, now long dead. My furniture fits in quite as neatly as in the Clinton St. place[. . . .] The house is immaculately clean, and inhabited only by select persons of the good old families—a miniature painter of some fame, an official of the School of Design Museum, etc. etc. The neighbourhood is perfect—all old Yankee Providence homes, with a good percentage of the houses colonial. There is a little white colonial cottage, just renovated for an artist, only three doors away at the corner of Prospect St., and from the upper windows one may see the great brick Halsey Mansion, built in 1801 and reputed to be haunted.[2] The vista from my pseudo-oriel desk corner is delectable—bits of antique houses, stately trees, urn-topp'd white Georgian fence, and an ecstatic old-fashion'd garden which will be breathlessly transporting in a couple of months. Westward, from the brow of the hill, the view is awesome and prodigious

—all the roofs, spires, and domes of the lower town, and beyond them the violet expanse of the far rolling rural meadows. The walk down town can be varied to suit one's mood, but it is always colonial. One may choose shady, stately Prospect St., past the mansions of the Sharpes and Metcalfes, (Kleinerus will recall the neo-Queen Anne brick manor-house in whose courtyard I photograph'd him) or select the narrow, crooked downhill lanes whose quaint doorways are so suggestive of Marblehead. In any case one has to the west the whole panorama of the lower town, with marble state house and exquisite 1st Baptist Steeple, (1775) and to the east (only a few blocks from my house) the colossal Roman bulk of the new Christian Science church, whose proud copper dome is the dominating feature of the Providence skyline. The view from this dome is said to be absolutely unparallelled—countless steepled towns, league on league of undulating countryside, and the beautiful blue bay to the south, gemmed with emerald islets. One can, the genial sexton says, see as far as Newport on good days; and he has promised to let me up there with a spy glass whenever I feel like making the climb.

Contented? Why, gentlemen, I am *home!* Up and down this colonial hill I have walk'd ever since I could walk at all—and it has always exerted upon me the greatest possible fascination, even though my native part of Angell St. is somewhat farther east, in a decidedly newer (middle and later Victorian) district. Let no one tell me that Providence is not the most beautiful city in the world! Line for line, atmospheric touch for atmospheric touch, it positively and absolutely *is!* Colour, shade, contour, diversity, quaintness, impressiveness—all are there; and nothing save an aesthetick blind spot could possibly prevent any cultivated observer of Yankee tastes from recognising and revering this supremacy at once. God knows I want no literature to feed my sense of beauty and variety when I live in the midst of this focus of scenick charm and historick richness! I must write about it—all other subjects seem flat and tame!

[2]   It is astonishing how much better the old head works since its restoration to those native scenes amidst which it belongs. As my exile progressed, even reading and writing became relatively slow and formidable processes; so that my epistles were exceedingly brief and labour'd efforts. Now I find something of my antique Providence fluency returning by degrees, and have been able to keep my correspondence in manageable shape without more than a fraction of the effort which I was forc'd to expend

when ingulph'd in the nightmare of Brooklyn's mongrel slums. That experience has already become the merest vague dream—and it is with difficulty that I can make myself realise, in any really convincing or subjective way—that I have ever been away for any length of time. I am Providence, and Providence is myself—together, indissolubly as one, we stand thro' the ages; a fixt monument set aeternally in the shadow of Durfee's ice-clad peak!

Reflections on Marriage

[It was only three years after his departure from New York—and his virtual abandonment of his wife, leading to their divorce in early 1929—that Lovecraft took occasion to reflect upon the institution of marriage and the causes for the failure of his own attempt at matrimony.]

[3]   As for domesticity—I'm no dealer in dogmatisms and blanket generalities. Some things suit some temperaments, others others. I haven't a doubt but that matrimony can become a very helpful and pleasing permanent arrangement when both parties happen to harbour the potentialities of parallel mental and imaginative lives—similar or at least mutually comprehensible reactions to the same salient points in environment, reading, historic and philosophic reflection, and so on; and corresponding needs and aspirations in geographic, social, and intellectual milieu—but I must add that I don't see how the hell any couple outside of professional psychiatrists can ever tell whether or not they possess this genuine parallelism until the actual test of two or three years of joint family life has brushed aside all the transient and superficial reactions due to novelty and rashly assumed adaptability, and revealed the basic, rock-bottom motivating mental and imaginative influences on each side—the influences actually constituting the inmost respective personalities involved, and forming inviolable nuclei of identity whose safeguarding is the inevitable and fundamental aim of every human being's intellectual-emotional mechanism. It is all a matter of chance—in greater or less degree as the parties have or lack a lifelong acquaintanceship, or are naturally good or poor judges of human temperament—whether a given marriage will develop into a true and lasting domestic harmony, or become an intolerable mental irritant until cancelled by a sane and benign court action. Fortunately people are beginning to realise this as time passes and philosophic outlooks broaden, so that in most enlightened states like Rhode Island the divorce laws are such as to

allow rational readjustments when no other solution is wholly adequate. If other kinds of states—such as New York or South Carolina, with their mediaeval lack of liberal statutes—were equally intelligent in their solicitude for the half-moribund institution of monogamy, they would hasten to follow suit in legislation; for certainly, the disillusioned future generations will never tolerate a blind trap which offers ten chances of disaster to one of success.[3] If the divorce laws of a region be not sufficiently intelligent to provide for the necessary readjustment of lives misplaced in good faith, then the result will be a gradual disuse of legal marriage and an almost complete reign of that type of semi-clandestine extra-legal relationship which has indeed already displaced the older system to some extent, yet which is infinitely less desirable from a social, political, economic, and aesthetic point of view. To my mind, any acceleration of this "new morality" is an unwise thing, even though the new system may be the normal rule in the remote future. Too quick a transition tends to uproot some of the deepest emotional anchorings of the Anglo-Saxon race—and the loss of the well-known values of domestic tranquillity seems very likely to outweigh the corresponding gain in erotic normality to such an extent that the net result will be an impoverishment rather than an enrichment of life as a whole. No—I am in favour of the established order; old-fashioned marriage with its Roman regularity of registration and its wholesome absence of the element of furtiveness. But if it is to survive, it must clean house—must purge itself of primitive superstition and Victorian hypocrisy, and reorganise itself as a rational institution adapted to human needs rather than remain an impossible Procrustean bed to which all human temperaments must be fitted through crippling and torture. It must allow for the mistakes and false starts which all but savants and clairvoyants are certain to make now and then, and must not pose as a romantic ideal when in truth it is at best merely a social compromise. The very intelligent and conscientious Judge Lindsey[4] has about the right idea. Marriage should aim at permanence, but should not be bound to it—especially in the case of the young and the inexperienced—with superstitious rigidity. And if any shudder at the possible abuses of such a liberalised system, let him reflect that an occasionally abused system is vastly better than a system contemptuously discarded in favour of no system at all. Nothing is abuse-proof, and the true conservative would prefer to see an intelligently historic background, possibilities of family harmony, and favourable conditions for offspring, even if it did lead to occasional cases of premeditated consecutive polygamy; rather than witness the total collapse and repudiation of lawful wedlock, and the adoption of an unregulated type of companionship perilous to posterity and to the state. Under a rational regime, a very fair number of persons would — according to the laws of chance — need only one plunge in order to hit the target of a passable permanent marriage. More, perhaps, would succeed at the second plunge — having learned much of their orientation-possibilities from the first. Others, like Paul J. Campbell,[5] would ring the bell only on their third shot. And anybody that tried more than three shots would be the sort of person to experiment anyway — under any system, or outside all systems! A good way to cut down the percentages of abuse would be to make divorces for purely temperamental reasons (i.e., for reasons other than those specific and acute ones already recognised by the laws of most states) available only for couples married long enough (say two or three years) to have truly demonstrated their essential incompatibility. The one kind of divorce which sometimes strikes me as a bit fishy and premature is where the marriage date itself is only a year or less in the past. Weed these out, and there is not the least modicum of sense in denying divorce to any couple who mutually desire it — custody of offspring to be determined by the court if not decided by the joint petitioners. And alimony is a relique of obsolescent economics and a source of ridiculous extortion which ought to be laughed off the statutes in favour of a very restricted programme of financial responsibility to be applied by the court when called for in a few individual cases. Ho, hum — it's easy to be a Lycurgus on paper! Descending to the merely concrete — I've no fault to find with the institution, but think the chances of success for a strongly individualised, opinionated, and imaginative person are damn slender. It's a hundred to one shot that any four or five consecutive plunges he might make would turn out to be flivvers equally oppressive to himself and to his fellow-victim, so if he's a wise guy he "lays off" after the collapse of venture #1 . . . . . . or if he's very wise he avoids even that! Matrimony may be more or less normal, and socially essential in the abstract, and all that — but nothing in heaven or earth is so important to the man of spirit and imagination as the inviolate integrity of his cerebral life — his sense of utter integration and defiant independence as a proud, lone entity face to face with the illimitable cosmos. And if he has the general temperament that usually goes with such a mental makeup, he will not be apt to consider a haughty celibacy any great price to pay for this ethereal inviolateness. Independence, and perfect seclusion from the futile herd, are things so necessary to a certain type of mind that all other issues become subordinate when brought into comparison with them. Probably this is so with me. And yet I didn't find matrimony such a bugbear as one might imagine. With a wife of the same temperament as my mother and aunts, I would probably have been able to reconstruct a type of domestic life not unlike that of Angell St. days, even though I would have had a different status in the household hierarchy. But years brought out basic and essential diversities in reactions to the various landmarks of the time-stream, and antipodal ambitions and conceptions of value in planning a fixed joint milieu. It was the clash of the abstract-traditional-individual-retrospective-Apollonian aesthetic with the concrete-emotional-present-dwelling-social-ethical-Dionysian aesthetic; and amidst this, the originally fancied congeniality, based on a shared disillusion, philosophic bent, and sensitiveness to beauty, waged a losing struggle. It was a struggle unaccompanied by any lessening of mutual esteem or respect or appreciation, but it nevertheless meant the constant attrition and ultimate impairment of two personalities revealed by time to be antipodal in the minor overtones and deep hidden currents that count. I could not exist except in a slow-moving and historically-grounded New England backwater—and the hapless sharer of the voyage found such a prospect, complicated as it was by economic stress, nothing short of asphyxiation! Trying to exist in N.Y. drove me close to madness, and trying to think of living in Rhode Island drove the late missus equally close to despair. Each, obviously, formed an integral and inextricable part of a radically different scene and life-cycle—so the distaff side of the outfit, for whom the initiative in such matters is traditionally reserved, proffered increasingly forcible arguments in favour of a rational and amicable dissolution. Without wishing to retreat from any historic responsibility of an English gentleman, I could not for ever be deaf to such logic; hence last winter agreed to do what I could to further a liberation and a fresh start all around. Rhode Island, as a really civilised commonwealth, did its duty—so oil returns to oil and water to water! And I would, despite my profound theoretical regard for the custom of wedlock, be rather a Nilotic saurian if I used peeled onions to register my emotions at getting back to the comfortable old Rhode Island basis of contemplative independence with congenial blood-kinsfolk hovering benignly by! After all, when a guy has been a secluded and set-in-his-ways bachelor for thirty-three-and-one-half years, as I had been when I risked the plunge in 1924, the chances are that he won't take kindly to any radical domestic change. A bird as old as that is past the age of weaving new kinds of nests, and had better not try it. Be a Benedick before twenty-five or not at all, is my grandpaternal advice to conservative youth. I don't try to advise the "flaming" kind, because I don't understand 'em.

Reflections on New England

[Lovecraft also quickly came to realize how essential his New England background was to his personality and to his writing; and his return to Providence marks the end of his attempt at cosmopolitan sophistication and his increasingly profound investigation for his own New England heritage.]

[4]   As to the effect of environment on work—I forget exactly what I said in my former letter, but in any case I think an author strongly reflects his surroundings, and that he does best in founding his elements of incident and colour on a life and background to which he has a real and deep-seated relation. This may or may not be his native and childhood environment, but I think it is generally better so unless that setting be more than ordinarily devoid of vividness or dramatic possibilities. If the latter be the case, then I think the author would do well to choose a new setting with great care; keeping in mind both his own psychological tastes and requirements, and the general truth that life has more available literary values in such places as possess a visible and continuous linkage with their own sources and development, and a well-defined relation to some dominant stream of civilisation. This would really exclude any such cosmopolitan chaos as New York—which has no central identity or meaning, and no clean-cut relationship either to its own past or to anything else in particular—but of course I realise that different minds have different requirements, and that there are those who find in the intense surge of artificial life a certain stimulation which brings out what is already in them. But one ought to be warned in advance that all life in New York is purely artificial and affected—values are forced and arbitrary, mental fashions are capricious, pathological, or commercial rather than authentic, and literary activity and conversation are motivated by a shallow pose, a sophistical concealment of ignorance, and a morbidly charlatanic egotism and cheap assertiveness far removed from the solid aesthetic intensity which ought to

underlie a life of art and letters. New York has, by force of sheer wealth and glitter and advertising, captured the *reputation* of a literary capital, but it is not a true one in the sense that Boston once was. The "aesthetes" of New York are less interested in art and beauty than in themselves; and their smart badinage and discussion savour much more of psychological exhibitionism and social gesture than of actual artistic insight, vision, and devotion. It is a case of inferior people trying to be conspicuous somehow, and choosing art as a form of ballyhoo more convenient and inexpensive than business or evangelism or sword-swallowing. Of the genuine flow of life, or the sincere recording of life and dreams which is literature, I can discern scarcely a trace. Whatever of value is produced there is merely the outcropping of things elsewhere nourished—except of course in the case of those few real native New Yorkers who survive in sadness from the dead and lovely old city that was; the gracious, glamorous elder New York of dignity and poise, which lies stark and horrible and ghoul-gnawed today beneath the foul claws of the mongrel and misshapen foreign colossus that gibbers and howls vulgarly and dreamlessly on its site. If you want to know what I think of New York, read "He". I was living there when I wrote it—and I had to get out of town to the quiet colonial shades of a New Jersey village in order to put it into coherent words. No—New York is dead, and the brilliancy which so impresses one from outside is the phosphorescence of a maggoty corpse. There can be no normal American life or thought in a town full of twisted ratlike vermin from the ghetto and steerage of yesterday—a town where for block on block one can walk without seeing a single face which has any relation to the life and growth of the Nordic, Anglo-American stream of civilisation. It is not America—it is not even Europe—it is Asia and chaos and hell—the sort of stinking, amorphous hybridism which Juvenal noted in Rome when he wrote "Syrus Orontes in Tiberim defluxit."[6] I don't think America has any real literary capital today—although Chicago may tone down some day into the nearest approach to one. I've never been there, but from what I hear and from what correspondents say I believe there's at least more real artistic and intellectual vigour there than in New York. Philadelphia, too, may come back; for it has history and standards and taste and wealth, and more and more influential people will settle there as New York becomes increasingly impossible for a white man to live in. Philadelphia has the loveliest art museum and public library—not yet finished, however—in the world. Boston is passé, but despite its artistic anaemia its old traditional life flows graciously on with a degree of dignity and high level of taste and scholarship which make it an alluring place of residence. Old Beacon Hill in the sunset is yet something to behold and worship. On the whole, I think that of all large cities Boston and Philadelphia are the best to live in. In the far west I believe only San Francisco is really stimulating and aesthetically habitable. Southern California is a desert of boobs, Babbitts, and "realtors", and the Oregon and Washington regions are places of homes and commerce rather than of art. The South probably has some really good spots, but I don't know it. I found Washington delightful in a brief trip, and imagine that Baltimore, Richmond, Charleston, and New Orleans—especially the latter—all have the sort of background and historic richness to stimulate a sensitive imagination. As for me—I have found from experience that Providence is the only place where I can be content. Here I was born, and here one-half of my ancestry has had its roots for nearly three centuries. The soil and the air are in my blood and cell-structure, and I have come to recognise myself as of the type that cannot live apart from its sources and background and historic reliquiae—in a word, the essential provincial as opposed to the cosmopolitan. In Providence are all the elements which appeal most poignantly to my spirit, with its joint love of beauty and antiquity. The old town dreams on seven green hills at the head of its lovely blue bay, crowned by great domes and venerable steeples, and preserving unchanged a vast proportion of the narrow, winding hill streets, the peaked Colonial gables and gambrel roofs, the exquisitely carved classic doorways with double flights of iron-railed steps, and the stately Georgian mansions in their archaic walled gardens, which made it splendid and colourful at the time of the Revolution. Something of the stately old life lingers, too— for the residence section is on a precipitous hill which shoots up just east of the many-bridged river, and which has stemmed the creeping tide of cosmopolitan decadence. The old families and the old ideals still dominate, and there are little ways and customs on every hand which attest an unbroken evolution from colonial times, and an absolute, vital identity with the Gothic town of Roger Williams and the Georgian times of Stephen Hopkins. Every night at nine, for example, the curfew still rings from the ancient steeple (1775—finest classic steeple in the United States) of the First Baptist Church, which all my maternal ancestors attended. One comes to love all the old lanes and the old buildings—and what a wealth are still standing! The 1761 Colony House, the 1770 College Edifice, the 1773 Market House, the four old churches dating from betwixt 1775 and

1816, the exquisite private homes with dates between 1770 and 1825, the smaller wooden houses in quaint hilly or labyrinthine rows dating from 1740 onward, and the vivid, glamorous waterfront with its rotting wharves and colonial warehouses and archaic lines of gambrel roofs and dark alleys with romantic names (Doubloon, Sovereign, Guilder, Bullion, &c.) and wondrous ship-chandleries and mysterious marine boarding-houses in ancient, lamplit, cobblestoned courts—that is Old Providence, the town that gave me birth and in which I have lived all but two of my thirty-six years. I am it, and it is I[7]—separation or disentanglement is impossible. You must *surely* see it when you come East—there is a fine and direct motor-coach service to Hartford, which you will find very convenient to patronise. Of course, it does not offer any brilliant opportunities for bizarre literary conversation; for it is very staid and traditional, and its aesthetic interests (which are many, and which include a fine museum system) run to music and pictorial art rather than to literature. But I have found from experience that for me, at least, it is better to do without actual conversation and depend on correspondence than to sacrifice this picturesque linkage with my own past and America's past in order to reside 'where poets most do congregate.'[8] A good nine-tenths of my best friends reside in New York from accident or necessity, and I thought three years ago that it was the logical place for me to settle—at least for several years.[9] Accordingly I transferred my belongings thither in March 1924, and remained till April 1926, at the end of which time I found I absolutely could stand the beastly place no longer. It is true that I had the advantage of daily contact and conversation with those whom I know best and whose work lies along the same lines—Long, Morton, Kleiner, Loveman, and so on—but in spite of all this, and of the delightfully informal club which we formed to meet each week at the home of one member or another, the deadly decadence, stridor, foreignism, and combined garishness and squalor of the parvenu and backgroundless metropolis became too much for me; so that I packed up and came home to "God's country" where one can see white men on the streets and behold about one the marks of gradual national unfolding and ancient tradition. Now, of course, I do not have frequent chances for the special literary conversation I then had—but after all, that formed but a small part of life. It is more important to live—to dream and to write—than to talk, and in New York I could not live. Everything I saw became unreal and two-dimensional, and everything I thought and did became trivial and devoid of meaning through lack of any points of reference belonging to any fabric

of which I could conceivably form a part. I was stifled—poisoned—
imprisoned in a nightmare—and now not even the threat of damnation
could induce me to dwell in the accursed place again. It may be that
younger, gayer souls than I can find something endurable in Manhattan.
They are welcome to it. All I can say is that it is no place for a quiet, old-
fashioned person strongly rooted in the past, and with an imagination depending on ancient, mellow things. During my last year there I did nothing
but search out old neighbourhoods and quaint rural suburbs in an effort to
find something to nourish my soul—something like venerable New England—a drowning man's straw. To give the devil his due, New York is a
fine place to *visit*—but only to visit. Its tall buildings seen from a distance
are an exquisite picture, and its museums, bookstalls, and general facilities
are very convenient for occasional consultation. But to try to *live* there!
May Pegāna's gods preserve me!

A Torrent of Fiction

[Lovecraft's return to Providence triggered a tremendous burst of
creative energy: in six months he wrote two short novels, two novelettes,
and several short stories. In the two following extracts, he tells of writing
The Dream-Quest of Unknown Kadath (1926–27) as a kind of "practice"
novel.]

[5]   I was delighted to hear that you like the "Strange High House",[10]
for that is by all odds my own favourite among my recent yarns. The two
elements in all existence which are most fascinating to me are strangeness
and antiquity; and when I can combine the two in one tale I always feel
that the result is better than as though I had only one of them. It remains to
be seen how successful this bizarrerie can be when extended to novel
length. I am now on page 72 of my dreamland fantasy, and am very fearful
that Randolph Carter's adventures may have reached the point of palling
on the reader; or that the very plethora of weird imagery may have destroyed the power of any one image to produce the desired impression of
strangeness. This tale is one of picaresque adventure—a quest for the gods
through varied and incredible scenes and perils—and is written continuously like "Vathek" without any subdivision into chapters, though it really
contains several well-defined episodes. It will probably make about 100
pages—a small book—in all, and has very small likelihood of ever seeing
the light of day in print. I dread the task of typing it so badly that I shall not

attempt it till I have read it aloud to two or three good judges and obtained a verdict as to whether or not it is worth preserving.

[6]   As for my novel—you'll be disappointed to hear that weirdness is the thing of which it ain't got nothin' else but! It is a picaresque chronicle of impossible adventures in dreamland, and is composed under no illusion of professional acceptance. There is certainly nothing of popular or best-seller psychology in it—although, in consonance with the mood in which it was conceived, it contains more of the naive fairy-tale wonder-spirit than of actual Baudelairian decadence. Actually, it isn't much good; but forms useful practice for later and more authentic attempts in the novel form.

[Immediately after completing the *Dream-Quest,* Lovecraft commenced another short novel, *The Case of Charles Dexter Ward.* Both works, however, remained unpublished until after his death, as Lovecraft made no attempt to market them.]

[7]   ♋   ♉

Y'AI 'NG'NGAH,	OG THROD AI'F
YOG-SOTHOTH	GEB'L—EE'H
H'EI—L'GEB	*YOG-SOTHOTH*
F'AI THRODOG	'NGAH'NG AI'Y
UAAAH	ZHRO

You don't know what these twin formulae mean? Ah, you are fortunate! Dr. Willett would give every hair of his well-trimmed white beard if he could only say the same—but God! *He knows! He has seen!* It all comes out on page 112 of the tale now drawing toward its close, and which I shall call either "The Case of Charles Dexter Ward" or "The Madness out of Time". Like Midas of old, curs'd by the turning to gold of everything he touch'd, I am this year curs'd by the turning into a young novel of every story I begin. You will in all likelihood see neither this nor "The Dream-Quest of Unknown Kadath" till you come hither in your new shiny Essex, for the typing of manuscripts of this length is utterly beyond the powers of a feeble old gentleman who loses interest in a tale the moment he completes it.

[8]   I have just finished one new tale which I'll send you in my next. This one has little flashes of the quasi-poetic, but is for the most part real-

istic; with a homely country setting "west of Arkham". Something falls from the sky, and terror broods. The thing is told by an old man forty years after, and the title is "The Colour Out of Space". It is a long-short affair — exactly as long as "Cthulhu".

[After his great burst of writing in 1926–27, Lovecraft became literarily quiescent. Finally, in the summer of 1928, a new work emerged.]

[9]   I have managed to snatch the time to write one new tale — which is now in Dwyer's possession and which I shall ask him to forward to you for ultimate return to me. It covers 48 pages, so that Wright would probably classify it as a "novelette". I haven't yet submitted it to him. The title is "The Dunwich Horror", and it belongs to the Arkham cycle. The Necronomicon[11] figures in it to some extent. Heaven only knows when I'll get the time to write another, for revision has struck me with full force again.

[In late 1927 Farnsworth Wright of *Weird Tales* began negotiations with Lovecraft about a book of his stories. Lovecraft wrote the following letter giving his preferences for the makeup of the volume; but the book never appeared, as a previous book published by *Weird Tales* sold very poorly and the depression made further thoughts of book publications by the magazine untenable.]

[10]   As to that problematical volume of my tales — I'm really not very particular about the contents, since of course it would have to be formulated with the *Weird Tales* clientele in view and couldn't represent any real choice of mine. However, it appears to me that a certain group of tales can be considered as definitely better than the rest from both popular and artistic points of view; and I will here record their names as I conceive them — together with my rough estimates of their length in words:

"Outsider"	2500
"Arthur Jermyn"	3500

("White Ape") — that title concocted by Baird, gives
me acute cervical agony. The original title is "Facts
concerning the Late Arthur Jermyn and His Family"
— but I think plain Arthur Jermyn is the best.

"Rats in Walls"	7500
"Picture in House"	3000
"Pickman's Model"	5500
"Erich Zann"	4000
"Dagon"	2000
"Randolph Carter"	3000
"Cats of Ulthar"	1400
	————
	32400

Here, then, is what I call the *indispensable* nucleus of any book purporting to represent the popular side of my fiction. I omit all things of any length—"Cthulhu", "Red Hook", etc.—because only one long tale can be included in a volume of this length. As for a *title*—my choice is "The Outsider and Other Stories". This is because I consider the touch of cosmic *outsideness*—of dim, shadowy non-terrestrial hints—to be the characteristic feature of my writing.

Thus we have 32,400 words accounted for. I would advise piecing out with one of the longish (10,000-word) tales and as many more shorter ones as are needed to fill the space you have in mind. Of my longer tales—exclusive of the two novelettes never typed or seen by anyone but Wandrei—I think the following classification in order of merit is possible:

1. "The Colour Out of Space"
2. "Cthulhu"
3. "Red Hook"

"The Shunned House" won't be available, since Cook wants to print that as a thin book uniform with Belknap's poems.[12] Incidentally—I have my doubts about the *popular* appeal of "The Colour". I advise choice of "Cthulhu", for in spite of what Belknap says and what the British anthologist chose, I think "Red Hook" is comparatively poor. Another alternative, though, is that thunderously melodramatic thing which I let Houtain publish in his nauseous *Home Brew* (ugh!) five years ago—"The Lurking Fear"—which of course I have the right to use again in a book. It is poor art, because it was written to order with certain limitations, but it ought to please the followers of Nictzin Dyalhis and his congeners.[13] I'll enclose a manuscript of it—which please return if you don't care for it.

Now as to shorter "fillers" to round out your 45 or 6 thousand words —
(32400 plus 10000 = 42400; 46000–42400 = 3600) = here are my suggestions:

"Festival"	3000
"Unnamable"	2500
"Terrible Old Man"	1400

These can be juggled around as you like, since the *exact* size of the
volume is not a fixed quantity. Incidentally, by the way — that 32400-word
essential nucleus is only my own estimate. I'm perfectly agreeable to any
changes in that which you may choose to make. Cut out anything you
fancy would decrease the book's profit, and insert anything you think
would increase it. If you want a touch of my other and more fantastic style,
try "The White Ship".

[Although Lovecraft was not writing much original fiction in 1928–29, he
was involved in revising or ghostwriting horror tales for clients. One of
the most persistent was Zealia Brown (Reed) Bishop, for whom Lovecraft wrote several substantial works that are tantamount to original stories of his own.]

[11]   By the way — if you want to see a new story which is practically
mine, read "The Curse of Yig" in the current W.T.[14] Mrs. Reed is a client
for whom Long and I have done oceans of work, and this story is about
75% mine. All I had to work on was a synopsis describing a couple of pio-
neers in a cabin with a nest of rattlesnakes beneath, the killing of the hus-
band by snakes, but bursting of the corpse, and the madness of the wife,
who was an eye-witness to the horror. There was no plot or motivation —
no prologue or aftermath to the incident — so that one might say the story,
as a story, is wholly my own. I invented the snake-god and the curse, the
tragic wielding of the axe by the wife, the matter of the snake-victim's identity, and the asylum epilogue. Also, I worked up the geographic and other
incidental colour — getting some date from the alleged authoress, who
knows Oklahoma, but more from books. As it stands, the tale isn't bad
according to W.T. standards; though of course it is absurdly *mechanical* and
artificial. I have no regrets at not being the avowed author. I got $20.00 for
the job, and Wright paid Mrs. Reed $45.00 for the completed MS.

[12] Yes—I hope to get at some more *signed* original fiction within a month. I say "signed", because the "revision" job I'm doing now is the composition of an original tale from a single paragraph of locale and subject orders—not even a plot germ. The only reason I do this kind of thing is that the pay is absolutely certain, whereas on signed original work one has to take one's chances of acceptance or rejection. I'll point out any tales which are unacknowledgedly mine, either wholly or in part, when or if they appear in print. My present job is a Reed yarn to be entitled "The Mound"—with the Oklahoma locale of "Yig," but with ramifications extending to blasphemously elder worlds, and a race of beings that came down from the stars with great Cthulhu. I also bring in a Spaniard who deserted from Coronado's party in 1541.[15] This job—and the two De Castro jobs preceding it[16]—will tend to limber up my fictional pen for the spontaneous effusions to follow!

[13] Tsathoggua made such an impression on my fancy that I am using him in the "revision" (i.e., "ghost-writing") job I am now doing—telling of some things connected with his worship before he appeared on the earth's *surface.* As you know my tale concerns a nether world of unbelievable antiquity below the mound-and-pueblo region of the American southwest, and the visit thereto in 1541–45 by one of Coronado's men—Panfilio de Zamacona y Nuñez. It is a place litten by a blue radiance due to magnetic force and radio-activity, and is peopled by the primal proto-humans brought down from the stars by Great Cthulhu—a forgotten, decadent race who cut themselves off from the upper world when Atlantis and Lemuria sank. *But there was a race of beings in the earth infinitely older than they*—the saurian quadrupeds of the red-litten caverns of Yoth which yawn underneath the blue-litten caverns of K'n-yan. When the first men came to K'n-yan they found the archaeological reliques of Yoth, and speculated curiously upon them. At the point where I introduce our friend Tsathoggua, the Spanish explorer has entered K'n-yan, has encountered a party of friendly natives led by one Gll'-Hthaa-Ynn, and is being escorted to the great city of Tsath—mounted on a monstrous horned and half-human quadruped.

[Unexpectedly, Lovecraft's poetic inspiration returned at the very end of 1929, and in a single week (December 27–January 4) he produced most of the thirty-six sonnets of the cycle *Fungi from Yuggoth*, generally considered his finest poetic work.]

[14]   Oh—here are my Yuggothian Fungi, to be returned at leisure. Nothing notable about them—but they at least embody certain moods and images. Some of the themes are really more adapted to fiction—so that I shall probably make stories of them whenever I get that constantly-deferred creative opportunity I am always hoping for. You will see something of my scenic or landscape-architectural tendency in these verses—especially suggestions of unplaceable or half-forgotten scenes. These vague, elusive pseudo-memories have haunted me ever since I was an infant, and are quite a typical ingredient of my psychology and aesthetic attitude.

[As both Lovecraft and some of his colleagues began to cite his invented pseudomythology in different stories, readers of *Weird Tales* began to wonder whether a real body of myth was being cited. Even the writer Robert E. Howard, having recently come into correspondence with Lovecraft, was curious about the matter.]

[15]   Regarding the solemnly cited myth-cycle of Cthulhu, Yog Sothoth, R'lyeh, Nyarlathotep, Nug, Yeb, Shub-Niggurath, etc., etc.—let me confess that this is all a synthetic concoction of my own, like the populous and varied pantheon of Lord Dunsany's "Pegāna". The reason for its echoes in Dr. de Castro's work is that the latter gentleman is a revision-client of mine—into whose tales I have stuck these glancing references for sheer fun. If any other clients of mine get work placed in W.T., you will perhaps find a still-wider spread of the cult of Azathoth, Cthulhu, and the Great Old Ones! The Necronomicon of the mad Arab Abdul Alhazred is likewise something which must yet be written in order to possess objective reality. Abdul is a favourite dream-character of mine—indeed that is what I used to call myself when I was five years old and a transported devotee of Andrew Lang's version of the Arabian Nights. A few years ago I prepared a mock-erudite synopsis of Abdul's life, and of the posthumous vicissitudes and translations of his hideous and unmentionable work *Al Azif* (called Tò Νεκρονόμικον by the Byzantine Monk Theodoras Philetas, who translated it into late Greek in A.D. 900!)—a synopsis which I shall follow in future references to the dark and accursed thing. Long has alluded to the Necronomicon in some things of his—in fact, I think it is rather good fun to have this artificial mythology given an air of verisimilitude by wide citation. I ought, though, to write Mr. O'Neail and disabuse him of the idea that there is a large blind spot in his mythological erudition![17] Clark

Ashton Smith is launching another mock mythology revolving around the black, furry toad-god *Tsathoggua,* whose name had variant forms amongst the Atlanteans, Lemurians, and Hyperboreans who worshipped him after he emerged from inner Earth (whither he came from Outer Space, with Saturn as a stepping-stone). I am using Tsathoggua in several tales of my own and of revision-clients—although Wright rejected the Smith tale in which he originally appeared.[18] It would be amusing to identify your Kathulos with my Cthulhu—indeed, I may so adopt him in some future black allusion.

[16]   In my unfinished "Whisperer in Darkness" I have the idea of trans-planted brains kept in metal cylinders for interplanetary transportation, and connected with sensory and speaking machines when arrived at their destinations. Thus a person becomes like a phonograph record—his intel-ligence easily transportable, and at once available for perception and ex-pression wherever apparatus of the standardised type exists. The race of things employing this method come from Outside, but they have an out-post in this solar system on the new 9th planet[19]—called by them Yug-goth—and a smaller and nearer outpost amidst the hills of Vermont. I must whip this yarn into final shape soon. The effect of striking scenery on one's creative concentration is evidently a highly variable thing. I have heard many refer to it—as you do—as a distraction, but in my case it seems to be precisely the opposite. Outdoor settings and impressive panoramas excite and awaken my faculties, so that I can do things twice as well in the woods and fields as in my study.

Theories of Literature and the Weird

[In the course of the 1920s Lovecraft developed a compelling theory of weird fiction, especially of the type of weird fiction he himself was writ-ing. This theory focused on the notion of "cosmicism"—the vastness of space and time and the resultant inconsequence of human beings—and is typical of much of Lovecraft's late work. Its most compact expression is in a letter to Farnsworth Wright of *Weird Tales,* who had asked to see "The Call of Cthulhu" in the summer of 1927, several months after he had ini-tially rejected it.]

[17]   In accordance with your suggestion I am re-submitting "The Call of Cthulhu", though possibly you will still think it a trifle too bizarre for a

clientele who demand their weirdness in name only, and who like to keep both feet pretty solidly on the ground of the known and the familiar. As I said some time ago, I doubt if my work—and especially my later products—would "go" very well with the sort of readers whose reactions are represented in the "Eyrie".[20] The general trend of the yarns which seem to suit the public is that of essential normality of outlook and simplicity of point of view—with thoroughly conventional human values and motives predominating, and with brisk action of the best-seller type as an indispensable attribute. The weird element in such material does not extend far into the fabric—it is the artificial weirdness of the fireside tale and the Victorian ghost story, and remains external camouflage even in the seemingly wildest of the "interplanetary" concoctions. You can see this sort of thing at its best in Seabury Quinn,[21] and at its worst in the general run of contributors. It is exactly what the majority want—for if they were to see a really weird tale they wouldn't know what it's all about. This is quite obvious from the way they object to the *reprints,* which in many cases have brought them the genuine article.

Now all my tales are based on the fundamental premise that common human laws and interests and emotions have no validity or significance in the vast cosmos-at-large. To me there is nothing but puerility in a tale in which the human form—and the local human passions and conditions and standards—are depicted as native to other worlds or other universes. To achieve the essence of real externality, whether of time or space or dimension, one must forget that such things as organic life, good and evil, love and hate, and all such local attributes of a negligible and temporary race called mankind, have any existence at all. Only the human scenes and characters must have human qualities. *These* must be handled with unsparing *realism,* (*not* catch-penny *romanticism*) but when we cross the line to the boundless and hideous unknown—the shadow-haunted *Outside*—we must remember to leave our humanity—and terrestrialism at the threshold.

So much for theory. In practice, I presume that few commonplace readers would have any use for a story written on these psychological principles. They want their conventional best-seller values and motives kept paramount throughout the abysses of apocalyptic vision and extra-Einsteinian chaos, and would not deem an "interplanetary" tale in the least interesting if it did not have its Martian (or Jovian or Venerian or Saturnian) heroine fall in love with the young voyager from Earth, and thereby incur the jealousy of the inevitable Prince Kongros (or Zeelar or Hoshgosh or Norkog) who at once proceeds to usurp the throne etc.; or if it did not have its Martian (or etc.) nomenclature follow a closely terrestrial pattern, with an Indo-Germanic *'—a'* name for the Princess, and something disagreeable and Semitic for the villain.[22] Now I couldn't grind out that sort of junk if my life depended on it. If I were writing an "interplanetary" tale it would deal with beings organised very differently from mundane mammalia, and obeying motives wholly alien to anything we know upon Earth —the exact degree of alienage depending, of course, on the scene of the tale; whether laid in the solar system, the visible galactic universe outside the solar system, or the *utterly unplumbed* gulfs still farther out—nameless vortices of never-dreamed-of strangeness, where form and symmetry, light and heat, even matter and energy themselves, may be unthinkably metamorphosed or totally wanting. I have merely got at the edge of this in "Cthulhu", where I have been careful to avoid terrestrialism in the few linguistic and nomenclatural specimens from Outside which I present. All very well—but will the readers stand for it? That's all they're likely to get from me in the future—except when I deal with definitely terrestrial scenes—and I am the last one to urge the acceptance of material of doubtful value to the magazine's particular purpose. Even when I deal with the mundanely weird, moreover, I shan't be likely to stress the popular artificial values and emotions of cheap fiction.

[Further reflections on weird fiction, as well as more general remarks on literature as a whole, are found in a 1930 letter to fellow fantaisiste Clark Ashton Smith.]

[18]   The more I consider weird fiction, the more I am convinced that a solidly realistic framework is needed in order to build up a preparation for the unreal element. The one supreme defect of cheap weird fiction is an absurd taking-for-granted of fantastic prodigies, and a sketchy delineation of such things before any background of convincingness is laid down. When a story fails to emphasise, by contrast with reality, the utter strangeness and abnormality of the wonders it depicts, it likewise fails to make those wonders seem like anything more than aimless puerility. Only normal things can be convincingly related in a casual way. Whatever an abnormal thing may be, its foremost quality must always be that of abnormality itself; so that in delineating it one must put prime stress on its departure from the natural order, and see that the characters of the narrative react to it with

adequate emotions. My own rule is that no weird story can truly produce terror unless it is devised with all the care and verisimilitude of an actual *hoax*. The author must forget all about "short story technique", and build up a stark, simple account, full of homely corroborative details, just as if he were actually trying to "put across" a deception in real life—a deception clever enough to make adults believe it. My own attitude in writing is always that of the hoax-weaver. One part of my mind tries to concoct something realistic and coherent enough to fool the rest of my mind and make me swallow the marvel as the late Camille Flammarion[23] used to swallow the ghost and revenant yarns unloaded on him by fakers and neurotics. For the time being I try to forget formal literature, and simply devise a lie as carefully as a crooked witness prepares a line of testimony with cross-examining lawyers in his mind. I take the place of the lawyers now and then—finding motivations with a greater care for probability. Not that I succeed especially well, but that I think I have the basic method calculated to give maximum results if expertly used. This ideal became a conscious one with me about the "Cthulhu" period, and is perhaps best exemplified in "The Colour Out of Space". Its general principle would not have to be suspended even in dream-like narrations of the "Randolph Carter" and "Erich Zann" type—a type to which I may return now and then in future— though it does of course vanish in phantasy of the Dunsanian or "White Ship" order. I think I mentioned in a P.S. that Wright has just accepted "The Whisperer" for $350.00, to use as a 2-part serial in the June and July issues.[24] This quick landing certainly pleases me mightily, and encourages me to cut down revision long enough to grind out a whole series of tales as I used to do in 1919 and 1920. Of such a batch, only about ¼ would be likely to land—yet the price of original work is so much higher than that of revision, that I might even at worst make as much as revision now brings. At any rate, an attempt will do no harm. I agree that very short pieces seem to lack effect—indeed, I seem less and less able to find anything which will go into a compact space. Every tale I tackle nowadays seems to spin itself out beyond all ordinary short story limits, nor can I find any way to make excision without ruining the whole thing. I think a novel must be much easier to write than a good short story. [. . .]

As for literary values in general—while my personal taste and interests coincide precisely with your own, I am not disposed to make any generalisations therefrom. The basic essence of art is too subtle and elusive to be defined hastily, and I have a strong objective conviction that realism can be very great art. Not that the mere photographic reproduction of unselected detail is real art. On the other hand, such a thing is *pure science*—psychology or anthropology. But I think that there is a profound aesthetic value in realism so developed as to give the reader a sense of the underlying rhythms of things—a realism which hints at longer streams of essence and vaster marches of pageantry than the span and substance of the outward events, and in which detail serves either to indicate basic trends or to enhance the convincing life-likeness of the foreground. Such a realism must be accurate in its depiction of life and motivations, and must be detailed enough to give a sense of actual substance to the outward events shewn, else it will not have enough contact with any deep sense of truth to form the unifying or liberating influence desired. No avenue can lead us away from the immediate to the remote or the shadowy or the universal unless it really does begin at the immediate—and not at any false, cheap, or conventional conception of the immediate. Now I am not saying that all realists succeed in leading away from the immediate toward anything else. There are futile exponents of every school of art. Nor do I claim to enjoy *personally* such master-realists as concern themselves wholly with the human scene and personality. Candidly, such masters (Dreiser, de Maupassant, Anderson, etc.) bore me acutely after brief doses—but at this point I pause to question my own authority to form snap judgments. Upon impersonal analysis, I come to conclude that this realism is actually sound and sometimes great art; and that my lack of fondness for it is due to a blind spot in my own makeup—like that which makes me a poor judge of music, or that which made Hawthorne almost devoid of architectural appreciation. I'll never be a Dreiser fan like Vrest Orton,[25] but just the same I think Dreiser is the greatest novelist America has yet produced. The *one* form of literary appeal which I consider *absolutely unsound, charlatanic, and valueless*—frivolous, insincere, irrelevant, and meaningless—is that mode of handling human events and values and motivations known as *romanticism*. Dumas, Scott, Stevenson—my gawd! Here is sheer puerility—the concoction of false glamours and enthusiasms and events out of an addled and distorted background which has no relation to anything in the genuine thoughts, feelings, and experiences of evolved and adult mankind. Its very essence is that one unforgivable disparity which forms the supreme crux of all cheapness and commonness—the investing of things and events with wholly disproportioned and inappropriate emotions. Heroic tales are not unsound so long as they adhere to the actual essentials of life and the human spirit; but when some sentimental poseur adopts their tone for artificial and trivial unrealities, the result is too nauseating and wearisome for words. As against romanticism I am solidly a realist—even though realising the dangerously narrow margin separating romanticism from certain acceptable forms of phantasy. My conception of phantasy, as a genuine art-form, is *an extension rather than a negation of reality.* Ordinary tales about a castle ghost or old-fashioned werewolf are merely so much junk. The true function of phantasy is to give the imagination a ground for limitless expansion, and to satisfy aesthetically the sincere and burning curiosity and sense of awe which a sensitive minority of mankind feel toward the alluring and provocative abysses of unplumbed space and unguessed entity which press in upon the known world from unknown infinities and in unknown relationships of time, space, matter, force, dimensionality, and consciousness. This curiosity and sense of awe, I believe, are quite basic amongst the sensitive minority in question; and I see no reason to think that they will decline in the future—for as you point out, the frontier of the unknown can never do more than scratch the surface of eternally unknowable infinity. But the truly sensitive will never be more than a minority, because most persons—even those of the keenest possible intellect and aesthetic ability—simply have not the psychological equipment or adjustment to feel that way. I have taken some pains to sound various persons as to their capacity to feel profoundly regarding the cosmos and the disturbing and fascinating quality of the extra-terrestrial and perpetually unknown; and my results reveal a surprisingly small quota. In literature we can easily see the cosmic quality in Poe, Maturin, Dunsany, de la Mare, and Blackwood, but I profoundly suspect the cosmicism of Bierce, James, and even Machen. It is not every macabre writer who feels poignantly and almost intolerably the pressure of cryptic and unbounded outer space.

Further Philosophical Ruminations

[One of Lovecraft's greatest philosophical triumphs of the later 1920s was the adaptation of his materialist thought to the radical findings of Einstein, Planck, and others. In contrast to other contemporary thinkers, who saw in these new discoveries an excuse to return to outmoded spiritual and religious views, Lovecraft took them in stride and evolved a philosophy of modified materialism similar to that of the two thinkers he came to admire at this time, Bertrand Russell and George Santayana.]

[19]   The actual cosmos of pattern'd energy, including what we know as matter, is of a contour and nature absolutely impossible of realisation by the human brain; and the more we learn of it the more we perceive this circumstance. All we can say of it, is that it contains no visible central principle so like the physical brains of terrestrial mammals that we may reasonably attribute to it the purely terrestrial and biological phaenomenon call'd *conscious purpose;* and that we form, even allowing for the most radical conceptions of the relativist, so insignificant and temporary a part of it (whether all space be infinite or curved, and transgalactic distances constant or variable, we know that within the bounds of our stellar universe no relativistic circumstance can banish the approximate dimensions we recognise. The relative place of our solar system among the stars is as much a proximate reality as the relative positions of Providence, N.Y., and Chicago) that all notions of special relationships and names and destinies expressed in human conduct must necessarily be vestigial myths. Moreover, we know that a cosmos which is eternal (and any other kind would be a paradoxical impossibility) can have no such thing as a permanent direction or goal; since such would imply a beginning and ending, thus postulating a larger creating and managing cosmos outside this one—and so on ad infinitum like a nest of Chinese boxes. This point remains the same whether we consider eternity as a measure of regular pattern-movements (time) or as a fourth dimension. The latter merely makes all these intimations of a cosmos which our senses and calculations present to us. We must admit at the outset that the spectacle gives us no indications of a central consciousness or purpose, and suggests no reason why a cosmos should possess such; that it renders the notion of special human standards and destinies absurd; and that it makes the idea of a permanent direction or goal improbable to the point of impossibility. *Theoretically* it *can* be almost anything—but when we have not the faintest shadow of reason for believing certain specific things exactly contrary to all the principles of probability and experience in our limited part of space, it becomes a piece of hallucination or affectation to try to believe such things. Here are we—and yonder yawns the universe. If there be indeed any central governor, any set of standards, or any final goal, we can never hope to get even the faintest inkling of any of these things; since the ultimate reality of space is clearly a complex churning of energy of which the human mind can never form any even approximate picture, and which can touch us only through the veil of local apparent manifestations which we call the visible and material uni-

verse. So far as analogy and probability go, there is strong presumptive evidence on the negative side — evidence based on the observation of small material systems like the electrons of an atom or the planets circling the sun. This evidence tells us that all small units of mass-energy are (that is, all humanly visible and conceivable presentations of such units are) rotating systems organised in a certain way and preserving a balance and dovetailing of functions, absolute regularity and the exclusion of chance, (and hence of volition or conscious action) and the infinite uniformity of this system of interlocking rotations and forms of regularity, seem to confront us wherever we delve beneath the surface; so that these circumstances actually form the sum total of all our knowledge of the composition and administration of infinity. To say that such an array of evidence suggests a central will, a one-way direction, and a special concern for any one of the infinitesimal temporary force-combinations which form incidents of the eternal cycles within cycles of constant rearrangement, is to utter simple and unadulterated damn foolishness. It is like saying that the descent of the thermometer on the 7th of January suggests a hot summer day on the morrow. It is simply self-hallucination to which no sane adult need feel obliged to listen without laughing. And there is scarcely less idiocy in the pitiful whine of the modern supernatural-dupe, that the discovery of the identity of matter and energy breaks down 18th century materialism and reopens the way for mystical myth-making. Nothing could be more contrary to fact. The collapse of cosmic dimensions supplies no iota of evidence or suggestion either for or against materialistic reason, whilst the elimination of matter as a separate entity is simply a step *toward the unification of all being and the consequent destruction of the myth of worker separate from work or goal separate from present position.* What these feeble-minded theists are howling about as a sudden victory for themselves is *really the materialist's trump card.* The poor fools think they have beaten him because they have seen the disappearance of that for which his *name* stood. It is characteristic of a tribe who have always dealt in words and myths alone to fancy their opponent is bound to the externals of an empty *word. Matter* indeed has been shewn to be a passing phase of *energy* — or the raw stuff of sheer entity as envisaged from our terrestrial and physical observation-point — *but what is this save a perfect confirmation of the basic essentials of Haeckelian monism?* Thus the *materialist,* now using that title in an historical sense only, emerges strengthened in his position as *an atheistical (or agnostic) monist.* He has sounded space a little deeper and found what he always finds on further penetration —

simply *a profounder disintegration, and a profounder mechanistic impersonality.*
Hitherto he has felt forced to *describe* entity somewhat; now he feels more
and more able to swear to the absence of any purposeful *riddle* in creation,
and to sum up all there is of cosmic existence and apparent purpose in one
final sentence—*entity is, always has been, and always will be.* Of its detailed design and minute operative secrets he will never know. Of his relation to it
he may guess very shrewdly *because his extreme insignificance makes him so
small a part even of the infinitesimal fraction of infinity he can envisage.* He
knows he is minute and temporary, because the local laws of his immediate
milieu and mode of entity can be *tested conclusively for their small positive radius;* and in consonance with their unfailing applicability to time and space
units which *even for human perception are small,* (that is, the earth's seasons,
effect of heat and cold on organic life, etc.) can be extended over a slightly
larger area in which the same conditions hold good (that is, the galactic
universe, and time-reaches involving the birth and death of suns) and in
which they shew with *absolute* accuracy the very brief span capable of
being occupied by the history of terrestrial life past and present. Here is
where the theist makes an ass of himself trying to catch the atheist by using
the jargon of relativity. He tries to erase all our physical knowledge by
pointing to the subjective nature of our relation to infinite time and
space—forgetting that *the history of terrestrial life is not being reckoned against
the background of infinity.* He is knocking over, for the purpose of crowing
over a fake victory, a man of straw which he himself has set up. Nobody is
trying to envisage infinity, for it very clearly can't be done. The atheist is
merely shewing that man cannot reasonably occupy any considerable
place in the scheme of things—relative or otherwise—and he is doing it *by
working outward from the physically known.* He doesn't have to get mixed up in
the impossible problem of what relation the apparent universe has to infinite reality, because his business is all within a small fraction of the apparent universe. *He aims to show that, no matter what the visible universe is or what
mankind is, mankind is only a transient incident in any one part of the visible universe.* Note that he is not risking any confusion of terms. He is working with
like quantities. He doesn't seek to learn the relation of either man or the visible universe to infinity, but simply to learn the relation of the apparent
entity man to the apparent entity called the visible universe. Only indirectly does this give him a hint of anything larger—the hint being that if
man can be proved temporary and insignificant *in his universe,* he cannot
very well be otherwise in infinity! As for the mode of proof—it is simply to

apply the local laws whose infallible working *on earth* prove them *absolutely correct for that part of space immediately around us.* We know these laws work here, because we have applied them in countless ways and have *never* found them to fail. Birth and death, heat and cold, weight and pulley, acid and alkali. Our whole life and civilisation and engineering are a proof of the *perfect certainty and dependability* of these laws. Now the line between earth and sky is only an arbitrary one—which aeroplanes are indeed pushing outward every day—and the application of suitable optical devices to the sky proves that for many trillion and quadrillion miles outward from us the conditions of space are sufficiently like our own to be comparatively unaffected by relativity. That is, these surrounding stellar regions may be taken as part of our illusion-island in infinity, since the laws that work on earth work scarcely less well some distance beyond it. Despite *minor* illusions caused by unknown factors in light transmission, it can be checked up, tested, and *proved* by the parallel application of *different* mensurational methods that the region of nearer stars is, practically speaking, *as much what it seems to us as the surface of the earth is.*

Don't let the Einstein-twisters catch you here! It may be illusion all right, but it's the same batch of illusion which makes you think New York exists and that you move when you walk. Distances among the planets and nearer stars are, allowing for all possible variations, constant enough to make our picture of them as roughly true as our picture of the distances among the various cities of America. You can no more conceive of a vastly varied distance between Sirius and the sun as a result of place and motion, than you can conceive of a practically varied distance between your house and honest old Mac's joint as a result of the direction and speed of the Interborough train you're riding in. The given area *isn't big enough* to let relativity get in its major effects—*hence we can rely on the never-failing laws of earth to give absolutely reliable results in the nearer heavens.* There's no getting around this. If we can study the relation of a race of ants to a coral atoll or a volcanic islet which has risen and will sink again—and nobody dares deny that we can—then it will be *equally possible* for us, if we have suitable instruments and methods, to study the relation of man and the earth to the solar system and the nearer stars. The result will, when obtained, be just as conclusive as that of a study in terrestrial zoölogy or geology. The radius is too small to give relativity or mysticism a chance. The universe may be a dream, but it cannot be considered a *human* dream if we can shew that it must antedate and outlast all human dreamers just as surely as an ocean must antedate and outlast the denizens of one of his alternately rising and submerging volcanic islands. The laws that work on earth work in the nearer sky; and if we can trace man's beginning and finish, we can say *absolutely* (a) that what corresponds to our universe is *not humanly subjective in essence,* (although our sensory picture of it is wholly so) and (b) that man and organic life, or at least man and organic life on this globe (or any like it, if we find the law of temporary worlds common to the visible universe), cannot be a central concern of infinity. This positively obtainable knowledge will knock the bottom out of any ideas of cosmic human destiny save those based on the self-evident insanity of immortality and spiritualism. Now what do find? Well—read what Harlow Shapley, A. S. Eddington, J. H. Jeans, or any contemporary astrophysicist has to say. We find a cycle of constantly shifting energy, marked by the birth of nebulae from stars, the condensation of nebulae into stars, the loss of energy as radiant heat and the radio-active breakdown of matter into energy, and the possible (cf. Millikan's "cosmic ray") building up of matter from free energy. Outstanding are the facts that *all stars are temporary in the long run,* that the birth of planets from them is comparatively rare, (induced by tidal action of other stars that pass by them under rare conditions) and that life on a planet can hardly survive the death of the star whose radiations made it possible in the first place. All this belongs to *positive physical knowledge*—as positive as the knowledge that an inkstand will fall if you drop it from the window to the ground, or that a rat will die if you keep it under water fifteen minutes.

It took a long time to work up to this simple statement—just as the mountain in labour took a long time to bring forth a mouse—but the primer stuff was necessary as a counteractive to the popular theological misuse of relativity. The point is, that we *know* organic life to be a rare, short, and negligible phenomenon. *Know* it beyond the reach of any trick metaphysics. If the cosmos be a momentary illusion, *then mankind is a still briefer one!*

One word on the silly attempt of spiritualists to argue that the non-solid and non-separate nature of matter, as newly proved, indicates the reality of their mythical "soul matter" or "ectoplasm", and makes immortality any less absurd a notion than it was before. Here, as in the case of their comment on the word materialist, they are merely evading facts in a cheap game of verbalism. Matter, we learn, is a definite phenomenon instituted by certain modifications of energy; *but does this cirumstance make it less dis-*

tinctive in itself, or permit us to imagine the presence of another kind of modified energy in places where no sign or result of energy can be discovered? It is to laugh! The truth is, that the discovery of matter's identity with energy — and of its consequent lack of vital intrinsic difference from empty space — is *an absolute coup de grace to the primitive and irresponsible myth of "spirit". For matter, it appears, really is exactly what "spirit" was always supposed to be.* Thus it is proved *that wandering energy always has a detectable form* — that if it doesn't take the form of waves or electron-streams, *it becomes matter itself;* and that the absence of matter or any other detectable energy-form indicates *not the presence of spirit, but the absence of anything whatever.* The new discovery *doesn't abolish matter,* or make it any closer to the occult world than it's ever been. If any mystic thinks that matter has lost its known properties because it's been found made of invisible energy, just let him read Einstein and try to apply his new conception by butting his head into a stone wall. He will quickly discover that matter is still the same old stuff, and that knowing more about it doesn't have much effect on its disconcerting solidity. It may be made up of something which is itself non-solid and non-material, just as heavy, harmless water is made up of airy, intoxicating oxygen and ethereal, explosive, and inflammable hydrogen — but it's pretty damn definite on its own hook, and there's no more use comparing it to thin mythical ectoplasm than there is in trying to breathe water for oxygen or burn water for hydrogen. The hard fact of the whole business is — and this is what the mystics close their eyes to — that *matter is a definite condition involving fixed and certain laws; the laws being known and invariable, applicable to no other phenomenon, and having nothing so do with any other hypothetical relationship between an invisible entity and actual effects.* We've known the laws of matter for a long time — does a new explanation of them enlarge their field of application? Because we have found that the body of a human being is composed of certain energy-streams which gradually undergo transformations (though retaining the form of matter in various decomposition-products) after the withdrawal of the chemical and physical process called life, are we any more justified in believing that these demonstrable streams are during life accompanied by another set which gives no evidence of its presence, and which at the cessation of the life-reactions retains its specialised grouping, contrary to all laws of energy, and at a time when even the solid streams of matter-energy — whose existence is really capable of proof — are unable to retain a similar grouping? Passing over for the moment the utterly puerile unjustifiedness of such a supposition in the first place, let us consider the only sane analogy the mystic could possibly draw—that is, the analogy of the bony shell or skeleton, which remains undestroyed and undissociated after the death of the organism. This ought not to stand up a moment when we consider *what it is* that spiritualists claim as surviving. That surviving element, they say, is *the personality*—a particularly unfortunate choice in view of the fact that we happen to know just what bodily parts involve the personality; modifying and guiding it in health, and unerringly impairing their respective sections of it when they are themselves injured. If we were really anxious for tangible suggestions that the dead still live, we would believe that they survive in the indestructible parts of their bodies, and would pray to and converse with their dried bones—as indeed many primitive peoples do. Or we would mummify their whole corpses—as indeed do many somewhat less primitive peoples. Either of these courses would be less flagrantly ridiculous than inventing out of whole cloth the notion of an airy near-matter which hovers around the real matter and acquires and retains complex configurations which we know are produced only through long aeons of evolution in the one specific substance known as the protoplasmic form of energy-acting-as-matter. Personality, we know, is a mode of motion in the neural tissue of highly evolved vertebrate animals; centreing in the brain and spine, and governed largely by glandular hormones conveyed by the blood. It suffers when its material medium suffers, and visibly changes as that medium alters with age. It has no demonstrable existence—and there is every reason why it couldn't have—after the cessation of the life-reactions in the matter on which it depends; nor could we conceive of it rationally as anything apart from the complex and slowly evolved biological mechanism which typifies so well its own rarity, delicacy, and subtlety, and complexity. And yet there are adults at large who associate his involvedly physiological-mechanical peak of bodily development with the thin air of a loosely unorganised ghost-substance which never gave any evidence of existence—and who perversely fancy that the existence of such a mythical spook-gas is less absurdly unlikely because matter itself—with all its certain evidences of existence—has been found to have a basis in phenomena not themselves solid or ponderable. Surely a triumph of fallacy and inverse reasoning! It is no more sensible to assume that personality exists and survives as a shadow beside the material human body, than to assume that every manifestation of matter has a parallel shadow of more tenuous substance to accompany and survive it.

[Lovecraft remained fully convinced that an omnipotent deity, an afterlife, and other religious conceptions were still highly unlikely, and that the new developments in astrophysics did not affect their fundamental improbability.]

[20]   We are bidden to accept, as the one paradoxical *certainty* of experience, the fact that we can never have any other ultimate certainty. All conclusions for an infinite time to come, barring wholly unexpected data, must be regarded as no more than *competitive probabilities*. So far as *actual knowledge* is concerned, the theistic myths of tradition are as *absolutely and finally dethroned from all pretension to authority* as are any of the earlier conclusions of science. Ancient tradition and earlier science must alike resign all *former* claims to truth which they may ever have put forward. They, together with every other possible attempt to explain the cosmos, now stand on a basis of *complete and fundamental equality* so far as their original claims are concerned. The old game is over, and the cards are shuffled again. Nothing whatever can *now* be done toward reaching probabilities in the matter of cosmic organisation, *except by assembling all the tentative data of 1930 and forming a fresh chain of partial indications based exclusively on that data and on no conceptions derived from earlier arrays of data;* meanwhile testing, by the psychological knowledge of 1930, the workings and inclinations of our minds in accepting, correlating, and making deductions from data, *and most particularly weeding out all tendencies to give more than equal consideration to conceptions which would never have occurred to us had we not formerly harboured ideas of the universe now conclusively known to be false.* Let this last point be supremely plain, for it is through *a deliberate and dishonest ignoring of it* that every contemporary claim of traditional theism is advanced. Nothing but shoddy emotionalism and irresponsible irrationality can account for the pathetick and contemptible asininity with which the Chestertons and Eliots, and even the Fosdicks and Eddingtons and Osborns,[26] try to brush it aside or cover it up in their attempts to capitalise the new uncertainty of everything in the interest of historical mythology. What this means—and it means it just as plainly, for all the jaunty flippancy of touch-and-go epigrammatists who dare not put their fallacies to the test of honest reason and original cerebration—is simply this: that although each of the conflicting orthodoxies of the past, founded on known fallacies among primitive and ignorant races, certainly has an *equal theoretical chance* with any other orthodoxy or with

any theory of science of being true, *it most positively has no greater chance* than has ANY RANDOM SYSTEM OF FICTION, DEVISED CAPRICIOUSLY BY IGNORANCE, DISEASE, WHIM, ACCIDENT, EMOTION, GREED, OR ANY OTHER AGENCY INCLUDING CONSCIOUS MENDACITY, HALLUCINATION, POLITICAL OR SOCIAL INTEREST, AND ULTERIOR CONSIDERATIONS IN GENERAL. If we could shave off the moustachelets of our Chestertons and rub their noses in this plain truth, we would have fewer spectacles of neo-obscurantism. It is this one crucial circumstance which renders utterly valueless all half-baked attempts to utilise the admitted uncertainty of knowledge in bolstering up obsolete lies whose natural origin and total emptiness are obvious to all psychologists, biologists, and anthropologists. Let us grant that *in theory* the doctrine of Buddha, or of Mohammed, or of Lao-Tse, or of Christus, or of Zoroaster, or of some Congo witch-doctor, or of T. S. Eliot, or of Mary Baker Eddy, or of Dionysus, or of Plato, or of Ralph Waldo Emerson, *has just as much or as little positive evidence for it as has any other attempted explanation of the cosmos.* So far, so good. *But this concession cannot possibly be made without extending equal theoretical authority to Chambers's Yellow Sign, Dunsany's Pegāna, your Tindalos, Klarkash-Ton's Tsathoggua, my Cthulhu, or any other fantastic concoction anybody may choose to invent. Who can disprove any such concoction,* or say that it is not "esoterically true" even if its creator did think he invented it in jest or fiction? What shall be our guide in deciding which, out of an infinity of possible speculations, is the most likely to be a correct explanation of surrounding entity? How shall we establish a test of comparative validity or authority for the various conflicting claims which present themselves? If the theism of Christus is "true" because our ancestors believed it, why is not the devil-worship of the Yezidis equally "true" because they and their ancestors have believed it? What is anything? Can any one explanation be deemed more acceptable than any other? If so, on what principle? At this point the moustacheletted fat neo-papists begin to crack brilliant and irrelevant jokes and spout emotional generalities designed to get the mind of the seeker off the facts and confuse him into the acceptance of ready-made traditional hokum. But men of sense pause a bit and try to see what *really can be done* toward a tentative elimination leading in the direction of general probabilities. The result, inevitably, is that conclusion stated a few paragraphs back — *that probabilities can now be reached only by assembling, all the data of 1930, and forming a fresh chain of partial indications based exclusively on that data and on no conceptions derived from earlier arrays of data;* meanwhile testing, by the psychological knowledge of 1930, the workings and inclinations of our minds in accepting, correlating, and making deductions from data, AND MOST PARTICULARLY WEEDING OUT ALL TENDENCIES TO GIVE MORE THAN EQUAL CONSIDERATION TO CONCEPTIONS WHICH WOULD NEVER HAVE OCCURRED TO US HAD WE NOT FORMERLY HARBOURED IDEAS OF THE UNIVERSE NOW CONCLUSIVELY KNOWN TO BE FALSE.

Specifically (for no sane human being disputes the *general* proposition just stated) our job is to test (a) the intrinsic probability, as judged by our contemporary observations of what we see of the universe, of any system which enters a claim; and more particularly (b) to investigate the sources of such a system, *and the probable reason why anybody believes or ever has believed in it,* the latter point to be worked at by the most thorough psychological analyses we can devise.

Get this straight—*for there is no other road to probability.*

First, what is the likelihood of a theory as judged by the general action of nature manifest in regular and predictable phenomena? (Day and night, heat and cold, seasons, laws of mechanics, etc. etc.)

Second, if it squares less readily with observed reality than does some other theory, then why was it proposed in the first place?

Third, if in answer to (2) it be said that certain persons at a certain time found this theory more in accord with nature than any other, then what relationship has the conception of nature at that time to our conception of it today?

Fourth, on what mental principles are all these conceptions of nature, and of the relation of this theory to any observed set of phenomena or parallel theory based on such phenomena, formed? How does contemporary psychology interpret the processes causing the formation of these conceptions?

Going back to the general proposition—what does the natural evidence of 1930 suggest, anyhow? Well, *uncertainty* in the first place. A definite limitation of our knowledge of what lies behind the visible aspects of the cosmos as seen by human beings from this planet. But how far can we extend this uncertainty? Certainly, it has no place in our immediate environment. Grandpa Theobald will never dodge a hateful northern winter because time and space are relative in infinity, nor will the planet Pluto ever revolve around the sun as swiftly as Mercury from the point of view of this part of space. No person in Providence, without circumnavigating the globe, will ever get to Charleston by starting for Quebec; nor will any projectile in the solar system ever hit Saturn by being aimed at the opposite part of its orbit. We live in a cosmos in which a certain amount of regularity is an essential part; and in which time and space, far from being illusions, have definite and recognisable functions so far as the relationship of any small unit to its immediate environment is concerned. Whatever be the relationship of our galactic universe to any larger unit—whether or not the totality of entity and extension—the relationship of our star-group to the galaxy, of our solar system to its star group, of our earth to the solar system, and of organic life to the earth, may and must still be regarded as *roughly* what it seems; or rather, as something with so limited a relativity-latitude that the underling "reality" rhythms cannot be out of all *quantitative* correspondence with the phenomena we observe. We see a certain interplay of patterned forces not discernibly dissimilar *in kind* from the formation of the smallest crystal to the shaping and kinetic balance of the whole immediate galaxy. The evidence on hand points to a sort of general rhythmic seething of force-streams along channels automatically predetermined in ultimate ends, though conceivably subject to slight variations in route (quantum theory) and with certain developments definitely unpredictable *although not, in the opinion of conservative physicists, forming actual violations of the basic principle of causation.* What most physicists take the quantum theory, at present, to mean, is *not that any cosmic uncertainty exists* as to which of several courses a given reaction will take; but that in certain instances *no conceivable channel of information can ever tell human beings which course will be taken,* or by what exact course a certain observed result came about.[27] There is room for much discussion on this point, and I can cite some very pertinent articles on the subject if necessary. Organic life, of which consciousness is an incidental process, and which rises and falls through varying degrees of complexity, (mankind being at present its most intricate example within our scope of vision) is a phenomenon of apparent rarity, though of so well-defined a type that it would be rash to deem it confined to this solar system alone in all the history of the cosmos. We know, roughly, the relationship it bears to our solar system, and realise that it must be a very transient phase in the history of such planets as contain it. We can look back geologically, on this earth, to a relatively recent time when it did not exist; (a time which is *not* an illusion *in the history of this system*) and forward to a comparatively early moment when it shall have ceased to be. In other words, we know it to be a matter of supreme indifference and impermanence so far as the immediate universe is concerned. In several trillion years it will be a matter of absolute indifference whether or not this phenomenon has ever existed on the planets in this part of space. If the laws governing this phenomenon are basically different from those governing other immediate and observed phenomena, we have yet to be shewn evidence based on anything but assumptions and conceptions without sources in ascertainable reality as recognised today. Proof—and even probability—is likewise required to justify the assumption that organic life, either as a whole or in that department known as consciousness, has any special or significant relationship to the pattern and motions of the cosmos as a whole; *even allowing for a radical and causation-disturbing interpretation of the quantum theory* (even proof of a cosmic "purpose" and "consciousness" would indicate nothing as to man's place therein. All life might well be a trifling pimple or disease). While it is perfectly true, in theory, that we require a mathematician's knowledge in order to test a mathematician's statement of a special resemblance between cosmic law and the cerebral processes of terrestrial organisms; it is equally true that common sense, after hearing the mathematician explain the basis of his claim, and after comparing this claim with the views of other and equally noted mathematicians, has a certain unofficial right to formulate concepts of probability or the reverse. And when we learn that the sole ground for the mind-and-cosmos-comparison is merely the possibility (certainly not the probability) that occasional chance tempers the dominant determinism of infinity, we are certainly justified in demanding confirmatory data before so palpably strained and artificial (and so obviously myth-and-tradition-suggested) an analogy is accepted. Is anyone so naive as to believe that the mind-cosmos comparison would have been made solely from the present evidence of 1930, if unsuggested by ancient mythology? Let us analyse the comparison in the exclusive light of contemporary evidence and see how great a part of it consists of mere words and artificially forced parallels. Let us not forget that Einstein and others do not attempt such merely poetic analogies. Einstein has much to say of "religion"—which to him means a human emotion of ecstasy excited by the individual's correlation of himself with the cosmos—but he does not use the language of Jeans. And it would be superfluous to point out—except to purblind neo-obscurantists amongst whom all distinctions are dead—that none of these modern cosmic views has anything in common with any interpretation of the cosmos, and man's relation to it, which has traditionally gone under the name of religion. These cosmic philosophers are using ancient names to describe a cloudy pantheism utterly unlike anything those ancient names ever stood for in their heyday. It is folly and hypocrisy to use the hack terms "God" and "religion" to describe things having no relationship to the original concepts back of those terms. Whilst certain of the valuecentric and teleological implications of these fellows may be said to form a pale echo of the obsolete theism, especially in some of its more mystical Hindoo phases, it is ridiculous to consider them as a prolongation of the highly dogmatic and childishly specific set of delusions constituting the nominal Christianity of the Western World. According to any person following the Christian religion in its basic essence, be he a Papist or Protestant, both Jeans and Einstein are definite atheists. Thus we see the element of puerile fashion and irrational mob-psychology in any popular trend inclusive enough to favour at once, and allegedly on the same grounds, the crazy archaism of a Chesterton and the indecisive word-juggling of a Jeans or an Einstein.

[In a discussion with Woodburn Harris about ethics, Lovecraft ingeniously outlines his own ethical thought but makes it a subset of aesthetics. He also enunciates some of his political theories.]

[21]   About my own attitude toward ethics—I thought I made it plain that I object only to (a) grotesquely disproportionate indignations and enthusiasms, (b) illogical extremes involving a reductio ad absurdum, and (c) the nonsensical notion that "right" and "wrong" involve any principles more mystical and universal than those of immediate expediency (with the individual's comfort as a criterion) on the one hand, and those of aesthetic harmony and symmetry (with the individual's emotional-imaginative pleasure as a criterion) on the other hand. I believe I was careful to specify that I do not advocate vice and crime, but that on the other hand I have a marked distaste for immoral and unlawful acts which contravene the harmonious traditions and standards of beautiful living developed by a culture during its long history. This, however, is not *ethics but aesthetics*—a distinction which you are almost alone in considering negligible. The mental and emotional forces behind this attitude, and behind the attitude of the religionist or abstract moralist, are leagues apart; as is clearly recognised by virtually all arguers on both sides. Before I get through I shall quote a very good description of my type of person, from the pen of a man very much on

the other side. You can't gauge differences like this by one's daily personal conduct, because personal conduct is largely a matter of response to instinctive stimuli wholly dissociated from intellectual belief. We do what we do automatically, and then try either to rationalise it according to some theory, or to conceal it if it clashes too much with the particular theory which happens to be fastened upon us. We are mostly puppets—automata—though of course the theories we happen to hold may sometimes turn the scales one way or the other in determining a course of action, when all the other factors are evenly divided between two alternatives. So far as I am concerned—I am an aesthete devoted to harmony, and to the extraction of the maximum possible pleasure from life. I find by experience that my chief pleasure is in symbolic identification with the landscape and tradition-stream to which I belong—hence I follow the honour expected of a descendant of English gentlemen. It is pride and beauty-sense, plus the automatic instincts of generations trained in certain conduct-patterns, which determine my conduct from day to day. But this is *not ethics*, because the same compulsions and preferences apply, with me, to things wholly outside the ethical zone. For example, I never cheat or steal. Also, I never wear a top-hat with a sack coat or munch bananas in public on the streets, because a gentleman does not do those things either. I would as soon do the one as the other sort of thing—it is all a matter of harmony and good taste—whereas the ethical or "righteous" man would be horrified by dishonesty yet tolerant of coarse personal ways. If I were farming in your district I certainly would assist my neighbours—both as a means of promoting my standing in the community, and because it is good taste to be generous and accommodating. Likewise with the matter of treating the pupils in a school class. But this would not be through any sense of inner compulsion based on principles dissociated from my personal welfare and from the principle of beauty. It would be for the same reason that I would not dress eccentrically or use vulgar language. *Pure aesthetics*, aside from the personal-benefit element; and concerned with emotions of *pleasure versus disgust* rather than of *approval versus indignation*. This is a highly important distinction. Advancing to the question of *collective* conduct as involved in problems of government, social organisation, etc.—I fully see your side of the matter, and would be the last person in the world to advocate any course of civic or economic policy which might tend toward the destruction of the existing culture. In accordance with this attitude, I am distinctly opposed to visibly arrogant and arbitrary extremes of government—but

this is simply because I wish the safety of an artistic and intellectual civilisation to be secure, not because I have any sympathy with the coarse-
grained herd who would menace the civilisation if not placated by sops.
Surely you can see the profound and abysmal difference between this emotional attitude and the emotional attitude of the democratic reformer who
becomes wildly excited over the "wrongs of the masses". This reformer has
uppermost in his mind the welfare of those masses themselves—he feels
with them, takes up a mental-emotional point of view as one of them, regards their advancement as his prime objective independently of anything
else, and would willingly sacrifice the finest fruits of the civilisation for the
sake of stuffing their bellies and giving them two cinema shows instead of
one per day. I, on the other hand, don't give a hang about the masses except so far as I think deliberate cruelty is coarse and unaesthetic—be it toward horses, oxen, undeveloped men, dogs, niggers, or poultry. All that I
care about is *the civilisation*—the state of development and organisation
which is capable of gratifying the complex mental-emotional-aesthetic
needs of highly evolved and acutely sensitive men. Any *indignation* I may
feel in the whole matter is not for the woes of the down-trodden, but for
the threat of social unrest to the traditional institutions of the civilisation.
The reformer cares only for the masses, but may make concessions to the
civilisation. I care only for the civilisation, but may make concessions
to the masses. Do you not see the antipodal difference between the two
positions? Both the reformer and I may unite in opposing an unworkably
arrogant piece of legislation, but the motivating reasons will be absolutely
antithetical. He wants to give the crowd as *much* as can be given them without wrecking all semblance of civilisation, whereas I want to give them
only as much as can be given them without even slightly impairing the level
of the national culture. When it's an actual question of masses versus culture, I'm for giving the masses as little as can be given without bringing on
a danger of collapse. Thus you see that the reformer and I are very different after all. He has a *spontaneous enthusiasm* for reform and democracy,
thinking it imperative to *urge* these things. I, on the other hand, have no
enthusiasm at all in this direction; thinking it the best policy not to urge
concessions, but merely to grant such things when the safety of the civilisation demands it. He is a democrat at all times, and because he *wants* to be.
I am one only occasionally, and when I *have* to be. Still—if you want to be
so concrete and pragmatical as to ignore all emotions and motives, and
judge persons by acts alone, I suppose you can say that the moderate re-

former and I have *something* in common. We are both generally for a safe middle course, although each strains toward opposite boundaries of that course. In terms of the late campaign—all moderates were either for Smith or Hoover,[28] though the reformer often wished the policies of Norman Thomas and the Socialists would work, whilst I would frankly prefer a landholding aristocracy with a cultivated leisure class and a return to the historic authority of the British crown, of which I shall always be spiritually a subject. But as men of more or less rudimentary sense, both the reformer and I know that we can neither of us get what we respectively want—hence last autumn he compromised on Smith whilst I compromised on Hoover. And that's the way of it. We want different things, but have enough sense of reality to take what we can get. He works for as democratic a government *as possible;* I for as aristocratic a one *as possible.* But both recognise the limitations of possibility. Incidentally, the developments of the machine age may conceivably make inevitable a third and altogether different sort of organisation equally dissatisfying to democrat and oligarch! As for the relative value or authority of the democratic and aristocratic ideals—there is not, cosmically speaking, a bit of preference to be given either side. It is all a matter of personal emotion. I happen to favour the system which permits the free exercise of the most complex and evolved vital forces, but I freely concede that there is just as much logic in advocating a system which keeps everything down to the animal level. I would, indeed, freely concede an equal cosmic standing to any design of the insect race to extirpate the mammalian world and bring to dominance the ideals and institutions of the disciplined and efficiently organised articulata. But I couldn't get exactly enthusiastic about it!

[Perhaps Lovecraft's most concise expression of his "cosmic" philosophy —as it relates to human life and action—is found in a letter to his long-time philosophical opponent James F. Morton.]

[22] As for the future of Western Civilisation—and of any other cultures which the planet may preserve or develop—far be it from me to be dogmatick. All I deal in is probabilities. In the last analysis, nobody don't know nothin' about nothin'. Contrary to what you may assume, I am *not a pessimist* but an *indifferentist*—that is, I don't make the mistake of thinking that the resultant of the natural forces surrounding and governing organic life will have any connexion with the wishes or tastes of any part of that

organic life-process. Pessimists are just as illogical as optimists; insomuch as both envisage the aims of mankind as unified, and as having a direct relationship (either of frustration or of fulfilment) to the inevitable flow of terrestrial motivation and events. That is—both schools retain in a vestigial way the primitive concept of a conscious teleology of a cosmos which gives a damn one way or the other about the especial wants and ultimate welfare of mosquitoes, rats, lice, dogs, men, horses, pterodactyls, trees, fungi, dodos, or other forms of biological energy. And I fear the meliorist is not altogether free from this illusion, either. But the *indifferentist* is. He alone of all thinkers is willing to view the future of the planet *impartially*— without assigning (as indeed there is absolutely no ground for assigning) any preponderance of evidential value to such factors as appear to argue a course pleasant to himself. Not that he is especially looking for anti-human outcomes, or that he has any pleasure in contemplating such. It is merely that, in judging evidence, *he does not regard the quality of favourableness to man as any intrinsic mark of probability.* Neither does he regard it as any intrinsic mark of *improbability*—he simply knows that this quality has nothing to do with the case; that the interplay of forces which govern climate, behaviour, biological growth and decay, and so on, is too purely universal, cosmic, and eternal a phenomenon to have any relationship to the immediate wishing-phenomena of one minute organic species on our transient and insignificant planet. At times parts of this species may like the way things are going, and at times they may not—but that has nothing to do with the cosmically fixed march of the events themselves. Human liking or welfare is no probability-factor at all—and no person has a right to express an opinion on the future of the world, so long as he has the least tendency to consider a man-favouring course as *intrinsically* more likely to be probable than any other course. If he lets the quality of man-favouringness serve in lieu of real evidence to predispose him toward belief in any direction, then his opinion is null and void as a serious philosophic factor. The real philosopher knows that, *other* evidence being equal, favourableness or unfavourableness to mankind means absolutely nothing as an index of likelihood—that is, that a future hostile to man is precisely as probable as one favourable to him. And of course this works the other way around as well—so that no one is justified in thinking a theory probable *merely because it opposes man.* The indifferentist laughs as much at irresponsible calamity-howlers and temperamental melancholiacs as he does at smirking idealists and unctuous woodrowilsonians. For example—nothing makes me more amused than the hypersensitive people who consider life as essentially an *agony* instead of merely a cursed bore, punctuated by occasional agony and still rarer pleasure. Life is rather depressing because pain and ennui outweigh pleasure; but the pleasure exists, none the less, and can be enjoyed now and then while it lasts. And too—many can build up a crustacean insensitiveness against the subtler forms of pain, so that many lucky individuals have their pain-quota measurably reduced. Uniform melancholy is as illogical as uniform cheer.

[While denying the cosmic importance of human emotions, Lovecraft nevertheless granted them great significance on the human scale; and in the following letter to August Derleth he poignantly chronicles his own reasons for continuing existence. While admitting his essential solitude, Lovecraft maintains that he would not feel comfortable except in a homogeneous milieu that provided a "system of anchorage."]

[23]   I certainly do not disagree with you concerning the essential solitude of the individual, for it seems to me the plainest of all truths that no highly organised and freely developed mind can possibly envisage an external world having much in common with the external world envisaged by any other mind. The basic inclinations, yearnings, and ego-satisfactions of each separate individual depend wholly upon a myriad associations, hereditary predispositions, environmental accidents, and so on, which cannot possibly be duplicated in any other individual; hence it is merely foolish for anybody to expect himself to be "understood" more than vaguely, approximately, and objectively by anybody else. For example, I am perfectly confident that I could never adequately convey to any other human being the precise reasons why I continue to refrain from suicide—the reasons, that is, why I still find existence enough of a compensation to atone for its dominantly burthensome quality. These reasons are strongly linked with architecture, scenery, and lighting and atmospheric effects, and take the form of vague impressions of adventurous expectancy coupled with elusive memory—impressions that certain vistas, particularly those associated with sunsets, are avenues of approach to spheres or conditions of wholly undefined delights and freedoms which I have known in the past and have a slender possibility of knowing again in the future. Just what those delights and freedoms are, or even what they approximately resemble, I could not concretely imagine to save my life; save that they seem to

concern some ethereal quality of indefinite expansion and mobility, and of a heightened perception which shall make all forms and combinations of beauty simultaneously visible to me, and realisable by me. I might add, though, that they invariably imply a total defeat of the laws of time, space, matter, and energy—or rather, an individual independence of these laws on my part, whereby I can sail through the varied universes of space-time as an invisible vapour might . . . . . . upsetting none of them, yet superior to their limitations and local forms of material organisation. The commonest form of my imaginative aspiration—that is, the commonest definable form—is a motion backward in time, or a discovery that time is merely an illusion and that the past is simply a lost mode of vision which I have a chance of recovering. Now this all sounds damn foolish to anybody else—and very justly so. There is no reason why it should sound anything except damn foolish to anyone who has not happened to receive precisely the same series of inclinations, impressions, and background-images which the purely fortuitous circumstances of my especial life have chanced to give to me. But as I look at it, the very naturalness and universality of this solitude remove that condition from the more or less painful state called "loneliness", in the conception of which there is implicit some suggestion of preventable ill, out-of-placeness, or resentment-meriting defeat. The cosmic solitude which we all share may justly breed a mood of wistfulness, but hardly one of acutely painful "loneliness". However—very possibly you realise all this as fully as I do, and merely use the word "loneliness" to signify exactly what I mean when I say "cosmic solitude". It is well, in exchanging ideas, not to get tangled up in mere nomenclature, as we are too often apt to do. As a safeguard against this bothersome verbal sidetracking I have often said that we ought to discard all the traditional terms of philosophy; which differently-thinking ages have invested with so many conflicting overtones of meaning that they have almost ceased to stand for any definite realities. "Good", "evil", "pleasure", "pain", etc. no longer define any exact concepts; whilst the very names of the different branches of intellectual approach have come to raise meaningless and irrelevant distinctions and images. We ought no longer to use words like "philosophy", "science", and so on, but should adopt some fresh term like "cognition", which has not yet picked up any misleading or ambiguous associations.

Where I begin to disagree with you is the place where you allow your sense of solitude to conflict, through a false sense of consistency, with the common sense of pattern-placement. I find this a rather odd conflict, insomuch as it is hardly to be expected in one who objects to the wholly cosmic perspective of Wandrei and Clark Ashton Smith. Their perspective, of course, repudiates pattern-placement from an angle opposite to yours—arguing against it because they consider the ego too small to place, rather than too large to need a pattern—yet I should think that the grounds on which you reject their view would at least incline you to be distrustful of any view not attaching significance to certain external points of reference. You require certain landmarks like your beloved hills and river-bends—and it is only a step from this requirement to the need of a certain alignment with the natural traditions and folkways of the social and geographical group to which one belongs. One does not have to take these traditions and folkways seriously, in an intellectual way, and one may even laugh at their points of naivete and delusion—as indeed I laugh at the piety, narrowness, and conventionality of the New-England background which I love so well and find so necessary to contentment. But however we may regard such a pattern intellectually, the fact remains that most of us need it more or less as a point of departure for imaginative flights and a system of guideposts for the establishment of the illusions of direction and significance. And experience seems to shew that the only way one can effectively use such a pattern, is to refrain from repudiating it so far as the lesser symbolic conformities are concerned. Of course exceptions exist, and you may very well be one of them; but for the average person there is a need for personal anchorage to some system of landmarks larger than the ego yet smaller than the cosmos-at-large—a system of anchorage which can supply standards of comparison in the fields of size, nature, distance, direction, and so on; as demanded for the fulfilment of the normal sense of interest and dramatic action. Probably everybody has to have such a system—the differences being in the way various people envisage and express it. Religious people seek a mystical identification with a system of hereditary myths; whereas I, who am non-religious, seek a corresponding mystical identification with the only immediate tangible external reality which my perceptions acknowledge—i.e., the continuous stream of folkways around me. I achieve this mystical identification simply by a symbolic acceptance of the minor externals whose synthesis constitutes the surrounding stream. I follow this acceptance purely for my own personal pleasure—because I would feel lost in a limitless and impersonal cosmos if

I had no way of thinking of myself but as a dissociated and independent point. And my particular way of following it is simply that dictated by relative ease and a natural economy of energy.

Travels

[The later 1920s saw Lovecraft at the height of his travels, as he roamed the length of the Eastern Seaboard in search of antiquities. In 1927 he stumbled upon the archaic Massachusetts town of Deerfield and then proceeded up to unspoiled Vermont.]

[24]   As for the trip . . . . . oh, boy! Hot dawg! I haven't had such a good time since the golden 1900's! I spent five days with Cook in Athol, and was tooken around to all the adjacent mountain vistas and agrestick landscapes—AND DEERFIELD! Man, them blasphemously primordial ellums and unwholesomely archaick houses! It's all there, kid—every inch what it's crack'd up to be! But the big trip in the Culinary chariot was the northward one—Vermont as far north as Bellows Falls, and then N.H. to Lake Sunapee. It was on this jaunt that we stopped to discover that last of nineteenth century Novanglia's Puritan Pleiade—Arthur Henry Goodenough,[29] Yeoman, unspoil'd amidst his native rural shades, and favour'd nursling of th' Aonian Maids. Honustly, 'bo, I never seen no country niftier than the wild hills west of Brattleboro, where this guy hangs out. Brat itself is the diplodoccus' gold molar, with its works of pristine Yankee survival, but once you climb the slopes toward the setting sun you're in another and an elder world. All allegiance to modern and decadent things is cast off— all memory of such degenerate excrescences as steel and steam, tar and concrete roads, and the vulgar civilisation that bred them. Evoë! Evoë! We wind rapt and wondering over elder and familiar ribbons of rutted whiteness which curl past alluring valleys and traverse old wooden bridges in the lee of green slopes. The nearness and intimacy of the little domed hills become almost breath-taking—their steepness and abruptness hold nothing in common with the humdrum, standardised world we know, and we cannot help feeling that their outlines have some strange and almost-forgotten meaning, like vast hieroglyphs left by a rumoured titan race whose glories live only in rare, deep dreams. We climb and plunge fantastically as we thread this hypnotic landscape. Time has lost itself in the labyrinths behind, and around us stretch only the flowering waves of faery. Tawdriness and commerce, futile activity and urban smoke, greasy

filling-stations and ugly billboards, are not there—but instead, the recaptured beauty of vanished centuries; the hoary groves, the untainted pastures hedg'd with gay blossoms, and the small brown farmsteads nestling amidst huge trees beneath vertical precipices of fragrant brier and meadow-grass. Even the sunlight assumes a supernal glamour, as if some special atmosphere or exhalation mantled the whole region. There is nothing like it save in the magick vistas that sometimes form the backgrounds of Italian primitives. Sodoma and Leonardo saw such expanses, but only in the distance and thro' the vaultings of Renaissance arcades. We rove at will thro' the midst of the picture; and find in its necromancy a thing we have known or inherited, and for which we have always been vainly searching. At the heart of this weirdly beautiful Arcadia Vermont's gentle poet dwells. Good ol' Arty! We found him in overalls and a bristle of bucolick whiskerage; but he insisted on a ceremonious toilet before greeting his distinguished guests, and appeared later in all the radiance of a rusty black Prince-Albert, misfit collar, and gay tie with enormous opal pin in its northern hemisphere. Sunday best or nothin', b'gosh! And what a delectable atavism the old boy is! Old New England forever! His wife, an ex-teacher, and his prepossessing son Rupert, have seen a little of the outer world; but Squire Goodenough knows only the paternal Sabine farm. He has never set eyes on a city, and goes but once or twice a year to quaint Brattleboro, three miles distant. In speech, thought, and gesture he reflects only the days that were, the simple Saturnian reign of our fathers, when primal Virtue hung o'er Tempë's slope, and swains and ploughmen dwelt in faith and hope. One with his hereditary hills and groves, with the spreading, venerable trees and the antient peaked roofs of the vine-bank'd cottages, he sounds the elder strain, and sings as the last of the long line of Puritan Oracles. Tilling his ancestral garth in the good old way, and keeping alive beside his daily hearth the well-lov'd thoughts and customs of our Golden Age, is he vastly more than a retrospective teller of bygone tales. Alone amongst the surviving choir he truly leads the pastoral life he breathes; so that we need not wonder at the flawless authenticity of his Dorick reed. He has prolong'd our old New-England in himself, and his stately charm and genial hospitality are as truly poems—if not more so—as anything his oaten pipe could sound 'neath beechen shade. Happy Tityrus! Lovely beyond words is the realm whereover the poet wields his rural sway. The antient house on the hillside, embower'd in greenery and shadow'd by a lone leafy monarch peopled by the feathery train; the dream-stirring slope to the westward, where earth's beauty melts into the cosmick glory of sunset; the narrow, beckoning road, the outspread, dew-glistening mead- ows, and the hint of spectral woodlands and valleys in the background— all these mark out a perfect poet's seat, and cause us to thank Fate that for once in history a man and his setting are well-matched. Cook took several pictures with a brand-new camera he had bought that morning, and I'll send you a set as soon as he furnishes me with some promised duplicates. I know you'll enjoy an intimate glimpse of the half-fabulous old faun whose simple strains you have seen for a quarter-century in the piquant pages of amateurdom. Northward from Brattleboro the charm still holds. There are glorious sweeps of vivid valley where great cliffs rise, New-England's vir- gin granite showing grey and austere thro' the verdure that scales the crests. There are gorges where untamed streams leap, bearing down to- ward the bordering Connecticut the unimagined secrets of a thousand pathless peaks. Narrow, half-hidden roads bore their way thro' solid, luxu- riant masses of forest, among whose primal trees whole armies of fauns and dryads lurk. Archaick cover'd bridges of a sort wholly extinct in Rhode-Island linger fearsomely out of the past in pockets of the hills, and here and there a summit bears a tiny hamlet of trim, clean old houses and steeples that time has never been able to sully. Idyllick Vermont! Fit cradle for Imperial power, and native seat of the sturdy Consul C. Culigius Calv- inus, whom Pollux bless![30] I'm writing up my general impressions of the province for the new amateur Walter J. Coates of North Montpelier, whose magazine—*Driftwind*—is devoted to Vermont and its literature.[31]

[In the spring of 1928 Lovecraft was forced to spend six weeks in Brook- lyn at the insistence of his wife, Sonia, as she was attempting to establish a new hat shop. But Lovecraft found occasion to explore further antiquar- ian sites in the area and to meet with his New York friends.]

[25]   When you perceive the foregoing temporary address, and correlate it with what I have quite frequently expressed as my unvarnished senti- ments toward the New York region, you will probably appreciate the ex- tent of the combined burdens and nerve-taxes which have, through malign coincidence, utterly disrupted my programs this spring, and brought me to the verge of what would be a complete breakdown if I did not have a staunch and brilliant colleague—my young "adopted grandchild" Frank B. Long— on whom to lean for cooperation and assistance in getting my tasks in shape.

Nothing but strong domestic pressure could ever have induced me to waste a spring in this accursed metropolitan pest-zone. What occurred was the unexpected commercial need of my wife's wish that I join her for a time. Her business affiliations usually take her to different sections of the country for indefinite periods; and when these sections are far away, there is of course no thought of my interrupting my quiet Providence life (I room on the lower floor of a sedate Victorian backwater, with my elder aunt rooming on the second floor and furnishing a reminiscent touch of old-home family atmosphere) in order to follow. New York, however, is so fatally *near* to Providence in a geographical way—"so near and yet so far", as it were—that this time my wife really thought it only right for me to transfer a little of the domestic background to her present scene of action. Impartially reflecting, I could not help conceding the essential justice of the opinion; hence decided that the least I could do would be to conquer my anti-metropolitan repugnance for a season and avoid that depressing household inharmony which forms the theme of so many works of fiction! Fortunately the present quarters are in the very *least offensive* part of the whole greater New York area—a part so homelike, village-like, and old-American, indeed, that there is really very little in the immediate environment to complain of. This benign oasis is the southwestern section of the ancient village of Flatbush, Long Island, now overtaken by and incorporated in the Borough of Brooklyn. The particular district in question, protected by real-estate restrictions and by mutual agreements among the old-time property-owners, has resisted the encroachments of decadence and modernity to an astonishing degree; so that it is even now a place of separate wooden houses, green lawns and back yards, quiet streets with generous shade-trees, and sleepy churches whose chimes weave music and magic on Sunday mornings. One of the enclosed postcards gives a fair idea of it—as you will see, the terrain could very well be mistaken for a fairly modern residence section in almost any small American city. From this unique vantage-point, New York seems remote and incredible indeed— and it is difficult to believe that the howling bedlam of 42nd St. is only a half-hour away on the subway. That is the one mitigating thing which makes it possible for me to remain here for any continuous time. I have not yet—during this visit—been above ground in the crowded mid-town district, save for one trip to the public library. I fluctuate altogether between the somnolent oasis of Flatbush and the far uptown section of Manhattan where my youthful colleague Belknap holds forth. I have twice seen Mr.

Loveman—who, by the way, has recently moved his Rowfant Book Shop from the downtown section to the famous bookstall colony in 59th St.— 103 East 59th St., to be exact, opposite the Anderson Galleries. I've not yet had a chance to examine this place with care. One thing I'm going to do as an antidote to this metropolitan ordeal is to take advantage of my two-hundred-mile-greater proximity to Philadelphia and Washington to accomplish some antiquarian exploration I've long wished to undertake. I hope to snatch a look at many colonial sights—perhaps as far south as Williamsburg, Virginia—before returning to Providence, and to explore certain old towns like Annapolis and Alexandria with the same thoroughness I have been able to exercise in exploring Salem, Marblehead, Portsmouth, and the other old towns of New England.

[After his New York stay Lovecraft returned to Vermont with Orton. In mid-June he visited a curious recluse named Bert G. Akley, whose name Lovecraft misspells in the following letter to his aunt, and who clearly served as the model for Henry Wentworth Akeley in "The Whisperer in Darkness."]

[26]   I last wrote Thursday, as I was about to go to the artist Akeley's. At the proper time Charley Lee called for me—on foot, since the Ford was broken down and would take some time to repair. We walked 'cross-lots, thereby seeing some exquisite scenery which I would otherwise have missed. Akeley—who lives alone in the ancient farmhouse shewn on the other side of this card, turned out to be a highly remarkable rustic genius. His paintings—covering every field, but specialising in the local scenery, are of a remarkable degree of excellence; yet he has never taken a lesson in his life. He is Talman's equal or superior in heraldic painting, and is likewise a landscape and still-life photographer of the highest skill and taste. In other fields, too, he is a veritable jack-of-all-trades. Through it all he retains the primitiveness of the agrestic yeoman, and lives in unbelievable heaps and piles of disorder. About 10 o'clock Bill and Henry called for us in the Ford, and I returned to Orton's, retiring early. Friday was wretchedly rainy, so I spent the time reading proofs till late afternoon, when the downpour eased up. I then took a pedestrian tour, found the lovely waterfall I had been seeking so long, and explored the sleepy hillside village of Guilford Centre, whose ancient roofs and white church tower would make a delectable picture. I returned through Hinesburg, whose

delicate steeple and breathless hillside vistas so deeply impressed me on a former occasion.

[Later in June the weird writer H. Warner Munn took Lovecraft to a remote spot in central Massachusetts named the Bear's Den. Lovecraft's impressions of the Bear's Dean were incorporated directly into "The Dunwich Horror."]

[27]   On Thursday evening Munn came down to dinner in his Essex
Roadster and afterward took Cook and me on a trip to one of the finest scenic spots I have ever seen—Bear's Den, in the woods southwest of Athol.
There is a deep forest gorge there; approached dramatically from a rising
path ending in a cleft boulder, and containing a magnificent terraced waterfall over the sheer bed-rock. Above the tumbling stream rise high rock
precipices crusted with strange lichens and honeycombed with alluring
caves. Of the latter several extend far into the hillside, though too narrowly to admit a human being beyond a few yards. I entered the largest
specimen—it being the first time I was ever in a real cave, notwithstanding
the vast amount I have written concerning such things. Munn says there is
another and still larger cave near Athol, to which he will take me the next
time I am there; and Cook promises to shew me the extensive caverns in
Cavendish, Vermont, when we go there in the early autumn. Having seen
Bear's Den with sufficient minuteness, we proceeded to Munn's house and
looked over the old books in the barn. Munn made me a present of a Bible
in the long s—something I have always wanted—printed at Edinburgh in
1795. That, and several other books I received or am borrowing, will be
brought down by Cook the next time he visits Providence in his car. After
this we returned to Cook's and chatted till quite late, when all dispersed
and retired.

[Lovecraft then proceeded to visit his old amateur associate Edith Miniter
in Wilbraham, Massachusetts. In a memorial essay on Miniter written in
1934, Lovecraft speaks of this visit, mentioning several details—such as
the legend of the whippoorwills and the large gathering of fireflies—that
he incorporated into "The Dunwich Horror."]

[28]   An eight-day visit to the household at Maplehurst in July, 1928,
formed my last personal glimpse of Mrs. Miniter. I had never seen the
Wilbraham region before, and was charmed by the vivid vistas of hills and

valleys, and the remote winding roads so redolent of other centuries. No better hierophants of the local arcana than Mrs. Miniter and Miss Beebe[32] could possibly have been found, and my knowledge of Central New England lore was virtually trebled during my short stay.

I saw the ruinous, deserted old Randolph Beebe house where the whippoorwills cluster abnormally, and learned that these birds are feared by the rustics as evil psychopomps. It is whispered that they linger and flutter around houses where death is approaching, hoping to catch the soul of the departed as it leaves. If the soul eludes them, they disperse in quiet disappointment; but sometimes they set up a chorused clamour of excited, triumphant chattering which makes the watchers turn pale and mutter — with that air of hushed, awestruck portentousness which only a backwoods Yankee can assume — "They got 'im!" On another day I was taken to nearby Monson to see a dark, damp street in the shadow of a great hill, the houses on the hillward side of which are whispered about because of the number of their tenants who have gone mad or killed themselves.

I saw the haunted pasture bars in the spectral dusk, and one evening was thrilled and amazed by a monstrous saraband of fireflies over marsh and meadow. It was as if some strange, sinister constellation had taken on an uncanny life and descended to hang low above the lush grasses. And one day Mrs. Miniter shewed me a deep, mute ravine beyond the Randolph Beebe house, along whose far-off wooded floor an unseen stream trickles in eternal shadow. Here, I am told, the whippoorwills gather on certain nights for no good purpose.

I was taken over the sightly Beebe acres by my hostess, Old Fats trotting dog-like at our heels; and beheld some of the silent, uncommunicative, slowly retrograding yeomanry of the region. Later the aged, courtly Stitchie and Mrs. Miniter were my joint guides to neighbouring Glendale and its ancient church and churchyard. Still another trip was up old Wilbra'm Mountain, where the road winds mystically aloft into a region of hushed skyey meadow-land seemingly half-apart from time and change, and abounding in breath-taking vistas. Through the haze of distance other mountains loom purple and mysterious. A line of fog marks the great Connecticut, and the smoke of Springfield clouds the southwestern horizon. Sometimes even the golden dome of the Hartford state house, far to the south, can be discerned. Though the slopes were much as Lieut. Mirick must have known them in his day, I saw no "pizen sarpients". On the way

Mrs. Miniter pointed out the home of the "Natupskis" immortalised in her novel.[33]

A subsequent day was devoted to a long walk around the mountain, over roads which included some of quite colonial primitiveness. On this occasion, for the only time in my life, I saw a wild deer in its native habitat. Wilbraham village, under the mountain's southern slope, is a drowsy, pleasant town with a quiet main street and giant elms. Mrs. Miniter displayed the moss-grown graveyards of the place—one of which, The Dell, includes a dank wooded declivity beside a stream that is said to wash away the earth and expose curious secrets at times. The old brick Academy, built in 1825 and still surviving after many vicissitudes, was another interesting sight. The return trip, beginning in the wild and picturesque woodlands behind the Academy, led over unspoiled colonial roads on the mountain's side, and revealed many of the brooding, unpainted houses of other generations. At one stage of the journey I saw the house where Mrs. Miniter was born—built in 1842 by her grandfather, Edwin Lombard Tupper, and still inhabited by his direct descendants. Among the varied and exquisite prospects along this route is one of a strangely blasted slope where grey, dead trees claw at the sky with leafless boughs amidst an abomination of desolation. Vegetation will grow here no longer—why, no one can tell.

[Lovecraft then proceeded south on an ambitious trek that led him to the Endless Caverns in Virginia, where he combined his fondness for nature, antiquity, and the weird.]

[29] [. . .] at last I put visiting behind me, and embarked upon the more kinetic part of my irresponsible wanderings. Glancing cursorily at Springfield [. . .] I rapidly ascended the Connecticut Valley by trolley and omnibus, passing through Holyoke, paying my respects to Mt. Tom, saluting Northampton, home of the Emperor Calvinus I, and revelling in ancient Deerfield—which I visited last year, and had also visited earlier this year on a side-trip from Vermont. At quiet Greenfield I took a west-bound stage-coach over the celebrated Mohawk Trail, and was forthwith enraptured by a greater display of scenic magnificence than my fancy had ever theretofore conceived. Endless leagues of hills and winding rivers outspread—and the ineffable sense of mountain mystery as the coach wound down precipitous slopes into the bowl-like valley containing the town of

North Adams. I kept on to Albany, N.Y., at which point I took a boat down the river, through the storied and scenic Catskill region so dear to the heart of Washington Irving. At New York City, compulsion being absent, I did not tarry except to exchange greetings with Little Belknap and young Donald Wandrei; (the latter weird writer being now emigrated to Brooklyn, and living only two blocks from the accursed scene of my own weary exile of 1925!) but kept on southward to my dearly-loved colonial haven of Philadelphia. There I communed as usual with the past; in the form of endless rows of Georgian brick, and endless alleys of labyrinthine archaism and mystery in the sinister, half-forgotten regions near the Delaware waterfront. Finally I moved on to Baltimore—travelling by omnibus through a region rather tame scenically except for small spots around Elkton and Havre-de-Grace. I had never seen Baltimore before, and therefore proceeded to give it an exceptionally thorough exploration. I saw Fort McHenry, birthplace of Mr. Key's celebrated ode to the tune of "Anacreon in Heaven",[34] but delighted chiefly in the melancholy grave of Edgar Allan Poe, in a neglected corner of Westminster Presbyterian Churchyard. I tried to purchase pictures of it, but could not locate any during the short time I had at my disposal. I regretted not having brought along a kodak. After Baltimore came historic and colonial Annapolis; and there I was forced to give vent to an almost childish enthusiasm over the marvellously preserved archaism of the place. It is utterly and vibrantly a part of the eighteenth century, redolent of the courtly life which after 1694 centred around the capital of the Proprietors' Colony of Maryland. The town itself is as purely Georgian as Newport, R.I., or the coast towns north of Boston; whilst the country-seats adjoining show the true southern type of colonial architecture, (steep roof, flat end chimneys, wings and arcades on each side of the main edifice etc.) as distinguished from the middle-colonies type prevailing in Pennsylvania and as far south as Baltimore. I also went through the naval academy buildings—of which the golden-domed chapel, with the body of John Paul Jones in its crypt, is by far the most interesting.

After Annapolis came Washington, D.C., which I made a base of operations for many side-trips into the adjacent parts of northern Virginia. Alexandria, with its venerable Christ Church and endless rows of colonial brick houses, was my favourite goal. In places like this, and Annapolis, one finds more of the old royalist spirit than in New England, where the sentiment for sedition was stronger in the unfortunate period of 1775–83. It did my ancient Tory soul good to walk along such thoroughfares as King St., Prince St., Royal St., King George St., Duke St., Prince George St., and Duke of Gloucester St. I have no sympathy with rebellion, but am still a loyal subject of His Britannick Majesty's Colony of Rhode-Island and Providence-Plantations. *God Save the King!*

But I did not permit my loyalist sentiments to deter me from visiting Mt. Vernon, country-seat of the late rebel leader General Washington. I have a hearty respect for the gentleman, who was a true Virginia aristocrat and man of taste for all his disaffection from his rightful sovereign. I left no part of the mansion or the grounds unvisited, and must express my most unqualified admiration and approval of the whole estate. Another trip of mine was to the quaint valley hamlet of Falls Church, Va., of whose venerable fane General Washington was a vestryman. Washington itself— mostly the older Georgetown section—claimed considerable of my attention. Of the newer buildings I think I was most impressed by the imposing temple of the Scottish Rite Masons at 16th and S. Sts. I saw this first at night; and something about the Cyclopean windowless facade, with its guardian Sphinxes and cryptical twin braziers burning beside the great bronze door, gave me an ineffably poignant sense of brooding, transmitted mystery—of terrible secrets and obscure arcana of an elder earth, handed down in nocturnal incantations amongst the ancient and privileged group whose meeting-place the temple is. I could understand the sensation of awe, sometimes amounting to fear and aversion, with which the masonic fraternity was generally regarded by outsiders in naiver ages than the present.

But the climax of the whole Odyssey was my excursion, by train, to the *Endless Caverns* in the exquisite Shenandoah Valley. Despite all the fantasy I have written concerning the nether world, I had never beheld a real cave before in all my life—and my sensations upon plunging into one of the finest specimens in the country may be better imagined than described. For over an hour I was led spellbound through illimitable gulfs and chasms of elfin beauty and daemonic mystery—here and there lighted with wondrous effect by concealed lamps, and in other places displaying awesome grottoes and abysses of unconquered night; black bottomless shafts and galleries where hidden winds and waters course eternally out of this world and all possible worlds of mankind, down, down to the sunless secrets of the gnomes and night-gaunts, and the worlds where web-winged monsters and fabulous gargoyles reign in undisputed horror.

[Lovecraft's travels of 1929 took him first to several spots in Virginia, then—after stops in Washington, Philadelphia, and New York— to visit Bernard Austin Dwyer in the ancient Dutch region of Kingston, Hurley, and New Paltz, New York.]

[30]   If my Yonkers epistle was a surprise, I fancy a note from the sun-swept bluffs of stately *Richmond* will be still more of one—yet to such an aestival clime has my antiquarian zeal led me! I meant to visit Old Philadelphia only; but a timely cheque empowered me to go farther, so I decided to pay my long-intended visit to the cradle of American civilisation—the banks of the York and James. Nor have I been disappointed in my expectations, for I have found here a wealth of colonial material rivalling that in my own New England—and in the Annapolis and Alexandria which gave me my first tantalising taste of Southernism. Fredericksburg is a treasure-house—Richmond seems like a second home-town—Williamsburg is an ecstacy of architecture rivalling even my favourite Marblehead—Yorktown is almost equal to Fredericksburg—and *James-town* is one of the most powerful imaginative stimuli I have ever received. To stand upon the soil where Elizabethan gentleman-adventurers first broke ground for the settlement of the western world is to experience a thrill that nothing else can give. Here has been a continuous civilisation since 1607—thirteen years before the landing of the Pilgrims or Plymouth Rock—and here developed a stately and mellow culture which at its ante-bellum apex may fairly be said to have eclipsed any other in the nation. The lone church tower, the Gothic walls of the ruined Ambler house, the various foundation stones visible here and there, and the tree-grown church-yard with its crumbling walls, all combine to produce an atmosphere which induces conversation in awed whispers. I have never seen anything like it before.

Williamsburg—now under careful restoration to its colonial state—was of course the architectural high spot. I spent much time in the Wythe house and Old Bruton Church and churchyard, and duly examined all the other notable buildings and sites—the gaol where Blackbeard's men were kept before their trial and hanging, the college hall designed in person by Sir Christopher Wren, the 1769 Courthouse, the foundations of the vanished colony house, and so on. All told, I came to know Williamsburg rather well in a single afternoon; and am now anxious to visit it 3 or 4 years hence, when the restoration will be complete.

In Richmond the chief object of interest for me is the Poe Shrine—an old stone house with the two adjoining houses connected as wings and used as a storehouse of Poe reliques. Here I have spent much time examining the objects associated with my supreme literary favourite—to say nothing of the marvellous model of Richmond in 1820, housed in one of the wings. On my final days in the town I am idling about the parks and getting my accumulated revision and correspondence done. Tomorrow or the next day—my cash being nearly exhausted—I shall face northward again.

[31]   My trip after leaving Washington proved as interesting as the preceding southerly portion, and spun itself out to an unforeseen length. I first paused in Philadelphia, always a favourite town with me, and went over my customary colonial haunts—besides inspecting the magnificent new art museum near the edge of Fairmount Park. This majestic Hellenic Acropolis, crowning an elevation and forming the apex of a long parkway vista, is positively the most impressive piece of contemporary architecture I have ever seen—a vast colonnaded temple of tinted marble, set high above broad flights of steps flanked by waterfalls and enclosing a tessellated courtyard at whose centre a many-jetted fountain plays. Silhouetted against the western sky it is one of the most stupendous and dream-exciting structures that the fancy can picture—a veritable gateway out of reality and into a timeless region of myth and beauty. The interior is not yet finished, but the one habitable wing houses a highly remarkable series of English Georgian and Colonial panelled rooms—including the only Pennsylvania-German specimens I have ever seen. Some of the rooms from England are from houses of the same style and period as Tharpe Hall.

From Philadelphia I proceeded to New York, where my young grandchild Frank B. Long and his parents gave me a motor lift up the Hudson shore to Kingston—the ancient town harbouring my artist-fantasiste friend Bernard Austin Dwyer, whom neither Long nor I had ever met in person before, despite long and interesting correspondence. Dwyer turned out to be as genial and pleasant in person as on paper, and I stayed at his house several days—though Long had to move on and collaborate with his father in a trout-fishing excursion (which turned out absolutely fruitless!). Kingston itself interested me prodigiously, for it is a highly venerable and historic place full of reliques of the past. The present city is a fusion of two once separate villages—Kingston proper, where my host lives and which is about a mile inland from the Hudson's west bank, and the river-port of

Rondout on the hilly bank itself, where the ferry from Rhinebeck lands and which is now a somewhat picturesque slum. The two were fused about 50 years ago when a municipal form of government was adopted. [. . .]

My other sub-pilgrimage was to New Paltz—which lies about 16 miles south of Kingston, by the Wallkill and Shawaugunk Creeks, and in the eternal shadow of the lordly and lovely Shawangunk Hills. It is a thriving village with shops, hotels, banks, a normal-school, and a newspaper, quite in contrast to the scattered and somnolent Hurley; but the modern (i.e., post-Revolutionary) town lies some distance from the heart of the ancient settlement. This has tended to preserve the original area in its pristine, early Hurley-like state; so that we may still see the place as it was in the early 18th Century. To reach the old town from the modern town one has to walk a considerable distance, descending a steep hill and crossing the railway track. The countryside between Kingston and New Paltz is as splendidly unspoiled as that between Kingston and Hurley—a typical sample of the quiet Dutch milieu so well exploited by Washington Irving. Any one of these drowsy old villages might well have been the abode of Rip Van Winkle. On this particular route lovely valleys abounded, and bends of streams in the lee of mountains produced a scenic effect hard to surpass. I saw at least one old-fashioned *covered bridge,* a type of survival usually associated nowadays with Vermont or western Massachusetts. At length the coach ascended a hill and delivered me at the principal tavern of New Paltz—the "modern" part, although even that is as quaint as Georgetown or Annapolis, and far more untainted as to original population. There are virtually no foreigners in this idyllic backwater, nearly all the inhabitants being descended from the first Huguenot settlers. Making judicious inquiries, I soon found my way down to the ancient section—Huguenot St.—and there revelled in the sparse line of old stone dwellings which has given the town so great an historical and architectural fame. There are not many— perhaps a half-dozen at best—but their fine preservation and isolation from modern influences give them a magnified charm. One of them (see accompanying postcard) is fitted as a museum and open to the public; others remain private dwellings, mostly in the hands of the families that built them more than two centuries ago. The museum—which is the old Jean Hasbrouck house built in 1712—is a large stone house of one full story and two attic stories under the immense sloping roof—an ideal storehouse for grain or other rural commodities. It is a fine type of early colonial construction under Dutch influence, (though Frenchmen built it) and I examined it with the utmost thoroughness and interest; visiting the attic and noting the massive exposed beams. It is called the "Memorial House", and a boulder monument to the town's founders stands on the small triangular green opposite it. Nearby is the quaint burying-ground housing those 'rude forefathers of the hamlet.' The other houses—of varied types, and having features as unique as transoms with double rows of lights—stretch southward along a broad shady street reminiscent of the main street of Deerfield, Mass., or Duke of Gloucester St. in Williamsburg, Virginia. All of these—the DuBois, Elbing, Abraham Hasbrouck, Freer, etc. houses— are of about the 1700 period, as can be well seen from every detail of their construction. The interior of the "Memorial House" has some highly primitive features such as the great plank doors—some unpanelled and some single-panelled. Oddly enough, there is just one of the ancient stone houses in the "modern" village—now used as a public library. In the old times it must have been an isolated farmhouse on a lonely hill.

[In 1930 Lovecraft encountered two transcendently moving sites. The first of them was the living antiquarian museum that is Charleston, South Carolina.]

[32]   I travell'd day and night from New York by stage-coach; stopping nowhere save to change vehicles at Washington, Richmond, Winston-Salem, N.C., and Columbia, S.C. This procedure turn'd out to be very well-advis'd, insomuch as every moment spent away from Charles-Town betwixt September 15 and May 15 must be accounted a sheer waste of time. Never in my eighty or ninety years of existence have I beheld a place which wou'd appeal to me so much if it were more like Providence! The climate is marvellous and summerlike—palmettos, live oaks, creeping vines, wisteria, jasmine, azaleas, etc., etc., everywhere, and the thermometer up around seventy-five degrees and eighty degrees. Near everyone is array'd in a straw hat, and it is possible to sit outdoors all day and enjoy it. Right now I am in antient Battery Park looking out across the harbour at Ft. Sumter of Civil War fame. The atmosphere makes me feel twenty years younger and one hundred percent better—and I really seem to have a surplus fund of energy for the first time since last August. The sea breeze is always blowing, and I have become as tanned as an Indian in less than a

week—I say less than a week after consulting the calendar; tho' I have seen so many sights since arriving on Monday last, that I feel as if I had been here a full decade.

But the climate, O Sage, is *only the beginning* of the miracle from an antiquarian point of view. Indeed—there is nothing about the place so wholly important and distinctive as the astoundingly eighteenth century atmosphere—for in all verity I can say that Charleston is the best-preserv'd colonial city of any size, without exception, that I have ever encounter'd. Virtually *everything* is just as it was in the reign of George the Third—indeed, 'tis easier to count the houses which are *not* colonial, than to attempt to count those which *are*. The inhabitants are by nature conservative, and have never chang'd their way of building houses thro' all the years—save for a trifling Victorian lapse in extending the northern fringe of the city, and in replacing the buildings burnt in the fire of 1861. (An event *not* connected with the Civil War.) On account of the climate, these edifices differ somewhat from the structures of the Northern colonies—usually having piazzas on all three storeys of the southern or western side. This is a feature develop'd shortly after 1750; houses before that date being more of the general colonial or British Georgian type. There are even a few cases of the familiar New England gambrel roofs—a design perhaps pick'd up by Charleston mariners on voyages to Salem or Newport, but soon abandon'd because of its unsuitability for a warm climate. Houses here are generally of brick with stucco exterior, and the general details and contours show more latitude and individuality than elsewhere. Tiled roofs are a distinctive feature—this fashion having been introduc'd subsequently to 1735. The publick buildings—dating from 1760 to 1800 and after—are of monumental magnificence; all in the classick Grecian manner, and of such solid workmanship as to be aeternal in duration. There are likewise many excellent churches and steeples—of which my chimes dominate the aural atmosphere of the city. This is visible from my Y.M.C.A. window. The most glamorous of all is the old Unitarian Church which I discover'd only this morning. This is one of those *very rare* specimens of *revived Gothick* built in *Georgian* times—perhaps as an echo of the antiquarianism which produc'd Mr. Walpole's Strawberry-Hill. It was erected in 1772, yet is in every detail a fine type of English pointed Gothick. The churchyard is the last word in glamorousness—a perfum'd green tropick twilight of overarching live-oaks and hanging vines, with antient headstones peeping through a vivid, odorous undergrowth threaded by curious winding walks. It is really something out of a *dream* of my oddly prescient "Randolph Carter"—such things do not belong to the waking world! In this enchanted spot are interr'd the last mortal reliquiae of the Rev'd. Samuel Gilman, author of the college hymn "Fair Harvard", who was long pastor of the church, and whose birthplace I beheld in 1927 at Gloucester, in the Province of the Massachusetts-Bay.

One of the most famous features of Charleston is its profusion of wrought-iron work—gates, balconies, window-grilles, railings, and the like; all of the finest craftsmanship. I will enclose among other views, a card showing one typical gate. These gates are especially numerous because of the prevalence of high-wall'd gardens in this land of luxurious flowers, rambling vines, and opulent trees that weave an omnipresent green twilight. Charlestonians endeavour to secure privacy and the open air at the same time.

Another phase of Charleston is represented by the sea islands that bound the harbour, one of which—the Isle of Palms—is reputed to possess the finest beach on the Atlantick Coast. Of these, my own chief interest centres in Sullivan's Island, which contains Ft. Moultrie, where Poe served in 1829 as "Corp. Edgar A. Perry" of the Quartermaster's Corps. Many of the scenes of "The Gold Bug" were laid upon this island, and it gave me a thrill to visit in person a region familiar to me in literature for above thirty years.

[By late May Lovecraft was back in New York, where he had one final glimpse of Hart Crane, two years before the latter's suicide.]

[33] After the museum we returned to 230; whence, after a brief period of discussion, I set out for my evening engagement at Loveman's. We had meant to devote most of the time to outdoor exploration; but after a sumptuous dinner prepared by young McGrath we observed the approach of a rainstorm, hence cancelled this feature and spent the time in general discussion and the viewing of some of Loveman's literary treasures. About 8 o'clock the bell rang, and there appeared that tragically drink-riddled but now eminent friend of Loveman's whom I had met in Cleveland in 1922, and once or twice later in New York—the poet Hart Crane, whose new book, "The Bridge", has made him one of the most celebrated and talked-of figures of contemporary American letters. He had been scheduled to speak over the radio during the evening; but a shipwreck off the coast

(demanding the use of the ether for important messages) had cut off all local radio programmes and left him free. When he entered, his discourse was of alcoholics in various phases—and of the correct amount of whiskey one ought to drink in order to speak well in public—but as soon as a bit of poetic and philosophic discussion sprang up, this sordid side of his strange dual personality slipped off like a cloak, and left him as a man of great scholarship, intelligence, and aesthetic taste, who can argue as interestingly and profoundly as anyone I have ever seen. Poor devil—he has "arrived" at last as a standard American poet seriously regarded by all reviewers and critics; yet at the very crest of his fame he is on the verge of psychological, physical, and financial disintegration, and with no certainty of ever having the inspiration to write a major work of literature again. After about three hours of acute and intelligent argument poor Crane left—to hunt up a new supply of whiskey and banish reality for the rest of the night! He gets to be a nuisance now and then, but Loveman is too conscious of his tragic importance and genuine genius as a man of letters to be harsh or brusque toward him. His case is surely a sad one—all the more so because of his great attainments and of the new fame which he is so ill-fitted to carry for any considerable time. He looks more weather-beaten and drink-puffed than he did in the past, though the shaving off of his moustache has somewhat improved him. He is only 33, yet his hair is nearly white. Altogether, his case is almost like that of Baudelaire on a vastly smaller scale. "The Bridge" really is a thing of astonishing merit.

[Then, in early September, Lovecraft took an excursion to Quebec—his first time out of the United States—and was overwhelmed by its archaic beauty. He would return there twice more in the next three years and would also write an immense travelogue, *A Description of the Town of Quebeck* (1930–31), his single longest literary work.]

[34]   Am beginning to get my revision under control, and hope to snatch time for some tales of my own before long. The coming week-end I shall take advantage of a cheap excursion to the quaint and ancient town of *Quebec*—which I have wished to see all my life, and which after all is not so very far from New England. This city, founded in 1608, is perhaps the most traditional and old-world-like place on the American continent, and I look forward to a marvellous time there. It will mark my first excursion

outside the territorial limits of the U.S., and my first treading of the soil of that British Empire to which my spirit has never ceased to be loyal despite the secession of the Rhode Island colony on May 4, 1776. Will continue this letter after my return, enclosing any good Quebec views I may happen to come across. Long has just been there, and says it will surpass my fondest expectations—except that I'll find it too French for my ingrainedly English soul.

Later

And it *did* surpass all my fondest expectations! Never have I seen another place like it! All my former standards of urban beauty must be abandoned after my sight of Quebec! It hardly belongs to the world of prosaic reality at all—it is a dream of city walls, fortress-crowned cliffs, silver spires, narrow, winding, perpendicular streets, magnificent vistas, and the mellow, leisurely civilisation of an elder world. The enclosed gives hardly more than a hint of the actuality. Horse vehicles still abound, and the atmosphere is altogether of the past. It is a perfectly preserved bit of old royalist France, transplanted to the New World with very little loss of atmosphere. My stay was perforce tragically brief, but in 3 days (from early morning till pitch dark) I managed to see about everything there was to see (aside from interiors) by keeping constantly on the move. I feel as if I had lived there for years—though I must go again and at greater length in order to absorb impressions to a really satisfying degree. The oldest house [. . .] was built in 1674, but most of the buildings date from the early or middle 18th century. All architecture is French—mostly brick and stucco—and the buildings strongly suggest those of Charleston, S.C.—perhaps because of the strong French Huguenot influence in the latter town. The 400-foot perpendicular cliff with its staircases and steep ascents, the massive and almost perfectly preserved city wall, the dominating citadel, and the strange, ancient tangled streets, all combine to make Quebec an almost unearthly bit of fairyland. Everything I have seen before seems tame in comparison. The only side trip I took was to the great falls of the Montmorency river—on the upper level of which stands the old house in which the Duke of Kent (Queen Victoria's father) lived whilst in military service here in the late 1790's. The countryside has some moderately quaint villages dominated by curious French churches, but is too much modernised to be really colourful. The real charm is all concentrated in Quebec City.

Colleagues

[During this period Lovecraft came into contact with an ever-increasing circle of like-minded literary colleagues, and their mutual association proved a source of both literary and personal inspiration to Lovecraft. Among the most important of these are August Derleth, Robert E. Howard, and Clark Ashton Smith. Although he never met any of these three colleagues, his voluminous correspondence with them testifies to the value Lovecraft placed on his relationship with them.]

[35]   Derleth impressed me tremendously favourably from the moment I began to hear from him personally. I saw that he had a prodigious fund of activity and reserve mental energy, and that it would only be a question of time before he began to correlate it to real aesthetic advantage. There was a bit of callow egotism also—but that was only to be expected; and indeed, a boy of his age would scarcely have been normal if he hadn't had it. And surely enough, as the years passed, I saw that the kid was truly growing. The delicate reminiscent sketches begun a couple of years ago were the final proof—for there, indeed, he had reached what was unmistakably sincere and serious self-expression of a high order. Nor did it take long to see that this was the real stuff, and not any mere flash in the pan. He kept it up—naturally, spontaneously, and without effort—and the various fragments began to fit splendidly into a larger organic unity. There was no disputing that he *really had something to say*—which is true of woefully few prolific and often cultivated aspirants—and that he was trying to say it honestly and effectively, with a minimum of the jaunty hack devices and stylistic tricks which went into his printed pot-boiling material. Undeniably, a writer of substance was in the making—and I have since had every reason to confirm and reiterate that dictum. Even his hack work is shewing the difference—though Wright persistently favours his poorest things, and accepts the better items only after a campaign of attrition on Derleth's part. As you say, his tendency toward mass production is hardly a good thing for his style; and Derleth shews the right idea in his reminiscent pieces when he seeks utter simplicity of language, and places accuracy and significance of mood and impression above everything else. He will be worth watching in the years to come, for very few of us have as clearly-defined and serious a mass of impressions demanding an outlet. With his sensitiveness to shades of experience, we can well picture the effect of added years and

wider life on his imaginative background and creative faculty. I doubt if he will be primarily a weird writer—though he will probably always retain an interest in the bizarre and the macabre. He actually believes in the supernatural—a circumstance which will tend to counteract any drift away from weird interests that realistic experience and the prose of life might otherwise bring.

[36]   I don't care what any bird's I.Q. is, so long as he is as original, independent, and sincere in his attitude and work as his own particular cerebrum will let him be. Of course, as I've said, I feel a bond of fellowship with the Bivonae and the Olsons, and a respectful admiration for the Aristotles, the Descartes, the Sterlings, and the Belknaps; but aside from these little partialities I'm scarcely less interested in the chap of average endowment *who is equally original and distinctive* in thought and expression. Let me see if I can cite a case. Well—take Bob Howard. There's a bird whose *basic mentality* seems to me to be just about the good respectable citizen's bank cashier, medium shopkeeper, ordinary lawyer, stockbroker, high school teacher, prosperous farmer, pulp fictionist, skilled mechanic, successful salesman, responsible government clerk, routine army or navy officer up to a colonel, etc. average—bright and keen, accurate and retentive, but not profound or analytical—yet who is at the same time one of the most eminently interesting beings I know. Two-Gun is interesting because he has refused to let his thoughts and feelings be standardised. He remains himself. He couldn't—today—solve a quadratic equation, and probably thinks that Santayana is a brand of coffee—but he has a set of emotions which he has moulded and directed in uniquely harmonious patterns, and from which proceed his marvellous outbursts of historic retrospection and geographical description (in letters), and his vivid, energised and spontaneous pictures of a prehistoric world of battle in fiction . . . . pictures which insist on remaining distinctive and self-expressive despite all outward concessions to the stultifying pulp ideal. It is, therefore, piquant and enjoyable to exchange ideas with Two-Gun or to read his stories. He is of about the same intelligence as Seabury Quinn—but Yuggoth, what a difference!

[Lovecraft had, of course, known Smith since 1922, but in 1929 Smith began producing weird stories at a rapid rate, thereby further cementing their bonds of friendship.]

[37]   Yes—I certainly would like to meet Smith, who is in some ways the most unusual person I know. I have been a close correspondent of his since August 1922, when I was 'put next' to him by my friend Samuel Loveman (the "Harley Warren" of my "Statement of Randolph Carter"), who in turn got in touch with him through the late poet George Sterling. Smith was born in Auburn, California, in 1893, and has never been out of his native state. He lives with his parents in a cottage on a hill side somewhat outside Auburn village—within easy access of a rather weird type of mountain scenery (Crater Ridge etc.—cf. "The City of the Singing Flame")[35] which has figured in some of his tales. His family has always been in very strait-ened circumstances, and his parents are now in the 80's—having married late in life. His father is a gentleman of a very ancient English Catholic family—born in England, and bearing the hyphenated name of Ashton-Smith. (C A S does not use the hyphen) The elder Smith in his youth was something of a soldier of fortune, and travelled in many odd corners of the earth, including the Amazon jungles of South America. Clark probably de-rives much of his exotic taste from the tales told him by his father when he was very small—he was especially impressed by accounts of the gor-geously plumed birds and bizarre tropical flowers of equatorial Brazil. On his mother's side Smith comes of American Southern blood—Huguenot and English. From childhood he was a poet, artist, and dreamer—obviously something of a boy wonder. He attended ordinary public schools and never went to a university, but has amassed an immense and curious erudi-tion through private study. When 17 he published his first book of po-etry—"The Star-Treader"[36]—[. . .] and attracted the favourable attention of George Sterling. At the same time he conducted his original and untutored experiments in art—evolving a fantastic style of drawing and painting which is really ineffably powerful despite its lack of technical smoothness. When he had an exhibition of paintings at Berkeley many critics highly praised his work. Smith's tastes have always inclined toward the cosmic and the fantastic, and his poetry is mainly concerned with bizarre themes despite occasional excursions into more mundane lyrical fields. Much of his verse shows the influence of Sterling; whom he has vis-ited many times, and who wrote prefaces for some of his books.[37] At one period—when he was about 18—Smith wrote several stories . . . . in a vein somewhat less non-terrestrial than his present work . . . . but he did not keep up the practice. His present series of tales dates from 1925. Until lately he suffered from very poor health—including a now-vanished touch

of tuberculosis. During his ill period he displayed the greatest disregard of
health rules—exposing himself recklessly to all kinds of weather—but his
rashness cured instead of killed him. I believe he was at one time inclined
toward a touch of artistic "pose"—wearing a picturesque shock of hair and
even growing a full beard—but that is all over now. Naturally, he is rather
misunderstood and unappreciated by the provincial villagers among whom
he lives, but as he gets into middle age this disturbs him less than it used to.
I can see a perceptible mellowing and growth of geniality in him during the
last five years. He no longer has the touch of active, cynical bitterness that
he once had. At one period Smith conducted a column—largely verse—in
his local paper, *The Auburn Journal.* At the age of 32 he took up the study of
French—at home, and without a teacher—and in six months was writing
French poems of marvellous power. He has since contributed verse to
some of the leading Paris magazines—the editor of one of which wrote him
that he could hardly believe he was not a Frenchman. And yet Smith has
never known any French-speaking person, and could hardly *pronounce* the
language intelligibly! His translations of Baudelaire—both free para-
phrases in verse, and literal ones in prose—are the best I have ever seen,
although they have not yet found a publisher. Smith has read the magazine
W T from the start—and was the first to direct my attention to it. At that
period he did not expect to contribute to it, but at my urging he sent in several poems—many of which were accepted. I kept urging the editors—first
Edwin Baird and then Wright—to use his art work, but they were very
slow to respond. Indeed, it was not till this year that any picture of his was
accepted. His new period of fiction writing was very slow in developing. In
1925 he wrote "Sadastor" and "The Abominations of Yondo",[38] but Wright
rejected both. Not till about 1930 did he become prolific—and persistent in
bombarding editors. Then his success as a fictionist began quite suddenly—both W T and the science-fiction magazines accepting his tales in
unlimited quantity. This unfortunately caused him to write many cheap
hack tales, but such pot-boiling has never spoiled his real style. When he
sets out to write something really serious, he *does* it! His pictorial work
would require a chapter in itself. Some of his hideous heads—proboscidian,
semi-reptile, semi-insect—are classics of their kind, and no one excels him
in drawing unearthly, abnormal, and poisonous *vegetation.* His large landscapes—scenes on Saturn, and on still remoter worlds—are full of a mysterious spell. If you'd like to see some of Smith's smaller drawings I'll
gladly lend you those in my possession—as soon as their present borrower

returns them. I have met two people who have seen Smith face to face—one friend of his in Auburn who visited the east last year,[39] and one easterner (George Kirk) who visited him in California in 1921. He is very kindly and likeable, and incredibly brave in his lifelong struggle against illness, poverty, and misunderstanding. He has at times helped out his revenues by fruit-picking, but is always forced to struggle hard. His home is a very small one, with no running water—just a primitive well outside. He writes in the open a good deal—at a table in his front yard—and takes many walking trips in the picturesque mountains of his region. The responsibility of his aged parents (who are inclined to domineer a bit) has kept him chained rather closely at home—if it were not for them, he would probably manage to see more of the world. Perhaps, though, his localism has been a blessing in disguise—his limited acquaintance with this world (San Francisco being the only metropolis he knows) giving his imagination all the keener force in depicting other worlds and other universes!

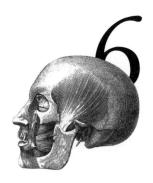

The Old Gentleman
(1931–1937)

Weird Fiction: Theory and Practice

[With the onset of the 1930s, Lovecraft gave increasing attention to the role of art—and of his own art, weird fiction—in
the modern world. Influenced by such works as Joseph
Wood Krutch's *The Modern Temper* (1929), Lovecraft came to
believe that weird art must depict not "contradictions" but
"supplements" to the known facts of the universe if it is to remain viable. As a result, he effected a union of old-time Goth-
icism with the new field of science fiction.]

[1] Some former art attitudes—like sentimental romance, loud
heroics, ethical didacticism, etc.—are so patently hollow as to
be visibly absurd and non-usable from the start. Others, like
those dependent on moods and feelings (pity, tragedy, personal
affection, group loyalty etc.) which are still empirical conduct-
factors though intellectually undermined, have an excellent
chance of survival. Fantastic literature cannot be treated as a
single unit, because it is a composite resting on widely diver-
gent bases. I really agree that *Yog-Sothoth* is a basically immature conception, and unfitted for really serious literature. The
fact is, I have never approached serious literature as yet. But I
consider the use of actual folk-myths as even more childish than
the use of new artificial myths, since in employing the former

one is forced to retain many blatant puerilities and contradictions of experience which could be subtilised or smoothed over if the supernaturalism were modelled to order for the given case. The only permanently artistic use of Yog-Sothothery, I think, is in symbolic or associative phantasy of the frankly poetic type; in which fixed dream-patterns of the natural organism are given an embodiment and crystallisation. The reasonable permanence of this phase of poetic phantasy as a possible art form (whether or not favoured by current fashion) seems to me a highly strong probability. It will, however, demand ineffable adroitness—the vision of a Blackwood joined to the touch of a De la Mare[1]—and is probably beyond my utmost powers of achievement. I hope to see material of this sort in time, though I hardly expect to produce anything even remotely approaching it myself. I am too saturated in the empty gestures and pseudo-moods of an archaic and vanished world to have any successful traffick with symbols of an expanded dream-reality. But there is another phase of cosmic phantasy (which may or may not include frank Yog-Sothothery) whose foundations appear to me as better grounded than these of ordinary oneiroscopy; personal limitation regarding the *sense of outsideness*. I refer to the aesthetic crystallisation of that burning and inextinguishable feeling of mixed wonder and oppression which the sensitive imagination experiences upon scaling itself and its restrictions against the vast and provocative abyss of the unknown. This has always been the chief emotion in my psychology; and whilst it obviously figures less in the psychology of the majority, it is clearly a well-defined and permanent factor from which very few sensitive persons are wholly free. Here we have a natural biological phenomenon so untouched and untouchable by intellectual disillusion that it is difficult to envisage its total death as a factor in the most serious art. Reason as we may, we cannot destroy a normal perception of the highly limited and fragmentary nature of our visible world of perception and experience as scaled against the outside abyss of unthinkable galaxies and unplumbed dimensions—an abyss wherein our solar system is the merest dot (by the same *local* principle that makes a sand-grain a dot as compared with the whole planet earth) *no matter what relativistic system we may use in conceiving the cosmos as a whole*—and this perception cannot fail to act potently upon the natural physical instinct of *pure curiosity;* an instinct just as basic and primitive, and as impossible of destruction by any philosophy whatsoever, as the parallel instincts of hunger, sex, ego-expansion, and fear. You grossly underestimate this physical instinct, which appears to be as undeveloped in you as superficial exhibitionism is in me; yet its potent reality is attested by the life-work of a Pliny, a Copernicus, a Newton, an Einstein, an Eddington, a Shapley, a Huxley, an Amundsen, a Scott, a Shackleton, a Byrd . . . . but hell! what's the use? Who can tell a blind man what sight is? At any rate, the lure of the unknown abyss remains as potent as ever under any conceivable intellectual, aesthetic, or social order; and will crop out as a forbidden thing even in societies where the external ideal of altruistic collectivism reigns. In types where this urge cannot be gratified by actual research in pure science, or by the actual physical exploration of unknown parts of the earth, it is inevitable that a symbolic aesthetic outlet will be demanded. You can't dodge it—the condition must exist, under all phases of cosmic interpretation, as long as a sense-chained race of inquirers on a microscopic earth-dot are faced by the black, unfathomable gulph of the Outside, with its forever-unexplorable orbs and its virtually certain sprinkling of utterly unknown life-forms. A great part of religion is merely a childish and diluted pseudo-gratification of this perpetual gnawing toward the ultimate illimitable void. Superadded to this simple curiosity is the galling sense of *intolerable restraint* which all sensitive people (except self-blinded earth-gazers like little Augie DerlEth)[2] feel as they survey their natural limitations in time and space as scaled against the freedoms and expansions and comprehensions and adventurous expectancies which the mind can formulate as abstract conceptions. Only a perfect clod can fail to discern these irritant feelings in the greater part of mankind—feelings so potent and imperious that, if denied symbolic outlets in aesthetics or religious fakery, they produce actual hallucinations of the supernatural, and drive half-responsible minds to the concoction of the most absurd hoaxes and the perpetuation of the most absurd specific myth-types. Don't let little Augie sidetrack you. The general revolt of the sensitive mind against the tyranny of corporeal enclosure, restricted sense-equipment, and the laws of force, space, and causation, is a far keener and bitterer and better-founded one than any of the silly revolts of long-haired poseurs against isolated and specific instances of cosmic inevitability. But of course it does not take the form of personal petulance, because there is no convenient scape-goat to saddle the impersonal ill upon. Rather does it crop out as a pervasive sadness and unplaceable impatience, manifested in a love of strange dreams and an amusing eagerness to be galled by the quack cosmic pretensions of the various religious circuses. Well—in our day the quack circuses are wearing pretty thin despite the premature senilities of fat Chesterbellocs and affected Waste Land Shantih-dwellers,[3] and the nostalgic and unmotivated "overbeliefs" of elderly and childhood-crippled physicists. The time has come when the normal revolt against time, space, and matter must assume a form not overtly incompatible with what is known of reality—when it must be gratified by images forming *supplements* rather than *contradictions* of the visible and mensurable universe. And what, if not a form of *non-supernatural cosmic art,* is to pacify this sense of revolt—as well as gratify the cognate sense of curiosity? "Dunt esk", as they say in your decadent cosmopolis! No, young Belloc, you can't rule out a phase of human feeling and expression which springs from instincts wholly basic and physical. Cosmic phantasy *of some sort* is as assured of possible permanence (its status subject to caprices of fashion) as is the literature of struggle and eroticism. But of course, as I have said before, its later and less irresponsible forms will doubtless differ vastly from most of the weird literature we have had so far. Like the lighter forms of dream-phantasy and Yog-Sothothery, it will require a delicate and precise technique; so that a crude old-timer like myself would never be likely to excel in it. Nevertheless, if I live much longer, I may try my hand at something of the sort—for it is really closer to my serious psychology than anything else on or off the earth. In "The Colour Out of Space" I began to get near it—though "Dunwich" and the "Whisperer" represent a relapse. In using up the ideas in my commonplacebook, I shall doubtless perpetrate a great deal more childish hokum, (gratifying to me only through personal association with the past) yet the time may come when I shall at least try something approximately serious.

[Lovecraft put his new principles into practice in the short novel *At the Mountains of Madness* (1931), which he came to regard as one of his most successful attempts at realism by the slow accumulation of detail.]

[2]   No—not even yet is the Old Man quite in his grave! But I may be before I'm through with what lies ahead of me . . . . . . which is nothing less than a siege of typing probably extending to nearly 100 pages! May Pegāna give me strength! The job in question is the new Antarctic thing which I was resolving in my mind when I last wrote you. Upon beginning the actual composition, I found additional incidents crowding in on me like pseudo-memories; so that the text spun itself out to 80 pages of my crabbed and interlined script before I could conscientiously call it a story. Judging from precedent, those 80 will expand to 100 in double-spaced Remington

work—making a novelette of 30,000 or 35,000 words. It is divided into 12 sections, and is capable of a major serial division in the exact middle. If I land it anywhere, it'll mean a marvellously welcome cheque—but with such length, the landing process won't be easy. It is entitled "At the Mountains of Madness", and treats of a hellish legacy from elder aeons amidst the eternal icy peaks of the polar waste—S. Lat. 76°10′, E. Lon. 113°15′. In a sense, it might be called a sort of pale "scientifiction"—but on the other hand, it belongs to the "Arthur Gordon Pym" tradition.[4] I mention Pym, and have something scream that hideous and cryptic word—"*Tekeli-li!*"

[Late in 1931 Lovecraft wrote the substantial novelette "The Shadow over Innsmouth," another triumph of verisimilitude based upon his recent excursion to the decaying backwater of Newburyport, Massachusetts. By this time, however, rejections of some of his best work were adversely affecting Lovecraft's self-esteem, and he felt that his new story was not a success.]

[3]   I certainly hope you can get to see Newburyport sooner or later, for its antiquity and desolation make it one of the most spectrally fascinating spots I have ever seen. It has started me off on a new story idea—not very novel in relation to other things of mine, but born of the imaginative overtones of such a place. My scene will not be called Newburyport, but will be the accursed sea-town of *Innsmouth*, between Newburyport and Arkham. However, this tale may never see the light, since that Putnam rebuff[5] has caused me to pause for a general stock-taking, and to review the question of whether my stuff really is any good except in a superficial way. All my tales, except for perhaps one or two, dissatisfy me profoundly on close analysis; and I have about decided to call a halt unless I can manage to do better than I am doing. I am using the new idea as a basis for what might be called laboratory experimentation—writing it out in different manners, one after the other, in an effort to determine the mood and tempo best suited to them. What I shall—or shan't—write hereafter depends to some extent on how I come out with these experiments. My latest move is to destroy all three versions written to date, preparatory to embarking on a fourth. The trouble with most of my stuff is that it falls between two stools—the vile magazine type subconsciously engrafted on my method by W.T. association, and the real story. My tales are not bad enough for cheap editors, nor good enough for standard acceptance and recognition. As

Putnam's pointed out, they tend to become too explanatory—to lack subtlety in the manner of Blackwood's "Incredible Adventures" or Machen's "White People." In choosing which direction to take for further efforts, I have little difficulty. Repugnance—and lack of natural cleverness and adaptability—definitely deters me from the popular "eckshun" field, so all I can do is to try honestly to write really better stories or give up the whole mess as a bad job—though possibly pulling off consciously mediocre yarns now and then for sheer amusement.

[By the mid-1930s Lovecraft had consciously articulated his own method of writing stories. He set down his principles in the essay "Notes on Writing Weird Fiction" (1933) and elaborated them further in a letter written two years later.]

[4]   In a way, it is impossible for me to give a detailed account of how I write a story—from the moment of conception till it is sent out to gain one of Wright's rejection slips—since I've scarcely ever used the same method for any two stories. It all depends on the individual circumstances.

The one thing I never do is sit down and seize a pen with the deliberate intention of writing a story. Nothing but hack work ever comes of that. The only stories I write are those whose central ideas, pictures, and moods occur to me spontaneously.

These ideas, pictures, and moods come from every possible source—dreams, reading, daily occurrences, odd visual glimpses, or origins so remote and fragmentary that I cannot place them. Naturally, they come in different stages of development—sometimes a bare incident, effect, concept, or shade of feeling which requires a whole fabric of deliberate story-construction to support it, and sometimes a sequence of incidents which forms a goodly part of the final story. One story I wholly dreamed—"The Statement of Randolph Carter" being a literal recording of what sleep brought me one night in December 1919.

If there is any one method which I follow, I suppose it is to be found by taking an average of my lines of procedure in all cases where I have done a great deal of deliberate construction. For example—behind "The Whisperer in Darkness" two initial impelling concepts: the idea of a man in a lonely farmhouse besieged by "outside" horrors, and the general impression of weirdness in the Vermont landscape, gained during a fortnight's visit near Brattleboro in 1928. Upon these notions I had to build a story—

and in doing that I followed a course which may or may not be typical. Here, then, is a rough idea of what I did in that case—and what I do more or less in similar cases.

First, a coherent story—or a rough approximation of one—must be thought out. This is a mental process, before pen and paper are approached. It is not often necessary to fill in details, or even to carry the plot forward to a definite end. The point is to think up some sort of definite series of developments which shall give the initial concept or concepts a plausible reason for existing, and make it or them appear to be the logical, inevitable outgrowth of some vital and convincing background. This "plot" or series of steps need not be a permanent one. Perhaps it will lose all its salient points during later manipulation—other and better ways of accounting for the central idea being discovered. But it is a useful starting point—something to work with and build upon. When it has attained some definite shape in one's head, the time has come to turn to writing materials.

Yet even the second—or first recorded state is not that of actual story-writing. Instead, one had better begin with a synopsis of the given plot—listing all developments *in the order of their supposed actual occurrence*, not the order in which they will finally reach the reader. This is to provide a logical working background for the writer, so that he can envisage his plot as something which has really happened, and decide at leisure on what narrative devices to adopt in preparing a dramatic, suspense-filled version for the reader. In writing such a synopsis I try to describe everything with enough fullness to cover all vital points and motivate all the incidents planned. Details, comments, and estimates of the *consequences* of certain points are often desirable. The result is rather like an official report of some chain of happenings—each event set down prosaically in precise order of occurrence. Often the previously-planned plot will suffer great changes in the course of this recording.

Then comes the next stage—deciding *how to tell* the story already thought out. This begins mentally—by thinking of various effective ways to arrange certain unfoldings and revelations. We speculate on what to tell first, and what to save for later presentation in order to preserve suspense or provoke interest. We analyse the dramatic value of putting this thing before that thing, or vice versa, and try to see what selection of details and order of narration best conduce to that rising tide of development and final burst of revealing completion which we call "climax." Having roughly made our decisions regarding a tentative arrangement, we proceed to write these down in the form of a *second synopsis*—a synopsis or "scenario" of events *in order of their narration to the reader,* with ample fullness and detail, and ultimate climax. I never hesitate to change the original synopsis to fit some newly devised developments if such a devising can increase the dramatic force or general effectiveness of the future story. Incidents should be interpolated or deleted at will—the writer never being bound by his original conception, even though the ultimate result be a tale wholly different from that first planned. The wise author lets additions and alterations be made whenever such are suggested by anything in the formulating process.

The time has now come to *write the story* in the approximate language the reader is to see. This first draught should be written rapidly, fluently, and not too critically—following the second synopsis. I always change incidents and plot whenever the developing process seems to suggest such change—never being bound by any previous design. If the development suddenly reveals new opportunities for dramatic effect or vivid story-telling, I add whatever I think advantageous—going back and reconciling early points to the new plan. I insert or delete whole sections when I deem it necessary or desirable—trying different beginnings and endings till the best is found. But I always take infinite pains to make sure that all references throughout the story are thoroughly reconciled with the final design. Then—in completing the rough draught—I seek to remove all possible superfluities—words, sentences, paragraphs, or whole episodes or elements—observing the usual precautions about the reconciliation of all references. So open-minded do I keep during this stage of writing, that several of my tales (such as "The Picture in the House", "The Dunwich Horror", and "The Shadow Over Innsmouth") end in a manner totally unforeseen when I began them.

Now comes the *revision*—a tedious, painstaking process. One must go over the entire job, paying attention to vocabulary, syntax, rhythm of prose, proportioning of parts, niceties of tone, grace and convincingness of *transitions* (scene to scene, slow and detailed action to rapid and sketchy time-causing actions and vice versa . . .), effectiveness of beginning, ending, dramatic suspense and interest, plausibility and atmosphere, and various other elements. That finishes the story—and the rest is merely the preparation of a neatly typed version . . . the most horrible part of all for me. I detest the typewriter, and could not possibly compose a story on one. The mechanical limitations of the machine are death to good style anyway—it being harder to transpose words and make the necessary complex interlineations when bound to keys and rollers, while delicate prose rhythms are defeated by the irrelevant regular rhythms of line-endings and roller-turnings. Nothing was ever composed on a typewriter which could not have been composed better with pen or pencil.

Well—as I have said, this list of composition steps is merely an average or idealised one. In practice, one seldom follows every step literally. Often one or more of the things supposed to be done on paper can better be done in one's head—so that many tales (such as my "Music of Erich Zann" or "Dagon") never had any kind of written synopsis.

Nor should the given method be followed even mentally in some cases. Sometimes I have found it useful to begin writing a story without either a synopsis or even a bare idea of how it shall be developed and ended. This is when I feel a need of recording and exploiting some especially powerful or suggestive mood or picture to the full—as in "The Strange High House in the Mist." In such a procedure the beginning thus produced may be regarded as a problem to be motivated and explained. Of course, in developing this motivation and explanation it may be well to alter—or even transform, transpose beyond recognition, or altogether eliminate—the beginning first produced. Once in a while, when a writer has a marked style with rhythms and cadences closely linked with imaginative associations, it is possible for him to begin *weaving a mood* with characteristic paragraphs and letting this mood dictate much of the tale. This is what I did with "The White Ship"—though it must be owned that the result was not very successful.

I try always to keep a supply of story-ideas on hand—recording all bizarre notions, moods, dreams, images, concepts, etc., (and keeping all press clippings involving such) for future use. I do not despair if they seem to have no logical development. Each one may be worked over gradually—surrounded with notes and synopses, and finally built into a coherent explanatory structure capable of fictional use. I never hurry, nor seek to emulate the commercial writers who boast of their wordage per day or week. The best stories sometimes grow very slowly—over long periods, and with intervals in their formulation. *Too long* intervals, though, are to be discouraged; insomuch as they often alienate the writer from the mood and tempo of his task.

Random notes: In a tale involving complex philosophical or scientific principles, I try to have all explanations *hinted* at the outset, when the thesis is first put forward (as in Machen's "White People"), thus leaving the narrative and climactic sections unencumbered.

I am always willing to spend as much time and care on the formulation of a synopsis as on the writing of the actual tale—*for its synopsis is the real heart of the story.* The real creative work of fiction-writing is originating and shaping a story in synoptic form.

In order to ensure an adequate climax it is in rare cases advisable to prepare one in considerable detail *first*, and then construct a main synopsis explaining it. I followed this plan in "The Tree", "The Hound", and other minor pieces. With one it works less satisfactorily than with others.

I always endeavour to read and analyse the best weird writers—Poe, Machen, Blackwood, James, Dunsany, de la Mare, Benson, Wakefield, Ewers, and the like—, seeking to understand their methods and recognise the specific laws of emotional modulation behind their potent effects. Such study gradually increases one's own grasp of his materials, and strengthens his powers of expression. By the same token, I strive to avoid all close attention to the prose and methods of pulp hack writers—things which insidiously corrupt and cheapen a serious style. I would advise all serious literary aspirants to cultivate a sort of defensive semi-blindness in skimming cheap magazine fiction—developing an ability to sift out incidents and follow a plot without closely paying attention to the language. And most plots of this sort had better be followed very lightly and emulated not at all. In a year's output of pulp magazines there are scarcely a dozen stories seriously conceived and artistically written to an extent justifying remembrance, preservation, or imitation. The genuine writer must forget editors and possible audiences, resign himself to very infrequent sales, and labour only to express himself and satisfy his inward standards of fiction. Commercialism and decent literature have no meeting-point except by accident.

[In a letter of 1934 Lovecraft harps—perhaps excessively—on his literary shortcomings (especially his inability to draw character), but emphasizes his central literary mission as depicting "violations of the natural order."]

[5]   Regarding my own stuff—it is a regrettable fact that I am never likely to produce anything of general acceptability. While having the highest respect for the authors of realistic fiction, and envying those who are able to accomplish the successful reflection of life in narrative form, I am sadly aware through actual experiment that this is a province definitely

closed to me. The fact is, that I have absolutely nothing to say where actual, unvarnished life is concerned. The events of life are so profoundly and chronically uninteresting to me—and I know so little about them as a whole—that I can't scrape up anything in connexion with them which could possibly have the zest and tension and suspense needed to form a real story. That is, I am incurably blind to dramatic or fictional values except where violations of the natural order are concerned. Of course, I understand *objectively* what those values are, and can apply them with fair success to the criticism and revision of others' work; but they do not take hold of my imagination sufficiently to find creative expression. When I try to think up some vivid sequence of actual events I simply come to nothing. The spark of creation and instinctive dramatic arrangement simply isn't there. I'm not deeply interested, and I can't get deeply interested. What is more—I don't know enough about life to be an effective exponent of it. On account of my early ill-health and naturally retiring disposition my contacts with mankind—and with its varied aspects, folkways, idioms, attitudes, and standards—have been extremely limited; so that there are probably very few people outside the extreme rustic class who are more fundamentally unsophisticated than myself. I don't know what different kinds of people do and think and feel and say—their lives, languages, values, and technical processes are as remote from me as the manners and customs of the Cingalese. Now it is impossible to write about one's spatial neighbours as one would write about the Cingalese—as remotely and objectively, that is—so that the would-be realist who does not know life well is perforce compelled to resort to imitation—copying what he picks up from the doubtful and artificial media of books, plays, newspaper reports, and the like. That is what Long does—but I am too actual a realist in psychology to be able to do this. I know so damned well that the pictures one gets from books are unreal and distorted, that I *can't* sit down and transcribe those second-hand (and probably erroneous) impressions with all the assumed convincingness of one who really knows about them. I know that I *don't* know about the people I'd be writing about, hence I can't put up a jaunty bluff that their ways and speech and thoughts are familiar to me. Let us say that I'm called upon to portray the way one of your dashing young clubman-detectives responds to a given situation. Now I'm not a dashing young clubman-detective and never was one—nor have I ever been acquainted with any. Obviously, I don't know how the hell one of them (assuming that there *are* such persons) would react to any given situation. How, then, can I portray any of their deeds? If I copy from other writers I'll probably be copying artificial gestures remote from reality—and *knowing* this, I can't put any zest into copying. And this is true of so many different types of person—there are so *few* types that I really understand (and I'm not sure that I understand even them)—that I could never piece out the dramatis personae of any well-rounded work of fiction. My handicap is—all apart from the basic lack of interest—really twofold. First, my acquaintance with varied phases of life is too small for effective literary use. Second, I lack the natural faculty of imagination which gives the genuine innate author the instinctive power to understand and portray what different sorts of people would feel and think and say and do in various given situations. Long also lacks this faculty, but he won't admit it. All his characters are little duplicate Belknaps in thought, manner, and speech. But I *realise* my lack and can't go ahead weaving vacuity when I *know* it's vacuity.

However—the crucial thing is my lack of interest in ordinary life. No one ever wrote a story yet without some real emotional drive behind it—and I have not that drive except where violations of the natural order . . . . defiances and evasions of time, space, and cosmic law . . . . are concerned. Just why this is so I haven't the slightest idea—it simply *is* so. I am interested only in broad pageants—historic streams—orders of biological, chemical, physical, and astronomical organisation—and the only conflict which has any deep emotional significance to me is that of the *principle of freedom or irregularity or adventurous opportunity against the eternal and maddening rigidity of cosmic law* . . . . especially the laws of *time.* Individuals and their fortunes within natural law move me very little. They are all momentary trifles bound from a common nothingness toward another common nothingness. Only the cosmic framework itself—or such individuals as symbolise principles (or defiances of principles) of the cosmic framework—can gain a deep grip on my imagination and set it to work creating. In other words, the only "heroes" I can write about are *phenomena.* The cosmos is such a closely-locked round of fatality—with everything prearranged—that nothing impresses me as *really dramatic* except some sudden and abnormal *violation of that relentless inevitability* . . . . something which cannot exist, but which can be imagined as existing. Hence the type of thing I try to write. Naturally, I am aware that this forms a very limited special field so far as mankind en masse is concerned; but I believe (as pointed out in that *Recluse* article) that the field is an authentic one despite its subordinate nature. This protest against natural law, and tendency to weave visions of escape from orderly nature, are characteristic and eternal factors in human psychology, even though very small ones. They exist as permanent realities, and have always expressed themselves in a typical form of art from the earliest fireside folk tales and ballads to the latest achievements of Blackwood and Machen or de la Mare or Dunsany. That art exists—whether the majority like it or not. It is small and limited, but real—and there is no reason why its practitioners should be ashamed of it. Naturally one would *rather* be a broad artist with power to evoke beauty from every phase of experience—but when one unmistakably *isn't* such an artist, there's no sense in bluffing and faking and pretending that one *is*. It being settled that I'm a little man instead of a big man, I'd a damn sight prefer to let it go frankly at that—and try to be a good little man in my narrow, limited, miniature fashion—than to cover up and pretend to be a bigger man than I am. Such a pretence can lead only to futile overreaching, pompous vacuity, and an ultimate loss of whatever little good I might have accomplished had I stuck to the one small province which was really mine. I am naturally a narrow specialist of very limited vision and power, and the only way I can ever create anything even half good is to stick to the area within which I have an actually genuine motivation—namely, the area of the cosmic and the weird. It I ever outgrow this area, it must be by very slow and gradual degrees; and only in the direction, and to the extent, that nature dictates. For example—it is barely conceivable that my longing for cosmic liberation might some time turn from the attempt to depict actual violations of nature to the realistic (but dream-overcast) portraiture of some fellow-dreamer with similar longings . . . . detailing dream-life *as* dream-life and constructing some half-mystical but non-supernatural narrative like Machen's "Hill of Dreams" or Dunsany's "Curse of the Wise Woman." But this must come only if it *wants* to come. Literature cannot be forced. Nothing really worth reading was ever deliberately or intentionally—or even wholly consciously—written. Art is not what one resolves to say, but what insists on saying itself through one. It has nothing to do with commerce, editorial demand, or popular approval. The only elements concerned are the artist and the emotions working within him. Of course, there is a business of magazine-purveying which is perfectly honest in itself, and a worthy field for those with a knack for it. I wish I had the knack. But this isn't the thing I'm interested in. If I had the knack, it would be something performed entirely apart from my serious work—just as my present revisory activities are. However, I haven't the knack, and the field is so repugnant to me that it's about the last way I'd ever choose to gain shelter and clothing and nourishment. Any other kind of a legitimate job would be preferable to my especial tastes. I dislike this trade because it bears a mocking external resemblance to the real literary composition which is the only thing (apart from sundry ancestral traditions) I take seriously in life.

Literary and Personal Setbacks

[The 1930s were a difficult period for Lovecraft, as a variety of literary and personal misfortunes affected him. In the summer of 1931 he received two nearly simultaneous rejections: Farnsworth Wright turned down *At the Mountains of Madness,* and G. P. Putnam's Sons declined on a collection of short stories.]

[6]   Yes—Wright "explained" his rejection of the "Mountains of Madness" in almost the same language as that with which he "explained" other recent rejections to Long and Derleth. It was "too long", "not easily divisible into parts", "not convincing"—and so on. Just what he has said of other things of mine (except for length)—some of which he has ultimately accepted after many hesitations. Those once-rejected and later-accepted things include "Cthulhu", "The Tomb", and many others. It is very possible that I am growing stale—that is for readers of the "Whisperer" and "Mountains of Madness" to judge—but if so it merely signifies the end of my fictional attempts. There is no field other than the weird in which I have any aptitude or inclination for fictional composition. Life has never interested me so much as the escape from life. However—there is a region on the border betwixt weirdness and "scientifiction" in which I might conceivably experiment. Indeed—the "Mountains of Madness" belongs largely to this type.

Yes—all the tales you mention were in the batch shot back by Putnam's. The grounds for rejection were twofold—first, that some of the tales are not subtle enough . . . . too obvious and well-explained—(admitted! That ass Wright got me into the habit of obvious writing with his never-ending complaints against the indefiniteness of my early stuff) and secondly, that all the tales are too uniformly macabre in mood to stand collected publication. This second reason is sheer bull—for as a matter of fact unity of mood is a positive asset in a fictional collection. But I suppose the herd must have their comic relief! The book editor—Winfield Shiras— added some slices of bologna about later discussions concerning a volume in which the heavier tales might be sandwiched in betwixt lighter ones . . . . but I'm not expecting to hear much from him. It satisfies me amply to let the incident remain a closed one. I don't think the John Day Co. would care greatly for anything of mine—they have not communicated with me concerning anything for their Hammett anthology.[6]

Neither do I think that Harpers would be any market for my stuff. The standard magazines take weird material only from the most famous and established writers—to say nothing of demanding a technical skill far in advance of mine. After all, the unreal is such a confoundedly *minor* phase of general human experience! It's place in the life of the majority is so slight, and the number of those to whom it is important is so small! Editors, having such an ingrained distrust of the whole genre, naturally confine their few acceptances to specimens in which the workmanship is of the highest possible level—and in which the weirdness is as mild and innocuous as possible. All of which lets me out.

[To the hard-headed professional writer August Derleth, Lovecraft's sensitivity to rejection seemed nearly incomprehensible, and in a letter of early 1932 Lovecraft made some attempt to explain it.]

[7]   As for my own latter-day attitude toward writing and submitting— I can see why you consider my anti-rejection policy a stubbornly foolish and needlessly short-sighted one, and am not prepared to offer any defence other than the mere fact that repeated rejections *do* work in a certain way on my psychology—rationally or not—and that their effect is to cause in me a certain literary lockjaw which absolutely prevents further fictional composition despite my most arduous efforts. I would be the last to say that they *ought* to produce such an effect, or that they would—even in a slight degree—upon a psychology of 100% toughness and balance. But unfortunately my nervous equilibrium has always been a rather uncertain quantity, and it is now in one of its more ragged phases—though I hardly fancy it portends one of the actual near-breakdowns as of 1898, 1900, 1906, 1908, 1912, and 1919. There are times when the experience of repeated rejections would mean little to me, but other times when the symbolism of the process grates harshly—and now is one of these other times. Later I may try sending again—especially after I have accumulated a stack of material and can make the submissions from stuff not so close to the actual process of writing. I feel tremendously ungrateful in not availing

myself of the generous encouragement and offers you have made, and could hardly blame you if you were to wash your hands of the old man as an altogether bad job—yet I feel sure that you realise how keenly I appreciate your interest and coöperation, and how much I regret having to seem stubborn, stupid, and a prey to second childhood's whims.

[In the summer of 1932, as Lovecraft was winding down an extensive series of travels, he was called suddenly home because of the terminal illness of his aunt Lillian. She died on July 3.]

[8]   I am sure that you will, upon learning the melancholy circumstances attending its writing, excuse the striking inadequacy of this attempted reply to your piquant and well-supplemented epistle of the first. Only the pressure of extreme nerve-strain could excuse the superficiality and neglectfulness I shall probably exhibit.

My return to Brooklyn from Richmond—via Fredericksburg, Washington, Annapolis, and Philadelphia—was carried out according to schedule; but upon the sixth day of my visit to Loveman I received a disastrous telegram which sent me hastening home on the first train, and caused 1932 to take its place as a black year for this household. It told of the sudden sinking of my semi-invalid aunt Mrs. Clark, (age seventy-six) whose decade-long neuritic and arthritic pains had produced an unexpected weakening and collapse of the general organic system. Hope of survival had been abandoned, though the pains themselves, after a burst of extraordinary acuteness, had mercifully subsided. When I reached home—eight hours after receiving the telegram on the morning of July first—my aunt was in a semi-coma out of which she never emerged. The next day showed no visible change, though the doctor thought she was weaker and gave her but twenty-four hours to live. Sadly enough, his prophecy was correct; for the end came at one-twenty p.m. Sunday the third—so peacefully and imperceptibly that I could not for some time believe that the dread change had actually taken place. Services were held on the sixth—for traditional reasons, according to the ancient Anglican ritual, though my aunt had no more belief in childish theology and immortality-myths than I have—and interment took place in the Clark lot in old Swan Point Cemetery (in another lot in which I shall myself be buried) among the sepulchres of Clark ancestors extending back to 1711. Green wooded slopes rise beside the mournful spot, and close by is a great hollow tree inhabited by a wood-pecker whose quaint twittering my aunt would have loved to hear in life.

The vacuum created in this household is easy to imagine, since my aunt was its presiding genius and animating spirit. It will be impossible for me to get concentrated on any project of moment for some time to come—and meanwhile there intervenes the painful task of distributing my aunt's effects—whose familiar arrangement, so expressive of her tastes and personality, I dread to disturb. The family is now reduced to my younger aunt—living a mile from here—and myself.

[In the summer of 1933 Lovecraft felt the need to give his fiction writing a fresh start by rereading the classics of the field in an analytical manner. Shortly thereafter he wrote "The Thing on the Doorstep," and he discusses the tale extensively in a letter to Clark Ashton Smith.]

[9]   Glad to hear that the "Doorstep" did not impress you as too inadequate—though I still feel a profound dissatisfaction with something about it. In everything I do there is a certain concreteness, extravagance, or general crudeness which defeats the vague but insistent object I have in mind. I start out trying to find symbols expressive of a certain mood induced by a certain visual conception (such as a sunset beyond fantastic towers, a steep, cobblestoned hill street, a great stone vault, a sense of alienage and ineffable antiquity in a house, a stirring of black wings over a black abyss, or a cryptic beam of light from a primordial stone turret in an Asian desert of rock), but when I come to put anything on paper the chosen symbols seem forced, awkward, childish, exaggerated, and essentially inexpressive. I have staged a cheap, melodramatic puppet-show without saying what I wanted to say in the first place. Whether the sensations I strive to utter are actually too nebulous or intangible for concrete utterance, or whether I am simply unequal to the task of uttering them, I have not yet been able to decide; although I tend to incline toward the latter explanation. And—adopting this theory—I am further unable to decide whether my incapacity proceeds from a lack of natural endowments, or whether it is a result of excessive familiarity with pulp fiction and its puerile crudities. But be all this as it may, the fact remains that whatever I write lacks the subtlety and maturity needed to give really effective expression to the mood behind the picture. For example—at present I am haunted by the cloudy notion of

brooding, elder forces surrounding or pervading an ancient house and seeking to achieve some sort of bodily formulation. Well and good. A real artist could make something of the idea. But when I sit down and try to think up the suitable elements — the nature of the elder forces, the reason for their concentration in this spot, the precise manner of their manifestation, their motive in seeking embodiment, and their procedure when embodied — I find that every idea occurring to me is hackneyed and commonplace. What I get is a mere catalogue of stock paraphernalia too crude and derivative to have any convincingness or adult significance. What I wanted to say remains unsaid — and the mystery of an old, shadowy house's suggestions remains unexplained. Thus I feel poignantly the truth of that observation in W. Compton Leith's "Serenica"[7] — "but woe to those who are made to dream the creator's dream without his finer understanding or his skill of capture." During the past week — and largely under the imaginative stimulus resulting from my trip to Plymouth's archaic lanes and bordering hills — I have been constantly attempting tales; though each one has been destroyed after a few pages because of the imaginative barrenness and cheap, concrete mechanicality revealed. After all, it may be that my relation to phantasy is that of the appreciative reader and spectator rather than that of the utterer or creator. At any rate, I shall not finish any more tales unless they are better than my previous attempts. Meanwhile the experimenting goes on . . . . . the quest for even half-way adequate images and incidents. I'll think over that possible change in the ending of the "Doorstep" tale. If there were any objection, it would be merely that the use of magic on Derby's part is *unnecessary*. The principle of *exchange* is so fully outlined before, that the existence of consciousness in the transferred victim is provided for without an additional element. However, it might be more effective — because less outrageously improbable in atmosphere — to go back and start the matter afresh by having the survival of consciousness in the corpse something resulting from a special and immediate sorcery rather than from the general mental mastery established by Ephraim-Asenath. In that case Asenath (as Edward would come to realise when the pull from the grave began to be apparent) would have had time during a death struggle to formulate a spell holding her consciousness to her soon-to-be-dead body. This would have to be indicated in Edward's final communication. *Then* it might be that Edward, when realising that his mind was being crowded out, could be represented as weaving a spell to preserve a trace of consciousness in the buried body after his mind-vibrations were transferred to that horrible vehicle. However—it is doubtful whether he could be willing to do this *voluntarily*, even to save the world from Ephraim, since the experience of being in a rotting body, with consciousness, would be so necessarily hideous. The transfer of *personality* to the corpse must of course be *automatic*, since *exchange* is the basic principle of the whole story. The dead Asenath could not take over Edward's body without sending his personality somehow into her own remains. It is this *inevitability* which creates the whole story. Also, it is unnecessary to invoke magic in the matter of the corpse's escape from its shallow grave. Asenath could have escaped had she wished to, but she did not so wish. There was no need of securing liberty for a dead and anyhow unwanted corpse when a good living body in the outside world was about to be seized. Indeed, Ephraim-Asenath probably took a grim pleasure in the idea of thrusting Edward's consciousness down into that corpse-pit of horror. She never thought the poor sap would have the stamina to escape, even though he had nerved himself up to the killing. And so it goes. There might be an increase in plausibility to have Asenath and Edward unable to survive consciously in a dead body without additional special spells—and yet this idea would involve an extra element easily capable of cumbrousness, besides subtracting measurably from the air of *inevitability* pervading and motivating the whole tale. There would be a sort of decrease in atmospheric *unity*—and a very sharp contradiction of the aura of *essential passivity* (except in simple, desperate lunges under direct and irresistible stimuli) surrounding Edward's character. In a word, I can see reasons both for and against the change; and will reflect carefully upon the matter. We'll see what Two-Gun Bob and the Peacock Sultan have to say about it.[8] I'm still undecided whether I'll let young Comte d'Erlette tear it to shreds. After two or three more verdicts I may consider a trial on Satrap Pharnabazus—though I don't want to overload him after his belated acceptance of the collaborated piece. And I don't like the psychological effect on myself of repeated rejections. L'affaire Knopf is still too damned recent.[9]

The Move to 66 College Street

[One event that buoyed Lovecraft's final years in spite of his setbacks was his move to 66 College Street in the spring of 1933. Although the move was made in the interest of economy, Lovecraft was delighted to be able at last to dwell in a house built shortly after his beloved colonial era.]

[10]   Here's just a line to apprise you of my changed address. I think I told you that economic pressure was forcing me to double up with my surviving aunt in a low-rent flat—but I have yet to tell you of the marvellous bargain we found . . . . . a bargain which makes our move *down* look like a move *up*, and which at last—after 40 years—places me for the first time in a *real colonial house.*

You no doubt remember our visit to the marble John Hay Library with its Harris Collection of Poetry. At that time it is just possible that I pointed out to you a yellow colonial house behind the library—at the back of a rather quaint rustic court leading off from the steep slope of College St.—mentioning that a friend of my aunt's lived in the lower half of it. Well—I live in the upper half of it now! My aunt's friend—a high-school teacher of German—had long wanted her to move in above her if ever the flat should be vacant. On May 1st. it *did* become vacant, and my aunt was duly informed. We looked it over, found it would be ideal for both, and at once clinched the bargain. You can imagine how I felt at the prospect of living in a real colonial home! Our respective quarters will be wholly separate except for dining room etc.—and yet the general effect will be that of a complete and homogeneous home—my study corresponding to the library and my aunt's living-room to the parlour. She has not yet moved in, although I am wholly settled. The place looks ineffably homelike with my belongings, and since I have 2 rooms of my own I don't have to crowd the furniture as I did at 10 Barnes. Arranging my books and files was a hellish job—I had to get 4 new cases and a cabinet for pamphlets—but it is done at last. Tomorrow my aunt moves in and completes the family circle.

The house is a square wooden edifice of the 1800 period—as you may possibly remember. The fine colonial doorway is like my bookplate come to life, though of a slightly later period with side lights and fan carving instead of a fanlight. In the rear is a picturesque, village-like garden at a higher level than the front of the house. The upper flat we have taken contains 5 rooms besides bath and kitchenette nook on the main (2nd) floor, plus 2 attic storerooms—one of which is so attractive that I wish I could have it for an extra den! My quarters—a large study and a small adjoining bedroom—are on the south side, with my working desk under a west window affording a splendid view of the lower town's outspread roofs and of the mystical sunsets that flame behind them. The interior is as fascinating as the exterior—with colonial fireplaces, mantels, and chimney cupboards, curving Georgian staircase, wide floor-boards, old-fashioned latches, small-paned windows, six-panel doors, rear wing with floor at a different level (3 steps down), quaint attic stairs, etc.—just like the old houses open as museums. After admiring such all my life, I find something magical and dreamlike in the experience of actually *living in one* . . . . . I keep half-expecting a museum guard to come around and kick me out at 5 o'clock closing time! And yet the whole thing costs only what I've been paying for one room and alcove at 10 Barnes. The house is owned by the university, and steam heat and hot water are piped in from the adjacent John Hay Library. Little did I think, when we were there last summer, that from that classic building would come my daily supply of caloric!

Daily Life

[Some of Lovecraft's most engaging letters are those in which he discusses, in minute detail and with self-deprecating humor, the details of his daily life. The following extracts regarding his finances, diet, and dishwashing bring his final years vividly to life.]

[11] You are profoundly lucky to have a regular job—I'd give my eye-teeth for one. The other day I had a chance at a reading and revisory post—but alas! it was in *Vermont,* which made it physically out of the question as a year-round matter.[10] But I hope you will find 1931 more profitable than its predecessor. Probably you will—especially if you expand your markets. Meanwhile I think you ought to learn to live on less money—for a writer is never likely to be very well fixed, and the sooner he gets his regimen scaled down to actualities, the more comfortable he is. It can be done—for I've done it myself. Up to 1910 or 1915 there was no one more recklessly careless of expenditures than I—even though the big collapse in family fortunes had come as far back as 1904. My mother used to say that I was absolutely ruined as a handler of money, and utterly spoiled as an endurer of poverty. However—as things grew still worse, the old man did manage to scale down everything; learning little by little what might best be eliminated without interfering with atmospheric continuity and freedom of imaginative life. Today I get along with a maximum expense of $15.00 per week, not counting the reckless antiquarian trips to which I irresponsibly blow myself about once a year. And this is not any squalid getting-along either—indeed, I'd feel damn lucky if I could always be sure of the hebdomadal fifteen which makes the present standard possible. It is a matter of caution and deliberation in the selection and

preservation of things, and in the judicious quest for lodgings at once cheap and in a reasonably select neighbourhood. In the course of years, by a system of trial and error, one learns what nourishing and palatable food is cheapest, and what system of clothes-choosing is likely to make replacements as far apart as possible. One learns, too, how to make public libraries serve instead of indiscriminate bookbuying. $15.00 per week will float any man of sense in a very tolerable way—lodging him in a cultivated neighbourhood if he knows how to look for rooms, (this one rule, though, breaks down in really megalopolitan centres like New York—but it will work in Providence, Richmond, or Charleston, and would probably work in most of the moderate-sized cities of the northwest) keeping him dressed in soberly conservative neatness if he knows how to choose quiet designs and durable fabrics among cheap suits, and feeding him amply and palatably if he is not an epicurean crank, and if he does not attempt to depend upon restaurants. One must have a kitchen-alcove and obtain provisions at grocery and delicatessen prices rather than pay cafes and cafeterias the additional price they demand for mere service. Of course, this applies only to the single man. My one venture into matrimony ended in the divorce-court for reasons 98% financial. But if one expects to be a man of letters one has to sacrifice something—and for anybody of reasonably ascetic temperament the interests and freedoms of imaginative and creative life more than overbalance the advantages of domesticity. $8.00 to $10.00 a week will get a very good-sized room in the best of neighbourhoods in the smaller cities, and $3.00 per week sees me fully fed. My dinners cost about 25¢ each, (a typical one—¼ lb veal loaf at delicatessen, 11¢; ½ lb potato salad, 8¢. Cake for dessert, 2½¢. Coffee—using condensed milk—averaging 2½¢) and my breakfast-lunches perhaps 10¢—a couple of doughnuts, cheese, and coffee. This is all I would eat even if wealthy, and it is just as palatable as the average programme. I also use Campbell's soups, 10¢ per can, and other inexpensive accessories. Then of course, now and then one blows oneself to a good restaurant gorge. As for clothing—buy plain designs, be careful of them, don't wear them out around the house when you can just as well be wearing any old spare rags, and you'll be astonished at the length of time they'll last. The important thing is to choose suits and overcoats so plain that no changes of style will make them conspicuous. I have an old topcoat (now relegated to rainy-day use) which I bought early in 1909— probably before you were born. My regular winter overcoat was bought in 1915, and my present topcoat in 1917—in April, just after the National

Guard doctors had denied me the honour of olive-drab habiliments. Of my suits — I always have four, a good heavy, a good light, and a second-best of each weight — three were purchased in 1925, and the other (scarcely used as yet) in 1928. None cost above $25.00. (although the overcoats did, since they date from the fringe of my "better days.") If I hadn't been robbed of all my clothing in a Brooklyn burglary in 1925, I'd have some still more venerable costume reliques. *Laundry* is an item which perplexes the beginner in economy, but one soon learns to have everything but shirts and collars done at a cheap "rough dry" rate — and more, one gradually picks up a facility in home laundering. The only way I ever take my long trips with a single small valise is by doing a good part of my own washing in YMCA lavatories and drying the results on chair-backs and opened dresser drawers. Shoe-leather wears fast, but the wise man can make splendid $6.60 replacements at a Regal store. I don't get shoes more than once in two years. And there are chain-stores like Truly Warner's where $3.50 will get you as good a felt hat as you could wish for — one, too, that will last a couple of years. For straws, the sagacious pauper waits till the end of a season before buying his next year's specimen. One solitary dollar got me my 1931 straw (easily a 3.00 one) last August. I picked up a good deal of this lore during my Brooklyn days, for at least two members of the "gang" there — Arthur Leeds and good old Everett McNeil, (dead now, but Wandrei remembers him) were in straits even more immediately dire than my own. They had worked out the problems of poverty before, and I gradually absorbed something of their spirit and methods. They were free-lance writers — and had found out what the game means to the average struggler! Poor old Mac is gone now — but Leeds has come on slightly better times, through his side-line of the drama. [. . .] Good old Leeds — he used to be pushed from lodging to lodging for non-payment of rent, and his coats were always bursting out at the shoulders if he moved around too violently; yet I never saw him in any state other than the most immaculate neatness — for somehow he had enough "pull" with barbers to get haircuts on credit, and never began a day without his bath, shave, and donning of home-washed-*and-ironed* (this latter is beyond me!) linen. It was Leeds who tipped me off to the cheap Jew clothing joints around 14th St. and 8th Avenue — places handling assorted remainders from which a keen critic with plenty of time might eventually pick something fit for a gentleman to wear . . . . as a spare suit, in artificial light. He found a suit for *$5.00,* but I couldn't quite duplicate that. $14.00 was the best I could do — for one's last residual aesthetic scruples aren't easily conquered. I have that $14.00 specimen still, for around-the-house wear. Not, of course, that one would deliberately choose a regimen of penury as close as this—but that it's damn useful to know how to wriggle along when one has to.

[12]   Speaking of industrio-economic matters—let me assure you that a 2-or-3-dollar-a-week dietary programme need not involve even a particle of malnutrition or unpalatability if one but knew what to get and where to get it. The tin can and delicatessen conceal marvellous possibilities! Porridge? Mehercule! On the contrary, my tastes call for the most blisteringly highly-seasoned materials conceivable, and for desserts as close to 100% $C_{12}H_{22}O_{11}$ as possible. Indeed, of this latter commodity I never employ less than four teaspoons in an average cup of coffee. Favourite dinners— Italian spaghetti, chili con carne, Hungarian goulash (save when I can get white meat of turkey with highly-seasoned dressing). If this be asceticism, make the most of it! As for the expense element—to begin with, I eat only twice daily from choice . . . or rather, digestive advisability. I adopted this two-meal programme long before I had to economise. The rest is merely a matter of judicious and and far from self-denying choice. Let us investigate a typical day's rations.

(a) *Breakfast* (whether I eat it before or after retiring
      depends on whether I retire at 2 a.m. or 9 a.m. or 3 p.m.
      or 9 p.m. or some other hour. My programme of sleeping
      and waking is very flexible.)

Doughnut from Weybosset Pure Food Market	0.015
York State Medium Cheese	
(for sake of round numbers)	0.060
Coffee + Challenge Brand Condensed Milk + $C_{12}H_{22}O_{11}$	0.025
	——
Total Breakfast	0.100

(b) Dinner (occurring vaguely betwixt 6 and 9 or 10 p.m.)

1 can Rath's Chili con Carne*	0.100
2 slices Bond Bread	0.025

*(or Armour's Corned Beef Hash or baked beans from delic., or Armour's Frankfort Sausage or Boiardi Meat Balls and Spaghetti or chop suey from delicatessen or Campbell's Vegetable Soup, etc. etc. etc.)

Coffee (with accessories as noted above)	0.025
Slice of cake or quadrant (or octant) of pie	0.050

Total Dinner	0.200

Grand Total for Entire Day	0.30
	7

Average Total per Week	2.10

Occasionally, of course, extravagant additions occur—such as fruit with breakfast, or cheese with pie at dinner, or a chocolate bar or ice cream at an odd hour, or a meat-course costing more than a dime, or other sybaritic luxuries. But even the most Lucullan indulgence seldom tops an hebdomadal 3 bucks. And the old man still lives—in a fairly hale and hearty state, at that! Oddly enough, I was a semi-invalid in the old days when I *didn't* economise. Porridge? Not for Grandpa!

[13]   Anent the art of vessel-cleansing. No—most emphatically—accumulation is the *precise and antipodal reverse* of my lifelong policy. On the contrary, I cannot endure dealing with more than one item at a time, or using any medium save running water direct from the faucet. As fast as one vessel or implement is used, I cleanse it for re-use—never having in the house any soiled item except that from which—or with which—I am taking nourishment. Thus I use but one plate, one fork, one knife, one spoon, one cup, one saucer, and so on . . . . . . washing and reëmploying as needed. This I considered the only civilised policy in the absence of a proper staff of servants—for a sink full of used and engreased objects is anathema to me. As once remarked, my policy is not uniformly endorsed at #66—but I nevertheless persist in it as far as possible. Thus, while appreciating in the extreme the philanthropick offer of yourself and the Chief Ailurophile to coöperate in an Augean-Stable ordeal, I am happy to state that the nonexistence of any accumulation makes it needless for the Board to impose on your joint generosity.

Cats!

[Lovecraft was a lifelong lover of cats, even though he did not own one after his family's cat ran away in 1904. Behind his lodgings at 66 College

Street was a boarding house upon whose shed many cats sunned themselves. Lovecraft would frequently borrow these creatures and spend hours with them as he worked. His many discussions of cats are among the most affecting passages in his correspondence.]

[14]   While I do not own a cat, I am very frequently a host to the young black gentleman, Mr. John Perkins (b. Feby. 14, 1935), who dwells at the boarding-house across the back garden. He is an elfin creature, with the long legs, large ears, and pointed nose typical of antique Ægyptus' sacred felines. His spirit is exceptionally valiant, and his courtesy to enemies sometimes limited. He has the curiously canine habit of keeping his tail in restless motion—when pleased more than when angered. Indeed, it is a truly eloquent appendage. Mr. Perkins's eyes are large and yellow, and his conversation holds much variety. For minor requests he retains the hesitant, apologetic little "eew" of his infancy—a characteristic almost amusing in so large a beast. For John has waxed mighty in size, and bids fair to form the leader of the local Kappa Alpha Tau fraternity.[11] The K.A.T., by the way, has fared badly of late. First (last spring) its dauntless fighting champion and Vice-President—the tiger Count Magnus Osterberg—was slain in battle with a vile crawling canine. R.I.P. . . . . he never feared any living thing, and is now doubtless dismembering dragons in Valhalla . . . yet he never attacked any adversary first. I weep as I think of his passing. And now—just this month—a further but less tragic loss has occurred—through the removal of the black and white President Peter Randall, Esq., and his tiger brother Stephen (Count Magnus's successor in the Vice-Presidency), from the neighbourhood in conjunction with their human family. Verily, I feel desolated—and the adjacent shed roof seems bleak and barren without the familiar furry forms sprawling in the sun! I must find out where the Messrs. Randall live, and pay them a call.

Some of my friends and correspondents have marvellous felines. Out in California Clark Ashton Smith's coal-black Simaetha has attained an astonishing age and matriarchal dignity—so that her wizard-master can scarcely recall a day when she did not exist. Not far away the weird writer E. Hoffmann Price has 2 cats, including old pure-white Nimrod, the most intrepid battler and fabulous eater who ever slew and devoured a million gophers in a single night. Down in Florida young Barlow has a teeming feline menagerie whose high spots are two Yellow Persians, Cyrus and

Darius; whilst in the Boston zone the amateur E. H. Cole boasts a truly royal tiger-angora companion—Peter Ivanovitch Romanoff—whose purr surpasses in volume any other recorded in history or zoölogy.

[15]   So I *hadn't* spoken about "Old Man" and my dreams of him! Well— he was a great fellow. He belonged to a market at the foot of Thomas Street—the hill street mentioned in "Cthulhu" as the abode of the young artist—and could usually (in later life) be found asleep on the sill of a low window almost touching the ground. Occasionally he would stroll up the hill as far as the Art Club, seating himself at the entrance to one of those old-fashioned courtyard archways (formerly common everywhere) for which Providence is so noted. At night, when the electric lights made the street bright, the space within the archway would remain pitch-black, so that it looked like the mouth of an illimitable abyss, or the gateway of some nameless dimension. And there, as if stationed as a guardian of the unfathomed mysteries beyond, would crouch the sphinxlike, jet-black, yellow-eyed, and incredibly ancient form of Old Man. I first knew him as a youngish cat in 1906, when my elder aunt lived in Benefit St. nearby, and Thomas St. lay on my route downtown from her place. I used to pet him and remark what a fine boy he was. I was 16 then. The years went by, and I continued to see him off and on. He grew mature—then elderly—and finally cryptically ancient. After about 10 years—when I was grown up and had a grey hair or two myself—I began calling him "Old Man". He knew me well, and would always purr and rub around my ankles, and greet me with a kind of friendly conversational "e-ew" which finally became hoarse with age. I came to regard him as an indispensable acquaintance, and would often go considerably out of my way to pass his habitual territory, on the chance that I might find him visible. Good Old Man! In fancy I pictured him as an hierophant of the mysteries behind the black archway, and wondered if he would ever invite me *through* it some midnight . . . . wondered, too, if I could ever come back to earth alive after accepting such an invitation. Well—more years slipped away. My Brooklyn period came and went; and in 1926, a middle-aged relique of 36, with a goodly sprinkling of white in my thatch, I took up my abode in Barnes Street—whence my habitual downtown route led straight down Thomas St. hill. And there by the ancient archway Old Man still lingered! He was not very active now, and spent most of his time sleeping—but he still knew

his fellow-elder, and never failed to give his hoarse, friendly "e-ew" when he chanced to be awake. About 1927 he took on a sort of final second youth and began to be awake more. He had been sticking rather close to the market, but now I met him farther and farther up the hill, and very often at the old archway. Good Old Man! In 1928 he seemed a trifle feeble, but his purring friendliness was unabated. Not long before my 38th birthday I saw him—him whom I had known at 16. Then in August I began to miss him. Always when turning the corner on to the hill I used to look down ahead and see if I could discern a familiar lump of black by the archway or at the market. Now I failed to see the graceful old furry lump. I feared the worst—but scarcely dared to enquire at the market. At last—in September—I did enquire and found that my fears were all too well founded. After more than two decades Old Man had gone through the archway at last, and dissolved into that eternal night of which he was a true fragment—that eternal night which had sent him up to earth as a tiny black atom of sportive kittenhood so long ago! Assuredly, I felt desolate enough without my old friend—without any black lump to look for on the ancient hill. I had dreamed of him—and the mysteries of the archway—before; but I now began to do so with redoubled vividness. He would greet me in sleep on a spectral Thomas Street hill, and gaze with aged yellow eyes that spoke secrets older than Ægyptus or Atlantis. And he would mew an invitation for me to follow him through the archway—beyond which lay (as saith Dunsany) "the unreverberate darkness of the abyss."[12] In no dream up to now have I actually followed him through—but I have often wondered what will happen if ever I do . . . . . whether, in such an event, I shall ever again awake in this tri-dimensional world? When I mentioned these dreams to Dwyer he wanted to make a story about Old Man, but he has not yet done so. If he doesn't, I may myself some day. Good Old Man! But I am sure that no world he would lead me to would be a world of horror. He is too old and true a friend for that! When little Sam Perkins appeared on the scene last summer I decided that he must be a great-great-great-great-great-grandson of Old Man—perhaps a messenger despatched from the Abyss by my old friend. As soon as his great violet eyes began to turn yellow, I occasionally addressed him as Old Man, and fancied I could sense a spark of recognition! Perhaps he was my friend himself in a new body! But, alas, he did not remain long. He, too, returned to that eternal Night of which he and all his kind are inalienable fragments!

[Now and again, tragedy struck Lovecraft's beloved felines.]

[16]   But the saddest news is yet to come. Alas—how can I impart it un-mov'd? Little Sam Perkins, the tiny ball of black fur whom you saw in August, is no more! He was ill then—but fully recover'd and was quite his novel dynamick little self. As late as Sept. 7 he spent the day with Grandpa—tearing about the place, shuffling the papers on the old gentleman's desk, and finally stretching out like a little ebony stick in the semi-circular chair, sound asleep. On the morning of the 10th, however, he was found peacefully lifeless in the garden—and from no apparent cause. Now he sleeps beneath the shrubbery amidst which he play'd in life. Blessed little piece of the Night! He liv'd but from June to September, and will never know what the winter's hellish cold is like. The Kappa Alpha Tau is in deep mourning, and President Randall often mews in elegiack numbers—

> The ancient garden seems tonight
> A deeper gloom to bear,
> As if some silent shadow's blight
> Were hov'ring in the air.

> With hidden griefs the grasses sway,
> Unable quite to word them—
> Remembering from yesterday
> The little paws that stirr'd them.[13]

During his later days Master Perkins was fully inducted into the K.A.T.—appearing frequently on the clubhouse roof. Eheu—the old place is not the same without him!

Travels

[In the 1930s Lovecraft continued his far-flung travels in search of anti-quarian sites. In 1931 he spent more than six weeks in Florida, visiting St. Augustine and Dunedin (staying with the weird writer Henry S. Whitehead), and proceeding all the way down to Key West.]

[17]   [. . .] now I am settled down for a week or two in one of the most delightfully quaint and reposeful subtropical towns—the oldest city in the United States—which the imagination can conceive. The climate braces

me up like a tonic, and I hate to think of ever going north again. I surely was made for the torrid zone! Charleston—though absolutely nothing can approach it for rich continuity of tradition and survival of 18th century life and architecture—is only an adumbration so far as real tropicality is concerned. There, I thought a few low palmettos and live-oaks with Spanish moss were remarkable. Here, one finds great palms overtopping buildings and creating a mystical haze of green twilight, and vast tangles of cypress and live-oak that dwarf anything in the Charleston region. Around me are the narrow lanes and ancient buildings of the old Spanish capital, the formidable bulk of ancient Fort San Marcos, on whose turreted, sun-drenched parapet I love to sit, the sleepy old market (now a benched loafing-place) in the Plaza de la Constitución, and the whole languorous atmosphere (the tourist season being over) of an elder, sounder, and more leisurely civilisation. Here is a city founded in 1565, 42 years before the first Jamestown colonist landed, and 55 years before the first Pilgrim set foot on Plymouth Rock. Here, too, is the region where Ponce de Leon fared on his vain quest of 1513. Varied fortunes—British rule 1763–83, sale to U.S. in 1821—yet much of the old Spanish architecture remaining. For the first time I am seeing structures built in the 1500's. The post office is the old Governor's Mansion—with unchanged exterior—built in 1591. At the north end of the narrow (19 ft) main street the ancient city gate still stands, though the rest of the walls are down. Nearly everything is built of coquina stone (small shells fused together in the sea) quarried from neighbouring Anastasia Island. A poor tourist season has made all rates comically low—the nonsybarite being able to get breakfasts for 10¢, dinners for 25¢ or 30¢, and *really good* rooms for almost nothing. I have a magnificent room in a fine section, with balcony fronting on the bay and giving a gorgeous vista of Anastasia Island, the great lighthouse, and the ocean beyond and how much to you think I pay? Don't call Grandpa a liar when I state that the price is exactly *four dollars per week!* It will be like pulling a tooth to break away from here—yet a week or two is my limit. I shall make a side-trip to Dunedin to visit Whitehead, since his invitations are too insistently cordial to admit of refusal. I feel sure I shall like him vastly personally. The trip down was made with a 2-day stopover at my beloved Charleston. From Providence to Charleston the bus ride took just 48 hours, and I stopped off at N Y to pay Belknap a call. He seems to be flourishing as usual. Charleston was chilly, but one gets the real subtropics here. Physically I am in my element. How can I ever endure the north again?

[18]   The trip down and across Florida was very pleasant, and has brought me to a region much more definitely subtropical than St Augustine. Dunedin is a very prettily planned and gardened residential town on a low bluff above the Gulf of Mexico, and it is only a few yards from Whitehead's front steps to the shore. Whitehead himself is absolutely delightful—a very prince of good fellows, whose solicitude as a host extends to such lengths as the bringing of an eye-opening grapefruit to my bedside each morning. He is—contrary to my previous assumption—rector of the small local Anglican church, and is a highly valued fixture in his community. He does a good deal of work with boys' clubs—last night he had a dozen kids from 9 to 11 over here, and they listened very politely when (at Whitehead's un-dodgeable request) I told them stories—such as the gist of "The Cats of Ulthar". He insists that I prolong my stay indefinitely, but I shall not impose on his spontaneous affability. His health has taken a slight upward curve, but is still very troublesome; so that he cannot remain standing for long continuous periods, and is obliged to rest in bed for a time each afternoon. He is 49 years of age, and now much thinner than the snap-shot sent to correspondents a year ago indicates. Apparently he is exactly my build, so that he wants me to wear his white drill tropical suits if the temperature rises spectacularly.

[19]   Greetings from the most southerly point in the U.S.! Climate agrees with me even better than St Augustine's and Dunedin's. This is a really tropical region—balconied, chimneyless houses amidst lush palm verdure. The view from the hotel roof looks exactly like pictures of West Indian towns. Fine old place—founded 1822, and so completely isolated that it has preserved a picturesquely simple early-American atmosphere! Cubans are very numerous—overflow from Havana, which is only 40 miles away. Damn sorry I'm too broke to get across there—I had retained hopes until the very last moment—the Florida Keys are some of the most fascinating sights in the world—green, low-lying coral isles in a clear, green and blue tropic sea—exotic fish and shore birds—waving palms, etc. Hate to think of turning north again! Saw Miami but was not impressed. Too modern and urban for me.

[20]   You have by this time received my Key West card, telling of the marvellous charm of that utterly remote place and sadly recounting my financial inability to get across to Havana. I hated to return, but it had to be

done. At Miami I took a side trip to the Seminole village where the Indians trade furs with the city merchants. A depressingly squalid place of pole-framed huts with peaked, palm-thatched roofs and wooden platforms. The Seminoles (who have infusions of Spanish and nigger blood and look like Chinese or Japanese) are ineffably dirty and odoriferous, and wear loose robes made of bright cloth fragments sewn together. I also took a trip over neighbouring coral reef in a glass-bottomed boat which gave splendid views of the exotic tropical flora and fauna of the ocean floor—grasses, sponges, corals, fishes, sea-urchins, crinoids, etc. A diver went down and brought up a bucket full of sea-urchins for distribution among the passengers, but I restored mine to its native element because I had no means of preserving it. Miami is set in a wretched landscape—flat sandy barrens, too far south for the subtropical live-oaks and Spanish moss, and too far north for a natural tropic growth like Key West's. Wealth and landscape gardening, however, have managed to create an artificial tropic growth which in places is highly spectacular and impressive. The ride up the east coast to St. Augustine was in places very picturesque—affording occasional glimpses of the open ocean. I shall stay here till Monday night—then on to Savannah, Charleston, Richmond, Philadelphia, and N.Y. Lack of cash will probably prevent me from staying very long at any one place, hence my next forwarding address will be in Belknap's care—230 W. 97th St., N.Y.C. I hate to think of going north—but of course actual summer is now close at hand.

[Two long trips enlivened the 1932 season: a visit to New Orleans (where he met E. Hoffmann Price) and other southern cities, and then, in late summer, his second visit to Quebec.]

[21]   The prime objective of trip #1 was New Orleans, which I wished to see before the destruction of the old French Market. On the way I stopped in N.Y. a week to visit Long, and afterward proceeded south via Washington and the exquisite Shenandoah Valley. From Roanoke, Va., I proceeded westward to Knoxville, Tenn., and thence south through splendid landscapes to Chattanooga. The latter is one of the most fascinating places I have ever seen—with its surrounding mountains and the sinuous windings of the yellow Tennessee River. I went all over Lookout Mountain, and explored the magnificent network of limestone caverns inside it—culminating in the vast and newly-discovered chamber called "Solomon's Temple", where a 145-foot waterfall bursts forth from the side—near the roof—and

dashes down to a pool whose outlet no man knows. From Chattanooga I proceeded west along the bluff-lined Tennessee, enjoying some of the finest landscapes I ever saw in my life. At Memphis (modern and unpicturesque) I beheld the mighty Mississippi for the first time—witnessing a splendid sunset over it. I then headed south through the alluvial cotton lands of Mississippi—where nothing but flat vistas and nigger cabins are found—finally reaching the Yazoo country and climbing the bluffs to picturesque old Vicksburg, which I like tremendously. Just south of Vicksburg I began to strike typically Southern flora—live-oaks and Spanish moss. Natchez—dreaming on its river-bluff—captivated me completely. It is one of those splendid survivals of the past exemplified by Quebec, Portsmouth, Newburyport, Salem, Marblehead, Annapolis, Fredericksburg, and Charleston. Founded in 1716 by the French, and later passing through British and Spanish hands, it came into the U.S. in 1798, and soon afterward became a great cotton port. Between 1800 and 1860 it was built up with a splendid type of classic architecture, nearly all of which survives to this day. The financial ruin attendant upon the Civil War stopped its growth, hence it remains today a bit of crystallised history. Its landscape setting is as fascinating as its architecture—live-oaks, moss, cypresses, rolling hills, and old roads deeply sunken in the friable yellow soil. Natchez is one of the few places I'd really like to live in. From there I descended straight to New Orleans—not pausing at the largely modernised Baton Rouge. South of Natchez the landscape grows flat and unpicturesque, and palm-like growths begin to appear. Later on the vast embankments and spillways of the levee system come into view, and occasional plantation houses (both of the slant-roofed French type and of the later pillared classic American type) are seen. At last New Orleans comes in sight—a large modern city with the ancient nucleus still surviving and imbedded close to the waterfront. Probably you've read a good deal about New Orleans. I stayed there over two weeks and came to like it immensely. It was founded by the French in 1718, and taken over by the Spaniards (though without any change in language and customs) in 1763. In 1788 a vast fire nearly wiped it out, but it was very solidly rebuilt—in a fashion slightly Spanish because of the aid furnished by government engineers. The American purchase came in 1803, but the Anglo-Saxon influx established itself south of the older city, leaving the former intact. In the course of years all activity and change centred in the newer American section, so that the original Creole city as rebuilt soon after 1788 still stands unchanged—as quaint a spectacle as Charleston or Quebec. It is a rectangle along the water front some 4000 ft. long and 1500 ft. deep, and now receives the name of "Vieux Carré", or "Old French Quarter." The houses are largely of brick and stucco, and have pointed roofs not unlike those of Charleston and Quebec. Wrought-iron grilles and balconies are everywhere present, and the Spanish influence shews itself in the many picturesque patios or courtyards. I spent most of my time in this ancient section, and came to know it very well. Outside toward the south is the modern American city of broad avenues and splendid gardens, and northward is the modern Creole (though English-speaking for the last two generations) district with houses shewing the hereditary French influence. New Orleans has some fine old live-oaks, and a wealth of tall palms. It is so low that only levees and an artificial drainage system can keep it dry—and until recently no cellars could be dug. Burials have to be above ground, and the ancient cemeteries with their tall tombs and thick walls pierced with oven-like vaults are highly picturesque. The drainage canals were formerly open ditches, but in latter years they have been covered over one by one to form boulevards. People of American and French descent still predominate in New Orleans, and niggers of every hue are numerous. There is a large Italian population, centreing chiefly in the northerly half of the Vieux Carré. The southerly half of the Quarter, somewhat reclaimed from slumdom, is a sort of mild Greenwich Village with antique shops and artists' studios.

New Orleans was, at the time of my visit, the home of the brilliant weird-taler E. Hoffmann Price; but since I had never been in touch with him I thought I wouldn't butt in and introduce myself. However, it happened that during my sojourn I wrote to Robert E. Howard of Texas—who, noting the hotel address on my stationery and being in epistolary touch with Price, took it upon himself to telegraph Price of my presence and whereabouts. The result was an unexpected telephone call from Price, followed by the longest call I have ever paid—or ever expect to pay—in my life . . . . . . a call lasting *25½ hours* without a break, from the middle of a Sunday evening to close upon midnight Monday. Price had a room in the Vieux Carré, and now and then his roommate would brew tea or coffee, or prepare a meal. Once we went over to the old French Market for professionally made coffee. Nobody seemed to get sleepy, and the hours slipped away imperceptibly amidst discussions and fictional criticisms. Later calls lasted 10 hours or so each—and I was in touch with Price until I left. Shortly after my departure Price himself moved out of town—to the quiet little village of Bay St. Louis across the line in Mississippi. Price is a remarkable chap—a West-Pointer, war veteran, Arabic student, connoisseur of Oriental rugs, amateur fencing-master, mathematician, dilettante coppersmith and iron worker, chess-champion, pianist, and what not! He is dark and trim of figure, not very tall, and with a small black moustache. He talks fluently and incessantly, and might be thought a bore by some—although I like to hear him rattling on. Up to last May he was well off—holding an important job with the Prestolite Co.—but the depression finally got him, and he is now depending on fiction for his income. The result is rather bad aesthetically, for he caters painfully to the pulp standard. I fear we shan't see anything more of the quality of "The Stranger from Kurdistan."[14] Still—he couldn't be as bad as most of the contributors to W.T. and its congeners. Just now he is trying to get me to collaborate on a sequel to my Silver Key—introducing a dimensional element suggested by his mathematical side.[15] I did not meet the other former New Orleans weird-taler—W. Kirk Mashburn—for he had previously moved to Texas.

Well—after New Orleans I proceeded to quaint old Mobile, which I liked exceedingly. Then up to Montgomery (original Confederate capital) and across to Atlanta. There was nothing in the latter modern city to hold me, so I hastened right on along the western Carolinas to Charlotte and Winston-Salem—and thence through Danville to good old Richmond. I love Richmond despite its fairly extensive modernisation. The landmarks of Poe's boyhood are readily traceable, and the bluff at the foot of Clay St. above old Shochoe Creek (near the White House of the Confederacy) is still unaltered—standing just as it did when little Edgar went swimming at its base. The creek, however, is filled in. As always, I visited Maymont Park on the banks of the James—a former private estate exquisitely landscaped and containing the finest Japanese garden in the U.S. After Richmond I paused at Fredericksburg, Annapolis, and Philadelphia—all favourite antiquarian havens of mine—and finally wound up by visiting a friend—Samuel Loveman—in Brooklyn. From this visit I was called home by a telegram announcing an acute attack on the part of my invalid aunt—an attack which terminated fatally on July 3d.

My second trip began Aug. 30 with a visit to W. Paul Cook in Boston. On the 31st we went to Newburyport to see the total solar eclipse, and had a most impressive view of that phenomenon. Two days later I started on a cheap rail excursion to Montreal and Quebec—thus entering the northern part of that New-France of which Louisiana formed the southern part. As perhaps you know, the French of Quebec Province are more retentive of their language and customs than those of Louisiana, so that they insist on an official bi-lingualism. All official signs are in the two languages, so that one comes on things like RAILWAY CROSSING / TRAVERSE DU CHEMIN DE FER or NO PARKING / NE STATIONNEZ PAS at every turning. Montreal (which I had never seen before) is more Anglo-Saxon than Quebec City, and does not seem at all foreign except in the French section east of St. Lawrence Blvd. It must be a great deal like the New Orleans of 75 years ago in its cultural division. Some parts are purely English, but in the French section all the store and street signs are in French. (as none are in New Orleans) There are really twice as many French as English in the city, though they have lost the real social and commercial dominance. Montreal is a highly attractive place, well set off by the towering slope of Mt. Royal, which rises in its midst. The ancient part—where I spent most of my time—is that closest to the southern waterfront, but it does not compare with the Vieux Carré of New Orleans or with the whole of old Quebec City. Montreal, taken all in all, would seem like any large high-grade American city but for the profusion of horse-drawn vehicles. I explored it thoroughly, and also visited the adjacent Lachine Rapids—beside which La Salle had his seigniory.

However—I was glad to move along to old Quebec at last, for that is utterly unique among the cities of this continent. As in 1930 I revelled in the atmosphere of massed antiquity—the towering cliff, frowning citadel, silver belfries, tiled red roofs, breath-taking panoramas, winding, precipitous alleys and flights of steps, centuried facades and doorways, venerable stone monasteries, and other picturesque reliquiae of bygone days—and I also took a ferry and 'bus excursion around the neighbouring Isle d'Orleans, where the old French countryside remains in a primitive, unspoiled state—just as when Wolfe and his men landed in 1759. There were endless brick farmhouses with curved eaves, wind and water mills, wayside shrines, and quaint white villages clustering around ancient silver-steepled parish churches. Nothing but French is spoken, and the rustic population live where their ancestors have lived for more than 200 years—seldom visiting even Quebec. I hated to go home, and when re-passing through Boston eased the transition by making a side-trip to ancient Marblehead.

[The year 1933 saw Lovecraft's last visit to Quebec.]

[22]   My Quebec trip was certainly a thorough success—and all the more so because of its unexpectedness. On the outbound voyage I paused in the Boston zone long enough to look up the ancient Deane Winthrop

house in a suburb. This edifice was built in 1637, and is one of the oldest structures in America. It is a simple farmhouse, but very solidly built. In the base of the colossal brick chimney is a secret room—of a sort very common in 17th century houses. An historical society maintains the place. I also called on W. Paul Cook—the Recluse man—while in Boston. The long train ride to Quebec was spent in reading and drowsing—and was unusually pleasant because there were no alcohol-seeking roysterers aboard as in '30 and '32. The return of King Gambrinus to the States has its compensations![16] Most of the passengers were honest, simple French peasants bent on visiting ancestral soil or on grovelling at the miracle-working shrine of La Bonne Ste. Anne de Beaupré. At last—after a post-auroral dash through the increasingly picturesque provincial landscape—came the mighty fortress of the North itself . . . . the rock-bound stronghold which defied the fleet of Phips and formed the Carthage of Cotton Mather's minatory thunderings! It gave me a tremendous hereditary kick to see our Old Flag—the time-hallowed Union Jack which greed and selfishness pulled down from the flagstaffs of the more southerly colonies—fluttering proudly from the lofty citadel and the towers of the Houses of Parliament. God Save the King!

I had four days—all delectably hot and sunny—in Quebec, and certainly made the most of them. What a town! Old grey walls, majestic citadel, dizzying cliffs, silver spires, ancient red roofs, mazes of winding ways, constant music of mellow chimes and clopping hooves over centuried cobblestones, throngs of cassocked, shovel-hatted priests, robed nuns, and tonsured barefoot friars, vistas of huddled chimney-pots, broad blue river far below, vivid, verdant countryside, and the dim, distant line of the purple Laurentians. . . . . I also took some suburban trips—a walk to Sillery, up the river (whose headland church is such an universal landmark), and a trolley ride to the upper level of the Montmorency Falls, where stands Kent House (enlarged and badly defaced as an hotel), the Georgian mansion inhabited in the 1790's by the Duke of Kent, Queen Victoria's father. I loafed, read, and wrote in all the parks and on the citadel embankment, and looked up the exact spot of Wolfe's ascent of the cliff— not an easy quest, since it is unmarked, and since the local Gauls are far from eager to point out the route of their great conqueror. One of the things about Quebec that always strikes me forcibly is the *sky*—the odd cloud formations peculiar to northerly latitudes and virtually unknown in southern New England. Mist and vapour assume fantastic and portentous aspects, and at sunset on Labour Day I saw one of the most impressive phenomena imaginable from a vantage-point on the ancient citadel overlooking the river and the Levis cliffs beyond. The evening was predominantly clear; but some strange refractive quality gave the dying solar rays an abnormal redness, whilst from the zenith to the southeastern horizon stretched an almost black funnel of churning nimbus clouds—the small end meeting the earth at some inland point beyond Levis. From a place midway in this cloud-funnel, zigzag streaks of lightning would occasionally dart toward the ground, with faint rumbles of thunder following tardily after. Finally—while the blood-red sun still bathed the river and cliffs and housetops in a supernal light—a pallid arc of rainbow sprang into sight above the distant Isle d'Orleans; its upper end lost in the great funnel of cloud. I have never seen such a phenomenon before, and doubt if it could occur as far south as Providence. Another striking thing is the almost perpetual mist which spectrally hovers about the mountains and valleys near Lake Memphramagog, at the Vermont-Quebec line. With such bizarre skies, I do not wonder that the northern races excel those of the south in fantastic imagination.

My ride back to the States was extremely pleasant—an apocalyptic sunset over a grotesquely steepled hilltop village, and a great round moon flooding strange plains with an eery radiance. Dawn came in New-Hampshire lake-and-mountain region of uncommon beauty, and I glimpsed Daniel Webster's early home from the train south of Franklin. Boston at 9 a.m.— and then good old Salem and Marblehead (Arkham and Kingsport).

In Salem I came upon some interesting new things, and got inside the fine old Richard Darby house (1762) for the first time. This structure— splendidly panelled—was rather old-fashioned even in its day. The Darbys were virtually the first of the great merchant princes of Salem—ship-captains and owners who established the thriving East-India trade. One high spot was the perfect reproduction of a gabled house of 1650 lately built on the grounds of the Pequot Mills. Every detail of the 17th century work is duplicated with scholarly fidelity, and I could hardly believe it was a modern fac-simile. But the climax was the splendid reproduction of the pioneer Salem settlement of 1626 et seq., carefully constructed and laid out in Forest Run Park. It consists of a generous plot of ground at the harbour's edge, painstakingly landscaped and covered with absolutely perfect duplicates of the very earliest huts and houses—dwellings of a sort now utterly vanished. All the early industries are also reproduced—there being such things as an ancient saw-pit, blacksmith shop, salt-works, brick-plant, fish-drying outfit, and so on. Nothing else that I have ever seen gives one so good a picture of the rough pioneer life led during the first half-decade of New England colonisation. Marblehead possessed its accustomed charm—though my inspection was broken by several showers. I finally got utterly drenched in Boston as I darted from the North Station to pay a farewell call on Cook. All told, it was a magnificent outing in spite of its brevity—and is probably the only first-rate voyage I'll get this year.

[In 1934 Lovecraft engaged in an extensive visit with his young friend Robert H. Barlow, whose family resided in a house outside of the town of De Land, Florida.]

[23]   In the evening I rode on to Jacksonville, Fla. and put up for the night. The next morning I proceeded onward to De Land, where my brilliant young host met the 'bus. I was now in the real subtropics, as the enclosed pictures will graphically hint. Through some chance incident of highway repair the coach did not proceed on its usual route, but detoured to ancient *St. Augustine*—that fascinating relique of 16ᵗʰ century Spain which I intend to visit for a week on my way back, and from which I'll send you some antiquarian material. On this occasion the 'bus did not stop or even enter the venerable town—but merely raced tantalisingly by the crumbling city gates . . . . those striking pillars of coquina-stone (stone formed by the coagulation of tiny shells and bits of shells by sea-water, and common on the east coast of northern Florida . . . different from the tapia or "tabby" stone formed of coral and common in Charleston) erected in 1730 or thereabouts. I had just a glimpse of old Fort San Marcos (or Marion) and the ancient Tolometo Cemetery with its strange slabs and spectral live-oaks. Of these you'll hear more when I stop there on my return.

As for De Land—it is a delightful town scenically, as you can see from the views; though just as modern as anything in your own state. The only *old* things are ruins which one sees on side-trips—such as old Spanish sugar mills antedating 1763, the old Turnbull plantation of 1768 at New Smyrna, and the ruins (great arches of coquina stone amidst great oaks and tangled vines—very picturesque) of a Franciscan mission of 1696. You would have been interested in the open sea as seen from Daytona Beach—

with no land between the spectator and the coast of North Africa far to the east! De Land was founded in 1876, contains a small college, and is an attractive though scarcely picturesque place.

The Barlow home is out in the open country 14 miles west of the village—in a region where the live-oaks give place to tall Australian pines which stand out against the sky like the trees of a Japanese print. The house is of 2 stories and log exterior—a rustic type—and is not yet quite finished. The grounds are still in the process of landscaping—pool, walks, rustic bridge, etc. Behind the house is a delightful lake on which we row, and across which is an impressive oak grove where we sometimes take our current reading and writing. Bits of typical subtropical jungle can be found here and there, and all sorts of snakes abound—Barlow shoots them for the sake of their skins, which he uses in bookbinding. The climate is absolutely ideal for me—temperatures of 85° or so every day—and I feel three or four times as well and active as I ever feel in the north. I habitually go hatless and coatless, and am preserving and augmenting the coat of tan I began to acquire in Charleston. A few points on the predicted programme have fallen through—for example, I shall not see Cummings, Hamilton, or Williamson, and shall probably not be able to get down to Dunedin.[17]

My young host—Robert Hayward Barlow—is a really brilliant boy prodigy only 16 years old but immensely mature for his age. He is the son of a retired army colonel now in poor health and on a visit in the north. An elder brother, also absent, is an active army officer. Young Barlow is extremely versatile—a writer, painter, sculptor in clay, pianist, landscape gardener, book collector, and scores of other things despite the handicap of desperately bad eyesight. In the autumn he is going north for a session with expert oculists who have promised him some relief. He is small, dark, and active in his mannerisms. [. . .] The present household consists of Barlow and his mother; and of a mother and son named Johnston, from Virginia, who keep house and attend to various duties. The son, Charles Blackburn Johnston, is a lean, tall, dark chap of 37 who possesses considerable talent in painting and in other directions. Somewhere amidst the current enclosures you'll find a crude sketch of the place—I've had no time to study out a good one. Later I hope to get a snap shot to send. There are four cats—all delightful. A veteran white Tom named Doodle-Bug, and three little tigers named "High", "Low", and "Jack". My especial favourite is High—the darkest of the three—who trots like a little dog with Barlow and me when we take our evening walks. Also in the household are four infant opossums—tiny creatures that have to be fed with a medicine dropper as yet. Their mother was slain by a passing motor. Barlow's collection of weird books and magazines would make you turn green with envy. He keeps it in a deep closet off his room, which he has christened—after Klarkash-Ton's story—"The Vaults of Yoh-Vombis." Since my arrival he has demonstrated his sculptural skill by making a marvellous clay bas-relief of Cthulhu and a fine statuette of the Hindoo elephant god Ganesa (probably the prototype of Long's "Chaugnar").[18]

[24] Last week I visited a marvellously impressive place—Silver Springs, about 60 miles from here. There is a chain of placid lagoons whose floor is riddled with great pits 30 to 80 feet deep—covered with curious growths and studied by means of a glass-bottomed boat. In some of these submarine chasms the bones of prehistoric monsters are found, and in one is the weed-grown outline of an ancient sunken boat. Out of this series of basins flows the Silver River—as typical a tropic stream as the Congo or Amazon. It winds through miles of lush, impenetrable jungle, with palms, cypresses, festoons of moss, and tangles of vines leaning into the water. Alligators, turtles, snakes, and strange birds abound throughout its length. It was here that all the jungle scenes in the Tarzan films featuring Johnny Weismuller were taken. I traversed this river for 10 miles in a launch, and could easily believe I was in the heart of Africa. At one landing a group of natives hailed the boat and exhibited a huge cotton-mouth moccasin snake that they had caught alive—and one of them got aboard with the quarry to bring it alive to the snake-house at Silver Springs. Quite a bizarre fellow-passenger! During this trip I saw, for the first time, alligators *in their native habitat.* Previously I had seen them only in zoos, or at the alligator farm on Anastasia Island opposite St. Augustine. At this latter place, though, the surroundings are made to look like a bit of real jungle. There's an alligator in the lake behind the house here—but I've never seen him, although Mrs. Barlow and Charles Johnston have.

[After returning to Providence, Lovecraft spent a week in Nantucket. Its colonial antiquities captivated him.]

[25] And what a place is Nantucket! I *thought* I had seen something of colonial antiquity before—but just wait till I take you and Old Jug to this utterly unchanged fragment of early America! Ædepol! There is absolutely

nothing else like it—and to think I never visited it before . . . . a place only
90 miles (6 hrs. by coach and ship) from my own door! Compared with
this town Providence and St. Augustine and the Vieux Carré are positively
modernistic! Whole networks of cobblestoned streets with nothing but
colonial houses on either side—narrow, garden-bordered lanes—ancient
belfries—picturesque waterfront—*everything* that the antiquarian would
ask! I'm seeing the whole thing in a week's sojourn. Have a 3d story room
at The Overlook (an ancient tavern with small-paned windows etc.), with
a splendid view of the town and harbour and sea. I've explored old houses,
the 1746 windmill, the Hist. Soc. Museum, the whaling museum, etc.—
and am doing every inch of the quaint streets and alleys on foot. Also took
motor sightseeing tour around the entire island—viewing ancient Siascon-
set (a fishing village with tiny cottages and rambling lanes, now a summer
resort) and other points. Yes—and just to echo faintly your Mt. Hamilton
astronomical experience I had a fine view of Saturn through the 5" refrac-
tor of the Maria Mitchell observatory. Yesterday I suffered greatly from
the cold, but today it is warm again. One thing I'm strongly tempted to do
is to follow the local fashion and hire a *bicycle* for a ramble around. I haven't
been on a wheel in 20 years, and the idea has a subtly rejuvenating quality
about it. In my youth I was a veritable bicycle centaur.

[In the summer of 1935 Lovecraft undertook his last major excursion,
spending several months again with Barlow in Florida.]

[26]   Well—as you see, the Southern trip *did* materialise despite all misgivings. Barlow got home June 3d, and I started on Wednesday the 5th.
Cut out N.Y. and Washington, and made my first stop in ancient Fredericksburg—a Virginia town of the 18th century where Washington virtually
grew up. Had 7 hours there, and saw all my favourite spots. Then straight
down to my beloved Charleston, where I likewise went the antiquarian
rounds. The moment I struck the steady heat of South Carolina I became
stronger and more active—indeed, this southern trip has caused me to feel
really comfortable for the first time in 1935. Had 2 days in Charleston,
then down to De Land via Jacksonville. Am now repeating my visit of
1934 with minor variations. The Johnstons have moved up the road, and
Bob's elder brother Lieut. Wayne Barlow has been here on a furlough from
Texas. The colonel—Bob's father—is also home. I mourn the absence of
Doodlebug, but High and Jack are great big boys now. Jack's neck is still
a bit askew from his mishap of last year. New cats are the yellow Per-

sians—Cyrus and Darius—and two kittens named Henry Clay and Pop-eye. Also a little dog—who got slightly hit by a motor the other night. Bob's new cabin is going up in the oak grove across the lake, and presents a fine appearance even in half-finished form. It will be occupiable before long. We are planning a number of things to do before I leave—perhaps some printing project connected with amateurdom. Bob has an excellent press. But time will tell what—if anything—we shall accomplish.

[27]   Occasional explorations diversify the programme. On June 17 we visited a fascinating place—Black Water Creek, a tropical river whose lush scenery suggests the Congo, Amazon, and other exotic streams found in history and legend. It winds through a steaming jungle of tall, moss-draped cypresses, whose grotesque, twisted roots writhe curiously at the water's edge. Palms lean precariously over the brink, and vines and creepers strow the black, dank earth of the bordering forest aisles. Sinister sunken logs loom up at various points, and pallid flowers and leprous fungi gleam whitely through the forest's perpetual twilight. It is much like the river at Silver Springs of which I think I wrote you last year—though I enjoyed it even more because of the more leisurely observing conditions. At Silver Springs I was whizzed ahead in a launch; this time we (R H B, Wayne, and I) went along slowly in a row boat. Each bend of the stream brought to light some unexpected vista of tropical luxuriance, and we absorbed the spectacle to the full. Serpents and alligators were somewhat in evidence—though none came near our boat. I hope for more trips of this kind, since I find myself especially sensitive to the beauty of subtropical scenery.

Revisionist

[Throughout his adult life, Lovecraft found a more regular income through professional revision or ghostwriting than through the sale of original fiction. In 1933 he outlines to a prospective client, Richard F. Searight, his terms for revision.]

[28]   Regarding critical and revisory work—I have been trying to cut down my quota of late in order to get some time for original writing, but might be able to coöperate in your enterprises—especially since your products would not appear to be in need of the most arduous kind of re-construction. I could tell better after seeing just what your stories need; hence if you will send along a few, I will be more definite about the matter.

My fees in such cases depend wholly upon the amount of work necessary, as reckoned in terms of time and labour. I have separate scales of prices for light revision, extensive revision, and actual reconstruction or "ghost-writing". I usually ask part in advance and the balance on delivery. What I cannot undertake—except in the very rarest cases—is *speculative* collaboration; that is, work done for a share of the proceeds in case of acceptance, and without a flat "win-or-lose" fee. My reason for this reluctance is that such an arrangement almost always results in loss rather than gain for the reviser—even when the story is accepted. Revision is really not only as hard as original writing, but (for me, at least) actually *harder.* It takes just as much (or more) of my time and energy to give a tale a thorough re-writing as to create one of my own—hence it would be absurd for me to do this, with only part of the proceeds as my greatest possible reward, when I could just as easily compose an original tale and have an equal chance of *all* the proceeds. My only object in accepting revision is to eliminate the element of chance—to accept lesser returns *because they are certain* instead of contingent upon acceptance. The sole exception to this rule is when a tale contains some absolutely sure-fire idea which makes sale almost certain—more nearly certain than with a thing of my own—but it is seldom that one finds an idea of which this can conclusively be said. Of course, even in those rare cases the speculative element is not absent, so that I have to ask a greater share of the proceeds than any flat fee, on a non-speculative basis, would amount to.

[29] **H. P. Lovecraft — Prose Revision Rates**

Reading Only—rough general remarks 1000 words or less 0.50
1000–2000 .... 0.65
2000–4000 .... 1.00
4000–5000 .... 1.25
20¢ for each 1000 wds over 5000

Criticism Only—analytical estimate in detail without revision
1000 words or less 1.50
1000–2000 .... 2.00
2000–4000 .... 3.00
4000–5000 .... 3.75
60¢ for each 1000 wds over 5000

Revision and Copying   (Per page of 330 words)

(a) Copying on typewriter—double space, 1 carbon. No revision
     except spelling, punctuation, and grammar   0.25

(b) Light revision, no copying (prose improved locally—
     no new ideas)   0.25

(c) Light revision typed, double-space with 1 carbon   0.50

(d) Extensive revision, no copying (thorough improvement,
     including structural change, transposition, addition, or excision—
     possible introduction of new ideas or plot elements. Requires
     new text or separate MS.) In rough draught longhand   0.75

(e) Extensive revision as above, typed, double space, 1 carbon   1.00

(f) Rewriting from old MS., synopsis, plot-notes, idea-germ, or
     mere suggestion—i.e., "ghost-writing". Text in full by reviser—
     both language and development. Rough draught longhand   2.25

(g) Rewriting as above, typed, double space, 1 carbon   2.50

Special flat rates quoted for special jobs, depending on estimated consumption of time and energy.

Continuing Philosophical Discussions

[Although by the 1930s Lovecraft had settled upon many of the fundamental tenets of his philosophy, he continued to debate issues with his correspondents. Religion—especially the indoctrination of religious belief in the young—particularly incurred his outrage.]

[30] The dull and devastating piety and literalism of the backwoods evangelical are destined to survive only in intellectually retarded areas like Tennessee, Mississippi, Iowa, etc., once the elder generation of childhood-biassed standpatters dies off in the ordinary course of events. That lower class among whom contemporary education is not diffused—and who will therefore continue to hand down a naively theistic tradition—are now overwhelmingly Catholic. To think clearly about the cosmos in the light of contemporary information is to abandon any possibility of believing in the fantastic and capricious orthodoxies of yesterday—be they Buddhistic, Judaic, Christian, Hindoo, Mahometan, or any other brand. More liberal wish-delusions, however, will undoubtedly last for several generations

more—or until the race has lost that emotional dependence on mythic values, and elogies, and immortalistics which the earlier centuries of primitive ignorance and fanciful speculation have bred into it. Some of us—as individuals—have lost this primitive dependence already; but we can more or less understand its survival in others—especially since we are ourselves full of primitive and vestigial feelings in other directions . . . . . feelings which (like worship of pageantry, exaltation of the family, love of hunting and fishing, etc.) are no less poignant because of our understanding of their purely mundane and fortuitous origin, and purely relative and transient significance as environmentally adjustive factors. Thus I know what you *mean* when you speak of the illusion of immortality as something emotionally "satisfying"; though to one of the contemporary milieu the element of emotional satisfyingness or its reverse *has nothing whatever to do with the question of a theory's truth or falsity* . . . . . experience and observation having taught us the complete unreliability of the emotions (which bring different and sometimes opposite conclusions to different persons) as a guide or interpreter of the external world. Moreover—the conventional emotional biasses toward immortality and cosmic purpose are themselves very largely accidental results of traditions rather than basic attitudes, as we may see by comparing the moods of different types and individuals—older and younger, unsophisticated and sophisticated. No level-headed modern either wants to be "immortal" himself (gawd, what boredom!) or to have his favourite characters immortal. Each appears for a second in the pattern and then disappears . . . . . and what of it? What more could anybody not filled up with infantile myth expect or even dream of? It is overwhelmingly true that no sane adult, confronted with the information of today, could possibly think up anything as grotesque, gratuitous, irrelevant, chimerical, and unmotivated as "immortality" unless bludgeoned into the ancient phantasy by the stultifying crime of childhood orthodox training. Religionists openly give away the fakery of their position when they insist on crippling children's emotions with specialised suggestion anterior to the development of a genuine critical faculty. We all know that *any* emotional bias—irrespective of truth or falsity—can be implanted by suggestion in the emotions of the young, hence the inherited traditions of an orthodox community are absolutely without evidential value regarding the real *is-or-isn'tness* of things. Only the exceptional individual reared in the nineteenth century or before has any chance of holding any genuine opinion of value regarding the universe—except by a slow and painful process of courageous disillusionment. If religion were true, its followers would not try to bludgeon their young into an artificial conformity; but would merely insist on their unbending quest for *truth*, irrespective of artificial backgrounds or practical consequences. With such an honest and inflexible *openness to evidence*, they could not fail to receive any *real truth* which might be manifesting itself around them. The fact that religionists do *not* follow this honourable course, but cheat at their game by invoking juvenile quasi-hypnosis, is enough to destroy their pretensions in my eyes even if their absurdity were not manifest in every other direction. Of course, their policy is the habitual ostrich-act of all primitive thinkers. When they see that honest openness to evidence does not incline their children toward the preferred system of myths, they do not behave like civilised beings and question the validity of the myths, but turn about and try to cripple the mental receiving apparatus of their children until the poor mites duplicate the accidental bias of their misinformed elders and forcibly acquire the same set of meaningless moods and obsolete prejudices. Thus each of the deeply-seated myth-systems carries on—the little Hindoo becoming a Brahma-worshipper like papa, the little Moslem continuing the ancestral whine to Allah, the little Yankee intoning nasal psalms to the god or demigods of the Christians, the little Jap burning more and more incense at Shinto shrines . . . . . and so on . . . . . and so on . . . . . ad infinitum . . . . . ad absurdum . . . . . and pretty soon the solar system will play out, and nobody in the cosmos will know that there has ever been any earth or human race or Brahmins or Moslems or Christians or Shintoists or such . . . . . dust to dust . . . . . and the ironic laughter of any entity which may happen to be watching the cosmos from outside . . . . . ho, hum!

[The belief that Lovecraft was chronically melancholy has sometimes been asserted, and as evidence his letters to Helen Sully are often cited. In reality, however, Lovecraft was merely attempting to encourage Sully (who was herself in a state of depression) by overemphasizing his own failings but nevertheless asserting that "There are dozens of things I can actually enjoy."]

[31]   Only a few persons ever attain acute and ecstatic happiness, and only a minority are even moderately happy. These degrees of felicity are simply chance boons which may or may not happen to befall any one person. If one stumbles upon happiness, well and good. That's just a piece of

luck. But if one doesn't, there's nothing which can be done about it. Most never do—so it is well not to *expect* any great good of existence. What most persons *can* rationally expect is a kind of *working adjustment* or *resignation* in which *active pain* is cut down to a minimum. It is likely that a *majority of persons* could attain such a state of *tolerable equilibrium* as this through the exercise of the intelligence and a disciplining of the emotions. This, therefore, *should be the only norm* in matters of expectation and endeavour. Half of our misery—perhaps more—comes from our mistaken notion that we *ought to be happy* . . . that we somehow, for some mysterious reason, "deserve" or "have a right to" acute happiness. The utter fallacy of this notion is something which should be widely inculcated—for just as long as people *think* they ought to be happy, they will extract an added unhappiness and bitterness from the fact that they are not . . . . and most are not and never can be. What they must learn is that *the highest consistent and practicable goal of mankind is simply an absence of acute and unendurable suffering*—a sensible compromise with an indifferent cosmos which was never built for mankind, and in which mankind is only a microscopic, negligible, and temporary accident. That is the most which the average person will ever get out of life, and he might as well trim his sails accordingly. Anything more is purely *accidental*—and while one may be at liberty to dream idly of such happy accidents, or to enjoy them in the rare event of their actually befalling one, it is certainly foolish to expect such things, or to feel sullen or envious when (as is usual) they fail to come. All in all, mankind's supreme folly lies in the general striving after excessively high and usually unattainable goals. Really good things *may* happen to one—but they don't very often. The sensible thing is not to expect them, but to consider them as mere "velvet" when through some rare chance they *do* happen along . . . . if they ever do. In the meanwhile we *can* ameliorate our condition, and eliminate certain active phases of pain, restlessness, and discontentedness, by adopting a philosophic and scientific attitude and making the most of our intellectual and aesthetic endowments. Through the cultivation of congenial interests, and the active exercise of one's mind and imagination in creative work and appreciative observation of the external world and the general field of human knowledge, we may gradually build up a fabric of resigned contentment amidst which we shall find it distinctly (even if not very markedly) better to be alive than dead. The *degree* of this advantage of living over non-living depends of course upon the individual, and his natural capacity for intellectual or aesthetic accomplishment, and for interested enjoyment of an objective survey of the external world. But even when the degree is slight, the state of resignation and contentment is none the less to be welcomed. There is no active discomfort in a life which is barely better than oblivion—and that is the kind of life most have. When we realise that we're damned lucky to escape acute pain, we more truly appreciate the condition of not-very-pleasant quasi-painlessness which falls to the lot of most. That is what life is—so why ask for more? Of the cases of *apparent* happiness which we see around us, about a quarter are accidental realities, and three quarters are false facades. Taking mankind as a whole, in relation to the state of happiness, I fancy one could say that half the people living are just about as well off alive as dead. Of the remaining half, about half (a quarter of all people) are *better off* alive than dead, while the rest would be better off dead than alive. Probably about 3 to 5% of the human race are actively happy—and 0.5 or 1% keenly and ecstatically happy. The real art of living is to become resigned to a mediocre muddling along, and to find enough things to do along the road to keep endurably contented. Once we realise that actual happiness is probably out of reach, we are better able to enjoy the little things and objective interests which make the average life tolerable. It helps us to realise that most people are just as miserable—or as lacking in acute happiness—as we ourselves are. That's what life is—and most of those who pretend to be happy are merely bluffing. [. . .]

In actual fact, there are few total losses and never-was's which discourage and exasperate me more than the venerable E'ch-Pi-El. I know of few persons whose attainments fall more consistently short of their aspirations, or who in general have less to live for. Every aptitude which I wish I had, I lack. Everything which I wish I could formulate and express, I have failed to formulate and express. Everything which I value, I have either lost or am likely to lose. Within a decade, unless I can find some job paying at least $10.00 per week, I shall have to take the cyanide route through inability to keep around me the books, pictures, furniture, and other familiar objects which constitute my only remaining reason for keeping alive. And so far as *solitude* is concerned, I probably capture all medals. In Providence I have never seen a congenial mind with which I could exchange ideas, and even among my correspondents there are fewer and fewer who coincide with me on enough points to make discourse enjoyable except on a few specialised points. The newer generation has grown away from me, whilst the older is so fossilised as to form very meagre material for argument or conversation. In everything—philosophy, politics, aesthetics, and interpretation of the sciences—I find myself more and more alone on an island, with an atmosphere almost of hostility gathering around me. With youth, all the possibilities of glamour and adventurous expectancy departed—leaving me stranded on a shelf with nothing to look forward to. Most distinctly, the picture is not an idyllic one—and I'd scarcely wish my worst enemy the fate of being no better off than I am. It might be said that I am just about two inches from the suicide level—among that vast majority for whom existence is the *barest shade* preferable to non-existence. But of course that bare shade makes a vast amount of difference. What keeps me alive is the ability to look back to the past and imagine I am still in 1902 or 1903. Of all my dreams, about 0.8 are of that period—with myself in short trousers and at the old home, with my mother, grandfather, black cat Nigger-Man, etc. still alive. Thus the world of the early 1900's still exists for me in about a third of the hours of my daily life. As long as I can retain the books and pictures and furniture and accessories of those days, as I still do, I have something to live for. When I no longer can, I shall move to that lot in Swan Point Cemetery which is reserved for me. Meanwhile, of course, I certainly *do* get a lot of pleasure from books, travel (when I *can* travel), philosophy, the arts, history, antiquarianism, scenery, the sciences, and so on . . . . and from such poor attempts in the way of aesthetic creation (= fantastic fiction) as I can kid myself into thinking I can sometimes achieve. The reason I have been more "melancholy" than usual in the last few years is that I am coming to distrust more and more the value of the material I produce. Adverse criticism has of late vastly undermined my confidence in my literary powers. And so it goes. Decidedly, Grandpa is not one of those beaming old gentlemen who radiate cheer wherever they go! However—I *do* escape the pits of genuine and extreme melancholy through a rational analysis of my situation—whereby I realise that my lot is no worse than the average, that there is no reason to think that it could have been better, and that there is nothing in particular to be done about it. My absence of acute happiness is in the main a direct result of my own limitations. My natural temperament, and lack of special intellectual and aesthetic abilities and personal graces—not the "evil" or "injustice" of the world around me—is largely responsible for the impasse in which my declining years find me. Other elements were contributed by *sheer chance*—but nowhere does human or cosmic malignancy figure. To be *bitter* or *resentful* over something for which only nature and chance are responsible, would be the apex of folly and irrationality. Who can be *angry* when there is no guiding consciousness to be "angry" at? Everything is just as blind and uncontrollable cosmic chance determines it. Therefore I simply say "Oh, what the hell" . . . . and let things muddle along as they will . . . . meanwhile trying to make the most of what meagre endowments, environmental advantages, and intellectual, aesthetic, and antiquarian interests I happen to have at my disposal. I couldn't help matters by brooding on the fact that some others are more happily situated. What's that to me? The happiness of *others* needn't make *me* any the more miserable! So I forego the masochistic luxury of mourning, and simply have as good a time as I can with the existing set-up. And at that, it isn't so bad. I'm no pining and picturesque victim of melancholy's romantic ravages. I merely shrug my shoulders, recognise the inevitable, let the world march past, and vegetate along as painlessly as possible. I suppose I'm a damned sight better off than millions. There are dozens of things I can actually enjoy.

Literature versus Hackwork

[Lovecraft never renounced a belief in art as pure "self-expression" that had no relationship to commerce. In long arguments with E. Hoffmann Price, the prototypical pulp hack, he sought to explain what writing meant to him, and why he could not write "to order" for a given market merely to make a sale.]

[32]   I can appreciate fully the extent to which an adroit and determined writer is able to circumvent the worst limitations of the pulp medium — although that does not alter the fact that this purely artificial burden (a burden not imposed by the legitimate demands of aesthetics, but by the ignorant, capricious, and irrelevant demands of those who have no interest in intrinsic merit and who, from their motives, have no right to make demands) represents a sheer waste of energy which any but a supercharged human dynamo would find disastrous. A writer with only the average store of energy has none to spare for things that are not essential. It may be that he could, through a dreary mental straining unrelieved by the zest which accompanies *artistically necessary* effort, succeed in the purely mechanical (but aesthetically meaningless and irrelevant) feat of producing a tale at once literally respectable and acceptable to the low-grade tradesman of the editorial racket; yet when he has done this, he has *achieved nothing whatever* in the direction of anything he wishes or respects. The excess of exhausting labour he has spent in suiting the freaks of illiterates has not carried him a

millimetre nearer to his one legitimate goal of emotional catharsis and harmonious expression, but has on the other hand lowered his vitality and creative energy, dampened the subconscious creative impulse which alone produces really powerful material, and confined him to a single set channel which—though he may have manipulated it till it does not flagrantly violate any aesthetic canon—is *certainly not better* than what he would have naturally used, and *probably much worse*. As an artist, he has flung away priceless strength to no purpose—wearing himself out in producing something *not as good* as he would otherwise have produced. No triumph is a real triumph unless it serves an end which the victor respects—and commercial advantage is an end which one can hardly respect unless one happens to be of a certain temperament. When so much ill-to-be-spared energy has to go into a field bringing no artistic return whatever, it is natural for the artist to prefer to *separate* his industrial from his personal life—using for honest, straightforward, non-pseudo-literary work of any sort the vast fund of energy which would have to be sunk futilely in his productions (and generally with a deleterious effect) in order to twist them into industrial material. All this, however, postulates the man of merely average or (like myself) sub-average energy—having no application to human dynamos like you and Derleth, who can pour out any amount of calculative cerebration independently of imaginative stimulus and without feeling the difference. Youse guys are damn lucky—but we plodders can't safely follow you any more than an average citizen can safely follow a tight-rope walker. What you are too lucky to be able to realise is that for a small-time writer *the whole bottom drops out of the creative process the moment it becomes consciously calculative.* Art is not the devising of artificial things to say, but the mere saying of something already formulated inside the artist's imagination and automatically clamouring to be said. That is the genesis of virtually every aesthetic product worth classifying as such. Art is potent only to the extent that it is unconscious. Of course, a great deal of careful conscious shaping is necessary, but this is always backed by a tense and effective emotional stimulus *as long as it is confined to the improvement and clarification of the original natural conception*—i.e., as long as it amplifies and promotes the basic subconscious desire which motivates and gives birth to the given aesthetic attempt. Even a comparatively sluggish and easily fatigued calculative intellect (like mine) can be spurred into fairly effective performances when the process promises to help in the fulfilment of the original subconscious expression-impulse. The hope of an adequate reward—a reward which seems adequate as measured by the then-ruling desire—is a stimulus of supreme potency. But set that same intellect to a calculative task *not* connected with the fulfilment of the dominant urge—a task such as the laborious arrangement of expression to suit an artificial end *not connected* with the intrinsic perfection of the expression itself—and all emotional stimulus is lacking. The negative stimulus afforded by the fear of starving is not at all like the positive stimulus afforded by the desire for expression, dream-capture, or imaginative expansion. It produces—or tends to produce—a sort of paralysing desperation *hostile* to clear thinking rather than the expansive glow which strengthens, quickens, and fertilises thought. Thus the under-energised artist who finds no difficulty at all in arranging literary details *conducive to his own aesthetic ends,* encounters an unscalable barrier of exhausting and repulsive toil when confronted with the profitless and irrelevant task of artificially twisting his product—without hope of improvement and with vast likelihood of debasement—into some meaningless shape dictated by empty conventions which his whole nature execrates as disgustingly uncivilised and outside the normal field of consciousness of a gentleman. What happens when such an average-energied or under-energied artist attempts to link his personal expression with business depends altogether on the man himself, and on the attendant circumstances. In cases where the person has varied interests and holds on life—where his sense of integrity and existence is not bound up in the task of saying something which desperately clamours to be said—the solution is often a complete surrender of self-expression. Then, when the writer (no longer an artist) has ceased to have anything to say, there is no longer any emotional obstacle to the commercial juggling of rubber-stamp situations in accordance with the low-grade market's whims. While still lacking any *stimulus* for work, there is at least no *handicap*—and if ordinary cleverness be present, the writer can often succeed in gauging and pandering to the fickle boob-market—which he will do without any of the efforts at compromise made by the super-energied man, since his 'victory' in cheap fields will have crushed within him that sense of integrity which makes the super-energied hack still wish to retain something of artistic verity. True, he is not likely to produce any more art. That side of his life has been killed off. But if it was not his dominant and pivotal side, the loss is no greater than other curtailments of personality common in a barbarism where the profit-motive is forced on large numbers of cultivated persons. When, however, the capture of dreams and the utterance of dimly adumbrated conceptions *is* the primary and crucial element in a man's life—as it indubitably is in a substantial number of cases—then the attempt to suit artificial and contemptible tradesman's whims is foredoomed to failure except among the super-energied. Vast and insuperable emotional dykes are subconsciously reared against the diversion of intellection to base and ulterior objects, so that the listless and reluctant struggle toward industrialism can hardly be more than a dull tragedy consuming all and yielding nothing. It may kill the artist, but it will never make a business-man of the corpse. Nothing which is forced out of one at the price of his imaginative life is ever likely to have enough substance and skill to suit even the mind-struck three-penny cynics of the pulp. Compromise is impossible when the artist has not enough excess energy to make the irrelevant intellectual manipulations other than a prostrating and usually self-defeating drain. Remember that the slightest departure from the single aim of self-expression puts an instant damper on the very springs of creative zeal and creative intellect in the person of average or sluggish energy. The obstacles are too great to get around. Thus (in cases of average energy or less) when one bases one's life and self-respect on imaginative sincerity, it is really a bad business policy to try to tamper with self-expression or fuse one's dreams with the hard-boiled job of squeezing money out of indifferent and stereotyped tradesmen. It is bad business because it gets one nowhere. There isn't any money in it . . . . . an argument which even a tradesman can recognise as valid. When the only thing in life that one wants to do is to express himself aesthetically, it is foolish to embark on any course which will almost certainly defeat that end (though of course a good business-man doesn't even suspect what this is all about)—and *doubly* foolish when (here the business-man assents) that suicidal sacrifice will never lead to even the hollow compensation of material profit! The gist, of course, is simply this; that for certain types of persons the energy which would have to go into the artificial and repulsive task of hack-adapting would be largely wasted, and in any case grossly *disproportionate* as compared with the potentialities in other commercial fields where no disgust-barrier operates. If I reserve a certain quantity of mental energy from my personal and creative life to devote to the shelter-and-nourishment-acquiring process, I want that energy to go as far as possible and to be wasted as little as possible . . . . and experiment seems to show that it would go farther and bring better returns in some simple, honest, and non-charlatanic occupation like drug-clerking or bookkeeping or bricklaying—an occupation of a straightforward, need-filling sort without the servile taint of pandering and wheedling—than in any field which involved the element of mockery, of degrading parody, or of the diversion of exhausting intellection to an ulterior, irrelevant, and aesthetically wasteful aim. That is why I'd give a good deal for a real job, if I only knew how to go about looking for such a thing. My great mistake was in my younger days, when I thought that actual literary effort would surely manage to earn me a living some how, some day. Had I known then what I know now, I would have hastened to fit myself for some steady routine work—of a sort mentally unexacting enough to leave my creative imagination free—as soon as my health became tolerable, and the ultimate exhaustion of drastically diminished resources apparent. But alas, these sensible perspectives generally come too late!

[As Lovecraft became increasingly concerned with political and economic issues with the onset of the depression, he came to realize that "bourgeois capitalism" had resulted in the transformation of much literary and artistic work into the realm of "amusement enterprises."]

[33] *Commercialism* forms the third aesthetically degrading factor of the present age, but is a parallel evil of different origin and nature. Instead of vitiating honest efforts at self-expression, as do decadence and social propagandism, it simply removes *human energy altogether from the field of honest expression,* and shackles it to a greedy and aesthetically and intellectually dishonest sort of charlatanry having no connexion with art. It is an older disease than chaotic decadence and systematic propagandism, and will persist as long as bourgeois capitalism remains a factor to be coped with. It was not so marked in the agrarian aristocratic age, because at that period the most unimaginative, philistinic, and under-educated elements did little or no reading or conscious artistic contemplation. When they did reach out aesthetically, they copied educated gentlefolk. Bourgeois capitalism gave artistic excellence and sincerity a deathblow by enthroning cheap *amusement-value* at the expense of that *intrinsic excellence* which only cultivated, non-acquisitive persons of assured position can enjoy. The determinant market for written, pictorial, musical, dramatic, decorative, architectural, and other heretofore aesthetic material ceased to he a small circle of truly educated persons, but became a substantially larger (even with a vast proportion of society starved and crushed into a sodden, inarticulate helplessness through commercial and commercial-satellitic greed and callousness)

circle of mixed origin numerically dominated by crude, half-educated clods whose systematically perverted ideals (worship of low cunning, material acquisition, cheap comfort and smoothness, worldly success, ostentation, speed, intrinsic magnitude, surface glitter, etc.) prevented them from ever achieving the tastes and perspectives of the gentlefolk whose dress and speech and external manners they so assiduously mimicked. This herd of acquisitive boors brought up from the shop and the counting-house a complete set of artificial attitudes, oversimplifications, and mawkish senti- mentalities which no sincere art or literature could gratify — & they so out- numbered the remaining educated gentlefolk that most of the purveying agencies became at once reoriented to them. Literature and art lost most of their market; and writing, painting, drama, etc. became engulfed more and more in the domain of *amusement enterprises*. Hence the *Saturday Evening Post*, the Hearst press, the "art" of Maxfield Parrish, the fiction of Robert W. Chambers (*after* his "King in Yellow" period) and Kathleen Norris, the happy ending tacked on to the cinema version of "Winterset" (to say noth- ing of the aimless mess of flickers which I drowsed through while waiting for "Winterset" to come on!), the heterogeneous pseudo-Colonial and pseudo-Tudor villas of our smart real-estate developments, the persistent sale of the late O. Henry's collected charlatanries, etc. etc. etc. And when bourgeois capitalism found it profitable to reach down to the still-sub- merged elements and cater to their crippled, repressed, and grotesquely unformed tastes with tabloid news rags, pulp "confession", "spicy", "love", "western", "horror", "scientifiction", "G-man" magazines, and the like, the opening-up of this huge market merely aggravated the trend away from real excellence toward showmanship and charlatanry. The suave bosses of a business "civilisation" have no wish to improve the masses — rather the reverse. Certainly, the spineless clod who sells himself into a pulp editor- ship under the present degenerate set-up cannot attempt to educate his circle of yokels and half-wits, or seek to cram meritorious literature down the reluctant gullets of people who simply continue buying trash from oth- ers. If he has chosen a cheap showman's job, he must stick to the pandering standards of his underworld or get out and make an honest living at some really constructive job of another sort if he can find such in a bourgeois world. Capitalism says, work the poor devils as cheaply as possible (throw- ing 'em out to starve when they're superfluous), and cash in on their present dwarfed tastes and faculties by selling 'em all the tabloids and Macfadden rags their decreasing store of pennies can pay for. Thus the noble cultures of well-mannered bank presidents, of Messrs. Hoover, Mellon, Mills, Al Smith, etc., and of other idealistic and disinterested upholders of our Sacred Constitution of the Founding Fathers. No wonder the Marxists exaggerate a *trend or influence* into an *immutable law*, and proclaim the eternal linkage of art and economics!

Problems of Politics and Economics

[The difficult decade of the 1930s saw Lovecraft make a remarkable revision in his political and economic attitudes, shifting from far-right conservatism to moderate socialism. But although he believed that a variety of socialistic policies (unemployment insurance, old age pensions, shorter working hours for all so that unemployment could be eased) were necessary as a means of rectifying economic inequities, he continued to champion a kind of "fascism" whereby only qualified citizens would be entitled to the vote.]

[34]   Democracy in a complex industrial civilisation is a joke — since it means nothing but the concentration of all resources in the hands of a few capable plutocrats, and the subterraneous rule of this group under the outward forms of democracy. Concerning unemployment — the present wave is the worst yet because it combines a new and permanent element with the recurrent depression-element which always comes at intervals in unregulated commercial nations. This new and permanent element is what we have come to call *technological unemployment,* and is the result of a very simple but profoundly important effect of mechanised industry — namely; that under all conditions, and to a constantly increasing degree as invention advances, *it now requires only a few persons, comparatively speaking, to produce all the materials which the total consumption of the world can possibly demand.* This is because of the infinite multiplying-power of the machine. Once make a pattern, and the apparatus to construct a given article from it, and there is no limit to the *number of such articles* which a mere handful of machine-tenders can produce. If more than the world's normal supply are made, there will be no one to buy them. Obviously, the old system of unregulated individual industry breaks down here. The manufacturer, under the traditional system, seeks to produce as much as possible with as little expenditure as possible; and therefore installs labour-saving machinery, discharging all but the few men needed to run it, and keeping these busy for as much time as he can in the face of labour-union pressure. This formerly gained him a

good profit, but now he finds that after his cheap, easy and inexhaustible producing mechanism has turned out a certain amount of goods, there is no market whatever for any more. People can use only a certain amount of any one thing, hence beyond that limit articles of the sort are useless. The so-called "saturation-point" has been reached, despite all artificial devices like style changes and "high-pressure salesmanship." Moreover—the manufacture *has restricted his own market* by trying to produce more and more cheaply—like the dog with a bone in his mouth who lost the bone through reaching for its reflection in the water. In discharging men and installing machines, he so swelled the pauper class that the remaining solvent elements, capable of forming a market, was materially decreased. If men can't be employed, they can't get money; and if they can't get money, they can't buy goods. Thus the manufacturer is caught in his own trap. By trying to produce goods more cheaply, he stripped so many people of their money that there are no longer enough solvent people to buy his goods! The eternal vicious circle—and a fine piece of grim cosmic irony. Then he closes down altogether and lives on his accumulated surplus while the masses live on charity or starve to death. Virtually no goods are produced. Prices fall, and eventually the few people who are not on charity manage to use up the existing stock of goods. This ends the *temporary* depression and gives the manufacturer a market once more. He reopens his factory and begins to produce again. *Formerly*, this brought safe prosperity, since the fresh start of industry required enough employed men to redistribute money, rescue the poor from charity, and expand markets once more. *But this recovery is less and less complete as the machine age advances, because the fresh start of industry and the virtually unlimited production of goods requires fewer and fewer employees.* The residue of the *permanently unemployed and unemployable* increases rapidly, and we have at last to face the situation that *all the possible business of the world can be performed by only a fraction of the world's population*—the rest remaining absolutely superfluous and without any natural function, whereby they can lay claim to food, clothing, and shelter. It is no longer a fact that there is always work for willing hands. The hands may be willing, but all the work that needs doing has been done. No matter what the size of a population, there is work for only a fraction of it so long as those in control of the power and industrial machinery are allowed to map out their own employing conditions and operate on the principle of minimum outlay. Those who have money will get more and more of it. The very brightest of those without money will get the few available jobs and receive whatever wages the owners will wish to pay. And the rest will starve or accept an increasingly impatient charity. The result of this unsupervised and unmodified drift is, of course, inevitable social revolution. No vast horde of people will endure long starvation if they have the physical force to seize food; and when the masses of the starving are large and desperate enough they will have the force and will use it. Then communism and chaos. *But*—the manufacturers know all this as well as anybody else, and will undoubtedly look for compromise-courses. Their goal is *greatest ultimate profit*, and when they see that *immediate* economy only restricts their market and imperils the whole system whereby they enjoy privilege, they will realise that good business demands less economy at the start. Better a costlier "overhead" and a sounder market and future. Thus you will see the moneyed groups making grudging concessions to the mob. Knowing that people can't buy things unless they have money, they will employ *more people for shorter hours* in the expectation that most of the money they pay will come back in the form of expanded markets. This will work a while, but not far enough. The extent of voluntary concession, as conditioned by visible profits, will not be enough to give permanent employment to enough people to remove the revolutionary menace due to starvation. If the existing social order is to last, more money must be distributed in some way or other, regardless of normal principles of profit. Socialistic measures like those already in force in England—old age pensions and unemployment insurance—the so-called "dole"—will be as necessary as fire-engines at a fire. As time passes, vested capital will have to "shell out" more and more in order to survive. It will be a painful thing for the plutocrats to yield up the latent surpluses which have hitherto given them absolute political power, but they will of course do this rather than sacrifice the social order which at least allows them enough profit to live in personal luxury and preserve the continuous traditions of the civilisation. Besides, if they are shrewd they can continue to rule as absolutely as at present—since they represent the sharpest brains, and will not be interfered with by a well-fed majority. All political administration in a machine age is so complex as to be beyond the comprehension of the common layman, and in time even the masses will come to realise this and be glad not to meddle in the business. Fed, clothed, housed, and amused, they will be content to leave bothersome problems to those better able to understand and deal with them. If social evolution gets this far without an explosion—as of course many doubt—the result will not be anything which one need lament. Of course, all familiar things and relationships—travel, housing, architecture, working conditions, social and family organisation, politics, etc.—will have changed so greatly that the present generation would find them bewildering and meaningless; but to those of the future they are likely to be as familiar and acceptable as earlier conditions have been to earlier generations. The amount of leisure possessed by all classes will necessarily—in view of the little work to be done by human agency—be prodigious; and it is barely possible that this enforced leisure, plus the collapse of the profit principle and the substitution of a production-for-use-only policy, will help to recreate the now-dying moods, perspectives, codes, and art-forms of non-commercial aristocracy among the governing classes. The gradual rise of the best brains to these classes will make them potentially very choice—and will leave the permanent masses correspondingly stupid and docile. The rebirth of the old paternalistic social order—ruling aristocracy and obedient proletariat—through a fruition of the very socialistic principle which moneyed reactionaries now decry, would be one of the richest ironies in the whole cosmic joke and muddle called life!

[35]   The extent to which "nice people" condone the suicidal policy of Hooverites is an eloquent commentary on the sway of emotion over reason. They have been conditioned to certain moods (as in religion), and are unable to see or think beyond them. Indeed, they suffer from just the same congenital stupidity and mass hysteria which they recognise and deplore in persons of lesser education and pretensions. If the present crisis has taught me anything, it is to ridicule the tragically emotio-traditional and basically anti-intellectual background of genteel "education". God! The utter ignorance and sappiness of the sniveling, myth-swallowing, church-going stuffed shirts who go about cackling dead slogans and spreading the heraldic tail-feathers that proclaim them self-conscious members of a close corporation of "best people"! Not that they're necessarily any *more* stupid and irrational than the rabble they hate, but that they add to an equal stupidity and irrationality the intolerable assumption of some mystical superiority unbased on personal merit. I'm all for personal merit, and used to revere aristocracy because it developed personal merit. Just as you revere your kindly plutocrats, so did I revere my kindly and honourable agrarian squires. But seven depression years in a hotbed of blind reactionaries has taught me things! . . . What some of these birds call *argument and logick!!* Now I'm beginning to wake up see that what I used to respect was *not re-*

ally aristocracy, but a set of personal qualities which aristocracy then developed better than any other system . . . a set of qualities, however, whose merit lay only in a psychology of non-calculative, non-competitive disinterestedness, truthfulness, courage, and generosity fostered by good education, minimum economic stress, and assumed position, and JUST AS ACHIEVABLE THROUGH SOCIALISM AS THROUGH ARISTOCRACY. It was the *fruits,* not the *mechanism,* which were worthy of respect — & today the decadent mechanism functions in vacuo, pavoninely proud of its mere skeletal essence, and no longer producing the fruits which once justify'd its existence. Hell! I'm done with it and its pretences. Best people! Best people my eye! I've reached the stage now where my aunt wants to hush me up in company, and keep me out of the sight of certain old friends. Last month, when she resignedly lamented the advent to the flat below us of a perfectly quiet and well-bred family "whom none of our friends know", I fear that my lack of sympathy was almost obtrusive. I almost went so far as to ask why I could find so little scientific vision, historic perspective, and disinterested logic in some of the precious old hens and unctuous stick-in-the-muds "whom we *do* know"! Goodbye, gentility, naïve idol of my callower years! Hallelujah, I'm a bum![19]

The present crisis in America is part of a fight that extends deep into the core of human standards and ideology. The real clash is betwixt two philosophies of life — one of which urges that the people coöperate and employ the fruits of invention and discovery in making the process of living as easy as possible for everyone in order to liberate energies for the real development of human personality, and the other of which urges that the struggle of the jungle be prolonged — life being made very hard for those not happening to inherit resources, so that the less shrewd will be forced into an intolerable position and have a high death-rate while the shrewd and calculative multiply, fight, and cultivate an ideal of dominant shrewdness. Upholders of this second philosophy argue that only by exalting shrewdness and aggressiveness, and trampling down the non-calculative, can a nation develop the harness necessary to excel or survive in the world-struggle. They have no confidence in the power of education, medical science, hygiene, character-training, and the discipline of legitimate work (i.e., non-profit struggle for the common welfare, or definite and rationally allocated service in exchange for an equitable stipend) to keep the race up to the necessary standard of stamina, material progressiveness, and survival-value. In other words, they ignore the modern world of science and hark back to the world of primitive man and the lower animals; where all the factors of evolution are accidental, and where consequently the prosperity of the acquisitively strong and the subordination and death of the weak are indeed elements making for progress. They evade entirely the question of different kinds of superiority. When they speak of favouring the "strong and efficient" they mean only the *industrially* acquisitively strong and efficient. The man of science, artist, or philosopher who is not a good money-maker is classed with the shiftless and consigned to suffering and extermination. All values but material values, apparently, are non-existent for these hardy upholders of "our historic pioneer Americanism". Well—I have already made it plain that I have thoroughly repudiated this primitive philosophy in favour of the more scientific and contemporary one. There is really nothing else for a thoughtful and disinterested person to do. I revere tradition—am in fact preëminently an antiquarian—but can hardly see why the coarsest and crudest element in pioneer life should be singled out and worshipped as "historic Americanism". I am likewise no friend of aimless idleness—but do not see why a savage and feverish scramble for bare necessities, *made artificially hard after machinery has given us the means of easier production,* is necessarily superior to a reasonable amount of sensible work plus an intelligently outlined programme of cultural development. Nor is my reluctance to starve and kill off the weak any indication that I worship weakness *per se.* I would advocate the improvement of backward groups through education, hygiene, and eugenics—nor do I think it especially naïve or ultra-idealistic in me to prefer these conscious and scientific methods to the blind, brutal, and accidental methods of primitive nature, in which real advances are merely the casual *by-products* of aimless, wasteful forces. The slyly and disingenuously raised question of "freedom" is of course a mere reactionary smoke-screen. Nobody wants to restrict the freedom of the individiual in America in anything but his large-scale economic organisation—& everyone who considers this single economic element synonymous with the whole of life stands revealed as occupying a rather crude philosophic plane. What is more—this very economic freedom does not exist any more under the old order than under a possible new one. As things are, the large economic interests completely enslave the small. Reform seeks merely to transfer restriction from one group to another—the reason being that the restriction of the large will have fewer bad effects on the whole social fabric than does the present and past restrictions of the small. *Some* kind of change *must* be established;

since old-time Hooverism was merely pauperising more and more individuals and piling up the gunpowder for a social revolution. Even the bulk of half-awake Republicans realise that something must be done—as in the times of Agis, Cleomenes, the Gracchi, Caesar, and Diocletianus—but the trouble is that they have no sympathy with a better state of things. All they want is to perpetuate as much of the old economic order as they safely can—their concessions to the needs of the times grudging and inadequate. [. . .]

[. . .] But the chief indictment of a capitalistic ideal is perhaps something deeper even than humanitarian principle—something which concerns the profound, subtle and pervasive hostility of capitalism, and of the whole essence of mercantilism, to all that is finest and most creative in the human spirit. As mentioned in the preceding pages, business and capital are the fundamental enemies of human worth in that they exalt and reward the *shrewdly acquisitive* rather than the *intrinsically superior and creative.* Pro-capitalists are prone to slobber over the "free competition" in economics which "rewards the worthy and punishes the shiftless". Very well. Let's see how the worthy are rewarded. Let us list a few of the most incontestably superior minds and personalities in the modern capitalistic world and see whether capitalism has given them its highest rewards. Albert Einstein. Romain Rolland. Bertrand Russell. H. G. Wells. George Santayana. Thomas Mann. John Dewey. W. B. Yeats. George Bernard Shaw. M. and Mme. Curie-Joliot. Heisenberg. Planck. Eddington. Jeans. Millikan. Compton. Ralph Adams Cram. Sigmund Freud. Ignacio Zuloaga. Theodore Dreiser. Julian and Aldous Huxley. Prof. G. Elliot Smith. Are these the world's richest people today? And in the past did capitalism award its highest benefits to such admittedly superior persons as Poe, Spinoza, Baudelaire, Shakespeare, Keats, and so on? Or is it just possible that the *real* beneficiaries of capitalism are *not* the truly superior, but merely *those who choose to devote their superiority to the single process of personal acquisition rather than to social service or to creative intellectual or aesthetic effort* . . . . . those, and the lucky parasites who share or inherit the fruits of their narrowly canalised superiority? "Capitalism fosters technological progress, etc. etc. etc." All right, Mr. Hoover, but just answer three questions for an old man: (a) is technological progress very important in the long run? (b) who *makes* the technological progress—the capitalists, or their underpaid inventors and engineers and research scientists? and (c) why has non-capitalistic Soviet Russia exceeded most of the capitalistic nations in technological progress during the past decade? What's that I hear in reply? "Oh, shut up, you goddam bolshevik, and don't ask such seditious questions!" Very well—we'll let history work out the problem in its own way. But as for anything *just* or *beneficent* in capitalism . . . . Pfooey! Equine plumage!

[36] I agree that most of the motive force behind any contemplated change in the economic order will necessarily come from the persons who have benefited least by the existing order; but I do not see why that fact makes it necessary to wage the struggle otherwise than as a *fight to guarantee a place for everybody* in the social fabric. The just demand of the citizen is that society assign him a place in its complex mechanism whereby he will have equal chances for education at the start, and a guarantee of just rewards for such services as he is able to render (or a proper pension if his services cannot be used) later on. Now this does not apply merely to the stevedore and elevator-boy. It applies equally to the artist and professor and administrator. The same social principle which assumes that positions should be artificially allocated to men of the factory-hand level of accomplishment, assumes also that positions should be artificially allocated to men of the trained executive level; each individual to be given a return determined by the kind and quality of the service he renders. The man of calibre benefits as much as the man of the factory-hand calibre in point of security, so we cannot truly call the principle a "class" issue. If *anybody* might call it a "class issue" it is the man of executive calibre, who feels that he loses more than he gains—since under the old order he was fairly sure of a job anyhow, and generally received a larger return (in unearned profits) than the just one which the new order would allot him. Well and good. If the enemy want to talk "class" (notice how the plutes complain that Roosevelt, in merely denouncing unjust special privilege and urging justice for *all*, "pits class against class" or "arouses class hatred"!), let them talk and be damned! But the *real aim* of the socialist is essentially a classless one. He is not thinking of benefiting this special group or harming that special group. He is simply thinking of ensuring just placement to *everybody*—and if his conception of just placement doesn't measure up to the wishes of any certain group, then the "class issue" is the "injured" group's—*not the socialist's*. This, I believe, is a far sounder conception than the "class-conscious" one. The war is not of any one "class" against any other "class". It is of *the people*—each human being considered as an equal unit irrespective of the amount of so-called "property" attached to him—against anybody and everybody who would obstruct a programme guaranteeing each member

of the people security and opportunities commensurate with his skill. This may, of course, mean—in terms of contemporary society—a struggle in which the low-paid wage-worker and the unemployed predominate on one side whilst the highly-paid businessman and inheritor of wealth predominate on the other side; but I think it is more socially wholesome—more favourable to a rational mood and perspective, and better adapted to the psychology of the future order aimed at—to think of the matter in general human terms than to think of it in terms of the *present* industrial status of the majority of participants on either side.

This may sound very sappy and attenuated, but I believe there is much to be said for it. It is better to fight *for a just deal for all the people* in the name of *all the people* (and who cares if some of the people refuse to be represented?) than in the name of any special "working class". In a decent society everyone is a "worker"—but if we use the term too narrowly today, we shall find that it creates mental overtones and images not at all favourable to the best type of development. There will be a tendency to exalt and idealise the contemporary low-grade worker *just as he is*, instead of to insist that his attributes be radically changed through the extension to him of a security and body of cultural privileges he has never possessed before. There will be a tendency to hate and injure the refinements and amenities of high-grade life, and to subordinate the cultural traditions which mean so much to sensitive persons, simply because these things have not hitherto been enjoyed by those classifiable as "workers". Excellence in human personality will be opposed, slighted, or jeered at as something hatefully "aristocratic" or "bourgeois"; whilst many of the crude and repellent folkways and attitudes of the *present* working "class" (folkways and attitudes which would not exist if justice prevailed) will be exalted as great national values. Now all this is very bad, and makes for increased bitterness. There ought not to be any rallying around the standards and ideals of the contemporary workman, together with a massed hatred of the standards and ideals of the contemporary aristocrat. Standards and ideals should not be associated with one "class" any more than with any other "class". Keeping well-groomed and talking grammatically and enjoying Horace and possessing sensitive honour—in brief, being a gentleman—ought not to be associated with the inheritor of a fortune any more than with an intelligent mechanic or miner. *We must learn to divorce the idea of human status and attributes from the relatively trivial concepts of remunerative occupation and financial position.* There will always be *natural* aristocrats and men of taste, and there will always be crude clods; but in a rational society it may be that the aristocrats will include people whose *purely economic* activities are relatively insignificant—miners, mill-hands, 'bus-drivers, etc.—whilst the crude clods will include highly-paid industrial administrators. The big idea is *to substitute the idea of personal excellence for that of economic position*—and in order to do that, we must not encourage any hatred or repudiation of those high qualities which are at present (through long injustice) associated with the "ruling class". Heaven knows, there is too much "class consciousness" in our *present* order! Listen to any average discussion of a stranger, and see how infallibly his economic status is brought up and dwelt upon! Read any news item about an accident, an arrest, a marriage, or a death, and see how infallibly a mention of *economic occupation* is tagged on to each person named . . . John Smith, grocer, age 50 . . . William Jones, insurance agent. . . . George Brown, labourer . . . etc. etc. etc. . . . . As if the principal thing about John Smith were the fact that he is a grocer . . . . as if he had no rounded individuality or complex personality of his own; no likes and dislikes; no taste in art or literature; no philosophic position or social belief . . . . . They never say "John Smith, admirer of Greek sculpture" or "John Smith, phenomenalist", or "John Smith, student of astronomy" . . . . it is, instead, always "John Smith, grocer"! This, mind you, is the vice of the *old* order—thousands of years old. I don't accuse the Marxians of inventing it. I merely think the rational socialist ought to *repudiate* it instead of *clinging to it and intensifying it!*

I'm not against any rational appeal to individuals who fare ill under the present system to join forces on the avowed basis of their common disadvantage—as a common bloc in a war (preferably parliamentary, otherwise if absolutely necessary) against the system. Really, I am quite with you in principle. My objection is to *the psychological and cultural effect of calling this struggle a war of "workmen" against another specific group of individuals.* Actually, the reluctance of many persons to line up with socialism against capitalism is because of this persistent identification of socialism with nigger roustabouts and surly coal-miners and illiterate bricklayers as opposed to people who shave daily, read *Harpers*, and live in tastefully furnished (even if cheap) homes. If the Marxians would lay less stress on the literal hammer and sickle and lay more stress on the *general circumstance of prevailing inequality and injustice,* they would win over more of the ill-paid professors and bankrupt small grocers and corporation-fleeced inventors and booted-around bookkeepers of whose continued capitalistic sympathies they so justly complain. *The big mistake of the Marxians is that they blind themselves to all non-economic factors.* They expect a man to act primarily according to his *economic* status, whereas in reality his primary reaction is determined wholly by his culture status. We act first and instinctively with *the sort of people whose tastes and background are like our own.* Only with difficulty and in mature years are we generally able to think and act independently of our hereditary culture-milieu—and all too few of us can ever achieve that independence. Most of the dispossessed non-workmen are products of the general culture-milieu which also produced the "ruling class", hence they can never be expected to act as enemies of that "class" *as a class*—especially if those who invite them to do so are conspicuously and avowedly the representatives of another and frankly inferior culture-milieu. If socialism wishes to create a really effective "popular front" against the system of special privilege, it must cease to represent any particular proletarian type. It must stand forth simply as the dispenser of real justice and best hope of the *economically* disadvantaged, and must abandon all traces of hostility toward the *culture* of the lucky propertied elements on whom, in practice, it will be waging war. This for two reasons: because that culture is one also shared by many of those it wishes to win over, and because that culture must eventually, in all essentials, form the general culture of all the people. Probably socialism *will* more or less broaden in the right direction. Even now the conscious "have-nots" are acquiring an increasingly impressive stream of recruits from the ranks of the traditionally cultured; and although many of these recruits profess to be converted to the one-sided ideology of proletarianism, the net influence of the influx is all in favour of reconciling the socialistic movement with the hereditary culture of the race. More and more a socialist may be a well-born person who thinks and feels as a gentleman, and whose warfare is that of a just and responsible gentleman upon a *system* (not a group of men) which viciously denies part of the community the basic rights which taste and logic demand for all. Look at such popular leaders as F D R, Bertrand Russell, Karl Marx himself, Oliver Baldwin, Norman Thomas, Leon Blum, Rexford G. Tugwell, and scores of others—all products of the general culture of the "ruling class", and none in all probability desirous of enthroning any new culture opposed to its non-economic phases. (Briffault and some of the extreme left theorists are another story). Persons of this general type are more numerous in the ranks of the socialists each year, and the result will probably be a good one. If there ever has to be something corresponding to a "class war", it will probably be

waged on purely economic lines, and not fall into the incidental tragic pattern of a war of plebeian coarseness and ignorance against patrician taste,
intellect, and refinement.

Yes—after all, I pretty much agree with you. There must be a widespread education of all types of people as to the need of new distribution-
patterns, and somehow the *blind fear of the word "socialism"* must be broken
down, so that progressive parties will not have to conceal, euphemise, and
compromise in order to secure any effective popular support. It is pathetic
to note how at present the New Deal's campaigning has to soft-pedal social
evolution and stress conservatism in order to rebut the dead-slogan per-
suasiveness of the reactionaries and stand a chance for success! Certainly,
the forward fight will be hard and long—and we can afford to be patient
with a little slowness if that will save us from what Russia has been
through and what Spain will be going through for the next few years. A
Popular Front is certainly a great desideratum—but in order to gain the
cautious and traditional, it will have to crack down on the wildest extreme-
lefters . . . the people who preach like Belknap and Briffault.

[Lovecraft found rich satisfaction in the election of 1936, in which
Franklin D. Roosevelt won a second term in a landslide, defeating the Republican Alf Landon and a third-party candidate, William Lemke.]

[37]   Whilst of course the general result was apparent long in advance,
the *extent* of the landslide surely was a pleasant surprise. The feeble arguments, obvious hokum, absurd accusations, and occasionally underhanded
tactics of the enemy reacted against them, while some obscure instinct of
common sense seemed to keep the extreme radicals from wasting their
votes on obviously hopeless tickets. It amuses me to see the woebegone
state of the staid reactionary reliques with whom I am surrounded. Around
election-time I came damn near having a family feud on my hands! Poor
old ostriches. Trembling for the republic's safety, they actually thought
their beloved Lemke or Langston or Langham (or whatever his name was)
had a chance! However, the alert university element was not so blind—
indeed, one of the professors said just before the election that his idea of a
bum sport was a man who would actually *take* one of the pro-Lansdowne
(or whatever his name was) bets offered by the white-moustached consti-
tution-savers of the Hope Club easy-chairs. Well—even the most stubborn
must some day learn that the tide of social evolution can't be checked for

ever. King Canute and the waves! Now—with the temper of the people definitely shewn—to see what the next four years will do! The unstable nature of capitalism should be made manifest through repeated object lessons, and the way paved for the gradual and peaceful extension of government proprietorship and non-profit operation over the basic industrial fields. Courage and foresight are demanded—and one hopes they will be forthcoming.

Supporting Hitler

[In spite of his leftist politics, Lovecraft in his later years continued to adhere to racist dogmas. While grudgingly forced to give up belief in the biological superiority or inferiority of any given race, he maintained an extreme belief in the cultural maladaptability of various racial or ethnic groups; and it was on this belief that he justified his reserved support of Hitler.]

[38]   The problem of race and culture is by no means as simple as is assumed either by the Nazis or by the rabble-catering equalitarian columnists of the Jew-York papers. Of course Hitler is an unscientific extremist in fancying that any racial strain can be reduced to theoretical purity, that the Nordic stock is intellectually and aesthetically superior to all others, and that even a trace of non-Nordic blood—or non-Aryan blood—is enough to alter the psychology and citizenly potentialities of an individual. These assumptions, most certainly, are crude and ignorant—but the anti-Hitlerites are too cocksure when they maintain that the fallacy of these points justifies a precisely opposite extremism. As a matter of fact—all apart from social and political prejudice—there indisputably is such a thing as a Nordic subdivision of the white race, as evolved by a strenuous and migratory life in Northern Asia and Europe. Of course, very little of it remains simon-pure at this date—after all the mixtures resulting from its contacts with other stocks—but anyone would be a damn fool to deny that certain modern racial or cultural units remain *predominantly and determinantly* Nordic in blood, so that their instincts and reactions generally follow the Nordic pattern, and differ basically from those of the groups which are predominantly non-Nordic. Anybody can see for himself the difference between a tall, straight-nosed, fine-haired dolichocephalic Teuton or Celt (be he blond or dark) on the one hand, and a squat, swarthy Latin, aquiline Semite, or brachycephalic Slav on the other hand. And even if a Teutonic

or Celtic group happens to pick up and assimilate substantial numbers of Latins, Semites, or Slavs, it will continue to think and feel and act in a characteristic Nordic fashion as long as the old blood remains predominant, and the culture-stream remains unbroken. It is of course true that the cultural heritage is more influential than the biological, but only a freakish extremist would reduce the biological to negligibility. Separate lines of evolution have certainly developed typically differing responses to given environmental stimuli. As for the question of superiority and inferiority — when we observe the whole animal kingdom and note the vast differences in capacity betwixt different species and sub-species within various genera, we see how utterly asinine and hysterically sentimental is the blanket assumption of idealists and other fools that all the sub-species of *homo sapiens* must *necessarily* be equal. The truth is, that we cannot lay down any general rule in this matter at the outset. We must simply study each variety with the perfect detachment of the zoölogist and abide by the results of honest investigation whether we relish them or not. And what does such study tell us? Largely this — that the australoid and negro races are basically and structurally primitive — possessing definite morphological and psychological variations in the direction of lower stages of organisation — whilst all others average about the same so far as the best classes of each are concerned. The same, that is, in *total capacity* — though each has its own special aptitudes and deficiencies. The races are *equal,* but *infinitely different* — so that the cultural pattern of one is essentially unadaptable to any other. The ancient civilisation of China is not inferior to ours — yet it could not possibly suit us, any more than ours could suit a race of essentially Mongol descent. And that is where the need of realistic intelligence as opposed to idealistic and sentimental flapdoodle in matters of racial policy comes in. The fact is, that a need for a certain rational amount of racial discrimination exists *apart from all questions of superiority or inferiority.* The effective development of a civilisation depends largely upon its *stability and continuity;* and these factors cannot be ensured unless (a) the culture-stream remains relatively undiluted by alien traditions or irrelevant and traditionless innovations, and (b) the race-stock remains approximately the same as that which evolved the culture and institutions now existing. The first point is of course very obvious. The second becomes so after a moment's thought. To take a concrete instance — we live in a social group and nation whose ingrained, hereditary folkways and types of thought and feeling are emphatically an outgrowth of a Teutonic-Celtic race-stock. That is, our institutions were evolved to fit the particular biological and psychological needs of persons who are predominantly Nordic Aryans, so that they cannot fit other races except in such respects as those others may happen to resemble ours. In many cases other race-stocks have decidedly different needs and feelings—hence if they try to settle en masse in our country they create a situation of mutual discomfort. They do not feel at home among us—and when they try to bend our institutions to fit themselves they make us uncomfortable, destroy our cultural equilibrium, and permanently weaken, dilute, and set back our whole civilisation. This should not be. Therefore *just this much* of Hitler's basic racial theory is *perfectly and irrefutably sound:* namely, that no settled and homogeneous nation ought (a) to admit enough of a decidedly alien race-stock to bring about an actual alteration in the dominant ethnic composition, or (b) tolerate the dilution of the culture-stream with emotional and intellectual elements alien to the original cultural impulse. Both of these perils lead to the most undesirable results—i.e.,the metamorphosis of the population away from the original institutions, and the twisting of the institutions away from the original people . . . . . . all these things being aspects of one underlying and disastrous condition—the destruction of cultural stability, and the creation of a hopeless disparity between a social group and the institutions under which it lives. *Now this has nothing to do with intrinsic superiority and inferiority.* That is what the howling sentimentalists and faddists can't get through their thick beans. It doesn't matter whether a race is our equal—or even our superior (as, in all probability, the ancient Greek race [a Nordic-Mediterranean blend] was); if it is in any way radically *different* from ours, then its blood ought not to pour by the wholesale into our nation, and its institutions (made to fit *it*, not *us*) ought not to be allowed to twist and dilute our own. Even *superior* importations can harm our culture if they break up the equilibrium existing between the people and the institutions under which the people live. Remember that a people cannot change its institutions lightly. These things, to be valid and satisfying, must be a deep-seated hereditary growth—and must above all be suited to the peculiar aptitudes of the race in question. Thus I sympathise warmly and completely with the general principle that northern nations like Germany and the United States ought to be kept *predominantly* Nordic in blood and *wholly* Nordic in institutions. This is not because Nordic blood and culture are necessarily superior to any other, but simply because the given nations happen to be essentially Nordic at the outset. I believe just as strongly that Japan ought to be kept predominantly Japanese; and would resent a wholesale influx of Aryans into Japan as keenly as I would resent a wholesale influx of Japanese into an Aryan nation. Indeed, I agree with those Japanese scholars who lament the existing dilution of Japan's art and folkways with European elements. As for this flabby talk of an "Americanism" which opposes all racial discrimination—that is simply god damned bull-shit! The ideal is so flagrantly unsound in its very essence that it would be a disgrace to any national tradition professing it. It is an ignorant, sentimental, impracticable, and potentially dangerous delusion—and any sophisticated person can realise that it belongs only to the insincere pseudo-Americanism of the spread-eagle illiterate or the charlatanic ward politician. It is what superficial Americans proclaim with their lips, while actually lynching niggers and selling select real-estate on a restrictive basis to keep Jews and Dagoes out. In other words, it is *not* a part of any "Americanism" which has any *real* existence. It is merely part of the cheap American bluff—and indeed, is not even nominally professed in that southern half of the country which was once the most important half and will probably become so again. Ever since 1924 American immigration legislation has, under the very thinnest of veils, discouraged the immigration of racial elements radically alien to the original American people; and I do not believe this sound policy will ever be rescinded. We had this much of "Hitlerism" before we had ever heard of Handsome Adolf!

Late Work

[Lovecraft wrote less and less fiction with the passing of years. One of his greatest late tales, however, was "The Shadow out of Time" (1934–35), whose genesis can be traced as far back as 1930, when he outlined its central concept in the course of a discussion on fantastic fiction with Clark Ashton Smith.]

[39]   Your idea for a time-voyaging machine is ideal—for in spite of Wells, no really satisfactory thing of the sort has ever been written. The weakness of most tales with this theme is that they do not provide for the recording, in history, of those inexplicable events in the past which were caused by the backward time-voyagings of persons of the present and fu-

ture. It must be remembered that if a man of 1930 travels back to B.C. 400, the strange phenomenon of his appearance actually occurred in B.C. 400, and must have excited notice wherever it took place. Of course, the way to get around this is to have the voyager conceal himself when he reaches the past, conscious of what an abnormality he must seem. Or rather, he ought simply to conceal his *identity*—hiding the evidences of his "futurity" and mingling with the ancients as best he can on their own plane. It would be excellent to have him know to some extent of his past appearance before making the voyage. Let him, for example, encounter some private document of the past in which a record of the advent of a mysterious stranger— unmistakably himself—is made. This might be the provocation for his voyage—that is, the conscious provocation. One baffling thing that could be introduced is to have a modern man discover, among documents exhumed from some prehistoric buried city, a mouldering papyrus of parchment *written in English, and in his own handwriting,* which tells a strange tale and awakes—amidst a general haze of amazement, horror and half-incredulity—a faint, far-off sense of familiarity which becomes more and more beckoning and challenging as the strings of semi-memory continue to vibrate. Re-reading awakes still more memories, till finally a definite course of action seems inevitable—and so on and so on. This idea has lain dormant in my commonplace-book for ages; and if you can find a use for it, you're certainly welcome to it. I might never develop it for years.

[40]   I have a sort of time idea of very simple nature floating around in the back of my head, but don't know when I shall ever get around to using it. The notion is that of a race in primal Lomar perhaps even before the founding of Olathoë and in the heyday of Hyperborean Commoriom— who gained a knowledge of all arts and sciences by sending thought-streams ahead to drain the minds of men in future ages—angling in time, as it were. Now and then they get hold of a really competent man of learning, and annex all his thoughts. Usually they only keep their victims tranced for a short time, but once in a while, when they need some special piece of continuous information, one of their number sacrifices himself for the race and actually changes bodies with the first thoroughly satisfactory victim he finds. The victim's brain then goes back to 100,000 B.C.—into the hypnotist's body to live in Lomar for the rest of his life, while the hypnotist from dead aeons animates the modern clay of his victim. Complications can be

imagined. I have no idea how—or from what angle—I shall elaborate the thing.

[Finally, in the fall of 1934, he began actual work on the tale.]

[41]   Just now I am experimenting with an old plot idea of mine which I may have described to you—that of a man who, in excavating ruins palpably of incredible antiquity, comes upon (as an unmistakable part of them) *a specimen of his own handwriting in English*. The explanation is that these ruins belong to a pre-human race of organic entities, infinitely above man in mental powers, who in their day ranged the whole gamut of time through mental transference. To learn of a future age, they would have one of their number project his mind ahead and displace the consciousness of somebody in the chosen period. Then the voyaging mind, in the body of its victim, would absorb all the information possible—and finally fly back through time to its original body, while the displaced mind returned to the vacated future body. In the meantime the displaced mind had occupied the body of the pre-human voyager, hence had had a brief life and consciousness in the immemorial past. And of course it could then leave a *record* which, in its proper body millions of years later, it could discover during the excavation of blasphemously ancient megalithic ruins. Well—I developed that story *mistily and allusively* in 16 pages, but it was no go. Thin and unconvincing, with the climactic revelation wholly unjustified by the hash of visions preceding it. So I've torn the whole damn thing up and am rewriting it in my usual latter style—with gradual hints and slowly built-up stages of unfolding. Am now on page 27, and fear it will run to 40 before I'm through. Naturally, I know what the majority will say—if I decide to type it and show it around. "Verbose—long-winded—slow—nothing happens—novelette length for short-story idea—etc. etc. etc." But the fact remains that it represents the best I can do with the given idea. The shorter treatment was wholly inadequate—not even scratching the surface of the many bizarre implications involved in the central assumption.

[42]   By the way—I finished "The Shadow Out of Time" last week, but doubt whether it is good enough to type. Somehow or other, it does not seem to embody quite what I want to embody—and I may tear it up and start all over again. It came to 65 pages in all—but I don't see how it could

be made any shorter without a loss of the essential effect. It is valueless to set down weird effects without adequate emotional preparation.

[In the fall of 1935 Lovecraft was momentarily cheered by the double sale of *At the Mountains of Madness* and "The Shadow out of Time" to *Astounding Stories*, resulting in net earnings of $595.]

[43]   Thanks for the congratulations—and you can double 'em if you like, for no sooner had the "Mts. of Madness" incident sunk into my consciousness than I was given a *second* pleasant surprise . . . . in the form of *another* cheque from Street and Smith. It seems that Donald Wandrei, to whom I had lent my newest novelette "The Shadow out of Time", had taken the liberty of submitting the MS. to *Astounding* without my knowledge—and through some inexplicable coincidence the editor was favourable again! This certainly was a life-saving windfall, and it is needless to say that I feel tremendously encouraged by the incident. I know that such "winning streaks" don't keep up—but the impression is pleasant while it lasts. This dual stroke gave me such a psychological boost that I've just written a new tale—a short specimen called "The Haunter of the Dark". From what I hear, the "Mts." will be a 3-part story in the February, March and April *Astounding*. I've no idea when the "Shadow" will appear.

[But Lovecraft's euphoria turned to disgust when he saw the printed version of *At the Mountains of Madness*, which had been severely edited by *Astounding*. The following long account shows the emphasis Lovecraft placed in fine points of style and diction.]

[44]   But hell and damnation! You ought to see the time I've had getting ready to release this lowly script! Iä! Shub-Niggurath! The Goat With a Thousand Young! In brief, that goddamn'd dung of a hyaena Orlin Tremaine has given the "Mts." the worst hashing-up any piece of mine ever received—in or out of Tryout![20] I'll be hang'd if I can consider the story as published at all—the last instalment is a joke, with whole passages missing. What I've had to do is virtually to write 3 new MSS. of the story—on the three printed copies I obtained! With infinite revision—and voluminous interpolation with finely sharpened pencil—I have at last 3 copies which are both correct and legible (with a magnifying-glass). But at what a cost

of labour! I started in Sunday noon (after being about worn out with a titanic file-cleaning and classifying which had become absolutely necessary
because of the growing chaos) — and now, Wednesday morning, I've only
just finished! And I was up working both Mon. and Tues. nights. Also did
"Shadow Out of Time" from memory, having no MS. It doesn't seem even
nearly as badly mangled as the Mts. . . . . . so you may congratulate yourself on *your* story![21]

But what I think of that decayed fish Tremaine wouldn't go in a wholesome family paper! I'll forgive him *real misprints*, as well as the lousy
spelling used by Street and Smith — but *some* of the things on his "style
sheet" are beyond tolerance! (He changes "Great God!" to "Great *Heavens!*")

Why, for example, are *Sun, Moon*, and even *Moonlight* (!!) always *capitalised?* Why must the damn fool invariably change my ordinary animal
name to its capitalised scientific equivalent? (dinosaurs = "Dinosauria"
etc.) Why does he change *subterrene* to *subterrane*, when the latter has no existence as an adjective? Why, in general, an overcapitalising and *overpunc-
tuating* mania? I've dulled my McCrory knife scratching out editorial com-
mas! I pass over certain affected changes in sentence-structure, but see red
again when I think of the *paragraphing*. Venom of Tsathoggua! Have you
seen the damn thing? *All my paragraphs cut up into little chunks* like the juvenile stuff the other pulp hacks write. Rhythm, emotional modulations, and
minor climactic effects thereby destroyed. If anybody writes in little
chunks to start with — as Belknap does — well and good. But if anyone
writes in full length paragraphs, then units have an organic structure
which can't bear division. Tremaine has tried to make "snappy action" stuff
out of old-fashioned leisurely prose. [. . .]

But the *supremely* intolerable thing is the way the text is cut in the last
instalment — to get an old serial out of the way quickly. Whole passages
(now written into my 3 copies on the margin) are left out — the result being
to decrease vitality and colour, and make the action mechanical. So many
important details and impressions and touches of sensation are missing
from the concluding parts that the effect is that of a flat ending. After all
the adventure and detail *before* the encounter with the shoggoth in the
abyss, the characters are shot up to the surface without any of the gradual
experiences and emotions which make the reader *feel* their return to the
world of man from the nighted aeon-old world of the Others. All sense of
the *duration and difficulty* of the exhausted climb is lost when it is dismissed

objectively in only a few words, with no hint of the fugitives' reactions to the scenes through which they pass. Among actual *plot* points omitted, is one where the explorers notice (through a dropped battery) that the re-vived Old Ones have been pausing perplexedly before that ominous and grotesquely crude *palimpsest carving* in the passage to the sunken sea. Well—all the text is back *now* in my 3 copies . . . . though it might take a mi-croscope to bring out some of the pencil interpolations.

Lovecraft as Mentor

[As he came into contact with a large array of young writers who sought advice and encouragement from him, Lovecraft naturally adopted the bearing of "the old gentleman" with his band of faithful disciples. Many of these novices later became highly distinguished authors in their own right, owing much to Lovecraft's tutelage in the fundamentals of their craft. Among the most noteworthy was Robert Bloch, who first wrote to Lovecraft when he was sixteen.]

[45]   I've read through your new story[22] with great interest, and must congratulate you on the dark suspense, lurking terror, and febrile pall of cosmic evil hanging over it. The way you lead up to the climax is delight-fully effective—having the evil abbot congratulate his guest sardonically on not having encountered the "other" monastery—and the climax itself is powerful . . . . . though I suppose you know there is a sort of taboo against cannibalistic stories among the cheap magazines. Regarding the story as a whole—you realise of course that the evil-monastery theme is a fairly often used one, though always excellent when deftly and originally handled. As for any points to criticise—it is always well to go over the text and see if there are places where one could eliminate awkward or naive phraseology. You are wise in deciding to recast the opening paragraph, and in the next one you might describe the building in less loosely generalised terms—being concrete about its aspect. Was it Romanesque? Gothic? Or a com-posite of Romanesque foundations and later Gothic work? (Ro-manesque—with rounded arches would be most ancient.) In describing the black servitors you might see if a less naive-sounding phrase than "in-trigued my romantic senses greatly" could be secured. Incidentally—the use of *intrigued* as a synonym for *fascinated* or *captivated* is a neologism which I really think ought to be discouraged. A little later on there is a slightly

naive sound in the paragraph where the narrator wonders why the abbey had been built in this wood. Lonely rural monasteries are not very uncommon. If any cause for wonder exist, let it be at certain ruins amidst the trees near the monastery, as if a village had once existed there and had been abandoned at some very remote date—vast trees having grown up inside ruinous foundation-walls. The incident of the strange chanting is *very good*. You get in a fine bit of genuine cosmic horror here. About the decorations—do you suppose you have laid on the richness and ostentation a bit thickly? That is, would not less emphasis on mere *luxury*, and a few vague hints of something bafflingly and subtly *outré* be more to the point? I don't know . . . it's a minor phase anyway. Also—is not the *gluttony* laid on rather heavily? Perhaps not, though. But when you come to the *roast* you must use care. Remember that the guest can see the process of carving—so that it isn't likely any *very well-defined* human member could be served him without his knowing it at the outset. Better let the roast be a flank or thigh which cannot well be identified—at least, let the *first* platter full be such. Of course, all this time the wine is rendering the guest less and less critical . . . . but let him have a certain curiosity regarding some of the bone fragments on the plates. Then have a second platter brought in—smoking hot and smothered in spices. The light tid-bits, as it were. By this time the ribaldry is started, and the guest isn't in a very critical shape. The company is getting sated now, and doesn't pick its bones very clean. And now begin to use your *very choicest subtlety*—for the abbot's sardonic congratulations and tale of the "other" monastery must be managed with the utmost care. Try to have the narration *more gradual*, more a matter of *suggestion*—with less bold and literal *explanation*. It would be just as well to devote a little more space to this sinister narration—making it *very indirect*, oblique, and full of *hints* rather than *statements*. The climax is excellent—it was a good idea to postpone the final revelation till after the narrator's emergence from the abbey, and also to suggest the dream possibility. All told, this is a distinctly strong and promising piece of work, and is well worth a bit of working over.

[Although Kenneth Sterling abandoned writing to become a distinguished physician, as a teenager he was interested in both science and science fiction. Lovecraft found him a remarkably precocious youth.]

[46]   One night last week I was reading the paper in my study when my aunt entered to announce (with a somewhat amused air) a caller by the name of Mr. Kenneth Sterling. Close on her heels the important visitor ap-

peared . . . . in the person of a little Jew boy about as high as my waist, with unchanged childish treble and swarthy cheeks innocent of the Gillette's harsh strokes. He *did* have long trousers—which somehow looked grotesque upon so tender an infant. It appears that he is one of the endless kid followers of *Wonder, Astounding,* F M, etc.—who had seen some of my stuff and learned my address from Hornig.[23] A typical N.Y. Yid—but his papa (a Harvard graduate, and evidently quite a brilliant scion of Moses' line) has just been made manager of a local fur store—so Leedle Kenneth iss ah Providentian now, and a star pupil by der Classical High School. And oy, vhat ah shild! Vhat ah shild! If they all come as precocious as this, I don't wonder that Hitler is afraid they'll juggle the shirts off the German people! Damme if the little imp didn't talk like a man of 30—correcting all the mistakes in the current science yarns, reeling off facts and figures a mile a minute, and displaying the taste and judgment of a veteran. He's already sold a story to *Wonder* (and *collected* from Hugo the Rat!), and is bubbling over with ideas. Two of his story plots are really splendid. Others in his family have reviewed books for the N.Y. *Herald Tribune* and written for various "slicks". And now he is prepared to conquer ancient Providentium! He vants he should organise an branch by der Science Fiction League here, etc. etc. I gave him some duplicate F F's and other items, and he says he's going to call again. Hope he won't prove a nuisance—but I wouldn't for the world discourage him in his endeavours. He really does seem like an astonishingly promising brat—and means to become a research biologist.

[Probably Lovecraft's most distinguished young colleague was Fritz Leiber, who would go on to write a body of superb weird and science fiction that rivals Lovecraft's own work. Although they corresponded for only a few months, Leiber has attested to the enduring value of association with Lovecraft. In late 1936 Lovecraft wrote a long letter examining in detail Leiber's novelette "Adept's Gambit," the first of a long series of tales involving two picaresque characters, Fafhrd and the Gray Mouser.]

[47]   My appreciation and enjoyment of "Adept's Gambit" as a capturer of dark currents from the void form an especially good proof of the story's essential power, since the style and manner of approach are almost antipodal to my own. With me, the transition to the unreal is accomplished through humourless pseudo-realism, dark suggestion, and a style full of

sombre menace and tension. You, on the other hand, adopt the light, witty, and sophisticated manner of Cabell, Stephens, the later Dunsany, and others of their type—with not a few suggestions of "Vathek" and "Ouroboros".[24] Lightness and humour impose a heavy handicap on the fantaisiste, and all too often end in triviality—yet in this case you have turned liabilities to assets and achieved a fine synthesis in which the breezy whimsicality ultimately builds up rather than dilutes or neutralises the tension and sense of impinging shadow.

The farther I read into "Adept's Gambit" the more I enjoyed it. You succeed abundantly in the difficult art of emotional modulation—heightening the tension and making each fresh turn more impressive—never less—than the preceding one. The picaresque chronicle is always in an ascending key. As the Viking and Mouser leave the low seacoast for the highlands of Turkestan and the mountains beyond the Lost City the feeling of latent evil and immanent alienage mounts, and a fascination creeps increasingly on the reader. Then—on p. 55, where the Elobeth section begins—you let the tempo change a bit and subordinate the cheerfully whimsical to the poignantly pathetic. The shift comes at the right time, and conveys the effect of the opening of some inner door. It is well synchronised with the complete following of the *current,* the vanishment of Ningauble's urchin-emissary, the steeper ascent, the wilder and more precipitous landscape, and the coming of a flaming sunset and purple twilight. Nor is there any letdown. Despite recurrences of the whimsical mood, the tension is always on the increase. The scenes within the castle are magnificently replete with cosmic fear and the sense of encroaching order upon order of alien outsideness. Nor is the ending anticlimactic—for the escape of the adept's soul in the traditional form of a mouse blends perfectly with the massed nature of what has gone before. Indeed, all the developments are gratifyingly plausible and inevitable according to the laws of that fantasy-touched world which you have chosen to depict. I could name dozens of especially tense and powerful high spots—such as the terrified glances in the Adept's sarcophagus in the lost city, the discovery of what was suspended in the box in the castle, etc. etc. etc. If anything in the plot would be the better for changing, I think it is perhaps the matter of the Adept's (or power-beyond-the-Adept's) motive in imposing an ignominious spell on Fafhrd and the Mouser. This is of course suggested on p. 29—but in view of the later doubtfulness of the source of Isaiah ben Elzhaz's volition I think the suggestion might well be a trifle more definite. Why was Isaiah—or That or

Those behind him—interested in Fafhrd and his companion? Was it indeed because the Mouser's superficial magical dabblings had attracted attention? Of course the Grey One's own explanation—about having insulted the Adept in Ephesus—is ruled out, since Elobeth's story-within-the-story reveals that Isaiah cannot have walked abroad in his own body as a magician. As for possible re-proportioning—if any sections would bear condensation, it is probably those referring respectively to the action of the spell in Tyre (the story's first 8 pages) and to the conversation and combat with the Adept's corpse in the Lost City. This latter section, however, should (as just stated) contain a very specific hint of the reason for the spell cast on the adventurers. However—all these observations are very minor matters. The novelette is really very much all right just as it is!

Certainly, you have produced a remarkably fine and distinctive bit of cosmic fantasy in a vein which is, for all the Cabellian or Beckfordian comparisons, essentially your own. The basic element of allegory, the earthiness and closeness to human nature, and the curious blending of worldly lightness with the strange and the macabre, all harmonise adequately and seem to express a definite mood and personality. The result is an authentic work of art—and I certainly hope it can eventually get published somewhere even though its genre makes it the hardest conceivable sort of thing to place. Picaresque fantasy of this type generally appears only in book form—which is of course a significant commentary on the vapid formula-following of even the best periodicals.

The End

[The last year of Lovecraft's life was a melancholy one, filled with personal tragedies, disappointments in writing, the illness of his aunt, and finally his own death. In the summer of 1936 Lovecraft was stunned to hear of the suicide of his close associate Robert E. Howard on June 11.]

[48]   Just had a most depressing and staggering message—a card from C L M[25] with the report (source not given) that good old Two-Gun Bob has committed suicide. It seems incredible—I had a long normal letter from him written May 13. He was worried about his mother's health, but otherwise seemed perfectly all right. If the news is indeed true, it forms weird fiction's worst blow since the passing of Whitehead in 1932. Nobody else in the gang had quite the driving zest and spontaneity of Brother Conan. I surely wish I could get a bulletin saying that the report is a

mistake. 1936 certainly is a hellish year! This loss will probably seem a more acute bereavement to you than to the others, since you are the only one of the group to have seen R E H in person. But if you can feel worse than I do about it, you'll be going some. Damnation, what a loss! That bird had gifts of an order even higher than the readers of his published work could suspect, and in time would have made his mark in real literature with some folk-epic of his beloved southwest. He was a perennial fount of erudition and eloquence on this theme—and had the creative imagination to make old days live again. Mitra, what a man! It is hard to describe precisely what made his stories stand out so—but the real secret is that *he was in every one of them,* whether they were ostensibly commercial or not. He was greater than any profit-seeking policy he could adopt—for even when he outwardly made concessions to the mammon-guided editors he had an internal force and sincerity which broke through the surface and put the imprint of his personality on everything he wrote. Seldom or never did he set down a lifeless stock character or situation and leave it as such. Before he got through with it, it always took on some tinge of vitality and reality in spite of editorial orders—always drew something from his own first-hand experience and knowledge of life instead of from the barbarism of desiccated pulpish standbys. He was almost alone in his ability to create real emotions of fear and of dread suspense. Contrast his "Black Canaan"[26] with the pallid synthetic pap comprising the rest of the current issue of W T. Bloch and Derleth are clever enough technically—but for stark, living fear . . . . the actual smell and feel and darkness and brooding terror and impending doom that inhere in that nighted, moss-hung jungle . . . . . what other writer is even in the running with R E H? No author can excel unless he takes his work very seriously and puts himself whole-heartedly into it—and Two-Gun did just that, even when he claimed and consciously believed that he didn't. And this is the giant whom Fate had to snatch away whilst hundreds of insincere hacks continue to concoct phony ghosts and vampires and space-ships and occult detectives! I can't understand the tragedy—for although R E H had a moody side expressed in his resentment against civilisation (the basis of our perennial and voluminous epistolary controversy), I always thought that this was a more or less *impersonal* sentiment—like Belknap's rage against the injustices of a capitalistic social order. He himself seemed to me pretty well adjusted—in an environment he loved, with plenty of congenial souls (like the "Pink" Tyson and Tevis Clyde Smith of whom he spoke so often . . . did you meet either of these when visiting Two-Gun?) to talk and travel with, and with parents whom he obviously idolised. His mother's pleural illness imposed a great strain upon both him and his father, yet I cannot think that this would be sufficient to drive his tough-fibred nervous system to self-destructive extremes. Nor was his financial state at all desperate as far as I know. I wonder if he was alive when my last letter arrived—that must have been a week ago. Probably he never saw its 32 pages, that ended with an enthusiastic tribute to his serial and to "Black Canaan", which I had just read. Hell!

[Later in the summer Lovecraft, in a discussion with a new round-robin group, the Coryciani, mentioned in passing what he would do if he knew he had only an hour to live. His remarks are prophetic.]

[49]   As for the general idea of what one would do if certain of death in an hour—I fancy most persons in normal health tend to sentimentalise and romanticise a bit about it. For my part—as a realist beyond the age of theatricalism and naive beliefs—I feel quite certain that my own known last hour would be spent quite prosaically in writing instructions for the disposition of certain books, manuscripts, heirlooms, and other possessions.[27] Such a task would—in view of the mental stress—take at least an hour—and it would be the most useful thing I could do before dropping off into oblivion. If I *did* finish ahead of time, I'd probably spend the residual minutes getting a last look at something closely associated with my earliest memories—a picture, a library table, an 1895 Farmer's Almanack, a small music-box I used to play with at 2½, or some kindred symbol—completing a psychological circle in a spirit half of humour and half of whimsical sentimentality. Then—nothingness, as before Aug. 20, 1890.

[Lovecraft's so-called "last letter," addressed to James F. Morton and found unfinished on his desk upon his death, had probably been written over a series of weeks beginning in early 1937. Here he outlines many of his activities of the previous months, including one final tramp in the woods near his home, where he met some of his beloved cats.]

[50]   As for outings—of course I kept in the open most of the time until the hellish chill of autumn finally began to shut down. Even after that I managed to take occasional trips to the woods and fields throughout October and just over the line into November. The unique feature of my autumnal

explorations was that I succeeded in discovering several splendid rural regions within a three-mile radius of here which I had never seen before. One is a wooded hill—Neutaconkanut—on the western rim of the town (much south of Friend Mariano), whence a series of marvellous views if the outspread city and adjacent countryside may be obtained. I had often ascended it before, but the exquisitely mystical sylvan scenery beyond the crest—curious mounds, hummocked pastures, and hushed, hidden valleys —was wholly new to me. On October 28th I explored this region still further—including the country west of Neutaconkanut and the western slopes of that eminence itself. At certain stages of this ramble I penetrated a terrain which took me half a mile from any spot I had ever trod before in the course of a long life. I followed a road which branches north and west from the Plainfield Pike, ascending a low rise which skirts Neutaconkanut's western foot and which commands an utterly idyllic vista of rolling meadows, ancient stone walls, hoary groves. and distant cottage roofs to the west and south. Only two or three miles from the city's heart, and yet in the primal rural New England of the first colonists! Just before sunset I ascended the hill by a precipitous cart-path bordering an ancient wood and from the dizzy crest obtained an almost stupefying prospect of unfolded leagues of farmsteads and champaigns, gleaming rivulets and far-off forests, and mystical orange sky with a great solar disc sinking redly amidst bars of stratus clouds. Entering the wood, I saw the actual sunset through the trees, and then turned east to cross the hill to that more familiar cityward slope which I have always known. Never before had I realised the great extent of Neutaconkanut's surface. It is really a miniature plateau or table-land, with valleys, ridges, and summits of its own, rather than a simple hill. From some of its hidden interior meadows—remote from every sign of nearby human life—I secured truly marvellous glimpses of the remote urban skyline—a dream of enchanted pinnacles and domes half-floating in air, and with an obscure aura of mystery around them. The upper windows of some of the taller towers held the fire of the sun after I had lost it, affording a spectacle of cryptic and curious glamour. Then I saw the great yellow disc of the Hunter's Moon (two days before full) floating above the belfries and minarets, while in the orange-glowing west Venus and Jupiter commenced to twinkle. My route across the plateau was varied—sometimes through the interior, but now and then getting toward the wooded edge where dark valleys slope down to the plain below, and huge balanced boulders on rocky heights impart a spectral, druidic effect as they stand out against the twilight. I did not begin to cover the full extent of the plateau, and can see that I have a field for several voyages of discovery when warm days return. Finally I came to more familiar ground—where the grassy ridge of an old buried aqueduct gives the illusion of one of those vestigial Roman roads in Machen's Caermaen country —and stood once more on the well-known eastward crest which I have gazed at since infancy. The outspread city was rapidly lighting up, and lay like a constellation in the deepening dusk. The moon poured down increasing floods of pale gold, and the glow of Venus and Jupiter in the fading west grew intense. Then down the steep hillside to the car line (too cold for enjoyable walking without scenery to compensate for shivers) and back to the prosaic haunts of man.

October 20 and 21 were phenomenally warm, and I utilised them in exploring a hitherto untapped region down the east shore of Narragansett Bay where the Barrington Parkway winds along the lofty bluff above the water. It is, in general, the area to the right of our usual route to Aunt Julia's. I found a highly fascinating forest called the Squantum Woods— where there are great oaks and birches, steep slopes and rock ledges, and breath-taking westward vistas beyond the trees. On both occasions there was a fine sunset—then glimpses of the crescent moon, Venus, and Jupiter . . . and the lights of far-off Providence from high places along the parkway. On my expedition of the 20th a particularly congenial bodyguard or retinue attended me through the sunlit arcades of the grove—in the persons of two tiny kittens, one gray and one tortoise-shell, who appeared out of nowhere in the midst of the sylvan solitudes. Blithe spirits of the ancient wood—furry faunlets of the shadowy vale! I wonder where their mother was? Judging by their diminutiveness, they could scarce have been fully graduated from her as a source of nourishment. Probably they appertained to an hospital whose grounds are contiguous with the mystical forest. Both were at first very timid, and reluctant to let Grandpa catch them; but eventually the little grey fellow became very purr-ful and amicable—climbing over the old gentleman, playing with twigs and with Grandpa's watch-charm, and eventually curling up and going to sleep in the grandpaternal lap. But Little Brother remained suspicious and aloof—clawing and spitting with surprising vehemence on the one occasion when Grandpa caught him. He hung around, however, because he didn't want to lose his brother!

Not wishing to wake my new friend, I carried him about when I continued my ramble—Little Tortoise-Shell Brother tagging along reluctantly and dubiously at a discreet distance in the rear. When the grey faunlet awaked, he requested to be set down; but proceeded to trot companionably after Grandpa—sometimes getting under the old gentleman's feet and considerably retarding progress. Thus I roamed the venerable forest aisles for an hour and a half—till the ruddy disc of the sun vanished behind the farther hills. As I emerged from the wood, I feared that my faithful retinue might follow me on to the broad park-way and incur the perils of motor traffic—and was considering expedients (such as putting Little Grey Boy a short distance up a tree) for discouraging their further attendance—but discovered that they were not without native caution. Or perhaps they were wholly genii loci, without real existence apart from their dim nemorense habitat. At any rate, Little Grey Boy paused at the edge of the grove with a mewed farewell—and naturally Little Tortoise-Shell had no great eagerness to follow. I bade them a regretful and ceremonious adieu—and on the next day looked for them in vain.

[By the end of February, when the following letter to Wilfred B. Talman was written, Lovecraft knew that his illness was terminal. Nevertheless, he carried on bravely, not letting any of his correspondents know the true severity of his condition.]

[51]   Yrs of the 15th found me completely knocked out with an acute intestinal trouble following 2 mos. of dragging grippe. Don't know how long or serious an ordeal I'm in for but Dr. Dustin plans to call in a stomach specialist Tuesday. Am in constant pain, take only liquid food, and so bloated with gas that I can't lie down. Spend all time in chair propped with pillows, and can read or write only a few minutes at a time. Taking 3 medicines at once.

But I must not delay answering yours of the 15th. Thanks immensely for the antiquarian travel bits, and for the new Texaco Star. No—I didn't get your Steel Number. The last Star I had before this new one was the Texas Centennial issue.

As for that book proposition—I'm devilish sorry to say that it looks rather stalled.[28] I've had no strength since the middle of December and could attend only to immediate things. Now it looks as if all bets were off. I've no idea what lies ahead of me—and any systematic effort seems fantastically remote. You and the firm are unbelievably kind and liberal—but what can a guy do when he hardly has strength enough to walk across the room? If I ever get through this damned mess, and the firm still feels receptive, we may be able to talk more to the point. All my correspondence and affairs are going to hell, though I'm dropping cards—or having my aunt drop them—in important cases.

Hope Belknap's magnum opus will be one of the sensations of 1937. His confidence at least is in his favour.

Good luck with your own pulp experiments. It all depends on what one's basic values and ambitions are. There is certainly vast economic advantage in the pulp field.

Well—I hope all is progressing well with you. Again let me apologise for the apparent letdown, and assure you that the cause is all too adequate. I'll see that you hear of any salient future development.

[Lovecraft was taken to Jane Brown Memorial Hospital in Providence ten days after writing this letter. He died there in the early morning of March 15, 1937.]

Appendix

Some Notes on a Nonentity (1933)

For me, the chief difficulty of writing an autobiography is finding anything of importance to put in it. My existence has been a quiet, uneventful, and undistinguished one; and at best must sound woefully flat and tame on paper.

I was born in Providence, R.I.—where, but for two minor interruptions, I have ever since lived—on August 20, 1890; of old Rhode Island stock on my mother's side, and of a Devonshire paternal line domiciled in New York State since 1827.

The interests which have led me to fantastic fiction were very early in appearing, for as far back as I can clearly remember I was charmed by strange stories and ideas, and by ancient scenes and objects. Nothing has ever seemed to fascinate me so much as the thought of some curious interruption in the prosaic laws of Nature, or some monstrous intrusion on our familiar world by unknown things from the limitless abysses outside.

When I was three or less I listened avidly to the usual juvenile fairy lore, and Grimm's Tales were among the first things I ever read, at the age of four. When I was five the Arabian Nights claimed me, and I spent hours in playing Arab—calling myself "Abdul Alhazred", which some kindly elder had suggested to me as a typical Saracen name. It was many years later, however, that I thought of giving Abdul an eighth-century setting and attributing to him the dreaded and unmentionable *Necronomicon!*

But for me books and legends held no monopoly of fantasy. In the quiet hill streets of my native town, where fanlighted colonial doorways, small-paned windows, and graceful Georgian steeples still keep alive the glamour of the eighteenth century, I felt a magic then and now hard to explain. Sunsets over the city's outspread roofs, as seen from vantage-points on the great hill, affected me with especial poignancy. Before I knew it the eighteenth century had captured me more utterly than ever the hero of *Berkeley Square* was captured; so that I used to spend hours in the attic poring over the long-s'd books banished from the library downstairs and unconsciously absorbing the style of Pope and Dr. Johnson as a natural mode of expression. This absorption was doubly strong because of the ill-health which rendered school attendance rare and irregular. One effect of it was to make me feel subtly out of place in the modern period, and consequently to think of *time* as a mystical, portentous thing in which all sorts of unexpected wonders might be discovered.

Nature, too, keenly touched my sense of the fantastic. My home was not far from what was then the edge of the settled residence district, so that I was just as used to the rolling fields, stone walls, giant elms, squat farmhouses, and deep woods of rural New England as to the ancient urban scene. This brooding, primitive landscape seemed to me to hold some vast but unknown significance, and certain dark wooded hollows near the Seekonk River took on an aura of strangeness not unmixed with vague horror. They figured in my dreams—especially those nightmares containing the black, winged, rubbery entities which I called "night-gaunts".

When I was six years old I encountered the mythology of Greece and Rome through various popular juvenile media, and was profoundly influenced by it. I gave up being an Arab and became a Roman, incidentally acquiring for ancient Rome a queer feeling of familiarity and identification only less powerful than my corresponding feeling for the eighteenth century. In a way, the two feelings worked together; for when I sought out the original classics from which the childish tales were taken, I found them very largely in late seventeenth- and eighteenth-century translations. The imaginative stimulus was immense, and for a time I actually thought I glimpsed fauns and dryads in certain venerable groves. I used to build altars and offer sacrifices to Pan, Diana, Apollo, and Minerva.

About this period the weird illustrations of Gustave Doré—met in editions of Dante, Milton, and the *Ancient Mariner*—affected me powerfully. For the first time I began to attempt writing—the earliest piece I can recall being a tale of a hideous cave perpetrated at the age of seven and entitled "The Noble Eavesdropper". This does not survive, though I still possess two hilariously infantile efforts dating from the following year—"The Mysterious Ship" and "The Secret of the Grave", whose titles display sufficiently the direction of my tastes.

At the age of about eight I acquired a strong interest in the sciences, which undoubtedly arose from the mysterious-looking pictures of "Philosophical and

Scientific Instruments" in the back of Webster's Unabridged Dictionary. Chemistry came first, and I soon had a very attractive little laboratory in the basement of my home. Next came geography—with a weird fascination centreing in the antarctic continent and other pathless realms of remote wonder. Finally astronomy dawned on me—and the lure of other worlds and inconceivable cosmic gulfs eclipsed all other interests for a long period after my twelfth birthday. I published a small hectographed paper called *The Rhode Island Journal of Astronomy* and at last—when sixteen—broke into actual newspaper print with astronomical matter, contributing monthly articles on current phenomena to a local daily, and flooding the weekly rural press with more expansive miscellany.

It was while in high-school—which I was able to attend with some regularity—that I first produced weird stories of any degree of coherence and seriousness. They were largely trash, and I destroyed the bulk of them when eighteen; but one or two probably came up to the average pulp level. Of them all I have kept only "The Beast in the Cave" (1905) and "The Alchemist" (1908). At this stage most of my incessant, voluminous reading was scientific and classical, weird material taking a relatively minor place. Science had removed my belief in the supernatural, and truth for the moment captivated me more than dreams. I am still a mechanistic materialist in philosophy. As for reading—I mixed science, history, general literature, weird literature, and utter juvenile rubbish with the most complete unconventionality.

Parallel with all these reading and writing interests I had a very enjoyable childhood; the early years well enlivened with toys and with outdoor diversions, and the stretch after my tenth birthday dominated by a persistent though perforce short-distanced cycling which made me familiar with all the picturesque and fancy-exciting phases of the New England village and rural landscape. Nor was I by any means a hermit—more than one band of local boyhood having me on its rolls.

My health prevented college attendance; but informal studies at home, and the influence of a notably scholarly physician-uncle, helped to banish some of the worst effects of the lack. In the years which should have been collegiate I veered from science to literature, specialising in the products of that eighteenth century of which I felt myself so oddly a part. Weird writing was then in abeyance, although I read everything spectral that I could find—including the frequent bizarre items in such cheap magazines as *The All-Story* and *The Black Cat.* My own products were largely verse and essays—uniformly worthless and now relegated to eternal concealment.

In 1914 I discovered and joined the United Amateur Press Association, one of several nation-wide correspondence organisations of literary novices who publish papers of their own and form, collectively, a miniature world of helpful mutual criticism and encouragement. The benefit received from this affiliation can scarcely be overestimated, for contact with the various members and critics helped me infinitely in toning down the worst archaisms and ponderosities in my style. This world of "amateur journalism" is now best represented by the National Amateur Press Association, a society which I can strongly and conscientiously recommend to any beginner in authorship. (For information address the Secretary, George W. Trainer, Jun., 95 Stuyvesant Ave., Brooklyn, N.Y.) It was in the ranks of organised amateurdom that I was first advised to resume weird writing—a step which I took in July, 1917, with the production of "The Tomb" and "Dagon" (both since published in *Weird Tales*) in quick succession. Also through amateurdom were established the contacts leading to the first professional publication of my fiction—in 1922, when *Home Brew* printed a ghastly series entitled "Herbert West—Reanimator". The same circle, moreover, led to my acquaintance with Clark Ashton Smith, Frank Belknap Long, Jun., Wilfred B. Talman, and others since celebrated in the field of unusual stories.

About 1919 the discovery of Lord Dunsany—from whom I got the idea of the artificial pantheon and myth-background represented by "Cthulhu", "Yog-Sothoth", "Yuggoth", etc.—gave a vast impetus to my weird writing; and I turned out material in greater volume than ever before or since. At that time I had no thought or hope of professional publication; but the founding of *Weird Tales* in 1923 opened up an outlet of considerable steadiness. My stories of the 1920 period reflect a good deal of my two chief models, Poe and Dunsany, and are in general too strongly inclined to extravagance and overcolouring to be of much serious literary value.

Meanwhile my health had been radically improving since 1920, so that a rather static existence began to be diversified with modest travels giving my strong antiquarian interests a freer play. My chief delight outside literature became the past-reviving quest for ancient architectural and landscape effects in the old colonial towns and byways of America's longest-settled regions, and gradually I have managed to cover a considerable territory from glamorous Quebec on the north to tropical Key West on the south and colourful Natchez and New Orleans on the west. Among my favourite towns, aside from Providence, are Quebec; Portsmouth, New Hampshire; Salem and Marblehead in Massachusetts; Newport in my own state; Philadelphia; Annapolis; Richmond with its wealth of Poe memories; eighteenth-century Charleston; sixteenth-century St. Augustine; and drowsy Natchez on its dizzy bluff and with its gorgeous subtropical hinterland. The "Arkham" and "Kingsport" figuring in some of my tales are more or less adapted versions of Salem and Marblehead. My native New England and its old, lingering lore have sunk deep into my imagination, and appear frequently in what I write. I dwell at present in a house 130 years old on the crest of Providence's ancient hill, with a haunting vista of venerable roofs and boughs from the window above my desk.

It is now clear to me that any actual literary merit I have is confined to tales of dream-life, strange shadow, and cosmic "outsideness", notwithstanding a keen interest in many other departments of life and a professional practice of general prose and verse revision. Why this is so, I have not the least idea. I have no illusions concerning the precarious status of my tales, and do not expect to become a serious competitor of my favourite weird authors— Poe, Arthur Machen, Dunsany, Algernon Blackwood, Walter de la Mare, and Montague Rhodes James. The only thing I can say in favour of my work is its sincerity. I refuse to follow the mechanical conventions of popular fiction or to fill my tales with stock characters and situations, but insist on reproducing real moods and impressions in the best way I can command. The result may be poor, but I had rather keep aiming at serious literary expression than accept the artificial standards of cheap romance.

I have tried to improve and subtilise my tales with the passing of years, but have not made the progress I wish. Some of my efforts have been cited in the O'Brien and O. Henry annuals, and a few have enjoyed reprinting in anthologies; but all proposals for a published collection have come to nothing. It is possible that one or two short tales may be issued as separate brochures before long. I never write when I cannot be spontaneous—expressing a mood already existing and demanding crystallisation. Some of my tales involve actual dreams I have experienced. My speed and manner of writing vary widely in different cases, but I always work best at night. Of my products, my favourites are "The Colour out of Space" and "The Music of Erich Zann", in the order named. I doubt if I could ever succeed well in the ordinary kind of science fiction.

I believe that weird writing offers a serious field not unworthy of the best literary artists; though it is at most a very limited one, reflecting only a small section of man's infinitely composite moods. Spectral fiction should be realistic and atmospheric—confining its departure from Nature to the one supernatural channel chosen, and remembering that scene, mood, and phenomena are more important in conveying what is to be conveyed than are characters and plot. The "punch" of a truly weird tale is simply some violation or transcending of fixed cosmic law—an imaginative escape from palling reality—hence *phenomena* rather than *persons* are the logical "heroes". Horrors, I believe, should be *original*—the use of common myths and legends being a weakening influence. Current magazine fiction, with its incurable leanings toward conventional sentimental perspectives, brisk, cheerful style, and artificial "action" plots, does not rank high. The greatest weird tale ever written is probably Algernon Blackwood's "The Willows".

Glossary of Names

Baird, Edwin (1886–1957), first editor of *Weird Tales* (1923–24), who accepted Lovecraft's first submissions to the magazine.

Barlow, Robert H[ayward] (1918–1951), author and collector. As a teenager he corresponded with Lovecraft and acted as his host during two long visits in the summers of 1934 and 1935. In the 1930s he wrote several works of weird and fantasy fiction, some in collaboration with Lovecraft. Lovecraft appointed him his literary executor. In the 1940s he went to Mexico and became a distinguished anthropologist. He died by suicide.

Bierce, Ambrose (1842–1914?), distinguished American author of tales of horror and of the Civil War. Lovecraft first read him in 1919.

Bishop, Zealia Brown (Reed) (1897–1968), Lovecraft's revision client. Basing his work on slim plot synopses, Lovecraft ghostwrote "The Curse of Yig" (1928), "The Mound" (1929–30), and "Medusa's Coil" (1930) for her.

Blackwood, Algernon (1869–1951), prolific British author of weird and fantasy tales whose work Lovecraft greatly admired when he read it in 1924.

Bloch, Robert (1917–1994), author of weird and suspense fiction who began a correspondence with Lovecraft in 1933. Lovecraft tutored him in the craft of writing during their four-year association.

Bush, (Rev.) David Van (1882–1959), prolific author of inspirational verse and popular psychology manuals, many of them revised by Lovecraft.

Clark, Dr. Franklin Chase (1847–1915), a medical doctor who had also translated some of the Latin classics. He helped Lovecraft considerably on his early prose and verse.

Clark, Lillian D[elora] (1856–1932), Lovecraft's maternal aunt. She married Dr. Franklin Chase Clark in 1902. From 1926 to her death she shared quarters with Lovecraft at 10 Barnes Street.

Cole, Edward H. (1892–1966), early associate of Lovecraft in the amateur journalism movement.

Cook, W. Paul (1881–1948), publisher of the *Monadnock Monthly*, the *Vagrant*, and other amateur journals. In 1927 he issued the *Recluse,* containing Lovecraft's "Supernatural Horror in Literature." He first visited Lovecraft in 1917 and remained a lifelong friend.

Crane, Hart (1899–1932), eminent American poet who met Lovecraft occasionally in Cleveland (1922) and New York (1924–26, 1930). Lovecraft admired his work, especially *The Bridge* (1930), on which Lovecraft saw him at work in 1924. He died by suicide.

de la Mare, Walter (1873–1956), English author and poet who wrote occasional weird tales much admired by Lovecraft for their subtlety and allusiveness.

Derleth, August W[illiam] (1909–1971), author of weird tales and also a long series of regional and historical works set in his native Wisconsin. Lovecraft much admired such of these works as *Place of Hawks* (1935) and *Evening in Spring* (1941), several drafts of which he read in manuscript. After Lovecraft's death, Derleth and Donald Wandrei founded the publishing firm of Arkham House to preserve Lovecraft's work in book form.

Dunsany, Lord (Edward John Moreton Drax Plunkett) (1878–1957), Irish writer of fantasy tales whose work, which Lovecraft first read in 1919, notably influenced him.

Galpin, Alfred (1901–1983), composer, French scholar, and longtime friend of Lovecraft.

Gamwell, Annie E[meline] Phillips (1866–1941), Lovecraft's maternal aunt. She shared quarters with Lovecraft at 66 College Street from 1933 to 1937.

Gamwell, Edward F[rancis] (1869–1936), Lovecraft's uncle. For a time he was editor of the *Cambridge (Mass.) Tribune.* He married Annie Gamwell in 1897, but the couple had separated by 1916.

Greene, Sonia Haft (1883–1972), Russian Jewish immigrant who became Lovecraft's wife in 1924. When Lovecraft returned to Providence in 1926, she continued to work in the millinery trade in New York. In early 1929 she forced Lovecraft to pursue divorce proceedings. Some years later she moved to California and married Nathaniel Davis. Her memoir of Lovecraft, first published in 1948, has been edited in its complete form as *The Private Life of H. P. Lovecraft* (1985).

Guiney, Louise Imogen (1861–1920), a once noted Massachusetts poet and essayist. Lovecraft claims that his family stayed with her at her home in Auburndale during the winter of 1892–93, but this has not been confirmed.

Howard, Robert E[rvin] (1906–1936), prolific Texas author of weird and adventure tales for *Weird Tales* and other pulp magazines; creator of the adventure hero Conan the Barbarian. He and Lovecraft corresponded voluminously from 1930 to 1936. He committed suicide when he heard of his mother's impending death.

Kirk, George [Willard] (1898–1962), member of the Kalem Club. He published

Twenty-one Letters of Ambrose Bierce (1922) and ran the Chelsea Bookshop in New York.

Kleiner, Rheinhart (1882–1949), amateur poet and longtime friend of Lovecraft. He visited Lovecraft in Providence in 1918, 1919, and 1920, and met Lovecraft frequently during the heyday of the Kalem Club (1924–26).

Leeds, Arthur (1882–1952?), an associate of Lovecraft's in New York and member of the Kalem Club.

Leiber, Fritz (1910–1992), distinguished author of weird and science fiction who corresponded with Lovecraft during the last few months of the latter's life.

Long, Frank Belknap (1901–1994), fiction writer and poet. He would become one of Lovecraft's closest friends and correspondents. Late in life he wrote the memoir, *Howard Phillips Lovecraft: Dreamer on the Nightside* (1975).

Lovecraft, Sarah Susan (Phillips) (1857–1921), Lovecraft's mother. She married Winfield Scott Lovecraft in 1889 and settled in Dorchester, Massachusetts, but returned with her son to her family home in Providence when her husband was institutionalized at Butler Hospital in 1893. From 1904 to 1919 she lived alone with Lovecraft at 598 Angell Street. She spent her last two years at Butler Hospital.

Lovecraft, Winfield Scott (1853–1898), Lovecraft's father. He attended an unspecified military college, then eventually became a salesman for the Gorham (Silversmiths) Co., based in Providence. He suffered a seizure in Chicago in 1893 and was placed in Butler Hospital, where he died of paresis (the term then used to denote syphilis).

Loveman, Samuel E. (1887–1976), poet and longtime friend of Lovecraft as well as of Ambrose Bierce, Hart Crane, and George Sterling. Author of *The Hermaphrodite* (1926) and other works highly regarded by Lovecraft.

McNeil, Everett (1862–1929), prolific author of historical and adventure novels for boys.

Miniter, Edith (1867–1934), amateur author who also professionally published a novel, *Our Natupski Neighbors* (1916) and many short stories. She hosted Lovecraft at her home in Wilbraham, Massachusetts, in the summer of 1928.

Moe, Maurice W[inter] (1882–1940), amateur journalist, English teacher, and longtime friend of Lovecraft.

Morton, James Ferdinand (1870–1941), amateur journalist, author of many tracts on race prejudice, freethought, and taxation, and longtime friend of Lovecraft.

Orton, Vrest (1897–1986), a late member of the Kalem Club. He was for a time an editor at the *Saturday Review* and later the founder of the Vermont Country Store. He compiled an early bibliography of Dreiser, *Dreiseriana* (1929).

Phillips, Whipple Van Buren (1833–1904), Lovecraft's maternal grandfather. A wealthy industrialist, he established the Owyhee Land and Irrigation

Company in Idaho. He provided strong guidance to Lovecraft in the absence of Lovecraft's father. His death in 1904 and the subsequent mismanagement of his estate forced Lovecraft and his mother to move from 454 Angell Street to smaller quarters at 598 Angell Street.

Price, E[dgar] Hoffmann (1898–1988), prolific pulp writer of weird and adventure tales. Lovecraft met him in New Orleans in 1932 and corresponded extensively with him thereafter.

Smith, Clark Ashton (1893–1961), prolific California poet and writer of fantasy tales. He received a "fan" letter from Lovecraft in 1922 and continued to correspond with him until Lovecraft's death.

Sterling, Kenneth (1920–1995), young science fiction fan who came into contact with Lovecraft in 1934. He later became a distinguished physician.

Talman, Wilfred Blanch (1904–1986), late member of the Kalem Club. He and Lovecraft collaborated on the story "Two Black Bottles" (1926). Late in life he wrote the memoir *The Normal Lovecraft* (1973).

Wandrei, Donald (1908–1987), author of weird and science fiction tales. He corresponded with Lovecraft from 1926 to 1937, visited Lovecraft in Providence in 1927 and 1932, and met Lovecraft occasionally in New York during the 1930s. After Lovecraft's death Wandrei and August Derleth founded the publishing firm of Arkham House to preserve Lovecraft's work in book form.

Whitehead, Henry S[t. Clair] (1882–1932), author of weird and adventure tales, many of them set in the Virgin Islands. Lovecraft visited him in Florida in 1931.

Wright, Farnsworth (1888–1940), editor of *Weird Tales* (1924–40). His involvement with Lovecraft was complex, as he rejected some of Lovecraft's best work of the 1930s.

Notes

Introduction

1. Maurice W. Moe, "Howard Phillips Lovecraft: The Sage of Providence" (1937), in *Caverns Measureless to Man: 18 Memoirs of H. P. Lovecraft*, ed. S. T. Joshi (West Warwick, R.I.: Necronomicon Press, 1996), p. 16.

2. "Extracts from H. P. Lovecraft's Letters to G. W. Macauley" (1938); rpt. *Lovecraft Studies* no. 3 (Fall 1980): 14.

3. Sonia Davis, *The Private Life of H. P. Lovecraft* (1985); quoted in S. T. Joshi, *H. P. Lovecraft: A Life* (West Warwick, R.I.: Necronomicon Press, 1996), p. 392.

1. Childhood and Adolescence (1890–1914)

1. Louise Imogen Guiney (1861–1920) had attended the Academy of the Sacred Heart in Providence from 1872 to 1879, and presumably at that time became acquainted with Sarah Susan Phillips, Lovecraft's mother.

2. A poem by Thomas Buchanan Read (1822–1872).

3. No doubt this was what Lovecraft was told by his family; but in fact Winfield Scott Lovecraft had contracted syphilis (then termed "paresis").

4. Lillian D. Clark.

5. Franklin C. Clark was a physician and writer on medicine and local and natural history. He translated Homer, Virgil, Lucretius, and Statius into English verse. Lovecraft possessed Clark's translations of the *Georgics* and *Aeneid* of Virgil and mentioned on several occasions his desire to see the work published.

6. Annie E. P. Gamwell, who lived with Lovecraft during his last years.

7. Edward Gamwell began courting Lovecraft's aunt Annie in 1895, and when they married in 1897, Lovecraft served as an usher at the wedding. Gamwell's affiliation with the Phillips family was not lasting, for he and Annie separated around 1916.

8. "Almost no sober person dances, unless by chance he is insane." In fact, the quotation is from Cicero's *Pro Murena* 13.

9. John B. Gough, *Sunlight and Shadow; or, Gleanings from My Life Work* (1880).

10. Thomas Bulfinch, *The Age of Fable* (1855), a celebrated retelling of the myths of ancient Greece and Rome.

11. The actual title (derived from the surviving manuscript of the "second edition" of November 8, 1897) is: "The Poem of Ulysses: Written for Young People." Two

alternate titles are found elsewhere in the manuscript: "The Young Folk's *Ulysses* or the *Odyssey* in plain Old *English* Verse" and "The New Odyssey or Ulyssiad for the Young."

12. Only Volume II of *Poemata Minora* (1902) survives. Volume I evidently dates to 1901.

13. Aside from the two mentioned, the following juvenile stories survive: "The Mystery of the Grave-yard" (1899?) and "The Mysterious Ship" (1902).

14. John Howard Appleton, *The Young Chemist* (1876).

15. A reference to Lovecraft's earlier enthusiasm for Arabian matters, derived from his reading of the *Arabian Nights* at the age of five.

16. Non-extant.

17. Lovecraft contributed monthly astronomy columns to the *Providence Tribune* (morning, evening, and Sunday editions) from August 1906 to June 1908.

18. *Pawtuxet Valley Gleaner,* October 12, 1906, p. 2.

19. "The Alchemist" (1908) appeared in the *United Amateur* for November 1916.

20. "Providence in 2000 A.D.," *Providence Evening Bulletin,* 4 March 1912, sec. 2, p. 6.

2. Amateur Journalism (1914–1921)

1. The *Conservative* would briefly resume with two issues in 1923.

2. The posts held by Lovecraft in the UAPA were First Vice-President (1915–16); President (1917–18); and Official Editor (1920–22, 1924–25). He was president of the NAPA in 1922–23.

3. Helene E. Hoffman, former president of the UAPA.

4. Lovecraft's colleague Maurice W. Moe had organized the Appleton High School Press Club in Appleton, Wisconsin.

5. John T. Dunn (1889–1983) was released shortly after the war and later became a Catholic priest.

6. Samuel Johnson, *The Rambler* no. 208 (March 14, 1752).

7. Thomas Campbell, *The Pleasures of Hope* (1799), Part I, line 7.

8. Graeme Davis had attacked the UAPA in his amateur paper, *The Lingerer,* leading to Lovecraft's rejoinder, "A Reply to *The Lingerer*" (*Tryout,* June 1917).

9. Maurice W. Moe, "The Church and the World," *Vagrant* no. 7 (June 1918): 17–22.

10. This dream was the basis for the story "Polaris" (1918).

11. Lovecraft refers to Ira A. Cole, a mystic who was part of the correspondence group the Kleicomolo, consisting of Rheinhart Kleiner, Cole, Maurice W. Moe, and Lovecraft.

12. Mr. Dooley was a character created in essays by the journalist and humorist Finley Peter Dunne (1867–1936). The expression was used as the last line of Moe's article.

13. Lovecraft refers to James Laurence Crowley, an amateur poet whose work Lovecraft revised, and Charles W. ("Tryout") Smith, an aged publisher of a long-running amateur journal, the *Tryout.*

14. Lovecraft refers to the submittal of a "credential," or proof of one's writing ability, in order to join the UAPA or the NAPA.

15. I.e., Lovecraft's friend and fellow amateur journalist W. Paul Cook.

16. "The Tomb" did not appear in Cook's *Monadnock Monthly*, but rather in the *Vagrant* for June 1922.

17. "Psychopompos" is a three-hundred-line poem (subtitled "A Tale in Rhyme") first published in the *Vagrant* for October 1919. Lovecraft frequently cited it in lists of his prose tales.

18. Lovecraft here recounts the writing of the collaborative tale "The Green Meadow" with the amateur writer Winifred Virginia Jordan (later Jackson).

19. Lovecraft's nickname for Alfred Galpin.

20. "The Green Meadow" appeared in Cook's last issue of the *Vagrant*, dated 1923 but not released until 1927.

21. F. F. Van de Water, "How Our State Police Have Spurred Their Way to Fame," *New York Tribune*, April 27, 1919, sec. VIII, pp. 2–3.

22. Lovecraft refers to his story "The Transition of Juan Romero." "Phil Mac" is the amateur writer Prof. Philip B. McDonald.

23. The reference is to Alice M. Hamlet, an amateur writer.

24. Actually, "Why the Milkman Shudders When He Perceives the Dawn," in *The Last Book of Wonder* (1916).

25. Philip Darrell Sherman (1881–1957) of Pawtucket, Rhode Island, was a drama critic and journalist.

26. *The Gods of the Mountain* is a play included in *Five Plays* (1914). "Bethmoora," "Poltarnees, Beholder of Ocean," and "Idle Days on the Yann" are in *A Dreamer's Tales* (1910); "How One Came, as Was Foretold, to the City of Never" is in *The Book of Wonder* (1912); "The Fall of Babbulkund" is in *The Sword of Welleran and Other Stories* (1908); "In the Land of Time" is in *Time and the Gods* (1906).

27. The following dream-account was, very slightly revised, rewritten as "The Statement of Randolph Carter" (1919).

28. The dream seems to have been partially the inspiration for "From Beyond" (1920), although that story is not set in Civil War times.

29. This image was incorporated into "The Rats in the Walls" (1923).

30. The following dream-account was eventually incorporated, with much alteration, into "The Call of Cthulhu" (1926).

31. Lovecraft refers to his prose-poem "Nyarlathotep" (*United Amateur*, November 1920).

32. David Van Bush was Lovecraft's most persistent revision client.

33. The "Department of Public Criticism" column appearing in the *United Amateur* for March 1919.

3. Expanding Horizons (1921–1924)

1. Sonia Greene had contributed fifty dollars to the "official organ fund," used to defray expenses in printing the *United Amateur*. *The Rainbow* was Greene's short-lived amateur journal.

2. The epithets "Bolingbroke," "St. John," and "Clynor" all refer to the amateur journalist Rheinhart Kleiner. Florence Carol Greene, whom Lovecraft called Sonia

Greene's "flapper offspring," did not succumb to Kleiner's charm as had so many others; nor did Florence approve of her mother's later marriage to Lovecraft.

3. "Nietscheism [*sic*] and Realism," *Rainbow* no. 1 (October 1921): 9–11.

4. Alfred Galpin. "Mocrates" in the next sentence is Maurice W. Moe; "Tibaldus" is Lovecraft himself.

5. Lovecraft had first met Sonia at the NAPA convention in July 1921, held at the Brunswick Hotel in Boston.

6. Lovecraft refers to his poem "Samuel Loveman, Esquire, on His Poetry and Drama, Writ in the Elizabethan Style," *Dowdell's Bearcat* 4, no. 5 (December 1915): [7]. In his essay "Howard Phillips Lovecraft," Loveman relates that Lovecraft's first letter to him was indeed written to establish whether Loveman was still living.

7. George Julian Houtain was an amateur writer who, with his wife E. Dorothy Houtain, established the short-lived humor magazine *Home Brew* in 1921. Lovecraft contributed two serials to it, "Herbert West—Reanimator" (1922) and "The Lurking Fear" (1923).

8. The lines come from Lovecraft's then unpublished poem, "The Isaacsonio-Mortoniad" (1915), a satire on two amateur writers, Charles D. Isaacson and James Ferdinand Morton. Morton would later become one of Lovecraft's closest friends.

9. The Blue Pencil Club, an amateur group in Brooklyn.

10. This passage is an imitation of the prose-poem on New York written by Lord Dunsany, "A City of Wonder," in *Tales of Three Hemispheres* (1919).

11. Frank Belknap Long, "Felis: A Prose Poem," *Conservative* no. 13 (July 1923): 3–4.

12. Paul Livingston Keil. His photograph of Lovecraft, Long, and Morton at the Poe cottage has been frequently reproduced. He later wrote a memoir, "I Met Lovecraft," *Phoenix* 3, no. 6 (July 1944): 149.

13. Lovecraft wrote to Smith shortly thereafter, establishing an association that lasted until Lovecraft's death.

14. A reference to ingrown facial hairs, which frequently bothered Lovecraft and also affected his self-esteem.

15. William Sommer, watercolorist and draftsman.

16. Edward Lazare, later to become the editor of *American Book-Prices Current*.

17. Lovecraft wrote "The Hound" (1922) as a result of this cemetery experience.

18. In the fall of 1923 Lovecraft wrote "The Festival" as a record of his impressions of Marblehead. In that story he uses many phrases and descriptive touches from this letter.

19. Alfred Adler (1870–1937), Austrian psychologist and founder of Individual Psychology, based on the theory that all human beings are striving for superiority.

20. The stories were "Dagon" (1917), "The Statement of Randolph Carter" (1919), "Facts concerning the Late Arthur Jermyn and His Family" (1920), "The Cats of Ulthar" (1920), and "The Hound" (1922). All were accepted.

21. *Black Cat* (1895–1923), a magazine that published some "unusual" stories, although it by no means specialized in weird or horror fiction.

22. Both "Beyond the Door" and "A Square of Canvas" appeared in *Weird Tales* for April 1923.

23. *Weird Tales,* March 1923. The story clearly influenced Lovecraft's "The Dunwich Horror" (1928).

24. "The Sin-Eater" was written by Fiona Macleod, the pseudonym of the Scottish writer William Sharp (1855–1905). It was reprinted in Joseph Lewis French's *The Best Psychic Stories* (1920).

25. As a matter of fact, somebody *did* note the difference. When the tale was reprinted in *Weird Tales* for June 1930, the young Robert E. Howard perceived this linguistic discrepancy and wrote a letter to the editor of *Weird Tales,* who forwarded it to Lovecraft. Howard and Lovecraft became voluminous correspondents until the former's death.

26. At the urging of his colleague C. M. Eddy, Jr., Lovecraft had submitted the story to the *Argosy All-Story Weekly.*

27. The story was published simply as by Houdini, since Lovecraft unexpectedly wrote the story in the first person as if narrated by Houdini, and J. C. Henneberger thought it would seem odd to have a first-person narrative with a dual by-line.

28. Lovecraft soon afterward discovered that Houdini's account was pure fiction, but he nevertheless used it as the nucleus of the story.

4. Marriage and Exile (1924–1926)

1. Lovecraft alludes to the need to prepare a new typescript of the Houdini story, "Under the Pyramids," because Lovecraft had lost the typescript at Union Station in Providence as he was leaving for New York.

2. This refers to some property in Bryn Mawr Park, a development in Yonkers, on which the couple had placed a down payment.

3. Mariano de Magistris was a tenant on some property in western Rhode Island owned by Lovecraft's family. He paid a rent of $37.08 every six months.

4. This of course is *The Bridge* (1930), which established Crane's reputation as a leading American poet.

5. The implication of this remark is that, up to this point, Lovecraft had been eating cold canned meals at home.

6. The "triumph" is Lovecraft's "good" suit, purchased in early July for twenty-five dollars.

7. A line from James Elroy Flecker's play *Hassan* (1922).

8. Lovecraft refers to Sidney H. Sime, illustrator of Dunsany's early works, and the artist and engraver Gustave Doré.

9. Lovecraft visited Washington in the company of George Kirk.

10. Lovecraft refers to several of the standard classics of Gothic fiction: Horace Walpole's *The Castle of Otranto* (1764); Clara Reeve's *The Old English Baron* (1777); Charles Robert Maturin's *Melmoth the Wanderer* (1820); William Beckford's *Vathek* (1786) and *The Episodes of Vathek* (1912); and Emily Brontë's *Wuthering Heights* (1847).

11. James F. Morton, who was about to become the curator of the Paterson (New

Jersey) Museum, was attempting to secure a position for Lovecraft as his assistant; but the trustees of the museum never authorized such a position.

5. Homecoming (1926–1930)

1. In the handwritten letter this word is printed in letters nearly an inch high and with four underscores.

2. Lovecraft set much of the action of *The Case of Charles Dexter Ward* (1927) in this dwelling at 100 Prospect Street. See further p. 191.

3. Lovecraft alludes to the fact that in New York state at the time, divorce was only possible on grounds of adultery or if one of the parties was sentenced to life imprisonment. For this reason, divorce proceedings had to be pursued in Rhode Island and initiated by Lovecraft himself under the guise that Sonia had "deserted" him.

4. Judge Benjamin Barr Lindsey (1869–1943) created tremendous controversy when he wrote a book (with Wainright Evans) entitled *The Companionate Marriage* (1927), arguing for a looser marriage bond, greater ease in securing divorces, and postponement of child-bearing for several years until the marriage had solidified.

5. An amateur writer.

6. "The Syrian [river] Orontes flows into the Tiber." Juvenal, *Satires* 3.62 (*Syrus in Tiberim defluxit Orontes* in Juvenal).

7. Robert Blake makes the identical utterance at the close of "The Haunter of the Dark" (1935), when his identity becomes fused with that of Nyarlathotep.

8. An adaptation of Shakespeare's "even there where merchants most do congregate" (*The Merchant of Venice* 1.3.49).

9. Note how Lovecraft here fails to mention to Donald Wandrei (who came into contact with him in late 1926, after his return from New York) the fact of his marriage. To many later correspondents Lovecraft was similarly reluctant to admit that he had ever been married.

10. "The Strange High House in the Mist," *Weird Tales* (October 1931).

11. A reference to Lovecraft's invented book of occult lore, purportedly written by the "mad Arab" Abdul Alhazred.

12. Although *The Shunned House* was printed by Cook in 1928, it was never bound or distributed by him. Copies were later bound and distributed by R. H. Barlow (1934–35) and Arkham House (1959–61).

13. Nictzin Dyalhis (1879?–1942) was a hack writer who published many stories in *Weird Tales*.

14. "The Curse of Yig," *Weird Tales* (November 1929); written in the summer of 1928.

15. "The Mound" was rejected by *Weird Tales*. It first appeared in abridged form in *Weird Tales* (November 1940) and was reprinted in *Beyond the Wall of Sleep* (1943).

16. "The Last Test" (*Weird Tales*, November 1928) and "The Electric Executioner" (*Weird Tales*, August 1930).

17. N. J. O'Neail had written a letter to the editor of *Weird Tales* (published in the March 1930 issue) asking whether Lovecraft's Cthulhu and Howard's Kathulos (an entity cited in "Skull-Face" [*Weird Tales*, October/November/December 1929]) were related.

18. The story in question was "The Tale of Satampra Zeiros," later accepted by Wright and published in *Weird Tales* for November 1931. As a result, however, Tsathoggua was first mentioned in print in Lovecraft's "The Whisperer in Darkness" (1930), published in *Weird Tales* for August 1931.

19. Pluto had been discovered in early 1930 by C. W. Tombaugh and announced in the *New York Times* for March 14, 1930.

20. The letter column of *Weird Tales*.

21. Perhaps the most prolific contributor to *Weird Tales*, Seabury Quinn (1889–1969) wrote dozens of stories involving a "psychic detective," Jules de Grandin, as well as other weird and science fiction tales. Lovecraft regarded most of Quinn's work as formulaic hackwork.

22. The chief target here seems to be the Martian novels and tales of Edgar Rice Burroughs, which Lovecraft had enjoyed fifteen years earlier when they appeared in the *All-Story*.

23. Camille Flammarion (1842–1925), French novelist and occultist. Lovecraft owned his *Haunted Houses* (1924).

24. This was the largest check that Lovecraft ever received for a single story. It in fact appeared entire in the August 1931 issue of *Weird Tales*.

25. Orton compiled the first Dreiser bibliography, *Dreiseriana* (1929).

26. Harry Emerson Fosdick (1878–1969), American clergyman and author; Arthur S. Eddington (1882–1944), English astronomer; Henry Fairfield Osborn (1857–1935), American paleontologist. All these thinkers attempted in various ways to harmonize the findings of modern science with religious belief.

27. But cf. Bertrand Russell, *Human Knowledge: Its Scope and Limits* (New York: Simon and Schuster, 1948), pp. 23–24: "In quantum theory, individual atomic occurrences are not determined by the equations; these suffice only to show that the possibilities form a discrete series, and that there are rules determining how often each possibility will be realized in a large number of cases. There are reasons for believing that this absence of complete determinism is not due to any incompleteness in the theory, but is a genuine chracteristic of small-scale occurrences. The regularity which is found in macroscopic phenomena is a statistical regularity. Phenomena involving large numbers of atoms remain deterministic, but what an individual atom may do in given circumstances is uncertain, not only because our knowledge is limited but because there are no physical laws giving a determinate result."

28. The reference is to Alfred E. Smith and Herbert Hoover, Democratic and Republican candidates for president in 1928.

29. A longtime amateur poet. Lovecraft modeled the Vermont home of Henry Wentworth Akeley in "The Whisperer in Darkness" in part upon Goodenough's home in Brattleboro.

30. President Calvin Coolidge was born in Plymouth Notch, Vermont.

31. "Vermont: A First Impression," *Driftwind* 2, no. 5 (March 1928): [5–9]. That essay incorporates passages from this letter, and they are in turn used with modifications in "The Whisperer in Darkness."

32. Miniter shared her house with Evanore Beebe.

33. The reference is to Miniter's novel *Our Natupski Neighbors* (1916), about Polish immigrants in Massachusetts.

34. Francis Scott Key had written the words of "The Star-Spangled Banner" to the tune of an old drinking song, "To Anacreon in Heaven."

35. Clark Ashton Smith, "The City of the Singing Flame," *Wonder Stories* (January 1931).

36. Actually, Smith was nineteen when he published *The Star-Treader and Other Poems* (1912). It created a sensation in California. Sterling had already known Smith since 1911, and in fact arranged for the publication of the volume.

37. George Sterling (1869–1926), author of numerous volumes of poetry, wrote prefaces to Clark Ashton Smith's *Odes and Sonnets* (1918) and *Ebony and Crystal: Poems in Verse and Prose* (1922).

38. Clark Ashton Smith, "Sadastor," *Weird Tales* (July 1930); "The Abominations of Yondo" was never published in *Weird Tales*.

39. Helen V. Sully.

6. The Old Gentleman (1931–1937)

1. Walter de la Mare (1873–1956), British author best known for his poetry, but recognized by many as an important novelist and short story writer. Lovecraft wrote with great enthusiasm of de la Mare's weird fiction in his correspondence and his essay "Supernatural Horror in Literature," ranking de la Mare just slightly behind Arthur Machen, Algernon Blackwood, Lord Dunsany, and M. R. James.

2. Lovecraft capitalizes the second *e* in Derleth because his correspondent, Frank Belknap Long, habitually and deliberately spelled and pronounced the name as "Derluth."

3. "Chesterbelloc" refers to G. K. Chesterton and Hilaire Belloc, who repudiated the findings of modern science in an attempt to justify religious belief. "Waste Land Shantih-dwellers" of course alludes to T. S. Eliot (whose *The Waste Land* [1922] concludes with the words "shantih shantih shantih"). The pun echoes the final lines in Lovecraft's parody of Eliot, "Waste Paper" (1923): "Nobody home / In the shantih."

4. Edgar Allan Poe, *The Narrative of Arthur Gordon Pym of Nantucket* (1838).

5. See p. 270.

6. The John Day Co. published Dashiell Hammett's anthology *Creeps by Night* (1931), which contained Lovecraft's "The Music of Erich Zann."

7. W. Compton Leith, *Sirenica* (Portland, Me.: Printed for Thomas Bird Mosher, 1927).

8. "Two-Gun Bob" is Robert E. Howard; "the Peacock Sultan" is E. Hoffmann Price.

9. A reference to the rejection of a collection of Lovecraft's stories by Alfred A. Knopf in the summer of 1933.

10. Lovecraft had an ailment (not fully understood) whereby exposure to temperatures below 20 degrees Fahrenheit for a prolonged period would result in loss of consciousness and probable death.

11. Because 66 College Street was on Brown University's fraternity row, Love-

craft devised the Greek name K.A.T. (standing for *Kompson Ailuron Taxis*, or "Band of elegant [or well-dressed] cats") for the array of cats at the boardinghouse.

12. From the final sentence of Dunsany's "Probable Adventure of the Three Literary Men," in *The Book of Wonder* (1912) ("blackness" for "darkness" in Dunsany). Also cited in Lovecraft's "The Nameless City" (1921).

13. This poem has frequently been reprinted under the title "Little Sam Perkins."

14. E. Hoffmann Price, "The Stranger from Kurdistan," *Weird Tales* (July 1925; rpt. Dec. 1929).

15. In October 1932 Price wrote a draft of a sequel to Lovecraft's "The Silver Key," entitled "The Lord of Illusion." After working on the story sporadically for months, Lovecraft rewrote it as "Through the Gates of the Silver Key" (*Weird Tales*, July 1934).

16. Lovecraft refers to the impending repeal of Prohibition on 5 December 1933.

17. The science fiction writers Ray Cummings, Edmond Hamilton, and Jack Williamson all lived at the time in Florida. Lovecraft never met any of them.

18. Frank Belknap Long's fictional god Chaugnar Faugn appeared in his short novel *The Horror from the Hills* (*Weird Tales*, January and February/March 1931).

19. This is the title of a working song by the turn-of-the-century radical labor organization, the Industrial Workers of the World (I.W.W.), a group Lovecraft had bitterly scorned in his earlier days.

20. It is unlikely that *Astounding* editor F. Orlin Tremaine personally edited Lovecraft's story; but no doubt he gave general approval to the editing. The *Tryout* was the perennially misprinted amateur journal edited by Charles W. Smith.

21. In fact, "The Shadow out of Time" (*Astounding Stories*, June 1936) was—as is revealed by the recently discovered autograph manuscript—also edited, although chiefly in matters of paragraphing and punctuation, not in the significant omission of text. Lovecraft in this letter to R. H. Barlow refers to "*your* story" because Barlow had secretly prepared the typescript of it when Lovecraft was visiting him in Florida in the summer of 1935.

22. "The Feast in the Abbey" (*Weird Tales*, January 1935).

23. Charles D. Hornig, youthful publisher of *The Fantasy Fan*.

24. Lovecraft refers to William Beckford's *Vathek* (see chap. 4, n. 10) and *The Worm Ouroboros* (1922) by E. R. Eddison.

25. The pulp writer C. L. Moore.

26. *Weird Tales*, June 1936.

27. Lovecraft did exactly that in the document "Instructions in Case of Decease."

28. Lovecraft refers to a proposal that Talman had made to the publisher William Morrow for a novel by Lovecraft.

Sources

Abbreviations

AHT = Arkham House transcripts
ALS = autograph letter, signed
JHL = H. P. Lovecraft Papers, John Hay Library, Brown University
NYPL = New York Public Library
SHSW= August W. Derleth Papers, State Historical Society of Wisconsin, Madison
TLS = typed letter, signed

Epigraph
"Biographical Notice." In Edward J. O'Brien, ed., *The Best Short Stories of 1928 and the Yearbook of the American Short Story* (New York: Dodd, Mead, 1928), p. 324.

1. Childhood and Adolescence (1890–1914)
1. To Maurice W. Moe, April 5, 1931 (AHT).
2. To Rheinhart Kleiner, November 16, 1916 (AHT).
3. To Edwin Baird, February 3, 1924 (TLS, JHL).
4. To Alfred Galpin, August 29, 1918 (ALS, JHL).
5. To Alfred Galpin, May 27, 1918 (TLS/ALS, JHL).
6. To August Derleth, February 17, 1931 (ALS, SHSW).
7. To Rheinhart Kleiner, November 16, 1916 (AHT).
8. To August Derleth, December 13, 1930 (ALS, SHSW).
9. To J. Vernon Shea, November 8, 1933 (ALS, JHL).
10. To the Gallomo, September 3, 1920 (AHT).
11. To Edwin Baird, February 3, 1924 (TLS, JHL).
12. To Rheinhart Kleiner, November 16, 1916 (AHT).
13. To J. Vernon Shea, February 4, 1934 (ALS, JHL).
14. To Robert E. Howard, March 25–29, 1933 (AHT).
15. To Rheinhart Kleiner, November 16, 1916 (AHT).
16. To R. H. Barlow, April 10, 1934 (ALS, JHL).
17. To Rheinhart Kleiner, December 4, 1918 (AHT).
18. To Rheinhart Kleiner, November 16, 1916 (AHT).

2. Amateur Journalism (1914–1921)

1. *United Amateur Press Association: Exponent of Amateur Journalism* [Elroy, Wis.: E. E. Er-
   icson, 1915].
2. "What Amateurdom and I Have Done for Each Other" (written in 1921), *Boys' Herald* 46, no. 1 (August 1937): 6–7.
3. To Edward H. Cole, November 23, 1914 (TLS, JHL).
4. To Alfred Galpin, August 29, 1918 (ALS, JHL).
5. "Editorial," *Conservative* 1, no. 2 (July 1915): 4–5.
6. "A Matter of Uniteds," *Bacon's Essays* 1, no. 1 (Summer 1927): 1–3.
7. "The Pseudo-United," *United Amateur* 19, no. 5 (May 1920): 106–8 (unsigned).
8. "Consolidation's Autopsy," *Lake Breeze* no. 19 (April 1915): 133 (as "El Imparcial").
9. To Rheinhart Kleiner, November 8, 1917 (H. P. Lovecraft, "By Post from Providence" [ed. Rheinhart Kleiner], *The Californian* 5, no. 1 [Summer 1937]: 14; rpt.
   H. P. Lovecraft, *The Californian: 1934–1938* [West Warwick, R.I.: Necronomicon
   Press, 1977], p. 47).
10. To Rheinhart Kleiner, May 23, 1917 (AHT).
11. To Rheinhart Kleiner, August 27, 1917 (AHT).
12. To Rheinhart Kleiner, December 23, 1917 (AHT).
13. To the Kleicomolo, August 8, 1916 (AHT).
14. To the Kleicomolo, [October 1916] (AHT).
15. To Maurice W. Moe, May 15, 1918 (AHT).
16. To Rheinhart Kleiner, March 7, 1920 (AHT).
17. To Rheinhart Kleiner, December 6, 1915 (AHT).
18. To Maurice W. Moe, December 8, 1914 (AHT).
19. To Elizabeth Toldridge, March 8, 1929 (ALS, JHL).
20. To the Gallomo, [January 1920] (AHT).
21. To Clark Ashton Smith, April 14, 1929 (AHT).
22. To Rheinhart Kleiner, November 9, 1919 (AHT).
23. To Rheinhart Kleiner, December 3, 1919 (AHT)
24. To Fritz Leiber, November 15, 1936 (AHT).
25. To the Gallomo, December 11, 1919 (AHT).
26. To the Gallomo, [January 1920] (AHT).
27. To Rheinhart Kleiner, May 21, 1920 (AHT).
28. To Rheinhart Kleiner, December 14, 1920 (AHT).
29. To Rheinhart Kleiner, September 27, 1919 (AHT).
30. To Rheinhart Kleiner, January 23, 1920 (AHT).
31. To Rheinhart Kleiner, January 18, 1919 (AHT).
32. To Rheinhart Kleiner, March 9, 1919 (AHT).
33. To Rheinhart Kleiner, March 30, 1919 (AHT).
34. To Anne Tillery Renshaw, June 4, 1921 (AHT).
35. To Rheinhart Kleiner, June 12, 1921 (AHT).

3. Expanding Horizons (1921–1924)

1. To Rheinhart Kleiner, August 30, 1921 (AHT).
2. To Rheinhart Kleiner, September 21, 1921 (AHT).

3. To Maurice W. Moe, June 21, 1922 (AHT).
4. To Maurice W. Moe, May 18, 1922 (AHT).
5. To Lillian D. Clark, August 4, 1922 (AHT).
6. To Lillian D. Clark, August 9, 1922 (ALS, JHL).
7. To Lillian D. Clark, September 29, 1922 (ALS, JHL).
8. To Rheinhart Kleiner, January 11, 1923 (AHT).
9. To James F. Morton, March 12, 1930 (AHT).
10. To Anne Tillery Renshaw, June 1, 1921 (AHT).
11. To James F. Morton, February 10, 1923 (AHT).
12. To James F. Morton, May 26, 1923 (AHT).
13. To Edwin Baird, *Weird Tales* 2, no. 2 (September 1923): 81–82.
14. To Edwin Baird, *Weird Tales* 3, no. 3 (March 1924): 89–92.
15. To Frank Belknap Long, November 8, 1923 (AHT).
16. To Frank Belknap Long, February 14, 1924 (AHT).

4. Marriage and Exile (1924–1926)
1. To Lillian D. Clark, March 9, 1924 (AHT).
2. To Lillian D. Clark, August 1, 1924 (AHT).
3. To Lillian D. Clark, May 28, 1925 (ALS, JHL).
4. To Lillian D. Clark, March 4, 1926 (ALS, JHL).
5. To Maurice W. Moe, June 15, 1925 (ALS, JHL).
6. To Lillian D. Clark, April 2, 1925 (ALS, JHL).
7. To Lillian D. Clark, April 11, 1925 (ALS, JHL).
8. To Lillian D. Clark, September 29–30, 1924 (TLS, JHL).
9. To Lillian D. Clark, November 4–6, 1924 (ALS, JHL).
10. To Lillian D. Clark, May 20, 1925 (AHT).
11. To Maurice W. Moe, January 18, 1930 (AHT).
12. To Lillian D. Clark, May 25, 1925 (AHT).
13. To Lillian D. Clark, May 28, 1925 (ALS, JHL).
14. To Lillian D. Clark, October 24–27, 1925 (ALS, JHL).
15. To Bernard Austin Dwyer, March 26, 1927 (AHT).
16. To Lillian D. Clark, November 4–6, 1924 (ALS, JHL).
17. To Lillian D. Clark, April 21, 1925 (TLS, JHL).
18. To Frank Belknap Long, August 2, 1925 (AHT).
19. To Clark Ashton Smith, October 9, 1925 (AHT).
20. To Lillian D. Clark, August 13, 1925 (ALS, JHL).
21. To James F. Morton, January 5, 1926 (AHT).
22. To Lillian D. Clark, January 11, 1926 (ALS, JHL).
23. To Lillian D. Clark, July 6, 1925 (ALS, JHL).
24. To Lillian D. Clark, January 11, 1926 (ALS, JHL).
25. To Lillian D. Clark, August 8, 1925 (ALS, JHL).
26. To Lillian D. Clark, December 22–23, 1925 (ALS, JHL).
27. To Lillian D. Clark, March 27, 1926 (ALS, JHL).
28. To Lillian D. Clark, March 29, 1926 (ALS, JHL).

5. Homecoming (1926–1930)

1. To Frank Belknap Long, May 1, 1926 (ALS, JHL).
2. To James F. Morton, May 16, 1926 (AHT).
3. To Maurice W. Moe, July 2, 1929 (AHT).
4. To Donald Wandrei, February 10, 1927 (ALS, JHL).
5. To August Derleth, [December 3, 1926] (ALS, SHSW).
6. To Wilfred Blanch Talman, December 19, 1926 (AHT).
7. To Frank Belknap Long, [February 1927] (AHT).
8. To Bernard Austin Dwyer, March 26, 1927 (AHT).
9. To Clark Ashton Smith, August 31, 1928 (ALS, private collection).
10. To Farnsworth Wright, December 22, 1927 (AHT).
11. To August Derleth, October 6, 1929 (ALS, SHSW).
12. To Clark Ashton Smith, December 3, 1929 (AHT).
13. To Clark Ashton Smith, December 17, 1929 (AHT).
14. To Clark Ashton Smith, February 2, 1930 (ALS, JHL).
15. To Robert E. Howard, August 14, 1930 (AHT).
16. To Clark Ashton Smith, September 11, 1930 (AHT).
17. To Farnsworth Wright, July 5, 1927 (AHT).
18. To Clark Ashton Smith, October 17, 1930 (AHT).
19. To Frank Belknap Long, February 20, 1929 (AHT).
20. To Frank Belknap Long, November 22, 1930 (AHT).
21. To Woodburn Harris, February 25, 1929 (AHT).
22. To James F. Morton, October 30, 1929 (AHT).
23. To August Derleth, [1930] (ALS, SHSW).
24. To Maurice W. Moe, October 6, 1927 (AHT).
25. To Zealia Bishop, May 1, 1928 (AHT).
26. To Lillian D. Clark, June 24, 1928 (ALS, JHL).
27. To Lillian D. Clark, July 1, 1928 (ALS, JHL).
28. "Mrs. Miniter — Estimates and Recollections" (written in 1934), *Californian* 5, no. 4 (Spring 1938): 47–55.
29. To Zealia Bishop, July 28, 1928 (AHT).
30. To Elizabeth Toldridge, May 4, 1929 (ALS, JHL).
31. To Elizabeth Toldridge, May 29, 1929 (ALS, JHL).
32. To Maurice W. Moe, May 4, 1930 (AHT).
33. To Lillian D. Clark, May 24–25, 1930 (ALS, JHL).
34. To Elizabeth Toldridge, [early September 1930] (ALS, JHL).
35. To Donald Wandrei, November 2, 1930 (ALS, JHL).
36. To Kenneth Sterling, December 14, 1935 (AHT).
37. To F. Lee Baldwin, March 27, 1934 (ALS, JHL).

6. The Old Gentleman (1931–1937)

1. To Frank Belknap Long, [February 1931] (AHT).
2. To August Derleth, March 24, 1931 (ALS, SHSW).
3. To Clark Ashton Smith, [November 20, 1931] (ALS, JHL).

4. To Alvin Earl Perry, October 4, 1935 (AHT).

5. To E. Hoffmann Price, August 15, 1934 (ALS, JHL).

6. To J. Vernon Shea, August 7, 1931 (ALS, JHL).

7. To August Derleth, March 4, 1932 (ALS, SHSW).

8. To Maurice W. Moe, July 12, 1932 (AHT).

9. To Clark Ashton Smith, December 13, 1933 (ALS, Northern Illinois University).

10. To Carl F. Strauch, May 31, 1933 (ALS, JHL).

11. To August Derleth, January 16, 1931 (ALS, SHSW).

12. To Jonquil Leiber, December 20, 1936 (AHT).

13. To Marion F. Bonner, April 4, 1936 (ALS, JHL).

14. To Alfred Galpin, January 17, 1936 (ALS, JHL).

15. To Duane W. Rimel, December 22, 1934 (ALS, JHL).

16. To James F. Morton, September 24, 1834 (AHT).

17. To August Derleth, May 9, 1931 (ALS, SHSW).

18. To August Derleth, May 23, 1931 (ALS, SHSW).

19. To August Derleth, [June 10–11?, 1931] (ALS, SHSW).

20. To August Derleth, June 17, 1931 (ALS, SHSW).

21. To J. Vernon Shea, October 13, 1932 (ALS, JHL).

22. To J. Vernon Shea, September 25, 1933 (ALS, JHL).

23. To Duane W. Rimel, May 13, 1934 (ALS, JHL).

24. To Duane W. Rimel, June 17, 1934 (ALS, JHL).

25. To E. Hoffmann Price, August 31, 1934 (ALS, JHL).

26. To Duane W. Rimel, June 30, 1935 (ALS, JHL).

27. To Richard F. Searight, August 4, 1935 (ALS, private collection).

28. To Richard F. Searight, August 25, 1933 (ALS, private collection).

29. To Richard F. Searight, August 31, 1933 (ALS, private collection).

30. To Maurice W. Moe, August 3, 1931 (AHT).

31. To Helen Sully, August 15, 1935 (ALS, JHL).

32. To E. Hoffmann Price, September 29, 1933 (ALS).

33. To C. L. Moore, February 7, 1937 (AHT).

34. To Elizabeth Toldridge, January 25, 1931 (ALS, JHL).

35. To C. L. Moore, [October 1936] (AHT).

36. To Kenneth Sterling, October 18, 1936 (AHT).

37. To R. H. Barlow, November 30, 1936 (ALS, JHL).

38. To J. Vernon Shea, September 25, 1933 (ALS, JHL).

39. To Clark Ashton Smith, November 11, 1930 (AHT).

40. To Clark Ashton Smith, March 2, 1932 (AHT).

41. To E. Hoffmann Price, November 18, 1934 (ALS, JHL).

42. To E. Hoffmann Price, March 14, 1935 (ALS, JHL).

43. To Lee White, December 20, 1935 (ALS, JHL).

44. To R. H. Barlow, June 4, 1936 (ALS, JHL).

45. To Robert Bloch, September 25, 1933 (ALS, private collection).

46. To R. H. Barlow, March 16, 1935 (ALS, JHL).

47. To Fritz Leiber, December 19, 1936 (ALS, JHL).

48. To E. Hoffmann Price, June 20, 1936 (ALS, JHL).
49. To the Coryciani, July 14, 1936 (ALS, JHL).
50. To James F. Morton, [early 1937] (AHT).
51. To Wilfred Blanch Talman, February 28, 1937 (ALS, JHL).

Appendix

"Some Notes on a Nonentity" (1933). In *Beyond the Wall of Sleep* (Sauk City, Wis.: Arkham House, 1943), pp. xi–xiv. Corrected text in *Autobiographical Writings* (West Warwick, R.I.: Necronomicon Press, 1992), pp. 32–37.

Further Reading

A. Primary

Fiction

The Annotated H. P. Lovecraft. Edited by S. T. Joshi. New York: Dell, 1997.

At the Mountains of Madness and Other Novels. Selected by August Derleth; texts edited by S. T. Joshi. Sauk City, Wis.: Arkham House, 1985.

The Call of Cthulhu and Other Weird Stories. Edited by S. T. Joshi. New York: Penguin, 1999.

Dagon and Other Macabre Tales. Selected by August Derleth; texts edited by S. T. Joshi. Sauk City, Wis.: Arkham House, 1986.

The Dunwich Horror and Others. Selected by August Derleth; texts edited by S. T. Joshi. Sauk City, Wis.: Arkham House, 1984.

The Horror in the Museum and Other Revisions. Edited by S. T. Joshi. Sauk City, Wis.: Arkham House, 1989.

The Shadow over Innsmouth. Edited by S. T. Joshi and David E. Schultz. West Warwick, R.I.: Necronomicon Press, 1994 (rev. 1997).

Poetry

The Ancient Track: Collected Poetical Works. Edited by S. T. Joshi. West Warwick, R.I.: Necronomicon Press, 2000.

Essays and Miscellany

Autobiographical Writings. Edited by S. T. Joshi. West Warwick, R.I.: Necronomicon Press, 1992.

Commonplace Book. Edited and annotated by David E. Schultz. West Warwick, R.I.: Necronomicon Press, 1987. 2 vols.

Marginalia. Edited by August Derleth and Donald Wandrei. Sauk City, Wis.: Arkham House, 1943.

Miscellaneous Writings. Edited by S. T. Joshi. Sauk City, Wis.: Arkham House, 1995.

The Shuttered Room and Other Pieces. Edited by August Derleth. Sauk City, Wis.: Arkham House, 1959.

Something about Cats and Other Pieces. Edited by August Derleth. Sauk City, Wis.: Arkham House, 1949.

To Quebec and the Stars. Edited by L. Sprague de Camp. West Kingston, R.I.: Donald M. Grant, 1976.

Uncollected Prose and Poetry. Edited by S. T. Joshi and Marc A. Michaud. West Warwick, R.I.: Necronomicon Press, 1978–82. 3 vols.

Letters

Letters to Richard F. Searight. Edited by David E. Schultz and S. T. Joshi. West Warwick, R.I.: Necronomicon Press, 1992.

Letters to Robert Bloch. Edited by David E. Schultz and S. T. Joshi. West Warwick, R.I.: Necronomicon Press, 1993.

Letters to Samuel Loveman and Vincent Starrett. Edited by S. T. Joshi and David E. Schultz. West Warwick, R.I.: Necronomicon Press, 1994.

Lovecraft at Last (with Willis Conover). Arlington, Va.: Carrollton-Clark, 1975.

Selected Letters. Edited by August Derleth, Donald Wandrei, and James Turner. 5 vols. Sauk City, Wis.: Arkham House, 1965–76.

Uncollected Letters. Edited by S. T. Joshi. West Warwick, R.I.: Necronomicon Press, 1986.

B. Secondary

Bibliographies and Catalogues

Joshi, S. T. *H. P. Lovecraft and Lovecraft Criticism: An Annotated Bibliography.* Kent, Ohio: Kent State University Press, 1981.

Joshi, S. T., and Marc A. Michaud. *Lovecraft's Library: A Catalogue.* West Warwick, R.I.: Necronomicon Press, 1980.

Biographies and Memoirs

Barlow, Robert H. "The Wind That Is in the Grass: A Memoir of H. P. Lovecraft in Florida." In Lovecraft's *Marginalia* (q.v.), pp. 342–50.

Bloch, Robert. "Out of the Ivory Tower." In Lovecraft's *The Shuttered Room and Other Pieces* (q.v.), pp. 171–77.

Brobst, Harry K., and Will Murray. "An Interview with Harry K. Brobst." *Lovecraft Studies* nos. 22/23 (Fall 1990): 24–42, 21.

Cannon, Peter, ed. *Lovecraft Remembered.* Sauk City, Wis.: Arkham House, 1998.

Cook, W. Paul. *In Memoriam: Howard Phillips Lovecraft: Recollections, Appreciations, Estimates.* North Montpelier, Vt.: Driftwind Press, 1941. West Warwick, RI: Necronomicon Press, 1977 (rpt. 1991).

Davis, Sonia H. *The Private Life of H. P. Lovecraft.* Edited by S. T. Joshi. West Warwick, R.I.: Necronomicon Press, 1985 (rev. 1993).

de Camp, L. Sprague. *Lovecraft: A Biography.* Garden City, N.Y.: Doubleday, 1975.

Derleth, August. *H. P. L.: A Memoir.* New York: Ben Abramson, 1945.

———. *Some Notes on H. P. Lovecraft.* Sauk City, Wis.: Arkham House, 1959.

Edkins, E. A. "Idiosyncraises of HPL." *Olympian* no. 35 (Autumn 1940): 1–7. In *The Lovecraft Collectors Library*, ed. George T. Wetzel, vol. 6, pp. 5–7. North

Tonawanda, N.Y.: SSR Publications, 1955.

Everts, R. Alain. *The Death of a Gentleman: The Last Days of Howard Phillips Lovecraft.* Madison, Wis.: The Strange Co., 1987.

Faig, Kenneth W., Jr. *H. P. Lovecraft: His Life, His Work.* West Warwick, R.I.: Necronomicon Press, 1979.

———. *The Parents of Howard Phillips Lovecraft.* West Warwick, R.I.: Necronomicon Press, 1990.

Galpin, Alfred. "Memories of a Friendship." In Lovecraft's *The Shuttered Room and Other Pieces* (q.v.), pp. 191–201.

Hart, Mara Kirk. "Walkers in the City: George Willard Kirk and Howard Phillips Lovecraft in New York City, 1924–1926." *Lovecraft Studies* no. 28 (Spring 1993): 2–17.

Joshi, S. T. *H. P. Lovecraft: A Life.* West Warwick, R.I.: Necronomicon Press, 1996.

———, ed. *Caverns Measureless to Man: 18 Memoirs of H. P. Lovecraft.* West Warwick, R.I.: Necronomicon Press, 1996.

Kleiner, Rheinhart. "A Memoir of Lovecraft." In Lovecraft's *Something about Cats and Other Pieces* (q.v.), pp. 218–28.

Koki, Arthur S. "H. P. Lovecraft: An Introduction to His Life and Writings." M.A. thesis: Columbia University, 1962.

Long, Frank Belknap. *Howard Phillips Lovecraft: Dreamer on the Nightside.* Sauk City, Wis.: Arkham House, 1975.

Loveman, Samuel. "Howard Phillips Lovecraft." In Lovecraft's *Something about Cats and Other Pieces* (q.v.), pp. 229–33.

Orton, Vrest. "Recollections of H. P. Lovecraft." *Whispers* 4 (March 1982): 95–101.

Price, E. Hoffmann. "The Man Who Was Lovecraft." In Lovecraft's *Something about Cats and Other Pieces* (q.v.), pp. 278–89.

Scott, Winfield Townley. "His Own Most Fantastic Creation: Howard Phillips Lovecraft." In Lovecraft's *Marginalia* (q.v.), pp. 309–31. In Scott's *Exiles and Fabrications.* Garden City, N.Y.: Doubleday, 1961, pp. 50–72.

Shea, J. Vernon. "H. P. Lovecraft: The House and the Shadows." *Fantasy and Science Fiction* 30 (May 1966): 82–99. West Warwick, R.I.: Necronomicon Press, 1982.

Sterling, Kenneth. "Caverns Measureless to Man." *Science-Fantasy Correspondent* 1 (1975): 36–43.

Talman, Wilfred B., et al. *The Normal Lovecraft.* Saddle River, N.J.: Gerry de la Ree, 1973.

Wandrei, Donald. "The Dweller in Darkness: Lovecraft, 1927." In Lovecraft's *Marginalia* (q.v.), pp. 362–69.

Critical Studies

Buhle, Paul. "Dystopia as Utopia: Howard Phillips Lovecraft and the Unknown Content of American Horror Literature." *Minnesota Review* 6 (Spring 1976): 118–31. In Joshi, *Four Decades* (q.v.), pp. 196–210.

Burleson, Donald R. *H. P. Lovecraft: A Critical Study.* Westport, Conn.: Greenwood Press, 1983.

————. "H. P. Lovecraft: The Hawthorne Influence." *Extrapolation* 22 (Fall 1981): 262–69.

————. "Humour beneath Horror: Some Sources for 'The Dunwich Horror' and 'The Whisperer in Darkness.'" *Lovecraft Studies* no. 2 (Spring 1980): 5–15.

————. *Lovecraft: Disturbing the Universe*. Lexington: University Press of Kentucky, 1990.

————. "The Mythic Hero Archetype in 'The Dunwich Horror.'" *Lovecraft Studies* no. 4 (Spring 1981): 3–9.

Cannon, Peter. *H. P. Lovecraft*. Boston: Twayne, 1989.

————. *"Sunset Terrace Imagery in Lovecraft" and Other Essays*. West Warwick, R.I.: Necronomicon Press, 1990.

Clore, Dan. "Metonyms of Alterity: A Semiotic Interpretation of *Fungi from Yuggoth*." *Lovecraft Studies* no. 30 (Spring 1994): 21–32.

Eckhardt, Jason C. "Behind the Mountains of Madness: Lovecraft and the Antarctic in 1930." *Lovecraft Studies* no. 14 (Spring 1987): 31–38.

Frierson, Meade and Penny, eds. *HPL*. Birmingham, Ala.: Meade and Penny Frierson, 1972.

Gayford, Norman R. "Randolph Carter: An Anti-Hero's Quest." *Lovecraft Studies* no. 16 (Spring 1988): 3–11; no. 17 (Fall 1988): 5–13.

Joshi, S. T. *H. P. Lovecraft: The Decline of the West*. Mercer Island, Wash.: Starmont House, 1990.

————. *Selected Papers on Lovecraft*. West Warwick, R.I.: Necronomicon Press, 1989.

————. *A Subtler Magick: The Writings and Philosophy of H. P. Lovecraft*. San Bernadino, Calif.: Borgo Press, 1996.

————. "Topical References in Lovecraft." *Extrapolation* 25 (Fall 1984): 247–65.

————, ed. *H. P. Lovecraft: Four Decades of Criticism*. Athens: Ohio University Press, 1980.

Leiber, Fritz. "A Literary Copernicus." In Lovecraft's *Something about Cats and Other Pieces* (q.v.), pp. 290–303. In Joshi, *Four Decades* (q.v.), pp. 50–62.

————. "Through Hyperspace with Brown Jenkin: Lovecraft's Contribution to Speculative Fiction." In Lovecraft's *The Dark Brotherhood* (q.v.), pp. 164–78. In Joshi, *Four Decades* (q.v.), pp. 140–52.

Lévy, Maurice. *Lovecraft: A Study in the Fantastic*. Translated by S. T. Joshi. Detroit: Wayne State University Press, 1988.

Mariconda, Steven J. *"On the Emergence of Cthulhu" and Other Observations*. West Warwick, R.I.: Necronomicon Press, 1995.

Montelone, Paul. "'The Rats in the Walls': A Study in Pessimism." *Lovecraft Studies* no. 32 (Spring 1995): 18–26.

————. "The Vanity of Existence in 'The Shadow out of Time.'" *Lovecraft Studies* no. 34 (Spring 1996): 27–35.

Mosig, Dirk W. *Mosig at Last: A Psychologist Looks at H. P. Lovecraft*. West Warwick, R.I.: Necronomicon Press, 1997.

Murray, Will. "The Dunwich Chimera and Others: Correlating the Cthulhu Mythos." *Lovecraft Studies* no. 8 (Spring 1984): 10–24.

Oates, Joyce Carol. "The King of Weird." *New York Review of Books*, 31 October 1996, pp. 46–53.

Onderdonk, Matthew H. "Charon—in Reverse; or, H. P. Lovecraft versus the 'Realists' of Fantasy." *Fantasy Commentator* 2 (Spring 1948): 193–97. *Fresco* 8 (Spring 1958): 45–51. *Lovecraft Studies* no. 3 (Fall 1980): 5–10.

———. "The Lord of R'lyeh." *Fantasy Commentator* 1 (Spring 1945): 103–14. *Lovecraft Studies* no. 7 (Fall 1982): 8–17.

Price, Robert M. *H. P. Lovecraft and the Cthulhu Mythos.* Mercer Island, Wash.: Starmont House, 1990.

St. Armand, Barton L. "Facts in the Case of H. P. Lovecraft." *Rhode Island History* 31 (February 1972): 3–19. In Joshi, *Four Decades* (q.v.), pp. 166–85.

———. "H. P. Lovecraft: New England Decadent." *Caliban* no. 12 (1975): 127–35. Albuquerque, N.Mex.: Silver Scarab Press, 1979.

———. *The Roots of Horror in the Fiction of H. P. Lovecraft.* Elizabethtown, N.Y.: Dragon Press, 1977.

St. Armand, Barton L., and John H. Stanley. "H. P. Lovecraft's *Waste Paper*: A Facsimile and Transcript of the Original Draft." *Books at Brown* 26 (1978): 31–47.

Schultz, David E. "The Origin of Lovecraft's 'Black Magic' Quote." *Crypt of Cthulhu* no. 48 (St. John's Eve 1987): 9–13.

———. "Who Needs the 'Cthulhu Mythos'?" *Lovecraft Studies* no. 13 (Fall 1986): 43–53.

Schultz, David E., and S. T. Joshi, eds. *An Epicure in the Terrible: A Centennial Anthology of Essays in Honor of H. P. Lovecraft.* Rutherford, N.J.: Fairleigh Dickinson University Press, 1991.

Schweitzer, Darrell, ed. *Discovering H. P. Lovecraft.* Mercer Island, Wash.: Starmont House, 1987.

Shreffler, Philip A. *The H. P. Lovecraft Companion.* Westport, Conn.: Greenwood Press, 1977.

Waugh, Robert H. "Lovecraft and Keats Confront the 'Awful Rainbow.'" *Lovecraft Studies* no. 35 (Fall 1996): 24–36; no. 36 (Spring 1997): 26–39.

———. "The Outsider, the Autodidact, and Other Professions." *Lovecraft Studies* no. 37 (Fall 1997): 4–15.

Wetzel, George T. "The Cthulhu Mythos: A Study." In Frierson, *HPL* (q.v.), pp. 35–41. In Joshi, *Four Decades* (q.v.), pp. 79–95.

———, ed. *H. P. Lovecraft: Memoirs, Critiques, and Bibliographies.* North Tonawanda, N.Y.: SSR Publications, 1955.

Index

Kleiner, Rheinhart, xi, 7, 88, 90, 92, 93, 94, 97, 98, 101–2, 103, 110, 128, 149, 159, 192, 200, 357 n. 2
Knopf, Alfred A., 275
Krutch, Joseph Wood, 257

Landon, Alf, 324
Lang, Andrew, 207
Lao-Tse, 222
Last Book of Wonder, The (Dunsany), 72
Lawrence, Carroll, 110
Lazare, Edward, 109
Lee, Charley, 238
Leeds, Arthur, 139–40, 145, 157–58, 159, 160, 178, 279
Leiber, Fritz, 71, 335–37
Leiser, Adeline E., 96
Leith, W. Compton, 274
Lemke, William, 324
Leon, Ponce de, 286
Leonardo da Vinci, 235
Lewis, Matthew Gregory ("Monk"), 96
Lindsey, Ben B., 194
Little, Myrta Alice, 86
"Little Glass Bottle, The," 13
Long, Frank Belknap, 122, 130, 187, 189, 200, 288, 348, 362 n. 2; collaborates with Lovecraft, 205, 236; explorations with Lovecraft, 151, 245; Lovecraft visits, 237, 242, 286; political views of, 324, 338; with Lovecraft in New York (1922), 93, 98–105, 110; with Lovecraft in New York (1924–26), 128, 140, 142, 145, 158, 159, 160; writings of, 267, 268, 270, 297, 332, 343, 363 n. 18
Longfellow, Henry Wadsworth, 64
Love, Dr., 165
Lovecraft, George, 5
Lovecraft, H. P.: and amateur journalism, x–xi, 37, 39–50, 61, 348; ancestry of, 3–7; and astronomy, 27, 29, 34, 347; attempted enlistment, 50–53; on cats, 281–85; and chemistry, 13, 15–16, 347; childhood of, viii–ix, 7–35, 345–47; and classical antiquity, 10, 12, 13–14, 27, 34–35, 95–96, 346; on clothing, 155–64; on commercialism, 311–13; diet of, 141–44, 278, 280–81; dreams of, 11, 57–58, 72–82; on economics, 313–25; as fiction writer, xii–xiii, xv, 13, 32, 35, 66–69, 71, 94, 120, 121–25, 167, 175–78, 201–5, 208, 211, 260–70, 273–75, 328–33, 346, 348, 349; health of, ix, xvii, 35, 36, 51, 52, 342–43, 347, 348; job prospects of, xi–xii, 134–41, 185, 186–88, 310–11; as let-

ter writer, vii–viii, xvi–xvii; on love, 82–83; marriage of, xiii–xv, 126–34, 193–97; and music, 17–18; and New England, xvi, 112–15, 167, 183–85, 187–88, 197–201; philosophical development of, xi, xv–xvi, 26–27, 53–62, 115–19, 214–34, 301–7; as poet, x, xii, 12, 36, 37–38, 64–66, 67–68, 206–7; on politics, 116–19, 228–29, 313–25; poverty of, ix, xii, 12, 143, 277–78; and prohibition, 55–56; and pulp magazines, xiii, 120–21, 270, 307–11; and racism, xiii–xiv, 63–64, 102–3, 179–81, 325–28; and religion, 12, 14, 54, 56–61, 221–26, 301–3; as revisionist, 157, 205–6, 299–301; robbery of, 152–55; school attendance of, ix, 12, 27–29, 33–35, 347; on suicide, ix, 30–32, 84–85, 182; theory of weird fiction of, xvi, 121–22, 208–13, 257–60, 349–50; travels of, xii, xv, 69–71, 93–115, 133–34, 168–75, 177, 190, 234–51, 285–99, 339–42, 348–49
Lovecraft, Joseph, 4–5
Lovecraft, Sarah Susan, ix–x, xi–xii, 8, 9, 11, 30, 51, 52, 53, 83–86, 196, 276, 355 n. 1
Lovecraft, Thomas, 4
Lovecraft, Winfield Scott, ix, 5, 7–8, 9, 11, 355 n. 3
Loveman, Samuel, xiv, 128, 152, 153, 154, 164, 164, 200, 254; as amateur writer, x, 43, 49, 358 n. 6; and Hart Crane, 147–49, 249–50; employment of, 140, 141; Lovecraft visits, 237–38, 249–50, 272, 291; in Lovecraft's dreams, 72–76, 81–82, 120; with Lovecraft in Cleveland, 106–8, 110; with Lovecraft in New York (1922), 93–105; with Lovecraft in New York (1924–26), 150, 151, 159, 178
Low (cat), 296
"Lurking Fear, The," 204

Macfadden, Bernarr, 312
Machen, Arthur, xii–xiii, 1, 121, 168, 213, 262, 266, 269, 341, 349
Macleod, Fiona (pseud. William Sharp), 123
Magistris, Mariano de, 138, 340, 359 n 3
Magnolia, Mass., 91–92, 127, 129
Main Street (Lewis), 106
Mandeville, Sir John, 31
Marblehead, Mass., xv, 113–15, 186, 188, 190, 238, 294–95, 348, 349
Martin, Harry E., 50
Marxism, 313, 322–23
Mary (Queen of England), 4
Mashburn, W. Kirk, 291